Doing Gender

Doing Gender

Franco-Canadian Women Writers
of the 1990s

Edited by
Paula Ruth Gilbert
and Roseanna L. Dufault

Madison • Teaneck
Fairleigh Dickinson University Press
London: Associated University Presses

© 2001 by Rosemont Publishing & Printing Corp.

All rights reserved. Authorization to photocopy items for internal or personal use, or the internal or personal use of specific clients, is granted by the copyright owner, provided that a base fee of $10.00, plus eight cents per page, per copy is paid directly to the Copyright Clearance Center, 222 Rosewood Drive, Danvers, Massachusetts 01923. [0-8386-3886-4/01 $10.00 + 8¢ pp. pc.]

Associated University Presses
440 Forsgate Drive
Cranbury, NJ 08512

Associated University Presses
16 Barter Street
London WC1A 2AH, England

Associated University Presses
P.O. Box 338, Port Credit
Mississauga, Ontario
Canada L5G 4L8

The paper used in this publication meets the requirements of the American National Standard for Permanence of Paper for Printed Library Materials Z39.48-1984.

Library of Congress Cataloging-in-Publication Data

Doing gender : Franco-Canadian women writers of the 1990s / edited by Paula Ruth Gilbert and Roseanna L. Dufault.
    p. cm.
Includes bibliographical references in index.
ISBN 0-8386-3886-4 (alk. paper)
  1. French-Canadian literature—Québec (Province)—History and criticism.
2. French-Canadian literature—Women authors—History and criticism.
3. French-Canadian literature—20th century—History and criticism.
4. Women and literature—Québec (Province)   5. Women in literature.
I. Gilbert, Paula Ruth.   II. Dufault, Roseanna Lewis.
PQ3917.Q3 D65 2001
840.9′9287′0971—dc21   2001018967

PRINTED IN THE UNITED STATES OF AMERICA

To Randy, Meredith, and Anne
To Catherine and Diana
To the memory of Jeanne Kissner

Marie-Claire Blais, Untitled, August 2000, mixed media.
By permission of the artist.

Kingsbury, le 22 août 2000

    Si j'aime dessiner, peindre, c'est surtout par jeu, c'est une détente agréable après le travail de l'écriture, lequel est toujours concentré et souvent douloureux. Le jeu avec les couleurs est un plaisir pour les yeux, une joie pour le coeur, c'est tout de suite limpide, séduisant. Pensons à quelques écrivains qui ont aimé dessiner et peindre, Victor Hugo dans ses magnifiques dessins hantés, Jean Cocteau, au trait léger et gracieux, les soeurs Brontë, Emily Dickinson, si je me souviens bien, le poète Elisabeth Bishop, l'écrivain Réjean Ducharme, au Québec, qui possède une maîtrise chagallienne de la peinture et de la sculpture. Ce qui m'a aussi fascinée dans la peinture c'est que j'ai eu le plaisir de rencontrer plusieurs peintres qui ont partagé avec moi leur amour de cet art et le mystère d'allégresse qui s'en dégage parfois.

—Marie-Claire Blais

[If I like to draw and paint, it's mainly for play; it is a pleasant way to relax after the hard work of writing, which is always concentrated and often painful. The play of colors pleases the eyes and is a joy to the heart. It is immediately clear and seductive. I'm thinking of several writers who liked to draw and paint: Victor Hugo, with his magnificent, haunting drawings; Jean Cocteau, with his light and graceful lines; the Brontë sisters; Emily Dickinson (if I am not mistaken); the poet Elisabeth Bishop; Réjean Ducharme, the Québec author with a Chagall-like mastery of painting and sculpture. Also, through painting, I have had the pleasure of meeting several artists who shared with me their love of art and the mystery of intense happiness that sometimes emanates from it.]

Contents

Preface MARY JEAN GREEN	11
Acknowledgments	13
Introduction PAULA RUTH GILBERT AND ROSEANNA L. DUFAULT	15
Marie-Josephte Becomes Ludivine: The Family Reformed in Anne Hébert's *La Cage* ANNABELLE M. REA	23
Myth and Memory in Nicole Brossard's *Baroque d'aube* and *Vertige de l'avant scène* ALICE A. PARKER	36
Writing and/in Mourning: The Legacy of Loss in Recent Texts by Madeleine Gagnon MILÉNA SANTORO	53
Rewriting Women into Historical Struggle as Transformative and Transformed Grace: Madeleine Ouellette-Michalska's *L'Été de l'Île de Grâce* MAUREEN F. O'MEARA	78
Gendered Migrations: History, Women, Class, and Urbanity in France Théoret's *Laurence* KAREN L. GOULD	95
Passionate Postmortems: Couples Plays by Women Dramatists JANE MOSS	108
It Takes Two to Tango: Pauline Harvey's *Un Homme est une valse* KARIN EGLOFF	130
The Future of Memory in Louise Dupré's *La Memoria* KAREN MCPHERSON	142
The Construction and Deconstruction of Gender in the Novels of Monique Proulx SANDRA BEYER	160

The Other Family Romance: Daughters and Fathers in
Québec Women's Fiction of the Nineties 169
 LORI SAINT-MARTIN

The Daughter's Revenge: Father-Daughter Incest in
Gabrielle Gourdeau's *L'Écho du silence* 186
 SUSAN IRELAND

The Legacy of Words: Mothers as Agents of Cultural
Subterfuge and Subversion 203
 LUCIE LEQUIN

Ying Chen's *Les Lettres chinoises* and Epistolary Identity 217
 EILEEN SIVERT

Feminine References and Feminine Space in *Entre les
fleuves* by Nadine Ltaif 235
 PEGGY DEVAUX

France Daigle's Postmodern Acadian Voice in the Context
of Franco-Canadian Lesbian Voices 248
 JANINE RICOUART

Memory, Sexuality, and Patriarchy: Emancipatory
Strategies in Contemporary Franco-Albertan Women's
Writing 267
 PAMELA V. SING

Giving Voice to the Body: (Pro)creation in the Texts of
Nancy Huston 288
 PATRICE J. PROULX

Feminist Discourse and Children's Literature in Québec:
Some Theoretical and Historical Foundations 306
 LUCIE GUILLEMETTE

Huguette Bertrand, "Internaute" Pioneer Poet: An
Introduction to *Entre l'ombre et la lumière* 322
 MYLÈNE CATEL

Marguerite . . . or She Who Sees Behind the Mirror: A
Translation of Hélène Rioux's *Marguerite . . . ou celle qui
voit derrière le miroir* 346
 JULIE RIEMAN

Contributors 356
Index 362

Preface

MARY JEAN GREEN

IF, AS JANE GALLOP HAS ARGUED, THE HISTORY OF FEMINIST CRITICISM can be traced through the various essay collections that form the stages of its development, Paula Gilbert's publication in 1985 of the essays in *Traditionalism, Nationalism, and Feminism* marked the moment when the writing of francophone women in Québec was recognized as constituting a corpus worthy of critical study. At that moment the complicated and contested identities of Québec, on the one hand, and women writers, on the other, were just emerging from a process of radical redefinition. The newly coined signifier of national identity, *Québécois*, had taken on meaning in the political debates of the 1960s and 1970s before being once again opened to question by the enigmatic outcome of the 1980 referendum on Québec independence. The active Québec feminist movement of the 1970s had proposed a new status for the woman writer in the term of *l'écrivaine*, prompting the rereading of texts by Québec women extending back to the nineteenth-century literary pioneer, Laure Conan.

As it was in the course of the 1980s that France Théoret felt able to bring these key terms together in her confident self-identification as "écrivaine et Québécoise," it was also in the 1980s that the work of Québec's women writers was able to make its generic claim to critical attention. It was in keeping with the feminist critical tradition, as it has taken form in the Americas, that this claim to critical recognition should assert itself through an essay collection, a fitting representation of the multiple voices that have come to characterize contemporary feminism.

The last fifteen years have seen the publication of a number of important books and articles on francophone women's writing, not only in Québec but in other regions of Canada. As a consequence, the topic is no longer perceived as marginal in the context of francophone literature or the interdisciplinary field of Canadian Studies. The writing of francophone women in Canada has entered the literary and cultural canon and has transformed it in many ways.

However, this writing itself has been transformed in the climate of the century's last decade. Although the terms through which it has been analyzed may remain in place, each has undergone significant definition, as has the concept of *Québécoise* itself. Traditionalism is still important, yet the traditions on which these writers draw, no longer those of an unchanging French, Catholic culture, have varied cultural roots. Francophone nationalist movements themselves, no longer the center of attention even in Québec, have undergone profound redefinition, finding expression in a sense of place that shapes heterogeneous cultural and personal experiences. Even the feminism that remains implicit in these texts by women has reduced its polemical charge and broadened its focus to encompass areas of experience largely untouched by earlier feminist theorists. These women writers of the 1990s seem curiously at ease in their unique position at the intersection of French intellectual tradition and American mediatic culture, of carefully preserved French-Canadian traditions and the transcultural world of a modern Montreal that has become a center of the international francophone community. Grounded in the shared contradictions of the postmodern condition, the writers who are the subject of this collection offer commentary pertinent to us all.

Acknowledgments

W<small>E WISH TO THANK HUGUETTE BERTRAND FOR ALLOWING US TO PRINT</small> her Internet poetry, *Entre l'ombre et la lumière;* Hélène Rioux for allowing us to print a translation of her short story, *Marguerite . . . ou celle qui voit derrière le miroir;* VLB for the use of excerpts from Madeleine Gagnon's novel, *Les Cathédrales sauvages;* and Leméac for permission to use excerpts from Ying Chen's novel, *Les Lettres chinoises*. We are deeply grateful to Marie-Claire Blais for the original artwork and short text that she graciously provided especially for this volume. Finally, we would like to give our thanks to Janine Ricouart for her invaluable assistance in working with Marie-Claire Blais and with us on this special artwork.

Marie-Claire Blais, Untitled, August 2000, mixed media.
By permission of the artist.

Introduction

PAULA RUTH GILBERT AND ROSEANNA L. DUFAULT

IF ONE WERE TO ATTEND AN ACADEMIC CONFERENCE ON CANADIAN OR Québec Studies, one would be struck by the number of sessions devoted to women writers—both francophone and anglophone. Why is it that so many scholars find themselves attracted to the writings of these women? Why do they present so many scholarly papers and publish so many articles and monographs on the texts of these writers? Why do they love to teach this literature? Why do so many students react so positively to the study of this fiction and poetry?

On the one hand, one can say that women writers of both English-speaking and French-speaking Canada have "grown up" with their country and with their province of Québec. Their concerns have mirrored the historical, social, cultural, linguistic, and political events of each passing decade. Of course they have created this mirror with their own special variation—that of the condition of being a woman and specifically a woman writer in this vast and fascinating land called Canada and in this complex and varied province called Québec. That complexity becomes even greater when one considers the fact that there are French-speaking writers throughout Canada, and not simply in Québec, and that the voices of these francophone women writers have become increasingly varied in their ethnic diversity.

It is beneficial to analyze some of the texts written by these women writers during the past decade in order to understand their issues and concerns and to try to see into the future of (their) literature as the new millenium begins. As one contributor (Lori Saint-Martin) has suggested, "Women's fiction of the 1990s tells new stories of 'detached daughters' working, sometimes painfully and problematically, toward new visions of the family, new solutions to old problems, even, perhaps, a new cultural canon."

Like the country of Canada and the province of Québec, these Franco-Canadian women writers are exploring transnational, postnational, and international issues. They are a plurilingual lot, representing a cultural diversity that is quite extraordinary for this

North American land: Québécoise; Chinese-Québécoise; Lebanese-Québécoise; Egyptian-Québécoise; Franco-Albertan; Franco-Acadian (New Brunswick); Haitian-Québécoise; Anglo-Canadian Parisian. They are immigrant writers as well as writers born and raised in Québec, in Alberta, in New Brunswick. They write about memory, cultural heritage, identity, gender, sexuality, maternity, the body, female space, family, children, relationships, aging, death, writing, creativity, and narrative voices. They write for adult audiences, children, and Internet users.

They are constantly searching for a link to the past, as they move into the next century with a certain uneasiness about their survival as Franco-Canadian women writers in a vast North America. They are, perhaps, less dour, angry, and pessimistic than the older generation was and that they themselves had once been, but then again they have grown up, just like their homelands—whether Québec, Canada, or the countries from which they have emigrated. Franco-Canadian women writers of the 1990s represent a marvelous study of women in the world of today.

Included in this volume are chapters treating a few "older," well-known writers, some well-established "mid-generation" authors, and several "most recent" writers, along with ethnic Franco-Canadian authors, often suggesting future directions for writing. Although the collection is not intended to be exhaustive or definitive, it is certainly rich, and it provides a substantial representation of fiction, poetry, and theater created by French-speaking women of Canada in the final decade of the twentieth century.

Many pioneers of women's writing in Québec—including Anne Hébert, Nicole Brossard, Madeleine Gagnon, Madeleine Ouellette-Michalska, and France Théoret—continue steadily to produce powerfully insightful works that illuminate women's experiences and perceptions of a world still largely dominated by patriarchal men.

Annabelle Rea's study of *La Cage* (*The Cage*) exposes the ways in which Hébert dramatically revised a legend, that of the criminal/witch known as "La Corriveau," in order to express her vision of joyful, creative women liberated from oppressive traditional family structures.

Alice Parker underscores the importance of myth and memory, and the necessity for women writers to "feminize" these resources, in her explication of Brossard's recent work in prose, *Baroque d'aube* (*Baroque at Dawn*), and poetry, *Vertige de l'avant scène* (*Vertigo of the Proscenium*), which deal with time, language, and creative memory.

Miléna Santoro analyzes the imprint of death on *Les Cathédrales sauvages* (*Wild Cathedrals*) and other recent prose by Gagnon, in which writing functions both as a form of mourning and as a creative inspiration that ultimately affirms life.

In her treatment of Ouellette-Michalska's novel, *L'Été de l'Île de Grâce* (*The Summer of Grace Island*), which reexamines the history of Grosse Île, a former quarantine station in the Saint Lawrence River, Maureen O'Meara underscores the importance of reversing the systematic erasure of women, especially those who made heroic sacrifices, from recorded accounts of significant events.

Théoret's recent novel, *Laurence*, also contains a historical element. As Karen Gould aptly demonstrates, the young female protagonist's experiences in Montreal in the 1930s epitomize problems associated with modernization, the shift from rural to urban society, and changing notions of women's roles and gender identity.

Québec's "mid-generation" women writers continue in the tradition established by their foremothers, adding elements of their own experiences, even more experimentation with language, and a greater reflection on contemporary societal issues.

Analyzing recent plays by Québec's women dramatists—including Elizabeth Bourget, Maryse Pelletier, Sylvie Provost, Carole Fréchette, and Marie Laberge—Jane Moss observes a trend toward exploring the difficulties of (failed) couples attempting to live together on equal terms. Further, Moss's essay addresses women's use of language in erotic discourse as well as the role of passion in human life and the quest for individual fulfillment and happiness.

Pauline Harvey's *Un Homme est une valse* (*A Man Is a Waltz*) also calls into question traditional gender roles in sexual relationships and the discourse of female desire. In her analysis of Harvey's novel, Karin Egloff examines the relationship between writing and sexual passion.

In her insightful examination of Louise Dupré's "prose en poésie" (prose in poetry), *La Memoria* (*Memoria*), Karen McPherson foregrounds the relationship between memory and mourning, and the role of creative writing as a means of working through the trauma of loss and the subsequent process of recovery.

Sandra Beyer observes ways in which Monique Proulx deconstructs notions of gender identity in her novel, *Homme invisible à la fenêtre* (*Invisible Man at the Window*), in which female characters invented by a woman writer are portrayed through the eyes of a disabled male narrator.

Since the 1970s, the implications of mother-daughter relationships have received considerable attention in literature, criticism, and theory. More recently, however, as Lori Saint-Martin demonstrates, some of Québec's women writers are focusing on the ambivalence inherent in father-daughter bonds. Saint-Martin presents two short stories, "La Gifle" ("The Slap") by Christiane Teasdale and "Friperie" ("Used Clothing Store") by Elise Turcotte, in addition to two novels, France Théoret's *Laurence* and Lise Tremblay's *La Danse juive* (*Jewish Dance*), as examples of recent works expressing daughters' conflicted emotions of resentment and gratitude toward their fathers.

Following the same theme, Susan Ireland illuminates the devastating effects of silencing and repression in her essay on father-daughter incest in Gabrielle Gourdeau's *L'Echo du silence* (*Echo of Silence*), which features five interlocking narratives that voice the victims' ineffable shame, their survival strategies, violent revenge, and eventual healing.

The past decade has seen a significant increase in immigration to Canada, prompting a heightened awareness of "otherness," questions of cultural and ethnic identity, nationality, exile, and the influence of geography and displacement on the individual's sense of self. At the same time, discussions surrounding the movement for political sovereignty in Québec have indirectly brought about a heightened awareness of significant francophone presences in Canada's other provinces. Several relatively "new" contemporary women writers offer a distinctly feminine perspective as they address these issues in their work.

Lucie Lequin's study of recent works by Célie Agnant, Ying Chen, and Abla Farhoud, originally from Haiti, China, and Lebanon, respectively, emphasizes the importance of women's cultural heritage as handed down from mother to daughter in the context of exile and relocation. As Lequin effectively demonstrates, these women authors portray immigrant mothers who defy the patriarchal legacy of submission and subordination by endowing their daughters with rich sensorial memories and a certain zest for life.

Eileen Sivert also examines questions of exile and cultural identity, especially as they relate to gender, in her essay on Ying Chen's *Les Lettres chinoises* (*Chinese Letters*), in which interwoven male and female voices convey their versions of certain transformations of the self intrinsic to the migratory experience.

Nadine Ltaif, an Arab-Canadian poet who writes in French, symbolizes experiences of exile and alienation in her long narrative poem, *Entre les fleuves* (*Between the Rivers*). Peggy Devaux's interpretation of this work reveals Ltaif's use of writing as a means of creating and entering a new, feminized space.

Introducing France Daigle, a lesbian novelist who writes in French in New Brunswick, within the context of a predominantly anglophone nation already strongly influenced by another, better-known Acadian author, Antonine Maillet, Janine Ricouart maintains that Daigle parallels her struggles as a lesbian member of a linguistic minority through her use of varied narrative voices and complex textual structures.

In her presentation of three Franco-Albertan women novelists—Marguerite-A. Primeau, Marie Moser, and Jacqueline Dumas—Pamela V. Sing exposes ways in which these authors use creative narrative strategies to subvert official authoritarian discourse.

Nancy Huston, who was born in Calgary to a French-speaking mother, found her own francophone voice through a self-imposed exile in Paris. Analyzing Huston's recent works, Patrice Proulx brings to light issues concerning the cultural construction of gender, the "baby versus book" myth of procreation for women, mind/body dualism as related to physical and/or mental disabilities, and the innovative incorporation of a nonfiction journal and a critical essay as narrative strategies.

With a view to the future, this volume concludes with an examination of children's literature that may strongly influence up-and-coming generations of young female readers, a discussion of Internet publishing with an example of possible new forms of multimedia creation, and a translation into English of a short story by Hélène Rioux, underscoring the increasing interest in translation throughout Canada.

Lucie Guillemette provides an inquiry into successful books for children and adolescents created by Louise Leblanc, Ginette Anfousse, and Marie-Danielle Croteau. In particular, Guillemette identifies the narratorial use of "Je" (I), the theme of feminine solidarity, and the quest for identity beyond preconceived notions of gender as positive trends in these works, which present strong, highly individualistic female protagonists.

Mylène Catel surveys the possibilities of the Internet as an alternative means of diffusing women's creative expressions in her introduction to Huguette Bertrand, a Québécoise multimedia innovator. Included with Catel's observations is a printed version of Bertrand's collection of poetry, *Entre l'ombre et la lumière* (*Between Shadow and Light*), which may be experienced more fully with music and images at Bertrand's Web-site address.

Finally, Julie Rieman provides a superb translation of a very powerful short story by Hélène Rioux, *Marguerite . . . ou celle qui voit derrière le miroir (Marguerite . . . or She Who Sees Behind the Mirror)*, which poignantly conveys an elderly woman's confrontation with solitude and, ultimately, death.

Based on the diverse representations of creative works by Franco-Canadian women writers collectively, we the editors conclude that, as a new millenium begins, women are still very much concerned with recording their contributions that were formerly omitted from historical accounts and/or perceived through a misogynist lens, and with re-presenting cultural mythology in ways that validate the female experience instead of suppressing it and replacing it with male interpretations. There is a distinct emphasis on memory and mourning, which may pertain particularly to beginning a new millenium, but which addresses specifically the singularly female ways of experiencing loss and the use of writing as both an inspiration and a means of recovery. A strong emphasis on the mother-daughter rapport appears to have been replaced, at least partially in the last decade, by tentative explorations of deeply conflicted father-daughter relations, which presuppose a full range of profound emotions. Multiethnic issues of cultural identity and exile versus belonging have also emerged as predominant themes, both in terms of affirmations of the francophone experience, in all its multiplicity on the North American continent, and in the ardent written expressions of francophone immigrants attempting to establish themselves in a drastically different geographical and climatic environment.

Overall, it appears, from the diversity of literary expressions of women, that Canada is an ideal place from which to enter the 21st century: Québec and Franco-Canadian women writers seem to define themselves as admirably flexible, fully capable of accepting (and revising, as necessary) the past in such a way as to affirm their presence and their long-standing right to exist, fully capable of coming to terms with incredibly painful memories, even those resulting from intolerable abuse, and fully capable of accepting and even expressing solidarity with women who have suffered and survived patriarchal oppression in other nations and cultures in order to reestablish themselves in Canada. As our collection affirms, Franco-Canadian women writers have a strong sense of their heritage as well as a vision for the future. Overall, we the editors hope that this volume will inspire many readers to investigate the amazing wealth of Franco-Canadian women's writing.

Doing Gender

Marie-Josephte Becomes Ludivine: The Family Reformed in Anne Hébert's *La Cage*

ANNABELLE M. REA

ANNE HÉBERT, A WRITER OF THE 1990s? UNQUESTIONABLY. WITH FIVE prose texts and two volumes of poetry between 1990 and 1999, in the various genres that she practiced since her first publications in the 1930s, the 1990s proved, in fact, to be Hébert's most productive decade. They also proved, alas, to be the final decade of her life; Anne Hébert died of bone cancer on 22 January 2000. Too little critical attention has as yet been given to the first of this impressive list of publications, the 1990 play, *La Cage* (*The Cage*), Hébert's revision of the story of Québec's legendary criminal/witch, or victim of the English, La Corriveau.[1]

Since her 1763 death by hanging ordered by a British military court, and, to instill fear in a newly conquered population, the exposure of her encaged corpse at a busy crossroads, Marie-Josephte Corriveau had haunted the popular imagination in Québec. Over the years, tales of murdered husbands—up to seven different men in some folk versions—of nocturnal apparitions, and of witches' sabbaths abounded in the oral tradition, as well as in works of literature, visual arts, music, and dance.[2] Hébert's version of the tale reinforces her long-standing criticism of family structure in Québec—and in human society in general. The 1990 work can best be understood with some background on the traditional family of Québec and with a close look at an early Hébert work, the ever-resonant "Le Torrent" ("The Torrent").

In French-speaking Canada until the mid-twentieth century, the family was considered the "final line of defense" (Gagnon 13) against the invasion of individualistic, Protestant, English-speaking culture.[3] It was seen, in other words, as the key to the survival of a Catholic, French-speaking population. No one who has studied Québec's history remains ignorant of the "revenge of the cradles," or the glorification of motherhood—"our mothers saved the nation" (Dumont, Hamelin, and Montminy 1981, 3:330). Because the men—the *coureurs de bois*, or trappers—were often absent, the *curé* delegated some authority for the transmission of moral values and rules to the mothers, who were later to cooperate with the school, over which the priest had total control. The ideological texts prove that the real power, however, remained with the priests, who, with the help of "battalions of women" (Malouin 1992, 27) in religious orders (and the support of the anglophone elite), governed the rural families that composed their parishes. Despite their glorification of motherhood, the priests taught that woman was Eve, the temptress. They preached that sexuality must be reserved for procreation and held woman alone responsible for what, outside of marital procreation, became Québec's obsessive sin.

The period's dominant literary expression, "the novel of the land," reflected this ideological landscape, as Janine Boynard-Frot, among others, has pointed out. An analysis of the recurring patterns of these stories of isolated rural families reveals the alliance formed by the priest and the father; the disappearance from the scene of the silent and self-sacrificing women once they have fulfilled their "religious and patriotic duty" (Dumont, Hamelin, and Montminy 1981, 3:333) to produce all possible offspring; and the familial goal of transmission of the heritage from generation to generation.

Anne Hébert's treatment of the family represents a powerful rejection of the official ideology. In order to assess that rejection in the 1990 play, we must first look at a novella written in 1945, based on an actual matricide. "Le Torrent" has been variously described as an allegory, a fable, or a parable. Like many of Hébert's works, it can also be seen as a variant of the detective novel, a genre dealing with "the labyrinths of family histories" (Pykett 1989, 25), where the spotlight focuses not on the crime itself, but on its motivation and its psychic consequences. Particularly interesting in "Le Torrent" in this regard is the use of the term "un manque" (26)—a blank, a lack, or a gap—by the first-person narrator, François Perrault.

François's expression "un manque" refers to his inability—or unwillingness—to remember details of the death of his mother, Claudine. The term, however, seems emblematic, for many more "manques"—or gaps—exist in the text. For instance, no explicit reason is given for the isolation of mother and son—"à l'écart de toute voie de communication" (12) [isolated from any means of communication]—except for the *suggestion* of François's illegitimacy.[4] No mention is made of a father, even of an inseminator. That absence is a particularly Québécois construct. Hébert affirmed that "Le Torrent" was "the story of the two forces that were the most powerful in Québec at that time. . . . The Church and the Mother" (McDonald 1981, 58).[5] The father in allegiance with the priest, the priest and the mother as a "couple" (Shek 1988, 29) are symbolically present in Claudine and François, the son in preparation for the priesthood, even though no priest actually appears in the text. The absent-father motif also characterizes the Christian Holy Family where Joseph is something of an "extra" in texts and iconography. It is the Virgin Mother who plays the essential role beside her infant son—and Ben Shek reminds us that the *infant* Jesus is one of the major religious symbols of Québec (29).[6]

Hébert translated the emphasis on the mother in Catholic theology and in Québec's history by portraying Claudine as a colossal figure. Certainly, from the point of view of the small child, parents—all adults—may be seen as powerful giants; Hébert's mother clearly represents more than this. The towering Claudine who repeats to her son, "Tu es mon fils. Tu me continues" (16, 40) [You are my son. You are my continuation], through her use of the first person singular—"mon fils," "me continues"—portrays herself as the sole ancestor, suggesting a parthenogenetic birth. Claudine is, however, the mother-monster—the Terrible Mother, Hecate, or Medusa, whose son cannot sustain her gaze.[7]

Claudine as mother may be analyzed as an ambitious woman, a keeper of accounts, the guardian of the keys, and an animal trainer. She has espoused the official ideology, with a vengeance—for the driving force behind her actions is indeed vengeance, against "eux tous" (16) (all of them). She will obey official authority, within what has been described as a "universe of submission."[8] Yet, she will do so full of rage, and that rage is inscribed on her face, with its "prunelles courroucées" (wrathful pupils), its "front . . . atrocement ravagé" (atrociously ravaged forehead), and its "bouche tourmentée" (11) (contorted mouth).[9] Claudine vows to realize her ambition through her son. Like many women in societies where motherhood has been glorified, the better to imprison them, she sees as the route to her goal the "prepar[ation] of a leader" (30), to borrow an expression from Colette Carisse. François will become a priest.

To assure success, armed with her "livre de comptes" (45) (account book), Claudine becomes a sort of bookkeeper. She will teach her child the prescribed rules and moral values, speaking to him only to chastise him for one of his "manquements" (10) (lapses or failures) or to transmit official ideology—"la parole n'entrait pas dans son ordre" (10) [Speech played no part in her world order].

Her bookkeeping mentality, her literal interpretations of the official ideology, led her to keep track of "l'argent du mal" (45) (the wages of sin) in a ledger so that she could pay for her sins in order to redeem herself—the French "se racheter" reveals the economic connotation more obviously than the English verb—in an attempt to bargain with God.

An important symbol of "Le Torrent," one neglected by critics, is the key, and the key represents one of the attributes of the Terrible Mother, Hecate.[10] For François, his mother's keys symbolize Claudine's domestic power, her absolute control over him. He sees his mother as possessing "toutes les clefs du monde" (21) (all the keys of the world). Those keys become the weapon with which she deafens her rebellious son, compounding his sensory deprivation, when he announces his decision not to return to the seminary, not to follow her plan for revenge. The significance of the key symbolism in Hébert's work is confirmed by a passage at the end of *Le Temps sauvage (The Savage Time)*, where another all-controlling mother, Agnès Joncas, abandoned by her children, desperately wants to "rétablir l'ordre saccagé par les fuyards. . . . Reprendre les clefs du monde dans un petit anneau passé à ma ceinture" (158) [reestablish the order plundered by the fugitives. . . . Take back the keys to the world into a little ring slipped onto my belt]. In this passage, we recognize the Hébertian motif of "l'ordre," already present in "Le Torrent" in Claudine's rigid obedience to the ideological order.

Claudine determined above all to exterminate "l'instinct mauvais" (16) (evil instincts), all sins of the senses, all sins of the flesh, those sins so central in Québec's psyche. To do so, she became an animal tamer to "dompter" (10, 24) (tame), "dresser" (18) (train or break in), or "mater" (24) (subdue) both herself and François, or the dirty drunkard on the road, a representative of Dionysian dis/order whom she beat with her cattle prod and termed "cochon" (15) (pig). Her death, attributable to unleashed animal passions represented by the horse Perceval, emblematizes her failure.

The mother-monster, sadistic bookkeeper, guardian of the keys, and animal trainer has produced a child deprived of childhood, deprived of laughter and joy. She passed on the reigning ideology to her son through her lessons and her textbooks, almost certainly written by priests representing the Jansenist program, books symbolic of this intergenerational transmission. François beats a man as Claudine had done; he too uses animal terminology for human beings—Amica is a "grosse dinde" (39) (silly goose; literally, "big turkey") and his "proie" (32) (prey). He uses his "right" to name Amica, in what he calls "le miracle du premier don" (32) (the miracle of the first gift). However, because he has known no gifts, only useful objects, later taken away, he has in reality suppressed her name (and the name is *essential* to self-identity in Hébert's works), depriving her, just as he was "dépossédé" (dispossessed).[11] He inherits Claudine's rage; it grows within him, taking the form of the horse Perceval and the swirling torrent, and leads to dreams of killing and torturing Amica.

The physical and mental destruction transmitted from generation to generation, within the "labyrinths of family histories," became a leitmotiv of Hébert's work. Links have been mapped between the familial violence and brutality of "Le Torrent" and the apocalyptic *Les Fous de Bassan* (*In The Shadow of the Wind*), for example.[12] *Le Temps sauvage*, with the controlling mother and the absent, or, rather, silenced father, reveals a similar pattern. As one of the Joncas children puts it, "La vie de famille est pourrie" (47) [Family life is rotten]. In contrast, Hébert did portray one happy family—a critic has referred to it as "a sort of Holy Family"—where the mother uses tones of endearment, and not terms of endearment, with her children, where the parents share enduring intimacy, where the children run free, play, and laugh, in the parodic *Les Enfants du sabbat* (*Children of the Black Sabbath*).[13]

Like other writers of Québec, Hébert mines—and undermines—the image of the Holy Family; she does so even more explicitly in *La Cage*. The necessity of reevaluating the family in Québec culture—and in human society in general—as I have said, seems to me to provide one of the motivating factors for Hébert's decision to rewrite the story of La Corriveau, and to change her protagonist's name from the historical Marie-Josephte, with its reference to the "Holy Family," to that of Ludivine.

The title suggests that *La Cage* has much in common with the deprivation, the restrictions on animality, and the locks and keys of "Le Torrent." However, from the first page, one realizes that the 1990 play is very different. Here Ludivine's adopted daughter declares proudly that she is her mother's daughter, "devant Dieu et devant les hommes" (11) (before God and mankind). She will frame her mother's story, but will not silence her as François did Claudine, and as Claudine did in her own self-censorship. As Ludivine finds her voice—to express her newly discovered "envie de vivre" (107) (urge to live)—the mother's voice too will be heard.[14] Marianne Hirsch has commented, in *The Mother/Daughter Plot*, "To speak for the mother, as many of the daughters in this book do, is at once to give voice to her discourse *and* to silence and marginalize her" (16). Later, Hirsch concludes, "Only in combining both voices, in finding a double voice that would yield a multiple female consciousness, can we begin to envision ways to 'live afresh'" (161). With her fantasy, her fairy tale, on the theme of La Corriveau—little of the historical reality subsists in the play—Hébert has done precisely that: "envision ways to live afresh."

As Neil Randall has pointed out, fantastic literature "often explores the created family, the newly-bonded family" (45). *La Cage* offers Hébert's created family, by contrasting it with several more traditional versions of family structure. An examination of the various families of the play would thus now be appropriate.

The first, that of John Crebessa, evokes the term "cellule familiale" (family unit; literally, "family cell").[15] As a male child, Crebessa was endowed with keys, the keys to power. Those keys will later enable him to control many things: first, his wife's person. After the wedding, where Rosalinde loses her name, he locks her in the home, in "une cage ordinaire, toute dorée, de celles qu'on offre habituellement aux femmes de qualité, le jour de leur mariage" (12) [an ordinary cage, all gilded, of the type generally given to high-born women on their wedding day]. He thus ensures her physical fragility and need to lean on him for support if she ventures outside the home. He locks up her personal possessions, now his by law, and allows her only to admire her jewelry as a reward—his "gift"—for finally producing for him a son and heir. Or he allows her to wear that jewelry in public to embellish *his* reputation. He has locked her in; he will also lock her out, by barring her from the family library so that she will no longer be able to develop her considerable mathematical talents.

John Crebessa, the male child, also tortured animals. That power over the weak will expand to sadistic power over the family, not just his wife. He alone will decide, as is his *right*, to send his young son to school in England. Crebessa knows his rights, for he is the English judge, the representative of the law, in the newly conquered territory. His colonizing power extends over all other families as well as his own, and he will seek to cage those who cross him.

Ludivine's origins contrast starkly with those of the wealthy Rosalinde. Misery reduces Ludivine's parents to child sellers; they will marry off their daughter because they cannot afford to feed her. The silent Ludivine is but an object handed over to the childless widower Elzéar, whose desire, like John Crebessa's, is to found a family for the transmission of *his* heritage. As Crebessa puts it, "Il fallait avant tout assurer la pérennité de mon nom et enraciner ma descendance" (67) [Above all, it was necessary to ensure the permanence of my name and put down roots for my descendants]. Elzéar's gift to his wife, established as a parallel to Crebessa's "gift" of jewelry, comes in the form of sadistic torment of Ludivine with a snake, which he relates to his sexual gratification from her screams. As a hunter, he too tortures animals. He plans to impregnate his wife and, his domestic responsibility ended, go off to follow his dream, "comme mon père et comme mon grand-père qui ont peuplé tout le pays, à dix lieues à la ronde, sans jamais perdre une bouffée d'odeur dans les bois, ni un poisson frétillant dans la rivière, ni la moindre bestiole éclatant dans son pelage fauve, comme une fleur rouge au bout du fusil fumant" (48–49) [like my father and grandfather, who populated the entire countryside, for ten leagues around, without ever missing a whiff of scent in the woods, a wriggle of a fish in the river, or the least creature, dazzling in its tawny fur, like a red flower at the tip of the smoking gun].

Elzéar has neither parents nor siblings. Hébert has created his support group, ironically, as "la belle-famille" (the in-laws).[16] Once again, the law is on the side of the male, for, during Elzéar's absence, his *in-laws* (the family of his deceased wife, with no blood ties to him, and no longer any legitimate reason to intervene) serve as rigid social bookkeepers to maintain the status quo. In a gesture that echoes Elzéar's hurling of the snake into Ludivine's face, his sister-in-law flings her "gift" of white wool and knitting needles onto the table as the "belle-famille" departs after a surveillance visit, disappointed at Ludivine's "manque" (lack), her nonexpectant status. Ludivine's monosyllabic responses throughout the visit suggest that she knows her lack of significance for them, as a poor woman of humble origin, except as a potential incubator.

At first, it is only in her dreams that Ludivine can reciprocate. Her gift, to provoke in Elzéar comparable shock, will be a baby carriage with an infant whose "tête de mort" (54) (death's head) suggests Ludivine's death wish for enforced maternity and the traditional family. This time, it is she who laughs in triumph. Able to speak freely in her dream, she confesses her truth: her submission to her husband's spousal rape has enraged her, "je vous dis 'vous' et je ne vous aime pas" (54) [I address you with the formal 'you' and I do not love you]. Only much later, with newfound confidence, will she dare to publicly confront the "belle-famille," calling them "tristes créatures." "Garez-vous, tristes créatures, c'est ma famille qui passe!" (62) [Move out of the way, pitiful creatures; my family is coming through!], she affirms.

In fact, in Elzéar's absence, Ludivine, like so many women alone before her, begins to delight in her solitude, in her responsibility for her own survival. Without her sadistic "lord and master," she develops her sensual reactions and her physical mobility. She begins to make independent decisions characteristic of her generous, life-affirming nature, shown in contrast to the males' traits; she adopts as her family those cast out by society's failed families. The illegitimate, the abandoned, the mentally handicapped, the orphaned, the elderly—in sum, the marginal—become Ludivine's *chosen* family: "la famille ad*opt*ive" (emphasis added; the adoptive family), working together with shared purpose, and with shared play and laughter. Here, I want to underscore what I hoped to make obvious with my title: the change of names from the historical Marie-Josephte to Ludivine. Ludivine represents the playful, laughing mother[17]—I refer to the Latin etymology of *ludere*, to play. Perhaps we can also tease out of the name "the light," from the Latin *lux*, of lucidity, and the vine (or "vigne") of fecundity and of Dionysian laughter and joy. Liberation of the body, the mind, and the voice to speak that mind, is *divine*. At any rate, her name no longer evokes the Virgin Mother, to quote Mieke Bal's words, "sadistic in its requirements imposed upon women" (335), and the surrogate father, Joseph.

Once Ludivine has become a responsible, articulate, sensual, playful, and powerful individual, the painter Hyacinthe enters the scene. Hébert's choice of a name here seems particularly interesting. The floral name identifies the character as what Annis Pratt calls a "green-world lover" (22), the ideal lover often imagined by women writers, who comes from the natural world, away from the restrictions of society. The mythological Hyacinthus is associated with sport and play—a good match for Ludivine's divine play. The name was originally masculine but, with the late-nineteenth-century fashion of flower and plant names for women, has also been used for women (Hanks and Hodges 160). Claudette Sartiliot points out that floral morphology "seems to invite this symbolic crossing of genders" (17).[18] The mythological tale of Hyacinthus has also been identified as an early homoerotic love story (Biedermann 180, Walker 427), and the legend has been conflated with that of the representative of self-love, Narcissus (Walker 427). All of these aspects suggest the complementary nature of the attraction between Ludivine and Hyacinthe, the breaking down of barriers, and the expansion of possibilities, parallel to the formation of the adoptive family.[19]

As a painter, Hyacinthe sees Ludivine's beauty. He offers a true gift: to create her portrait, to help her see herself as a beautiful woman, in both body and soul. He desires, not cries of fear, nor to pass on his name to future generations—that he has no patronymic underscores the point—what he wants is Ludivine's rebirth and his own. As he says, in a reversal of the genders of the Orphic myth, "Je voudrais la mettre au monde une seconde fois dans la joie et qu'elle me fasse surgir à nouveau des ténèbres de la terre" (108) [I want to give birth to her a second time, with joy, and have her bring me forth again from the darkness of the earth]. His maternal intention elicits in her the fullness of her sensual potential.

The play does not end, however, with the traditional "old marriage plot" (Heilbrun 1988, 121). Elzéar has been killed by Ludivine, in obedience to his own orders. She is put on trial for his death. The trial scene shows how far Ludivine has come during her independent management of her family's affairs. She is now capable of speaking eloquently in her own defense. She will brave the law, represented by the jealous and vindictive Crebessa, with his religious allies, the Péchés Capitaux (The Seven Deadly Sins), warning: "Ma vie est entre vos mains, M. le juge, et peut éclater d'un moment à l'autre, comme une grenade, et vous brûler jusqu'aux os, si vous n'y prenez garde" (107) [My life is in your hands, Your Honor, and can blow up at any moment, like a grenade, and burn you down to your bones, if you're not careful]. The French "grenade" has two distinct meanings here. "Grenade," as pomegranate, symbol of the womb, symbol of female fertility (Walker 1988, 493), recalls the many associations of Ludivine with the bountiful harvest of food ("la récolte abondante et mûre" [62] [the abundant, ripe harvest]), and with the family of rescued individuals ("tu cueilleras l'enfant sauvage" [26] [you will harvest the wild child]). In addition, the "grenade"—the weapon so named by association with the fruit—reveals Ludivine as ready to wage war against the established order, the hegemony of British patriarcho-religious law. Let it not be forgotten that, although Judge Crebessa is in charge, the trial has been held, not in a courtroom, but in nature, on Ludivine's "turf"—if one will allow the pun.[20]

John Crebessa dies of a heart attack, just as he was to sentence his powerful rival, La Corriveau, to death by hanging and exposure to public view in an iron cage. Once saved, Ludivine thinks first of claiming the keys of power, held by Crebessa, to use them, not to imprison, but to liberate. She leads the procession to free the fragile intellectual locked in the gilded cage, Rosalinde, now represented as an owl, the symbol of the goddess of wisdom, Minerva or Athena. The liberation of woman's intelligence, Ludivine's final act of female solidarity—such acts are rare in Hébert's work—closes the play.[21]

In the years between "Le Torrent" and *La Cage*, Hébert explored numerous family relationships, most of the "pernicious" (32) variety described by Ben Shek in his essay, "The Family in Québécois Fiction." Yet, Hébert came to understand much since "blaming the victim" in 1945. In creating a family headed by Claudine Perrault, a rage-filled, monstrous Medusa or Hecate, a rule-bound and sadistic maimer of childhood, and, in killing her off, both by silencing her in her son's narration and by the act of matricide, Hébert remained, paradoxically, despite her violent opposition, close to the treatment of family in the "novels of the land." Marianne Hirsch encapsulates this powerlessness of mothers (and women in general), explaining, "Inflating maternal influence has the effect of blaming mothers, rather than society" (18).

La Cage, with its title in the singular, concretizes the traditional version of the family as a rigid prison, a literal "cellule familiale" (family unit/cell). By contrast, in Ludivine's extended, inclusive, fairy-tale family by choice, with the mutual efforts of a joyful, playful collection of individuals, with a dis/orderly, new vision of the androgynous couple, and of altruistic solidarity, one finds "plenitude," rather than "lack" (manque). One perhaps also gains the understanding that, as Amy Swerdlow has put it in *Families in Flux*, "As we perceive that the family is not only a product of the larger society, but also its producer and reproducer, we begin to realize that changing the family can help change the society" (xv). Using the family as a microcosm, Anne Hébert probed deeply into society's ills throughout her writing career, for she refused to accept evil as inevitable.

Notes

1. A later work, *L'Enfant chargé de songes* (1992) (*Burden of Dreams*), has, by contrast, attracted much—and excellent—analysis.

2. Luc Lacourcière published his extensive research on the legend of La Corriveau in a series of articles in the 1960s and 1970s. Nicole Guilbault's essential volume surveys La Corriveau–inspired materials. With the help of these works, one can see the importance of the legend in Hébert's writing. I wish to thank Kathryn Slott for informing me about the Lacourcière articles.

3. All translations are mine. A published translation exists of "Le Torrent" (in *The Torrent: Novellas and Short Stories by Anne Hébert,* trans. Gwendolyn Moore [Montreal: Harvest House, 1973]). However, because it was completed over a quarter-century ago, before many of Hébert's themes, like "l'ordre" (order), had become clear, I would have had to modify the translation significantly on several occasions had I chosen to cite it.

4. "T'as quitté le village à cause du petit, hein?" (14) [You left the village because of the boy, eh?]. Recent research by historian Marie-Paule Malouin (see Turenne) shows that it would have been unlikely that an "unwed mother" and her "illegitimate child" could live alone together: "a mother cannot keep her baby

without the father's legal recognition of the child" (54). Most of these children were sent to orphanages because "prejudice against illegitimate children hindered adoption" (54).

5. In *Le Temps sauvage*, Hébert spells out, in a similar manner, the essence of Québec's traditional culture: "le culte de la mère fait pendant au culte du prêtre [dans ce pays]" (64) [the cult of the mother matches the cult of the priest (in this land)].

6. Shek credits Jean Le Moyne for the insight that the infant Jesus and the decapitated Saint John the Baptist are Québec's two major symbols. Amica's head swirling in the torrent recalls the latter.

7. See Vanasse for an analysis of the Medusa theme in works of several male writers of Québec.

8. The expression comes from the narration of the film on Hébert, in the "Profession écrivain" series, *Dompter les démons* (*To Tame the Demons*, Claude Godbout, 1982). In documents on women's education, "submission" is a leitmotiv. Historically, it was, as M. Dumont describes it, "the feminine virtue *par excellence*" (18).

9. Québec's men had outlets for their rage, such as hunting and the use of "sacres"—curses based on religious terminology, characteristic of the culture of Québec. Women's behavior required modesty in all areas. See especially Thivierge.

10. Cirlot lists the key as an attribute of Hecate (159), "the Terrible Mother" (137). Another attribute, the lash, may be associated with Claudine's desire to "dompter," "mater," or "dresser" (tame, break in, subdue).

11. *Le Premier jardin* (*The First Garden*) provides perhaps the best examples, with Guillemette Thibault (86–87) and the three identities of the heroine: Pierrette Paul, Marie Eventurel, and Flora Fontanges.

12. See, for example, two excellent articles: Côté/Mitchell, and Paterson.

13. See François Hébert.

14. In a 1982 interview with Jean Royer, Hébert insisted on the importance of the woman speaking for herself: "pour elle-même en son nom propre" (21) [for herself, in her own name].

15. I use the French term because the English translation, "family unit," lacks the connotation of the prison cell, important to Hébert's focus.

16. In English, the equivalent expression would be the "in-laws." Hébert, however, capitalizes on the irony of the adjective "belle" (beautiful).

17. Susan Suleiman speaks of the "playful (laughing) mother in contemporary feminist experimental writing" (145); see also her entire chapter 7, "Feminist Intertextuality and the Laugh of the Mother."

18. As Sartiliot explains, "the receptacle-shaped corolla readily becomes a symbol of the womb, whereas the pistil with its erect style points to phallic symbolism" (17).

19. Randall sees in fantastic literature the denial of "the male-female duality on which the traditional family relies" (149).

20. My analysis of Ludivine's behavior during the trial was enhanced by a comment by Kathleen Rowe in her study of "unruly" American figures, such as Mae West, Roseanne Arnold Barr, and Miss Piggy: "Courtrooms offer ideal sites for unruly challenges to patriarchy and the authority of the law . . ." (182). For their disturbance of the established order, I prefer to call such women in Hébert's works dis/orderly, rather than "unruly."

21. Bishop mentions Ludivine's feminist solidarity, without giving specific examples (213; see also his Introduction, 21).

Works Cited

Bal, Mieke. "Sexuality, Sin and Sorrow: The Emergence of Female Character (A Reading of Genesis 1–3)." In *The Female Body in Western Culture: Contemporary Perspectives*, edited by Susan R. Suleiman, 317–38. Cambridge: Harvard University Press, 1986.

Biedermann, Hans. *Dictionary of Symbolism*. 1989. Translated by James Hulbert. New York: Facts on File, 1992.

Bishop, Neil B. *Anne Hébert, son oeuvre, leurs exils*. Talence: Presses de l'Université de Bordeaux, 1993.

Boynard-Frot, Janine. *Un Matriarcat en procès: Analyse systématique de romans canadiens-français, 1860–1960*. Montréal: Presses de l'Université de Montréal, 1982.

Carisse, Colette. *La Famille: mythe et réalité québécoise*. Vol. 1. Sillery: Gouvernement du Québec, 1974.

Cirlot, J. E. *A Dictionary of Symbols*. Translated by Jack Sage. New York: Philosophical Library, 1962.

Côté, Paul Raymond and Constantina Mitchell. "*Les Fous de Bassan* and 'Le Torrent': At the Crossroads of Desire and Delusion." *Modern Language Studies* 21, no. 4 (1991): 78–89.

Dumont, Fernand, Jean Hamelin, and Jean-Paul Montminy. *Idéologies au Canada français: 1940–1976*. 3 vols. Québec: Presses de l'Université Laval, 1981.

Dumont, Micheline and Nadia Fahmy-Eid. *Les Couventines: l'éducation des filles au Québec dans les congrégations religieuses enseignantes, 1840–1960*. Montréal: Boréal, 1986.

Gagnon, Mona-Josée. *Les Femmes vues par le Québec des hommes: trente ans d'idéologies, 1940–1970*. Montréal: Editions du Jour, 1974.

Green, Mary Jean. "The Novel in Québec: The Family Plot and the Personal Voice." In *Studies on Canadian Literature: Introduction and Critical Essays*, edited by Arnold E. Davidson, 178–92. New York: Modern Language Association, 1990.

———. "The Witch and the Princess: The Feminine Fantastic in the Fiction of Anne Hébert." *American Review of Canadian Studies* 15, no. 2 (1985): 137–46.

Guilbault, Nicole. *Il était cent fois la Corriveau: Anthologie*. Québec: Nuit Blanche, 1995.

Hanks, Patrick and Flavia Hodges. *Dictionary of First Names*. Oxford: Oxford University Press, 1990.

Hébert, Anne. *La Cage*, suivi de *L'Ile de la Demoiselle*. Montréal: Boréal, 1990.

———. *Les Enfants du sabbat*. Paris: Seuil, 1975.

———. *Les Fous de Bassan*. Paris: Seuil, 1982.

———. *Le Temps sauvage*. Montréal: HMH, 1967.

———. *Le Torrent* 1950. Ville La Salle: L'Arbre HMH, 1976.

Hébert, François. Article from *Le Jour* 13 September 1975. In *Anne Hébert: Dossier de presse 1942–1980*. No pagination. Sherbrooke: Bibliothèque du Séminaire de Sherbrooke, 1981.

Heilbrun, Carolyn. *Writing A Woman's Life*. New York: Norton, 1988.

Hirsch, Marianne. *The Mother/Daughter Plot: Narrative, Psychoanalysis, Feminism*. Bloomington: Indiana University Press, 1989.

Lacourcière, Luc. "Le Destin posthume de la Corriveau." *Les Cahiers des Dix* 34 (1969): 239–71.

———. "Le Triple destin de Marie-Josephte Corriveau (1733–1763)." *Les Cahiers des Dix* 33 (1968): 213–42.

Malouin, Marie-Paule. "La Laïcisation de l'école publique québécoise entre 1939 et 1969: un processus de masculinisation." *Historical Studies in Education/ Revue d'Histoire de l'Education* 4, no. 1 (1992): 1–29.

McDonald, Marci. "Anne Hébert: Charting the Rage Within." *City Woman* (Spring 1981): 54–61, 74.

Moss, Jane. "'All in the Family': Québec Family Drama in the 1980s." *Journal of Canadian Studies/Revue d'Etudes Canadiennes* 27, no. 2 (1992): 97–106.

Paterson, Janet M. "A la source de l'énigme: 'Le Torrent' d'Anne Hébert." *Tangence* 50 (mars 1996): 7–19.

Pratt, Annis. *Archetypal Patterns in Women's Fiction*. Bloomington: Indiana University Press, 1981.

Pykett, Lyn. "Seizing the Crime: Recent Women's Crime Fiction." *The New Welsh Review* 21, no. 5 (1989): 24–27.

Randall, Neil. "The Makeshift Family in Canadian Fantastic Fiction." In *Family Fictions in Canadian Literature*, edited by Peter Hinchcliffe, 45–55. Waterloo: Waterloo University Press, 1988.

Rea, Annabelle M. "La Danse chez Anne Hébert: un demi-siècle de corps féminins." *Europe Plurilingue*, numéro spécial (mars 1997): 191–205.

Rowe, Kathleen. *The Unruly Woman: Gender and the Genres of Laughter*. Austin: Texas University Press, 1995.

Royer, Jean. *Ecrivains contemporains: entretiens 3*. Montréal: L'Hexagone, 1985: 11–22.

Sartiliot, Claudette. *Herbarium, verbarium: The Discourse of Flowers*. Lincoln:University of Nebraska Press, 1993.

Shek, Ben-Z. "The Family in Québécois Fiction." In *Family Fictions in Canadian Literature*, edited by Peter Hinchcliffe, 26–32. Waterloo: University of Waterloo Press, 1988.

Suleiman, Susan R. *Subversive Intent: Gender, Politics and the Avant-garde*. Cambridge: Harvard University Press, 1990.

Swerdlow, Amy, Renate Bridenthal, Joan Kelly, Phyllis Vine. *Families in Flux*. New York: The Feminist Press, 1989.

Thivierge, Nicole. "Modes et modestie féminines." *Cultures du Canada Français* 8 (1991): 18–29.

Turenne, Martine. "La Véritable histoire des Orphelins de Duplessis." *L'Actualité* July 1997 (54–56, 58)

Vanasse, André. *Le Père vaincu, la Méduse et les fils castrés: psychocritiques d'oeuvres québécoises contemporaines*. Montréal: XYZ, 1990.

Walker, Barbara G. *The Woman's Dictionary of Symbols and Sacred Objects*. Edison, NJ: Castle, 1988.

Myth and Memory in Nicole Brossard's *Baroque d'aube* and *Vertige de l'avant scène*

ALICE A. PARKER

WHAT IF "WOMEN" WERE NOT ONLY "DISCONTENTS" (FREUD), BUT ACtively "disloyal to civilization" (Lillian Smith/Adrienne Rich)? What if they experienced their immersion in language and discourse as sites of resistances? For Nicole Brossard as for many feminist theorists, gender itself is an enabling violence, written on our bodies and inscribed in our psyches long before we become conscious agents, but equally productive of resistances at every level.

What interests me in Brossard's last two works—*Baroque d'aube* (1995) (*Baroque at Dawn* [1997]) and *Vertige de l'avant scène* (1997) (*Vertigo of the Proscenium*)—is the way she works with myth and memory.[1] I will also look at the recent addendum to her *Journal intime* (*Personal Journal*), "Oeuvre de chair et métonymies" (1998) ("Bodywork and Metonymies"). Myth and memory are complementary dimensions, hedges against misogyny on the one hand and mortality on the other. Beyond the obvious potential for actual violence and abuse, misogyny results in the exclusion of women's material lives and accomplishments. A phallo(go)centric worldview reifies sexual difference, misrepresenting women's perceptions and their values, their relationships to themselves and to others. Mythic constructions counterbalance negativity, death, and destruction by expanding spiritual consciousness, by linking us to forces larger than our personal egos. Myths permit us to glimpse the awesome mysteries of life, of the universe, of creation. In order to play such a role, however, myths must remain fluid, protean, adapting to the constantly changing worlds in which we live and breathe.

Memory in *Baroque d'aube* is complex. It is intertextual, referring back to Brossard's own works and to those of other writers. Memory is also personal and cultural: Brossard investigates how memory works to produce identity, its roles in constructing and policing sexual difference. Myth and memory are not separable, but rather work in tandem as textual and cultural process. Thus the female voices in her works both inflect and shape the buried treasures of myth and memory. Characters themselves are mythic embodiments: "la naissance d'un personnage ... peut se comparer à la naissance d'un mythe" (*BA* 227) [the birth of a character ... can compare with the birth of a myth (*BD* 223)]. The goals of Brossard's efforts to "feminize" the resources of myth and memory are to refurbish both the imaginary and the symbolic potential of our cultural languages.

In her three recent texts, Brossard deals not only with relationships between the individual and the community in terms of gender and sexuality, but also how the cultural imaginary embodied in language and fictional representations affects women's potential for creative work. *Baroque d'aube* uses multiple geocultural locations as well as an oceanographic expedition on the high seas to reconfigure myth and memory, to open them out and permit new imagining literally to *take place*. Brossard's concerns are with the constraints of millennial histories affecting women's material lives and ambitions, and with the creative potential to deconstruct limiting boundaries both of the real and the imaginary. Her strategies range from the ironic portrayal of masculinist discourses to an exploration of virtual reality, incorporating new configurations of time/space and of collaborations/communities of women. Both the terms "baroque" and "aube" (dawn) are "charged like meteorites in the text," in accordance with Brossard's project to "divert the course of fiction" (*Picture Theory* 130, 99).

Myths are public dreams as dreams are private myths (Campbell 1988, 48). We know that myths are culturally inflected, reflecting geocultural and historical circumstances. I believe that all literature obeys an impulse toward mythmaking—stories that relate us to our mortality, to the community, to the earth and the cosmos, to poetic figures that plumb the depths of the psyche. In the liminal areas where myths are reconceived, lines between the private and the public blur. Myth is also political, intertwined with history and power. Poets and other creative artists understand the connections. In a recent companion piece to her *Journal intime*, entitled "Oeuvre de chair et métonymies" ("Bodywork and Metonymies"), Brossard writes: "Nous vivons tous au bord d'un roman-fleuve" (102) [We all live at the edge of an immense story]. Cultural artifacts have a profound influence on our sense of reality. The work is a fictional dialogue, a meditation on generations of women. "Écris-moi" [Write me], urges the daughter. "Sois ma mère encore un temps. Le temps de te lire et de comprendre la vérité que dans l'ensemble les femmes inventent comme des solutions de bonheur qui grisent l'esprit" (103) [Be my mother for a while still. The time it takes to read you and to understand the truth that women as a whole invent like solutions of happiness that make the mind reel].

The polysemous implications of "generations" leads the writer to thematize the relativity of time, the dimension in which desiring creatures of the flesh are suspended, swimming often against the current. As a mythic event, the birth of a child reminds us "du riche mystère des lois chimiques et physiques qui nous gouvernent et nous tiennent en haleine comme des créatures aimant la vitesse et rêvant, sens dessus dessous, de lenteur et d'extase sous la voûte céleste" (104) [of the rich mystery of chemical and physical laws that govern us, keeping us breathless like creatures in love with speed, who dream, topsy-turvy, of slowness and ecstasy beneath the celestial vault]. Generations also conjure up acts of violence, which the daughter refuses to contemplate, remembering instead the sounds of the maternal tongue from which she is now exiled, and the landscapes of her childhood (111). "Écris-moi encore" [Write me again], she repeats. Writing, for Brossard, is the very figure of creative memory that links the individual and the species, hope and desire.

Cybil Noland, the writer-protagonist of *Baroque d'aube*, is a multilingual world traveler, addicted to cities and to the frenetic images of the information age. "Elle avait ainsi appris à se déplacer entre les croyances et les rêves dispersés au fil des générations et des siècles" (15) [Thus she had learned to navigate among beliefs and dreams dispersed over generations and centuries (7)]. Like her creator, she is also concerned with *presence*, and the endless questions raised when we try to make sense of our senses (27). She relies on her intellect and her imagination to lead her beyond the bloodbath of history and the facile clichés of everyday reality. The reader enters the story at dawn, in a room in the Rafale Hotel, in a North American city that is "armed to the teeth." A chance encounter has brought Cybil together with a young violinist whom she calls La Sixtine. The virtues of anonymity permit the women to know each other first through their senses, without preconceptions, suppressing the biographical in favor of unedited pleasures. Enjoyment erases boundaries, converting the present into a mythic event, a synthesis of memory and desire.

As she situates Montreal on the map of Western culture, Brossard insists on a literary space for women's memory, desire, pleasure, agency, and creativity. Traditionally we have regarded myths either as false or unscientific information, or as narratives frozen in time, referring principally to origins. From his study of religion, philosophy, anthropology, and psychology, Joseph Campbell defines myths as facts of the mind. Telling/retelling/interpreting stories that relate us to each other, to our mortality, and to the world beyond seems to be part of our hardwiring. Mythmaking is an ongoing process, which begins with language itself. One could say that all of Brossard's work is about writing, and thus refers to the medium of writing, language. Generically, the mythos is the telling; thus the words as rituals (re)enact the deeds. However, words, the base units of language, are always/already located in a symbolic system.[2] The signifying chains of meaning to which we are heir bear the imprint of those who came before, including those who were refused a voice and whose silence moves us to attempt a translation. This, again, is where myth and memory collide/collude.

Perhaps, as Barbara Johnson observed, if there had not been two sexes, if sexual difference had not been a founding sociocultural category, there would have been no need for literature (1980, 13). Literature cannot tell what difference this makes, since (sexual) difference is firmly installed within literature itself. Is this a reason for the resistance to narrative on the part of proponents of modernity—analogous to a resistance to history—the fact that narrative so often propagates the same old story? "Si nous continuons à nous parler le même langage, nous allons reproduire la même histoire" [If we keep on speaking the same language together, we're going to reproduce the same history], observed Luce Irigaray. "Recommencer les mêmes histoires" (1977, 205) [Begin the same old stories all over again (1985, 205)]. From her earliest prose fiction, Brossard has written against the grain of narrativity, against the causality that imprisons women in stifling roles, absurd stereotypes, androcentric values. Yet, she continues to explore the work of time and of language.

For Brossard, the problematic of gender has to be analyzed first at the radical/ root level, that of the smallest unit of thought/expression, the words themselves. According to a genealogy of evil recounted in *Baroque d'aube* by an early mentor of la Sixtine, "Une fois installé dans les mots . . . le mal avait le pouvoir de circuler librement" (34) [Once established in words . . . the evil was empowered to circulate unimpeded (26)]. For example, "Le machisme . . . fait des trous dans l'âme des femmes et les femmes doivent remplir de leurs larmes chacun de ces trous. Quand les femmes n'ont plus de larmes, leurs filles prennent la relève. A leur tour, elles se penchent au-dessus des trous pour les emplir de leurs cris" (34) [Machismo leaves deep cavities in women hearts . . . and each cavity must be filled with women's tears. When the women have no tears left, their daughters take their place; then the daughters bend their heads over the cavities so as to fill them with their laments (26)]. Literature, a handmaiden to myth, is gender-inflected in all of its semiological operations, from the smallest units of meaning to grammar and syntax to narratology and figuration.[3] We can thus expect Brossard to offer multiple sites of resistance to various modes of literary discourse. By the same token, she stretches her imagination to counter the negativity of contemporary civilization.

Brossard fractures the narrative, furnishing us bits and pieces of women's memories, juxtaposed with mythic symbols of modernity. From the Rafale Hotel, the excursion into the city is risky; "Rafale" (literally a gust of wind, but also a volley of gunshots) suggests physical and spiritual dangers, whereas the several hotels in the fiction figure the transience of modern life. Questions provoked by urbanity, gender, and violence occasion daily acts of survival. The perpetrators of violence are qualified as *le bourreau* (the executioner), "un prince qui ne compte pas les gouttes de sang sur son front libre et solitaire" (38–39) [a prince who does not count the drops of blood on his free, lonely brow (31)]. Youth leaves its graffiti on the walls or tattooed into its flesh. Fear is everywhere; a lapse of attention could signal death, as in *Le Désert mauve* (*Mauve Desert*) where Angela Parkins forgot to look around. Mortality is the ultimate mythic theme. The strategies required to deal with death are countered in the text by conscious practices of creativity and pleasure. Characters negotiate between the real and the virtual by means of their imaginations and their wits, while temporal and spatial boundaries blur, as do those between writer and character.

Launching her enigmatic text from a Samuel Beckett quote that proclaims "Je ne raconterai pas mon raisonnement" (7) [I shall not recount my reasoning], and another from Alejandra Pizarnik stating that she wants to celebrate "celle qui possède mon ombre: celle qui dérobe au néant noms et figures" (11) [the woman who owns my shadow; she who rescues names and faces from obscurity (3)], Brossard situates her reader in a mythic time and space. "D'abord l'aube. Puis la femme avait joui" (13) [First the dawn. Then the woman came (5)]. In the heart of a civilization of "gangs, artists, dreams and computers," in the midst of a "night that swallows all countries," Cybil hears her lover cry out: "dé vaste moi, m'ange moi" [Devastate me. Eat me up] as she leaves the earth behind in "un énorme réflexe de vie aérienne" (13) [a stupendous aerial life reflex (5)]. Simultaneously, the sea slips into Cybil's thoughts along with the poet, Louise Labé, and immeasurable questions (13). Neither of the women think of speaking, each of them savoring instead the sensations of the present along with the sense of the elsewhere ("ailleurs") of their lives, like a former life (14).

Although Brossard, like Beckett, conceals the "raisonnement" (reasoning) undergirding the construction of the fiction, a sense of doubleness or shadowing operates on all levels in the text. The reader finds complements rather than polarities, both/and rather than either/or, in consonance with contemporary theories of space/time or particle/waves. Brossard's text breaks free of the gravity of ordinary reality that ties us to the phenomenology of everyday existence, the mechanical, mundane activities of our linear, goal-oriented lives. In mythic time and space the simultaneity of past and present impart a profound significance to rituals, allowing the participants to reenact spiritual dramas that ensure continuation and connection. Memory and collaborations among women, as well as the cultivation of pleasure and desire, elicit their creative resources, putting them in touch with the sea and with aerial levels of existence. Along with a suggestion of mythic prototypes and mysterious gifts of prophecy, Cybil and la Sixtine are charnel creatures. Their lovemaking represents a bodily wisdom that connects them not only to a microcosmic level of cells and neurons but to a larger communicative/ performative network of psychic, emotional, and mental exchange. Such intermingling of ontological spaces operates also at the level of the text. La Sixtine figures in Cybil's novel, while Cybil discovers that Nicole Brossard will be lecturing in Buenos Aires. Cybil and la Sixtine meet in room 43, the year of Brossard's birth. The effect of these (co)incidences is to reinforce boundary violations, notably between "reality" and fiction.

Baroque d'aube is a work of fiction in that it deals with narrativity and time, while manipulating language and blurring registers. The power to activate the many resources of the language in order to touch all of our senses simultaneously is the ultimate power of the writer. The text blends the explicit and the imaginary, the literal and the symbolic, the canny and the uncanny, juxtaposing semantic levels, playing with syntactical, temporal, and spatial arrangements. The principal conceit is an oceanographic mission aboard a vessel aptly named the *Symbol,* a mission to chart/reclaim the sea *before it is too late.* A collaboration among three women, a scientist and two artists, to produce a commemorative album of the voyage provokes a baroque profusion of ideas and feelings. The two artists, Cybil and Irène Mage, must confront fears and anxieties related to scientific methodologies and virtual technologies, and to a claustrophobic environment, as they are confined first to the library and then to meals with the all-male crew, who regale themselves with pornographic films. Meanwhile the (male) doctor and priest use the "god-trick of seeing everything from nowhere" (Haraway 1991, 189) to discourse omnisciently on Western "civilization."

Argentina, from which the *Symbol* will depart, has only recently emerged from the terror that runs through its historical veins, of which we are reminded in the persona of a suave arms dealer who funds the expedition. Yet, Buenos Aires also represents the seduction of the arts, the tango, and the accomplished women of la Sixtine's youth. Reading cultural texts disloyally, however, the many signs of machismo and misogyny command at least a portion of our thinking lives:

> Il y avait trop de sensations, de savoirs. Trop de signes. Trop de la même vie au milieu des bêtes de tout acabit qui entraient dans le présent après être sorties de la mer, puis de la forêt et du désert comme de puissants symboles chargés de décorer l'imaginaire pendant que les hommes avançaient péniblement vers la ville à coups de récits et de nouveaux outils. Les peaux avaient été tatouées, tannées, les têtes couronnées, les crânes assemblés, les os travaillés pour jouer, compter, décorer et blesser. Les récits avaient transformé les femmes en masses myst*érieuses* et fertiles, puis en proies silencieuses, puis en choses bronzées et électriques qui excitaient les passants des grandes villes. Tout ce temps les sexes d'hommes avaient été scuptés droits dirigés vers le ciel implorant Dieu de nettoyer lui-même le sexe des femmes de toute impureté afin que les fils puissent enjamber le présent et chevaucher les étoiles. Bestiaire. . . . Turf. (151)

> [There were too many feelings, too many bodies of knowledge. Too many signs. Too much of the same kind of life, with creatures of all shapes and descriptions coming into the present out of the sea, then out of the forest and the desert, like powerful symbols responsible for providing background to men's imaginations as they toiled toward cities by dint of narrative and new tools. Skin had been tattooed and tanned, heads crowned, skulls collected, bones carved for game-playing, counting, decorating, and wounding. The narrative had turned women into blobs of *mirth*stery and fertility, then into silent prey, then into suntanned, electrical things that turned on big-city passersby. All this time, the sexes of men were being carved to point straight at the sky, imploring God to do the dirty work of cleansing women's sexes of all impurities so that sons could step over the present and ride off on the stars. Bestiary. . . . Surf.] (145)

The reader remembers the surrealistic canvases of Max Ernst, with monsters emerging from primeval forests. Such an evolution gives us pause rather than pride in our humanity. Traversed by networks of power, we sort out the fictions that control our lives, while expanding frames of reference, the meanings we can assign to our desires. The latter, the regenerative part, is the work of good art and literature, to nourish our minds and our spirits. To be (re)connected to mythmaking is to (re)experience the wonder of life.

Therefore, relying upon the expertise of Occident Desrives to guide them, the women leave the boundaries of the known world behind them as they set sail on a journey toward the unknown. In *Vertige de l'avant-scène* (1997), her next work, Brossard writes: "si c'est un livre c'est un espace pour durer" (11) [if it's a book it is a space to endure]. The potential for a work of art to endure relates it to the sacred. We must respect the mystery, the silence, she notes, as it is "our reservoir of hope" (13). Words can grab hold of our lives without us knowing it, but we keep our equilibrium in the present by caressing the future. Thus in our best moments we preserve our balance, as night disappears into a mirror that retains no image (19).

The women on the ship live intensely, preserving their balance in the midst of a strange, new environment, registering unedited impressions and thoughts. However, it is not without anger that Cybil confronts Occident once they are finally permitted on deck. The night, like the imageless mirror, is of a density like none other, so frightfully dark that Occident will finally lose her breath and die. Yet, the night also yields an apocalyptic voice that promises creativity and renewal. Cybil and Irène Mage will complete their work; it will be translated and it will endure. The insights they have acquired will have been transformed and preserved, along with Occident's knowledge.

Beyond their negative forms, resistances take advantage of the (hitherto) unthought, unsaid, the many exclusions women have experienced from the so-called historical record, the silences entombed in words and phrases. In *Vertige* the poet writes: "les silences creusent / dans la phrase une ouverture / nos chances de ferveur à ciel ouvert" (20) [silences excavate / an opening in the sentence / our chances for fervor under an open sky]. Memory is a significant resource in the effort to fill the lacunae, personal memories as well as a substantial intertext of women's words and deeds. Symbolic names in *Baroque d'aube* reactivate cultural memories; they function like double-acting leavening agents, imparting a fresh vitality to the text. Mythic resonances abound: there is of course the *Symbol* itself, the ship that will carry the women and crew into unexplored waters, *au fond* (into the depths) as well as *ailleurs* (elsewhere), terms suggestive of philosophical as well as phenomenological concerns. Cybil and la Sixtine evoke learned women and sibylline prophesies of antiquity, reawakened by Michelangelo; Irène Mage (image) conjures up the figurative possibilities and prestige of photography, the ultramodern artistic medium.

The most perplexing character/voice/persona is that of the scientist Occident Desrives, who grew up in her father's casinos (193). How does game theory factor in to the strengths and weaknesses of Western cultural values? What have we made of our Enlightenment heritage, master discourses, and scientific pretensions that were to have provided the rationale for unraveling the mysteries of the universe? What logic persuaded us to make our lives more comfortable by exploiting the earth and non-Western populations? Is life essentially a gamble, a game of chance based upon educated guesses, like science? In this patrilineal scenario Occident has no firsthand knowledge of her mother, and lacks a talent for intimacy (192). As she puts it, aside from certain biological and chemical information she has acquired about self-preservation, she is emotionally illiterate (193). Ironically, she portrays the field of her oceanographic endeavors as a "desert," pointing to the derivation of the word "mare" in the Sanskrit "maru" (194). However, although she is slated to expire as a new era dawns, Occident has used her power to "change the horizon" of Cybil's life (195). The gifts she has imparted with her difficult discipline will remain present in the creative work that results from the voyage.

If not all memories are regenerative in the dark night of the patriarchy that closes in on the women the last evening out, there are always possibilities for rewriting, for radical world travelers to use their knowledge to rework the myths that nourish individual and collective psyches. The mysterious, sibylline messages of the siren that come to Cybil on deck the last night on the ocean recall the famous "Voix du Québec" (Voices of Quebec) that speak to Maria Chapdelaine, the early-twentieth-century heroine of Louis Hémon. However, the tonality and messages are quite different in Brossard's work; the poet resists the condescending voices of male authorities, as well as "ordinary" sexism and misogyny, while providing spaces in which to further women's energies and creativity. The Siren tells Cybil that she will write her book:

> Tu refuseras de choisir entre la voix, la nuit et la mer, t'enduisant de leur parfum, de leur immensité qui réveillent le corps dans l'abondance des serments d'amour. Dans cette langue qui te fut donnée, tu *réveilleras* les monstres, les légendes ... tout le vrai de réalité incrusté comme

une poussière du temps entre les ailes des anges et des madones sculptées. . . . Tu iras toutes les chercher ces voix dont tu entends les hautes et les basses, la mélopée, le modulé d'angoisse et de la peur, les cris de joie et de plaisir, les chuchotements énigmatiques, le murmure amoureux au matin clair. . . . Tu garderas l'équilibre au-dessus de l'âbime et de l'eau, vivras dans ton vertige. (190–91)

[You will refuse to choose from among this voice, the night and the sea, and will anoint yourself with their perfumes and immensity which awaken the body amid abundant declarations of undying love. In this language that was given to you, you will awaken dream monsters and legends . . . all the truth of reality incrusted like the dust of time between the wings of angels and on carved madonnas. . . . You will seek out every one of these voices, the high and low whose tones you hear even now, the recitative, the modulated strains of anxiety and fear, the cries of joy and pleasure, the enigmatic whisperings, the amorous murmurs in the pale light of morning. . . . You will teeter above the abyss and the water, and live in your vertigo.] (187)

The baroque splendor of Brossard's fiction lies in the beauty of her design, in the arrangement of voices, tonalities, images, events, and themes. Baroque also might qualify the complexity of narrative strategies, the interplay between fictional worlds, the juxtaposition of locations, the doubling of voices, and the repetition of images and motifs. At the dawn of a new millennium, Occident tells the artists that they must reinvest the sea with its symbolic potential. We might say the same of the dawn itself, of the horizon, of the immensity of the evening sky, of the vertigo of loving bodies, of prose fiction itself as Brossard has reconceived it. In a redesigned fictional space and language, *Baroque d'aube* has the energy of mythic dimensions, of cosmic discoveries that link what appears radically new to what we have always known.

Published two years later, *Vertige de l'avant scène* (*Vertigo of the Proscenium*) is also a work with which to enter the millennium. Equally enigmatic, it seems more philosophical, more classical in tone, in part because of the difference in genres. The volume is meditative and introspective, while avoiding, like the fiction, anecdote and biography. Some of the same concepts recur, like *vertige* (vertigo) itself, *immensité, réalité, silence, présent/futur, beauté, visions, solitude*, and familiar Brossardian terms like *horizon, nuit* (night), *corps* (body), *désir*. As in earlier texts, the poet plays with the first person, redefining subjectivity and gender. "L'avant scène" of the title suggests a "fore-scene," a proscenium in its generic meaning, or again the portion of the stage on which introductions/expositions occur before the curtain is raised. Vertigo comes from the immensity of space and the ever-increasing speed of postmodern life, a good portion of which is now spent with the electronic signals of cyberspace. The future is always already upon us, which we confront "la tête remplie d'inventions / . . . un vent souple d'ivresse et de silence / dans les yeux" (30) [our head full of inventions / . . . a supple breeze tipsy with silence / in our eyes].

Where might we go with a preference for the moment, for surprises? (7). A series of responses that are not, of course, answers, resonates with echoes of earlier works. The poet continues to refine her language, to expand her concerns with the philosophical and spiritual implications of women's lives. She continues to register the phenomenology of life, thought, and writing, to probe the depths of psychic and cultural existence, as well as relationships between the body, the language, and the text ("cortex"). Myth and memory as they affect women's lives and creativity continue to intrigue her, along with time and eternity, the complexity and speed of existence as we enter the millennium. As always, she is the explorer, factoring in the mysteries of contemporary scientific theory, of virtual reality, and of the mother tongue that is her medium.

In the second part of *Vertige* entitled "Paumes flexibles" ("Flexible Palms"), the poet muses about the pleasure principle: "j'ai longtemps cru que la lumière en nous renversant d'un souffle rendait nos pensées si souples que nous pouvions, goûtant l'étreinte et le climat, changer de corps et d'identité" (77) [I have long believed that the light we have inside, bending with a breath, made our thoughts so supple that we could, thanks to an embrace and the climate, change bodies and identities]. The transformativity of bodies and identities is matched by textual operations, bending syntax, jumping semantic levels, juxtaposing unlikely terms, digging around in words and phrases for unexpected meanings. With a fine ear for the harmonies and dissonances of the language, sonorities reinforce sense. The surprises we encounter are at once sensual and significant, expanding understanding, setting new possibilities in motion, possibilities for more (re)writing of women's lives, more creativity. Thus we read: ". . . en tenant des mots simples au creux de sa main, elle admirait la manière dont chaque femme en appuyant sa bouche sur le présent tenait à la vie, au fracas des lèvres sur les bas-reliefs de mémoire de ventre et de culture" (78) [. . . holding simple words in the crux of her hand, she admired how each woman, by pressing her mouth to the present, could hold on to life, in the fracas of lips on the bas-reliefs of internal memory and culture]. Cupping our hands to hold the precious words, with a slight pressure of the lips we can access the present forms of existence, the bas-relief of memory, the womb that nurtured us, culture itself; with flexible palms we can grasp almost anything.

Of course, all accomplished poets work in a liminal space where new imagining can occur.[4] Each has a particular location, however. From her worktable in Montreal, Brossard continues to interrogate the "real," which counterbalances the obscurity of memory. "Notre visage d'actualité s'émeut" [Our visage is moved by the moment], she writes in the last piece of "Paumes flexibles," "que l'on en soit encore là à imaginer la vérité comme une explosion du silence et de la lumière dans la bouche" (84) [that we are still at the point of imagining truth like an implosion of silence and light in our mouths]. Hers is a corporeal writing, a writing of desire, even when the poet addresses an abstraction like "truth," which provokes an explosion of light and silence, bright as a quasar, dense as a vanished star. In the aura of words that collide is the sustained afterglow of sense and meaning, which the reader will continue to reinterpret.

Composed with the fluidity of free verse followed by dense textual blocks, *Vertige de l'avant scène* is elusive, vertiginous, requiring sustained attention to decode. Although mythic names and figures may not be as evident as in *Baroque d'aube*, the poet's project is analogous, to open a space in the cultural imaginary and on the horizon for women to dream. Feminists have been well aware of the damage to women's psyches and spirits in the West for prestigious religious icons to have been gendered male.[5] Brossard is not the only feminist poet to turn to preclassical pagan or nonbiblical sources for inspiration. Obviously, heroes' voyages and odysseys concern her less than the historical circumstances of women's lives or the material texture of the language. Her texts seek a corporeal wisdom, reclaiming what has been abjected from phallocentric reality and truth claims, knowledges that have always haunted the borders of cultural discourses.

A prime figure for such a reclamation project is lesbian love, woman-to-woman communication. Brossard never Platonizes such relationships.[6] In "nos vies de miniatures" (8) [our lives like miniatures], as in baroque poetry, the eyes are a threshold for pleasure:

> circonstance des yeux le plaisir se répéterait
> parfois nous dirions adieu on dirait du silence
> un acte de pure volonté pour revenir
> au début (8)

> [circumstance of the eyes pleasure would repeat itself
> sometimes we would say adieu one would say silence

an act of pure will to return
to the beginning]

The beginning of a life, of a relationship, of a poem: the reader is left to wonder as s/he reads on. With a "wildly beating heart," it seems as if we are on a "new planet," as we pass through reality with "such a taste for fiction," our tongues are ready to spring "émeutes sémantiques / entre les paradoxes et les beaux jours" (9) [semantic uprisings / between the paradoxes and fine days]. Nothing gives the poet (or the reader) such a "feverish" sense of presence as writing, while the book will activate metaphors and fiction, myth and memory in order to endure (11). Vertigo comes from an infatuation with language, with writing, with books that comes from the depths of a personal and cultural imaginary, from tradition and difference (12–14).

The poet admits to a "passion" for a "futur traduit en une immense version" (23) [future translated into an immense example], as every summer reawakens desire (24). When tempted by utopia or eternity, the poet factors in "un peu de réalité" (25) [a bit of reality], words like "larmes et genoux" [tears and knees], an adverbial expression of temporality such as "demain / le siècle cinq heures" [tomorrow / the century five o'clock], syllables with the flavor of "olive" and "apéro" (apéritif, before-dinner drink), a *self-portrait* of life (25). Art can intercept "un bruit qui secoue l'imaginaire" in "le nerf du réel" [a sound that shakes up the imaginary in the nerves of reality]. At a corporeal level, "l'art taille dans nos os / des visions" (26) [art sculpts visions / in our bones]. By jumping semantic registers, juxtaposing nouns, pronouns, abstractions, and bodily referents, the poet takes in all of existence in kaleidoscopic fashion:

> le sens de la vie à toute allure
> échine nerveuse goût de toi
> un siècle entre nous un récit
> les grands mythes
> et la rue Saint-Denis . . .
> de vieilles questions la chaleur (27)
>
> [the sense of life at top pace
> nervous spine a taste of you
> a century between us a story
> the great myths
> and Saint-Denis Street . . .
> the heat of old questions]

As she ponders the great myths, seated in the warmth of the summer sun on the rue Saint-Denis, a major artery of Montreal's cultural/culinary life, old questions recur. While she enriches the maternal tongue with a woman's visions and thoughts, a hefty "dose de cybernuit" (38) [dose of cybernight] worries her: what will tomorrow bring? What if a "digital / . . . forêt de signes rumeurs . . . écorchent / vive la lumière" (39) [digital / . . . forest of rumbling signs . . . strip / light bare]? When memory turns upon itself, every narrative fragment leads directly to fiction. In Brossard's lexicon "narration" and "fiction" represent dangerous, traditional scenarios for women. Thus her project is to rewrite them, to "exit fiction by means of fiction."

Here and elsewhere merge while the poet faces the horizon like a screen full of images, exploring the truth "d'un monde si fragile qu'on le dirait surah / entre les planètes" (43–44) [of such a fragile world one might call it fine silk / among the planets].[7] Writing has an erotic quality for Brossard: when she writes she is fully alive, in touch with the deepest centers of thought and feeling. This is the abode of silence, the *elsewhere* to which *jouissance* through lovemaking or creative work provide access. With the dictionary beside her, she has her finger on the pulse of the language as if she were touching her lover. An entire poem or verse may result from the discovery of a single word, whose root, overlays, and sonorities stimulate a flood of other words and figures. Most often, however, the surprises in the Brossardian text result from syntactical arrangements, layering and juxtapositions, as the lexicon remains of a classical purity. The poems in *Vertige* are precisely crafted, with the clarity and order of fractals.

I began by asserting that women practice a certain disloyalty to civilization, which is perceived as androcentric, hierarchical, and oppressive.[8] Unequal power relations provoke women writers and artists to return to the sources, to perform a radical analysis of the cultural imaginary, the myths and memories that nourish creative work. Toward the end of "Vertiges," the poet writes: "c'est quand on touche à ma liberté / que je compare d'où vient la mort" (63) [it's when they touch on my freedom / that I compare where death comes from]. Differential subject positions allow thinking individuals to contest the truth and reality claims of those whose cultural location permits them to exert control or to abuse power. Further, feminist theory alerts us to the disingenuous claims of unmarked locations. There are no innocent identity positions, even our own. Given an understanding of the "politics of location" (Rich 1986), we are responsible for where we are, whether the places we occupy are assigned or freely chosen.

In reinvesting myth and memory with feminist desire, Brossard never loses sight of the need to *rewrite* the female body, to liberate women from centuries of phallocentric representation. Such corporeal recoding has to effect a thorough inventory and reordering of the language, in order to produce a balance between the mother tongue and the Nom/non du Père. I do not mean to suggest a break between the "semiotic" and the symbolic (Kristeva), between the feminine and the masculine, but rather an ongoing negotiation between the inherited representations and stories of the past that reified sexual difference and a future that leaves the boundaries uncertain and fluid. Brossard insists on the creativity of women, once they are able to envision themselves as producers of knowledge and values. Writing, in particular, symbolizes renewal.

> le futur serait poème serait
> des yeux de silence et d'aéroport
> des yeux guetteurs de vaste et de vitesse (62)
>
> [the future would be a poem would be
> about the eyes of silence and the airport
> eyes watching space and speed]

The eyes figure a threshold of understanding and vision, a depth (of silence) within, and a seer-like capacity to read and interpret texts as yet unwritten. Women's love unsettles laws that favor a (libidinal) economy of abnegation and scarcity. Thus will subjects reclaim their life, their use value (62).

At the end of *Baroque d'aube*, during a night "in the eye of the hurricane," Cybil resists the temptation to explain her silence and the seduction of her translator. The two women absorb the present, "tango after tango" recalling Buenos Aires, as the questions return. At dawn, the images flood in (258–60). We have only one body, which changes without our knowing it. Similarly, in the fiction, narrative and poetic elements shift continuously, remain unpredictable—like a hypertext? As phallocentric messages deconstruct (themselves), the questions serve to raise our consciousness, to stimulate more writing, to make the most of our terrible freedom (260).

Notes

1. Although I devoted a chapter of my book, *Liminal Visions of Nicole Brossard* (Peter Lang, 1998), "The Speed of Silence," to *Baroque d'aube*, the work is so rich

in interpretive potential that I feel that I have only begun to explore the possibilities. A note on the translations: I have used Patricia Claxton's excellent translation of *Baroque d'aube* (*Baroque at Dawn*) for citations from the novel. Translations from *Vertige de l'avant-scène* and other works are my own. Note: I will use *BA* and *BD* in the text to refer to the original and to the translation.

2. The Symbolic represents the Word, or, as Lacan puts it, le Nom/non du Père.

3. Thus to argue, as does Julia Kristeva, that poetic discourse represents a maternal/feminine language not only plays into gender stereotypes, but is a vast oversimplification of the pervasive influence of sexual difference at every linguistic/semiotic level of thought and expression.

4. I discuss liminality at some length in the monograph on Brossard, the threshold where perceptions begin to become conscious (as opposed to the subliminal), and the use of the term in contemporary theory to refer to borderline states and ambitions.

5. These include the Father, the Son, and the Holy Spirit—not to mention the fathers of the Church or the priests and ministers of the various cults. Such a patriarchal heritage inflects Judaism and Islam as well. Irigaray addresses the problem of religion and gender directly in *Sexes et parentés*, especially the exclusion of women from theological texts and concepts. See "Femmes divines" and "Les Femmes, le sacré, l'argent." In *The Power of Myth*, Joseph Campbell discusses with Bill Moyers the significance of the diminution or elimination of the feminine principle in modern (especially Protestant) Christianity. See "The Gift of the Goddess." Kristeva addresses in particular the psychic impact of the Virgin Mary and its relation to motherhood, as well as psychoanalysis, faith, and gender in various works, including "Stabat Mater," "Maternité selon Giovanni Bellini" (*Polylogue*), and *In the Beginning Was Love: Psychoanalysis and Faith*.

6. Adrienne Rich argued in "Compulsory Heterosexuality and Lesbian Existence" (1980) in favor of a "lesbian continuum" that would qualify many relationships and networks as "lesbian," to the dismay of many (possibly homophobic) readers. Lesbian writers such as Monique Wittig and Catharine Stimpson advanced counterarguments insisting on an erotic component to the category "lesbian." Recently, Judith Butler (1990) and others have added a performative element to definitions of lesbian behaviors, while insisting that the category remain fluid, open to future reconceptualization.

7. Surah: a light, supple Indian silk, used for foulards (Petit Robert 1973, 1719). Yet, the explanation only partly accounts for the sensual quality of the word as Brossard uses it.

8. Thus the ideologies that resulted in the canonization of such works as *Maria Chapdelaine* and other *romans du terroir* [novels of the land], encouraging women to sacrifice themselves for their family and country, in the *revanche du berceau* ("revenge of the cradle") that reduced generations of women to breeders, in the hegemonic power of the Catholic Church in Québec that kept women ignorant and submissive, and in many other kinds of social control that silenced women's voices, resulted in diverse strategies for resistance, some conscious and some almost instinctual.

Works Cited

Brossard, Nicole. *Baroque d'aube*. Montréal: l'Hexagone, 1995. Translated by Patricia Claxton under the title *Baroque at Dawn* (Toronto: McClelland and Stewart, 1997).

———. *Journal intime* suivi de *Oeuvre de chair et métonymies*. Montréal: Les Herbes Rouges, 1998.
———. *Picture Theory*. Montréal: Nouvelle Optique, 1982.
———. *Vertige de l'avant scène*. Trois-Rivières: Écrits des Forges, 1997.
Butler, Judith. *Gender Trouble*. New York: Routledge, 1990.
Campbell, Joseph (with Bill Moyers). *The Power of Myth*. New York: Doubleday, 1988.
Haraway, Donna J. *Simians, Cyborgs and Women*. New York: Routledge, 1991.
Irigaray, Luce. *Ce Sexe qui n'en est pas un*. Paris: Les Éditions de Minuit, 1977. Translated by Catherine Porter with Caroline Burke under the title *This Sex Which Is Not One* (Ithaca, NY: Cornell University Press, 1985).
———. *Sexes et parentés*. Paris: Les Éditions de Minuit, 1987.
Johnson, Barbara. *The Critical Difference*. Baltimore: Johns Hopkins University Press, 1980.
Kristeva, Julia. *Polylogue*. Paris: Éditions du Seuil, 1977.
———. *In the Beginning Was Love: Psychoanalysis and Faith*. Translation by Arthur Goldhammer of *Au commencement était l'amour*. New York: Columbia University Press, 1987.
———. "Stabat Mater." In *Histoires d'amour*. Paris: Denoel, 1983. Translated as *Tales of Love* by Leon S. Roudiez. New York: Columbia University Press, 1987.
Le Petit Robert: Dictionnaire alphabétique & analogique de la langue française par Paul Robert. Edited Alain Rey. Paris: Société du Nouveau Littré, 1973.
Parker, Alice A. *Liminal Visions of Nicole Brossard*. New York: Peter Lang, 1998.
Rich, Adrienne. "Compulsory Heterosexuality and Lesbian Existence." In *Blood, Bread, and Poetry*. New York: Norton, 1986.
———. "Disloyal to Civilization: Feminism, Racism, Gynophobia." In *Lies, Secrets, and Silences*. New York: Norton, 1979.
———. "Notes Toward a Politics of Location." In *Blood, Bread, and Poetry*. New York: Norton, 1986.
Smith, Lillian. *The Winner Names the Age: A Collection of Writings by Lillian Smith*. Edited by Michelle Cliff. New York: Norton, 1978.

Writing and/in Mourning: The Legacy of Loss in Recent Texts by Madeleine Gagnon

MILÉNA SANTORO

En notre siècle la mort est devenue tabou . . . la mort est cachée. Et muette. Elle a été refoulée dans un no man's land. La mort habite maintenant un désert . . . Désert de pensées et désoeuvrement . . . d'aridité et de froidure tout à la fois. Très peu d'humains de nos jours peuvent et savent parler de la mort. Ou écouter celle qui se dit.

[In our century death has become taboo. . . . death is occulted. And mute. It has been relegated to a no man's land. Death inhabits a desert . . . A desert of thought and apathy . . . of aridity and indifference at the same time. Very few humans today are able and know how to speak about death. Or to listen to the death that is being spoken.]

—Madeleine Gagnon

IN A CENTURY MARKED BY TWO WORLD WARS AND SUCCESSIVE AND CONtinuing waves of genocide and interethnic conflicts, it seems almost aberrant that death could be so absent from Western discourse as to motivate writers like Madeleine Gagnon to qualify our collective silence as a desertlike aporia of thought.[1] In his own recent meditation on mourning—significantly entitled *Aporias*—, Jacques Derrida also notes the many voices that seem to "deplore and denounce . . . a sort of disappearance of death in the modern West and in industrialized societies," to which he adds, with his characteristic wry humor, that "the dominant feeling for everyone is that death, you see, is no longer what it used to be. And who will deny it?" (Derrida 1993, 57, 58). Such a rhetorical question, coming from one of Europe's most celebrated contemporary philosophers, would indeed seem to confirm Gagnon's observation, pointing as it does to the decline of traditions, or what Gagnon herself calls the current "quasi-absence de rituels signifiants, avant, pendant et après la mort" (DS 150) [the quasi-absence of signifying rituals before, during, and after death]. We have, it would seem, evolved into a culture where death is kept at a safe distance, confined to nursing homes, hospitals, and the sound bites of headlines, so that we may more blithely pursue the instant gratification promised and promoted by the fantasy factories of Hollywood studios, advertising agencies, and television networks.

And yet, this occultation or deliberate distancing of death is but an impression, a partial truth increasingly undercut in recent years at least by the renewed focus on dying and our attitudes to it that is gradually finding a voice in a variety of forms of artistic expression.[2] In the arena of philosophical and cultural criticism, Derrida's recent work is itself an example of this,[3] as is the 1992 issue of the French journal *Autrement* (*Otherwise*) devoted to "Deuils" ("Mourning"). Indeed, one might even consider the contemporary spate of autobiographical writings as a paradoxical confirmation of the increasing weight accorded to the idea of death, for the writing of a life is one way to preserve that which the writer's death would erase. The thought of or actual approach of one's own death galvanizes a process of remembering, which in turn finds its expression in a writing intended to inscribe memory for posterity and thus, by anticipation as it were, overcome the loss associated with one's mortality. If, as André Comte-Sponville affirms in his contribution to "Deuils," "le deuil est comme une mort anticipée" [mourning is like an anticipated death], then the recent increase in life writings can be seen as a kind of mourning process, a way of coming to terms with and even circumventing the fact that to be mortal is to be "ouvert dans l'ouvert, passant dans le passage" (Comte-Sponville 1992, 14, 16) [open in open-endedness, passing in the transitory]. Overall, however, one would have to agree with Gagnon's view that there are few who "are able and know how to speak about death" in a North American society so preoccupied with its own amusement and so trusting in the power of technology and medicine to prolong and improve the quality of life. For her part, Gagnon's writing has always been informed by thoughts of death and memories of "les êtres en allés" (DS, back cover) [those who have passed away], which is no doubt why she is so sensitive to this seeming lacuna in the works of her contemporaries. As the critic Madeleine Boulanger notes in her brief study of *Les Morts-vivants* (*The Living Dead*) (1969), from the beginning of Gagnon's career death constitutes "the trigger mechanism for her writing ... Actual and imagined death, death of the individual and of the group" (Boulanger 1985, 33).[4] The accuracy of this critical insight is even more evident now than it was in the early 1980s when Boulanger made her initial remarks, for, as I intend to show, Gagnon's most recent prose texts all bear witness to the fundamental imprint of death on her writing. It would seem that, at the century's end, Gagnon is one who sees death and mourning as both a source of meaning and an impetus for her pursuit of what she calls "Le Livre rêvé" (The Ideal Book).[5]

It is interesting to note that, after more than a decade of publishing poetry almost exclusively, a period of writing culminating in a Governor General's award for *Chant pour un Québec lointain* (*Song for a Far-off Québec*) (1991), Gagnon has put out three thematically related works of prose in a row. The "narrative" (the cover calls it a "récit") of *Les Cathédrales sauvages* (*Wild Cathedrals*) (1994), the novel *Le Vent majeur* (*The Dominant Wind*) (1995), and the autobiographical *Le Deuil du soleil* (*Mourning for the Sun*) (1998) are all essentially prose texts that explicitly explore the link between death and writing. In all three, death seems indeed to constitute a "trigger" for creation, but it is also more than just a stimulus, bound up as it is with the very process of mourning and of remembrance, and of "coming to writing" them both in words that offer insight, solace, and even rejuvenation. It seems that Gagnon has not forgotten the meditation on death with which she concluded her feminist essay "Mon corps dans l'écriture" ("My Body in Writing"), where she affirms that "nos manques, nos morts, sont cela même qui nous mène à la reconnaissance et à la vie" [our lacks, our deaths, are precisely what leads us to recognition and to life].[6] To put it in the psychoanalytic terms that continue to inform Gagnon's thought, "la pulsion de Mort se tisse avec celle de la Vie" (CS 134) [the Death drive is interwoven with that of Life]. Writing demonstrates this point with particular clarity, because language is based on loss (the absent referent), even as it provides a way to mediate that loss by enabling the writing subject to find a voice, and thus the promise of endurance.[7] As Peggy Phelan suggests in her recent study entitled *Mourning Sex: Performing Public Memories*:

> What psychoanalysis makes clear is that the experience of loss is one of the central repetitions of subjectivity ... Severed from the placenta and cast from the womb, we enter the world as an amputated body whose being will be determined by the very mortality of that body. Prior to recognizing the specific context of an affective grief, perhaps the human subject is born ready to mourn. (Phelan 1997, 5)

In other words, to borrow the philosopher Comte-Sponville's reshaping of a famous phrase, "le deuil est le propre de l'homme" (Comte-Sponville 1992, 15) [mourning is peculiar to man].

But, one is tempted to add, so is writing. It is thus no wonder that performing mourning in and through writing is a gesture that haunts the work of writers like Gagnon, whose firsthand experience of loss began at a time when she was actively pursuing an academic interest in psychoanalysis but had as yet not thought to publish her own writings. As she recounts it in *Le Deuil du soleil*, the suicide of her cousin Régis in 1964 made it difficult for Gagnon to write at all for several years, until at last she experienced a breakthrough that allowed her to recover her memories, overcome the violence of his death, and publish her work (DS 41–45, 54–59, 64–67). Significantly, one of Gagnon's conclusions about this early encounter with mourning is that "le travail de deuil en son accomplissement même fait passer la mort à l'oeuvre" (DS 58) [the work of mourning by its very completion makes death (into the) work]. It would seem that, from Gagnon's early career to the autobiographical testimonials of loss that make up *Le Deuil du soleil*, mourning is a process intimately connected to writing, and one that finds its ultimate expression and resolution in the act of translating memory and experience into words. For Gagnon, "l'écriture est raccommodage, cicatrisation, expiation et compensation. Ce qui tisse entre les fils dispersés d'une mémoire trouée par les âges. Ce qui referme, guérit, d'anciennes blessures dues à l'érosion de la venue au monde symbolique" (Gagnon, "Prétexte," ts. 152) [writing is mending, healing, expiation, and compensation. What weaves between the scattered threads of a memory tattered by time. What closes up and heals old wounds caused by the erosion of our coming into the world of the symbolic].

In Gagnon's *Les Cathédrales sauvages*, the titles of the book's two parts—"Voyage au bout d'un mot"("Voyage to the End of a Word") and "L'Après-livre" ("The After-book")—as well as most of the chapter names—"Histoire vraie" ("True Story"), "Le Livre de Samuel" ("The Book of Samuel"), "Le Manuscrit" ("The Manuscript"), "L'Ecriture, c'est ma mère" ("Writing is My Mother"), "Le Livre rêvé" ("The Ideal Book") and "Post-scriptum" ("Postscript")—make explicit from the outset that this fictional narrative is about the particular "venue au monde symbolique" that is writing. Still further, as each successive chapter reveals, it is more precisely the circumstances that impel the release of writing that are at the heart of the text. Given the context of Gagnon's own inaugural experience of loss, it is perhaps not surprising that the scenes of coming to writing in this narrative are almost all associated with death or mourning.

In the "creation story" of "Genèse" ("Genesis"), the first chapter of *Les Cathédrales sauvages*, the female narrator begins with her own birth, where "un premier poème sans mots s'écrit tout seul" (CS 11) [a first wordless poem writes itself]. After this joyous inaugural moment, however, she quickly skips forward in time, because her infancy, as she says, contains "rien qui ne soit digne d'un roman" (CS 12) [nothing worthy of a novel]. Precociously conscious of the potential literary value of her life, she moves directly to the moment where she has a *real* story to tell, when, as she puts it, "ce que je vis est si extraordinaire qu'il me faut le raconter" (CS 12) [what I am living is so extraordinary that I must tell it]. The experiences that follow, narrated in the present tense, are indeed unusual, for on the day in question this four-year-old girl witnesses a fire, a child's death, the molestation of her friend Marie, and a possible drowning. What is most interesting here, although the events are clearly dramatic in and of themselves, is rather the way in which they are interconnected and become the impetus for the telling of the story.

In the narration of "Genèse," the fire that consumes the mill and a neighboring house with a helpless girl in it is also the fire of desire, literal and figurative fires conflated by the narrator as she comes upon an older man molesting her friend near the riverbank path she takes toward the mill: "Il y a du feu dans [les] yeux [de l'homme] . . . C'est le visage transformé de Marie qui me fait peur. C'est Marie et ce n'est plus Marie. J'ai chaud, les flammes sont proches. Je brûle, j'ai peur" (CS 13) [There is fire in (the man's) eyes. . . . It is Marie's transformed face that scares me. It is Marie and it is no longer Marie. I feel hot, the flames are close. I am burning up, I am scared]. Once at the mill, the narrator's eyes meet those of the trapped child whose screams are inaudible in the roar of flames. This traumatic encounter leads the narrator to conclude that "la plus belle image de ma vie a tué la petite fille et effacé maison, moulin et tant de choses que j'aimais" (CS 14) [the most beautiful image I have ever seen killed the little girl and wiped out the house, the mill, and so many things I loved], which is no doubt why we see her stop to stamp out the last stray sparks of the fire as she encounters them on the path back toward home.

After the narrator's fear subsides, she is able to assess the lasting effects of the scenes she has witnessed:

> J'entends le grand silence après la mort et la destruction. . . . Je suis attentive au silence et à l'obscurité d'après le feu. Ce qui était lumineux

soudain n'a plus de formes. Ou plutôt, je vois maintenant la forme des ombres. . . . Je comprends la noirceur. Et aucune illusion d'optique ne vient altérer ma vision des choses qui ne se voient plus jamais de la même façon. (CS 15)

[I hear the great silence after the death and destruction. . . . I am attentive to the silence and the obscurity after the fire. What once was luminous suddenly no longer has a shape. Or rather, I see now the shape of the shadows . . . I understand blackness. And no optical illusion comes to alter my vision of things that can never be seen in exactly the same way again.]

It is clear from these remarks that the "extraordinary" events that the narrator has seen are what makes her feel she has a story to tell, words to find that, in a sense, give a voice to those moments for which "on n'a pas de mots" (CS 14) [one has no words], such as when she exchanged looks with the dying little girl. The latter's incineration, immediately following such a disturbing scene of molestation, clearly results in the loss of the narrator's innocence. Still further, given the explicit metaphorical linking of the two events, one could see the girl's death in the house fire as a symbolic figuration of the end of Marie's sexual innocence also, for, as the narrator affirms, "personne ne peut entrer dans la maison sans risque de mourir" (CS 14) [no one can enter the house without risking death].[8] Desire, like fire, can be a destructive force, and certainly is one in Marie's case ("Marie . . . is no longer Marie").

For the narrator who witnesses such death and destruction, the concomitant genesis of storytelling becomes a kind of compensatory gesture that allows her to negotiate her own loss of innocence. In this respect, the philosopher Comte-Sponville's remarks seem particularly pertinent, for he notes:

Une fois que la mort a passé, ce n'est plus pareil: rien n'a changé, et plus rien pourtant n'est comme avant. C'est l'entrée dans l'âge adulte, si l'on veut, quoique les adultes fassent tout, le plus souvent, pour l'oublier. Disons que c'est l'accès à l'humanité véritable: le deuil marque que nous ne sommes pas Dieu, et de quel prix il faut le payer. (Comte-Sponville 1992, 15)

[Once death has passed, it is not the same: nothing has changed and yet nothing is like before. It is the entry into the adult world, so to speak, although adults do everything, most of the time, to forget it. Let us just say that it is the door to our true humanity: mourning reveals that we are not God, and the price we must pay for it.]

Writing about death and loss is thus part of the price to be paid for the experience that reveals one's own mortality. It is the legacy that this survivor, in any case, chooses to accept, for she strives, as do many of Gagnon's narrators, to embrace and "faire tenir ensemble les choses les plus mystérieuses de la vie avec le mot 'mort' qui jusque-là n'avait rien signifié" (CS 27) [hold together the most mysterious things of life with the word "death" that until then had meant nothing].

In "Genèse," there is one final and more positive figuration of death that contrasts with the traumatic nature of those we have discussed so far. At the very end of the story, the narrator, after crossing the river via a footbridge, turns and notices a beautiful woman poised there who eventually lets herself fall into the flowing water. In what is surely more a vision than a veritable drowning, the child describes how the reflections of the moon and the woman's shadow give the impression that the woman is first walking on the water, and then that she melts into her reflection and "devient la même, la même femme dans l'eau" (CS 16) [becomes the same, the same woman in the water]. After all that has preceded, this vision seems to soothe the narrator, and can be read, both literally and figuratively, as an externalized reflection of what the narrator has faced in what can surely be called the "baptism of fire" of the day's events.[9] Like the falling woman, the narrator has taken a symbolic plunge, into the world of death and loss, but also into storytelling, the flow of narrative that allows her to manage and mediate the violence and destruction she has seen. The narrator is thus perhaps seeing a vision of herself in this river scene, which she concludes by saying, "et je vois dans le rayon sans plus rien entendre une forme filer" (CS 16) [and I see in the moonbeam, without hearing anything, a form spin away]. It bears recalling here that in French the verb "filer" can mean both to spin (both literally and figuratively, as the mythical Fates do the lives of mortals) and to escape. Just as one can jump into the water to escape fire, so may the narrator escape into writing and thus envision a way to spin a story from the experience of death and loss that otherwise would, like Marie and her homologue in the burning house, never find a voice.

It is as surprising as it is significant that the same disturbing events that mark the first chapter of *Les Cathédrales sauvages* also figure in the opening of Gagnon's next work, *Le Vent majeur*. In this novel, the protagonist, Joseph Sully, begins his first-person narration with a scene that conflates sexual violence and death even more directly than does "Genèse." Here, it is an adult woman who is assaulted, and an adopted eleven-year-old boy who becomes the agent of death, for Joseph kills the man who gags and rapes his foster mother. This murder is clearly suggestive of an Oedipal scene as outlined by Freudian psychoanalysis, for even though the boy kills a rapist, and not his father (his "real" rival, as Freud would have it), the shock of the event seems to trigger a heart condition that will result in the father's premature death a mere three years later, effectively leaving Joseph and his mother alone (VM 19, 42.). Unlike the traumatic experiences that motivate the girl's narration in "Genèse," however, this boy's "catastrophe" (VM 20) is apparently not immediately transformed into the creative, life-affirming compensatory gesture of storytelling seen in Gagnon's earlier text. The reason, as Joseph explains, is that: "les mois qui suivirent le viol et le meurtre furent un cauchemar quasi indescriptible, vu qu'en ce temps-là je n'avais pas encore tous les mots pour traduire" (VM 17) [the months that followed the rape and murder were an almost indescribable nightmare, given that at that time I did not yet have all the words to translate] the effects of such an experience. In this justification for Joseph's silence, the "pas encore" (not yet) is what retains our attention, however, as it indicates quite clearly that Joseph will eventually find solace in writing about the consequences of this traumatic event.

The reader does not have to wait long, in fact, for a clear connection between death and creation to emerge. When Joseph is twelve, his biological father takes him to see the grave of his birth mother. At the grave site, Joseph is somewhat disoriented and, beside this father he has never known (VM 27), has the first of what he calls his "visions":

> Sur le versant ouest du cimetière, dans le violacé du soleil couchant d'août, je *vis* une ville inconnue . . . puis des petits bateaux à l'horizon, au port, là où la ville s'échouait dans la mer. . . . J'étais à la fois fasciné et angoissé. Fasciné par les beautés qui s'offraient, comme ça, à ma vue. Angoissé par cette étrangeté, qui, soudain, m'était révélée. (VM 27–28)

> [On the west slope of the cemetery, in the violet of the August sunset, I *saw* an unknown city . . . then some small boats on the horizon, in the port, where the city ended up in the sea. . . . I was at once fascinated and distressed. Fascinated by the beauties that presented themselves so to my eyes. Distressed by this strangeness that, suddenly, was revealed to me.]

These visions, which at first are interpreted by his foster parents as a form of mental instability resulting from the "catastrophe," are ultimately what will furnish the inspiration for Joseph's art. As the following chapters reveal, painting, which depends on visualization if not visions, will become the principal form of creative expression and fulfillment in his life. More interesting here, however, is that, much as in "Genèse," traumatic death and loss seem to contribute to awakening the creative faculty in the young narrator. Although it is true, since Joseph did not really know his biological parents, that he cannot be said to mourn his dead mother in this passage, what it does show is that the primal scene of rape and murder he has experienced is in fact not absent from his mind as he contemplates his "family plot" for the first time. Here, the "*violacé*" (my emphasis) of the setting sun, a time of day itself symbolic of death, becomes the backdrop for a vision of a city by the sea, the "mer" that is a homonym for "mère" and that thus recalls by association the rape ("*viol*") of his foster mother by the unidentified, bestial man. Indeed, how can one avoid seeing the act of the "vil inconnu" (the vile stranger) in the "ville inconnue" (unknown city) of Joseph's vision, given these suggestive word choices? Clearly, the death of this narrator's innocence in his traumatic encounter with violence (a word also evoked by "violacé") is linked to the earliest signs of his creative genius, born, as it were, under the aegis of the symbols of death that he contemplates in the cemetery. As in the case of the fearful narrator of "Genèse" who sees both beauty and death at work in the fire, so Joseph, overtaken by an uneasiness and fear (VM 27), also feels an ambivalent fascination for this seductive yet alarming vision that, as I have shown, bears the dramatic imprint of the violence and death that have already marked his life.

Where these two remarkably similar inaugural passages from *Les Cathédrales sauvages* and *Le Vent majeur* diverge, however, is in the gender of the narrator and their involvement in the violence against women that they witness. Whereas in "Genèse" the narrator is not directly involved in the scenes of loss she comes upon, because she is merely a chance witness to the death of the little girl and the molestation of her friend Marie, in Joseph's case he is an active participant, for he himself steps in to stop the violent rape of his adoptive mother by stabbing her attacker. While we will return subsequently for a closer look at the question of gender in *Le Vent majeur*, it bears noting here that a comparison of these two texts seems to suggest that gender makes a difference in the violence that unleashes the creative impulse. While death and loss have a similar effect on the two children, as they both respond creatively to such trauma, only the little boy actually responds in kind to the violence perpetrated by the adult man, as if such violence were a purely male attribute, of which women inevitably become either victims or witnesses, not agents.

To return to *Les Cathédrales sauvages*, it must be underscored that the link between death and writing is not always mediated by violence in Gagnon's recent work, even though the liminal text of "Genèse" demands to be read as a significant inaugural moment for her narrative. What is salient, however, is that almost every chapter of this text revolves around a female narrator's relationship to words, and how she comes to writing through an encounter with death or loss. The one exception to this is "Histoire vraie," the book's second chapter, in which a ten-year-old narrator shares a love of words with her father and learns from him the value of doing one's best and pursuing an education (CS 22–27). When the narrator reveals that she wants to become a writer some day, the autobiographical resonance of this child's "Histoire vraie" becomes clear: Gagnon herself pursued both a doctorate and a writing career, and was encouraged in this by her father.[10] As Gagnon confirms in her explicitly autobiographical *Le Deuil du soleil*: "ce que m'a légué de plus précieux mon père, je l'ai écrit dans" 'Une histoire vraie' [*sic*], chapitre du livre *Les Cathédrales sauvages*" (DS 96) [the most precious thing my father left me I wrote about in "A True Story," a chapter in the book *Wild Cathedrals*].

The idea of an intergenerational legacy, where writing becomes a form of inheritance and a vehicle for transmitting that heritage, is another thematic thread that binds the otherwise disorienting plethora of narrative voices in the chapters of *Les Cathédrales sauvages*. As I have shown elsewhere, this theme, developed in part through the use of a multiplicity of narrative voices, is not new to Gagnon, for it lies at the heart of her "roman archéologique" (archaeological novel), *Lueur* (*Glimmer*, 1979) (Santoro, "Feminist Translation"). In *Les Cathédrales sauvages*, Gagnon offers several variations on this motif. "Le Livre de Samuel," for example, is the first-person narration of a little girl (Samuel's daughter) whose mother died when she was eleven. The mother's death is clearly figured as a moment of transmission that leads to writing, for, as the narrator says: "ce jour-là, je suis sortie de l'enfance par la grande porte éternelle du silence . . . et dans le même temps, j'apprenais d'où je venais. . . . Ainsi j'appris l'écriture" (CS 33) [that day, I exited childhood through the great eternal door of silence . . . and at the same time, I was learning where I came from. . . . Thus I learned to write]. The effect of this moment of transmission on the narrator is profound, for throughout her life she carries her mother's "mots d'agonie . . . comme on porte un enfant qui resterait toujours dans le ventre" (CS 35) [words of agony like one carries a child that will forever remain in the womb]. Her writing is a way to inscribe "dans un rouleau d'immortalité les récits de maman" (CS 37) [Mamma's stories in a scroll of immortality] as well as her own, although she does allow herself to wonder how "immortal" her novel will be, in a world on the brink of destruction (CS 39). Now a terminally ill adult, the narrator laments the fact that she herself does not have a daughter to tell her story to, adding: "maintenant, j'ai plus que jamais la mémoire de ma mère, ma fille est l'écriture et par elle je fixe mes mots dans le temps" (CS 35) [now more than ever I have the memory of my mother, my daughter is writing and through it I fix my words in time]. Significantly, however, Gagnon frames this narration in such a way that it is clear this narrator has ultimately found an inheritor for her story. Her narration is in fact in quotation marks, delivered to us by another first-person narrator (her spiritual daughter?) who, by presenting it as direct discourse to the reader, effectively inscribes the transmission of this legacy of words. Moreover, there is also a performative aspect to this framing device, for in handing us this story with a commanding "voici" (see here) (CS 33), the "reporting" narrator makes the reader into another potential legatee, an heir to the words of loss and love that originate in the transmission of a tradition from mother to daughter, through the symbolic "child" of writing.

In the chapter "L'Ecriture, c'est ma mère," where the title points to writing's generative role in the construction of the writing self, the central story is also one of a death and of the impetus mourning gives to the release of words onto the page. Here, the death from cirrhosis of Alice, an alcoholic novelist, occurs not long after a disastrous visit she pays on the woman writer who narrates this story. Although "Malice," as the narrator secretly baptizes her vitriolic visitor, wreaks havoc on the serenity of the summer cottage where the narrator and her companions are staying, there seem to be no lasting traces of animus after the event. Indeed, when the narrator is apprised of Alice's death, she has no hesitation in traveling to her friend's funeral in Matapédia, for she has already recognized that Alice's violent passage has helped her return in her writing to the "seul chemin de l'écriture qui se déroule, là où plus rien n'est clair ni certain" (CS 95) [only path of writing, that unfolds where nothing is clear or certain at all anymore]. In fact, Alice's passing becomes a coalescence of many losses, a mourning process that finds a voice in the narrator's primal wail for "tous ceux, disparus souvent de façon tragique et gisant un peu partout dans des cimetières perdus et tous ceux-là, vivants, qui se retrouveraient dans le deuil d'Alice" (CS 100) [all those (who) often had died tragically and were lying here and there in lost cemeteries, and all those, still alive, who would find themselves and each other in mourning for Alice]. This inarticulate cry, the beginning of the mourning process, leads in fact, after the funeral, to an entirely new project for the writer-narrator. When she stays on in the hotel in Matapédia, in the valley of her childhood home, this woman finds the solitude so inspiring, so fecund, that she is able to write a new novel from beginning to end. In this way, much as in the narrative of Samuel's daughter, the reader sees an important legacy transmitted by one woman to another, a legacy in which the release of writing becomes a form of mourning, but also an affirmation of life, a new beginning. As Comte-Sponville puts it, recalling the interconnection of life and death drives that Gagnon herself affirms: "autant le deuil est du côté de la mort, comme événement, autant il est du côté de la vie, comme processus" (Comte-Sponville 1992, 20) [as much as mourning is on the side of death as an event, it is on the side of life as a process].

In a more subtle way, the chapter entitled "Le Manuscrit" also elaborates on the intertwined themes of death and the legacy of women's words. Typical of the tenuous diegetic coherence of *Les Cathédrales sauvages*, the links between this chapter and the others are suggested by similarities of situation and experiences rather than established by the direct connections of continuing characters or shared settings.[11] Here, the principal narrator discusses a manuscript she finds that purports to be the transcription of some notebooks written by "Pauline," a terminally ill woman who has decided to write, in part as a way of working through the accidental death of her son, in part as a way of preparing for her own. Although this impulse, along with her experience of rape, certainly recalls the story of the narrator in "Le Livre de Samuel," we are given no explicit confirmation that the two women are one and the same. Moreover, the use of embedded narratives in "Le Manuscrit" only serves to render the identity of the various "authors" and their relationships highly problematic.

In essence, what can be pieced together from the fragments of text clearly belonging to different narrative voices is the following chain of transmission: Pauline's original notebooks are passed on to a friend, whose transcription and development of their contents comprise the found manuscript that inspires the principal narrator to write. The latter is clear about the importance of this chance finding to her own work, as she affirms that her own novel would not have been started without the discovery (CS 44). In what can surely be read as a metatextual concession to the "real" reader's reaction to this intricate narrative, the narrator wistfully considers the complexity of this legacy of writing: "J'aimerais pouvoir penser que Pauline et la scriptrice du manuscrit sont un seul et même personnage et plus encore, que ces deux-là, confondues, forment, avec moi qui écris, une seule et même personne. Tout serait plus simple si tel était le cas" (CS 62) [I would like to be able to think that Pauline and the writer of the manuscript are one and the same character and, moreover, that these two, conflated, form one and the same person with the me who is writing. Everything would be simpler if this were the case]—which of course it is not. What is the case, however, is that this story, like that of "Le Livre de Samuel," is about how a legacy of words can transform a woman's life, inspiring in her time and again the desire to return to this narrative (CS 62). For the principal narrator of "Le Manuscrit," Pauline's death had such a profound effect on her life that writing becomes for her, as it did for the dying woman and the friend who first transcribed her notebooks, "une question de survie" (a question of survival) (CS 65).

"L'Après-livre," which constitutes the second part of *Les Cathédrales sauvages*, seems to perform a postmodern "mise en abyme" of the narratives of the previous section, creating an effect similar to that of the embedded narratives in "Le Livre de Samuel" and "Le Manuscrit."[12] In "Le Livre rêvé," the opening chapter of "L'Après-livre," a new narrator appears and shifts the frame of reference for the reader when she explains that this book project was conceived long ago (CS 119). With this new, apparently metatextual level of narrative authority, the reader is led to believe that *Les Cathédrales sauvages* is itself her "livre rêvé," an attempt on her part to "inventer une forme neuve d'autobiographie . . . qui eût déjoué toutes les stratégies inventives de ce Je prétendant écrire sa vie" (CS 121) [invent a new form of autobiography . . . that would have foiled all the inventive strategies of this I pretending to write her life]. Moreover, this narrator seems haunted by the voices of the dead, "dozens" of them, who make her feel haunted and who appear in the margins of her writing project (CS 119). Given the many narrative voices inhabiting the previous chapters in this book about writing, it is tempting to read "Le Livre rêvé" as an explanation or at least a clarification of what precedes. Nonetheless, it bears noting that where Gagnon's text contains two parts, this narrator had rather planned three:

> L'une en "Je" pour . . . celle qui pense et qui écrit. . . . La seconde (partie) en "Elle" pour . . . celle . . . qui fut enfant et qui se serait métamorphosée, le temps d'un livre, en une espèce de prophète de l'écriture. . . . Enfin, la troisième partie se fut écrite en l' "Autre."
> . . . Je. Elle. L'Autre. Ainsi se divisait le livre rêvé. Comme tout rêve, il s'est défait. Ne reste que des miettes, des lambeaux. (CS 121)

> [One using "I" for . . . the one who thinks and writes. . . . The second (part) using "Her" for . . . the one . . . who was a child and who would have been transformed, for the space of a book, into a kind of prophet of writing. . . . Finally, the third part would have been written using "the Other."
> . . . I. Her. The Other. The ideal book was thus divided up. But as with all dreams, it came undone. All that is left is some pieces, some tattered remnants.]

Perhaps the "remnants" of this narrator's innovative autobiography are indeed contained in the two parts of *Les Cathédrales sauvages*, this fragmentary text narrated by a multitude of children's and adults' voices that all seem to have an autobiographical status. Such insoluble questions aside, what is clearly indicated by the conditional and past conditional verb tenses in this passage, is that writing never coincides perfectly with its object, but rather escapes us, expressing both more and less than we intend. It leaves one forever hungering, as the writer-narrator of this chapter does, for "quelque chose qui se referme, comme un oeuf ou un jardin ou un livre ou une main! . . . Quelque chose qui ne risquerait pas de chuter soudain dans les abîmes. Qui serait fermé comme un ventre, mais d'où l'on pourrait s'expulser, fusée glissante, le temps venu. Quelque chose comme un chapitre" (CS 125–26) [something that would be enclosed, like an egg or a garden or a book or a hand! . . . Something that would not risk opening onto the abyss all of a sudden. That would be closed like a womb, but out of which one could eject oneself, like a slippery projectile, at the right time. Something like a chapter]. In language that recalls Phelan's metaphor of the violent "amputation" of birth, Gagnon here reveals the fundamental feeling of incompleteness that haunts her narrator, for whom the mere possibility of achieving the writing of closure and plenitude she longs for is enough to keep her working, for, as she says: "L'être meurt s'il n'accomplit pas la traversée du ventre au col pour venir respirer" (CS 124) [A person dies if he does not manage the journey from the womb to the cervix in order to breathe].

Significantly, Gagnon's narrative does not offer the comfortable closure or deliverance from postmodern ambiguity some might hope for, because this chapter about "the ideal book"[13] is followed by two more, "Qui?" and "Post-scriptum," also narrated in the first person by women who may or may not be the same person, and who thus further problematize the source and narrative cohesion of the text. In the search of the writer of "Le Livre rêvé" for an "outre-genre où mentir n'a plus lieu" (CS 122) [beyond-genre where there is no longer any need to lie], what becomes incidental and indeterminable is precisely "who" is writing, making the question of "Qui?" an appropriate one indeed in the context of *Les Cathédrales sauvages*. The only certitude in this text seems to be that the gesture of transmission, the search to inscribe dreams and ideas in writing, is a valued end in itself. In this collection of first-person narratives, writing offers a means to affirm life and to create a legacy inspired yet untouched by mortality, and, indeed, ultimately freed from any notion of possession as well. How else are we to understand the final scene where a mother and daughter read each other old letters, in which one writes: "le destin de ces lettres, n'est-il pas toujours outre-tombe?" (CS 157) [the destiny of these letters, is it not always beyond the grave?]? Our experiences are destined to be "dead letters" unless, as in the women's stories of *Les Cathédrales sauvages*, we can find a way to transmit them, through speech or writing, to a willing recipient who will pass them on to others in turn. In *Les Cathédrales sauvages*, where the principal narrators are exclusively women,[14] it would seem that this writing of transmission is a mission that women are the most likely to undertake and pursue.

Even in *Le Vent majeur*, where the protagonist is male, an argument can be made that the legacy of writing born of death and mourning is still associated with women and with a distinctly feminine subjectivity. Interestingly enough, this novel seems to explore and respond to two questions left hanging in the latter chapters of *Les Cathédrales sauvages*—namely "comment écrire sans meurtre?" (CS 130) [how to write without killing?] and "comment peut-on vivre sans écrire?" (CS 150) [how can one live without writing?]. As I have already shown, with regard to the first question, murder is not merely figuratively but also literally the traumatic inaugural event that marks Joseph's creative destiny. The psychiatrist consulted because of Joseph's subsequent "visions" explains to the mother that Joseph's recent emotional trauma has unleashed his imagination "comme si s'ouvraient, sous un choc . . . les vannes d'une puissante écluse sur un territoire . . . non endigué" (VM 39) [as if the floodgates of a powerful lock had, due to a shock, opened up onto a territory without dikes]. This specialist suggests painting as a creative outlet that will provide Joseph with a way to negotiate the consequences of the violence he both witnessed and committed. Thus, during his adolescent years, Joseph buries himself in his art, although he never seems to forget that its source lies in the death that haunts his past. On a return trip to the cemetery with a girlfriend who encourages him to paint the scene, he will make reference to this, feeling, "sans avoir les mots exacts, qu'il fallait encore plus de passé pour atteindre cette Beauté venue subrepticement du royaume de la Mort dans celui de la Vie" (VM 56) [without finding the precise words, that it was necessary to have even more of a past in order to attain this Beauty coming surreptitiously from the realm of Death into that of Life]. Much as in Gagnon's earlier text, here death becomes a source of inspiration, even if this narrator has not yet fully come to terms with its legacy at this point in his trajectory.

Unlike many of the narrators in *Les Cathédrales sauvages* who immediately turn to writing after an encounter with death, in *Le Vent majeur* it actually takes not one but two deaths before Joseph will begin to tell his story. The second death is that of "Muette" ("Mute"), a woman whose real name is Véronique and with whom Joseph falls in love in "L'Hôpital des esprits" ("The Hospital for Minds"), which furnishes the title of the book's second part. In an effective change of narrative focalization, the asylum stay is narrated in the third person, setting up the meaningful return to Joseph's voice once he "finds himself" and decides to write a letter to his mother after his release from the hospital. His "coming to writing," heralded by an initial letter from "Muette" (who at least briefly does have a voice in this narration), is in effect a coming to terms with his past, as he explains in a revealing postscript:

> Etre meurtrier à onze ans . . . , avoir vu sa propre mère assaillie par une brute violeur m'avait fait basculer . . . dans une *autre* vie souterraine pour laquelle je ne pouvais naître. Cela . . . est vraiment difficile à traduire en mots. Comme si ça s'était passé dans un lieu du monde où il n'y a plus de mots. Il me semble qu'on n'en a pas assez parlé . . . (VM 114)

> [To be a murderer at eleven . . . , to have seen one's own mother attacked by a brutal rapist had toppled me . . . into an *other*, subterranean life in which I was unable to be born. This is . . . truly difficult to put into words. As if it had happened in a place in the world where there are no longer any words. It seems to me we did not talk enough about it . . .]

Joseph's relationship with Véronique and his fruitful sessions with the professionals in the asylum certainly help him face his past more directly, but it is not until Véronique is killed in a horrible car accident, leaving him with their son David, that the artist will truly begin to find the words to translate his encounters with death and the legacy they leave in his life.

Joseph's letters to his dead wife almost exclusively comprise the book's third part, "C'est quoi, la mort?" ("What Is Death?"), and constitute this text's resounding answer to the second key question of *Les Cathédrales sauvages*, "comment peut-on vivre sans écrire?" (CS 150) [how can one live without writing?]. In the case of this artist, writing an epistolary journal becomes the only way he can live through his loss and complete the mourning process. As Joseph explains, since "seuls les mots m'apaisent, j'adresse ces mots écrits à la morte" (VM 133) [only words calm me, I address these written words to the dead woman]. Even five years later, this need has not changed, "car t'écrire m'aide encore à vivre" (VM 172) [for writing to you still helps me live], as he writes to his beloved. Véronique's death leaves Joseph with a child to take care of, but also with a creative legacy he cannot ignore, one that requires expression in words despite the fact that he also continues to paint. Indeed, even Joseph's painting soon involves a kind of writing, for he starts to include in his canvases what he calls "des espèces de pétroglyphes, sortes de *lettres illisibles* . . . gravées sur les parois par un feu . . . qui me viendrait peut-être de cette partie méconnue de mes origines, celle de ma mère biologique amérindienne" (VM 154) [a kind of petroglyph, some sort of *illegible letters* . . . engraved on the walls by a fire . . . that comes to me perhaps from that unrecognized part of my heritage, that of my Amerindian biological mother]. It would seem that Véronique's death has finally enabled Joseph to return to the "family plot" he saw in the cemetery when he was younger. So strong is the imperative to write in the face of death that, after attending his biological father's funeral, Joseph will even undertake the story of his childhood (VM 165), an autobiographical project that the reader recognizes retrospectively as *Le Vent majeur*'s first section. In this way, much as in *Les Cathédrales sauvages*, we see the linking of death, mourning, and writing as processes vital to life, for writing is one way to "redonne[r] vie" (restore life) (VM 151) even as it allows one to face its opposite, to "soutenir les morts dans LEUR mort" [to support the dead in THEIR death], as Gagnon will put it in *Le Deuil du soleil* (DS 17).

Le Deuil du soleil is of some assistance in articulating the difference that gender makes in Joseph's writing gesture in *Le Vent ma-*

jeur, for if "[é]crire la mort, c'est toujours écrire l'Autre" (DS 40) [writing death is always writing the Other], then this novel explicitly puts into play alterity in its most obvious form, that of sexual difference. Unlike *Les Cathédrales sauvages* where the legacy of writing was largely passed from one woman to another, the main transmission in this novel occurs between Véronique and Joseph. The letters inspired by his beloved's death are Joseph's way to reach out to her, to keep her memory alive and also to better understand himself. As Gagnon explains it in *Le Deuil du soleil*, "[r]êver l'autre peut parfois être le seul chemin qui nous conduit de l'autre à soi. Il s'agit d'un trajet risqué entre l'autre et soi où la mort de l'autre devient le ferment de la rencontre de soi. Cette rêverie comporte un travail: celui du deuil qui ramène autrement au sens pluriel d'une écriture et de sa vérité propre. Ou d'une vie" (DS 55) [Dreaming the other can sometimes be the only path that leads us from the other to the self. It is a risky journey, that between the other and oneself, where the death of the other becomes the ferment of an encounter with the self. This reverie involves work: that of mourning which confronts us in another way with the multiple senses of writing and of its honest truth. Or of a life]. The other is thus necessary to the discovery of the self, a point that is clear in the work of mourning that Joseph is able to perform only by writing to the woman he has lost.

What Joseph discovers about himself in this process, however, is in part his own femininity. Clearly a heterosexual man, Joseph is nonetheless the stereotypically sensitive artist, whose professional and personal contacts include many homosexuals, but whose closest friends are mostly women. Because Joseph's period of mourning coincides precisely with the feminist movement of the 1970s in Québec, it is perhaps not surprising that his women friends are the first to point out to him the "quelque chose de féminin dans [s]on tempérament" (VM 157) [feminine side of his character]. Despite the fact that Joseph claims that "toutes ces questions [lui] semblent plutôt mystérieuses" (VM 157) [all these questions seem rather mysterious to him], elsewhere he will often use the images and language associated with women's experiences. In his final letter to Véronique, for example, he writes: "comme dans les accouchements, dans la plainte et le cri, j'ai enfanté tous mes chagrins et m'en suis délivré, me sentant chaque fois devenir la foule des femmes du monde, tout en me sachant homme, le deuil ultime est androgyne, c'est ce que j'ai éprouvé au long de ces années" (VM 182) [as in childbirth, in moans and screams, I have given birth to all my sorrows and have delivered myself of them, feeling myself each time become the multitudinous women of the world, even as I knew I was a man, the ultimate mourning is androgynous, that is what I have felt for all these years]. In this way, while Joseph may claim that mourning is "androgynous," his frequent use of the childbirth metaphor highlights the "feminine" penchant of his imagination, and thus his ambiguous gender identity.[15]

In fact, Joseph's internal other, his inner self, is clearly aligned with the feminine, as is shown in a dream he has of Véronique and Giovanna, the new lover whose impact on his life enables him to end his mourning process. In this dream, as he describes it in his final letter to Véronique, Joseph sees two women seated in a Parisian café and:

> soudain, la première se retourne: elle est mon double. Exactement moi, mais au féminin. La seconde fait de même et c'est pareil, cette femme est ma copie. Nous nous regardons tous trois et savons d'emblée, sans mots, que nous nous aimons. Je me vois femme en elles, elles se voient homme en moi et nous nous aimons. Puis, la première . . . disparaît, laissant une ombre sur sa chaise. La seconde va s'asseoir dans l'ombre bleutée qui se dissipe comme un nuage. Elle me regarde, me sourit et c'est Giovanna. (VM 189)

> [suddenly, the first turns around: she is my double. Exactly me, but feminine. The second does the same and it is the same, this woman is my carbon copy. All three of us look at each other, and we know right away, without words, that we love each other. I see myself as a woman in them and they see themselves as a man in me, and we love each other. Then the first woman . . . disappears, leaving a shadow on the chair. The second goes to sit in that bluish shadow that dissipates like a cloud. She looks at me, smiles at me, and it is Giovanna.]

To Joseph, the narcissistic aspects of this dream of identificatory love and self-recognition are revealing of his true nature, for, as he says, "il y en a qui trouvent leur complément antipodal et qui se recréent sur le terreau de la différence. D'autres qui, comme moi, vont au semblable pour trouver au fond d'eux-mêmes leur étrangeté fuyante" (VM 190) [there are those who find their complementary antipode and who recreate themselves in the loam of difference. Others who, like me, go to their own kind to find in their own inner depths their fleeting otherness]. In effect, what this passage makes clear is that, although coming to terms with Véronique's death is initially why he writes, the process has also helped Joseph to face his own "fleeting otherness," as if that too were a part of the legacy of his beloved. In this way, Gagnon seems to preserve the gender-coded nature of the transmission gesture that appears in so many of her texts. Even in *Le Vent majeur*, the inheritance is clearly a feminine one, a writing out from death and mourning that speaks with particular clarity to the feminine side of the male protagonist.

Nevertheless, the ending of *Le Vent majeur* shows that there is yet another nuance that must be teased out in the complicated gender issues at stake in Gagnon's writings. Whereas the women in *Les Cathédrales sauvages* (and also in the earlier *Lueur*) all work toward ensuring the transmission of their stories as an important part of the legacy of words they have inherited, Joseph ultimately resolves to burn both his letters and Véronique's on the latter's grave, once he feels he has completed the mourning process that motivates his writing. The violence of this gesture of closure, recalling as it does the destructive fire of "Genèse," is reinforced in the novel's last part by the final image of him walking away from the grave "sans penser plus avant" (VM 200) [without thinking any further ahead]. Unlike Gagnon's women narrators who work to preserve their heritage of words and memories for the future, this male protagonist ultimately destroys the legacy of his old love, "fired" as he is, thanks to Giovanna, with the renewed desire to "ne plus céder. Avancer, créer, aimer. Etre du côté de la seule pulsion de vie dans ce monde où la pulsion de mort s'infiltre de tous côtés" (VM 174) [no longer give in. To move forward, to create, to love. To be on the side of the life drive alone in this world where the death drive filters in from all sides].

As both philosophy and psychoanalysis show us, however, "vivre et mourir vont ensemble, du même pas" (Comte-Sponville 1992, 16) [living and dying go together, in lockstep]. Thus Joseph's gesture of rupture with the past, which he sees as affirmative of life, is in truth the opposite, a fact underscored by the cigarette he lights after scattering the ashes of the little bonfire he has made on Véronique's grave. In Gagnon's textual economy, it is hard not to see the bonfire and the burning cigarette as symbols of the destructive desire and violence of men, so eloquently figured by their symbolic conflation in the fires of "Genèse." Ultimately, then, Joseph's ambivalent character reinforces the paradigm of the creative, healing legacy of writing passed on by women, and yet, at the same time, confirms that men's role in the chain of transmission is one of rupture rather than continuity. Even as Joseph's coming to writing, like that of many of Gagnon's female narrators, is impelled by death, one must also recognize that he in particular embodies the idea that writing "sans meurtre" (CS 130) (without killing) is impossible, for his act of murder is where the writing of this story literally begins, and his ostensible destruction of that writing is where his story ends. The only ironic compensation for the finality of his actions is that the novel itself preserves the letters and the autobiography that Joseph incinerates, a gesture of recuperation and bequest that clearly reveals Gagnon's own position in and on the transmission of textual legacies she thematizes.

Given her extensive personal experience of loss and mourning, Gagnon's focus in her recent work on the legacy of death in writing is as natural as it is compelling. In the poignant elegies that make up the autobiographical *Le Deuil du soleil*, Gagnon reveals that at one point she was faced with mourning nine deaths in a mere ten months in the mid-1990s (DS 47). It is no wonder, then, that the central theme of her three most recent works is death, and the way it can inspire us to turn to the work of creation and life as much as to the remembrance of what has been lost. As she will write in the liminal chapter of *Le Deuil du soleil*, for which she coins the beautiful title "Moraisons" ("Orisons for the dead"): "la mort s'est installée dans la maison du temps intérieur. . . . Je l'écoute et la regarde, et dois écrire ce qu'elle me dicte. . . . Je déroulerai le fil pour que ne se perde pas l'écriture traductrice à venir" (DS 11) [death has moved into the house of internal time. . . . I listen to it and look at it, and must write what she tells me to. . . . I will unwind the thread so that the future translator that is writing is not lost]. The legacy of death, for Gagnon, is thus a creative one, for, like one of her narrators in *Les Cathédrales sauvages*, she seems haunted by ghosts who seem to exhort her, saying: "Avance! Rêve! Ecris!" (CS 114) [Go forward! Dream! Write!].

In *Le Deuil du soleil*, where each chapter offers a prose version of the traditional "tombeau" (elegy) form so brilliantly illustrated by poets like Baudelaire,[16] it is clear that the process of mourning is completed through the process of writing, which becomes a "prière" (prayer) (DS 21), an offering as well as a vessel for the preservation of that "Mémoire veilleuse" ("Watchful Memory") that graces one chapter's title. In this, the writing of mourning is an expression of our "désir, ce manque initial, cette absolue tension vers l'autre, cette offrande ultime à celui ou à celle qui ne répondra plus, jamais" (DS 17) [desire, that initial lack, that absolute straining toward the other, that ultimate offering to the one who will never answer anymore]. If death thus incites the desire to write as the only way to reach out and touch the absent other, it is also true in Gagnon's texts that this outward gesture of transmission and communication is accompanied by an equally important inward movement toward self-creation and self-knowledge. This is why the narratives of her recent texts all seem to link the work of mourning not just to writing but more specifically to the autobiographical impulse, for "les vivants endeuillés . . . peuvent amorcer un véritable travail de deuil à travers lequel ils ne tendront à rien de moins qu'à la création, encore et toujours, de leur propre vie. . . . Chaque mort . . . donne lieu à une autre première naissance. . . . Un avènement primordial au monde, originel et fondateur de sens" (DS 83) [the living who are mourning . . . can begin true mourning work through which they will strive toward nothing less than the creation, again and eternally, of their own life. . . . Each death . . . makes way for another first birth. . . . A primordial coming into the world, inaugural and originating meaning]. Writing about loss and endings is thus also one way to give birth to meaning, and to create oneself in the pursuit of that meaning, which is no doubt why Gagnon continues in her writing to "se mesurer à la mort dans toutes directions" (Gagnon 1977, 107) [to confront death in all directions], even twenty years after first articulating this primordial impulse.

It is of course a pure coincidence that, at the end of the twentieth century, Gagnon finds herself, to use her own words, "à l'orée de la dernière tranche de vie" (CS 153) [at the threshold of the last phase of life], facing death in a way that few writers are prepared to do, as she puts it in the epigraph with which this discussion began. Nonetheless, that does not make the three texts studied here of any less symbolic value on this millennial threshold that gives us all pause, if not outright anxiety. Beyond the beauty and brutality of these three texts that deal in such nuanced and poetic ways with death and mourning, attentive readers may also see an ethics of both writing and life (and indeed, life writing) at work, in the creative gesture of recovery that is turned toward the future even as it does not forget the past. That women so often seem to be at the heart of this mission is also significant, for has our procreative potential not always placed us in a particularly direct relation to questions of birth, heritage, and death? Indeed, if, as Comte-Sponville asserts, "le deuil est le propre de l'homme" (Comte-Sponville 1992, 15) [mourning is peculiar to man], after reading Gagnon it seems that it is even more so "le propre de la femme" (women's territory). Except that death and mourning are not a question of property at all—which is why reading Gagnon's recent work calls us so compellingly into a space of exchange, for "ouvert dans l'ouvert, passant dans le passage" (Comte-Sponville 1992, 16) [open in open-endedness, passing in the transitory], Gagnon's writing bequeaths us all with the creative possibilities of our own mortality.

Notes

1. The above epigraph is from Gagnon's *Le Deuil du soleil* (*Mourning for the Sun*), 149–50. All future references to this work will be indicated by the abbreviation DS and will appear in parentheses after the quotation. Parenthetical references to *Les Cathédrales sauvages* (*Wild Cathedrals*) will be designated by the abbreviation CS, and those from *Le Vent majeur* (*The Dominant Wind*) by VM. All translations are my own. Titles will be translated only at the first occurrence.

2. One could, for example, point to the various serious treatments of death and mourning sparked by the AIDS epidemic, as seen in the ever-expanding "Quilt," the Broadway success of "Angels in America," or the 1992 French film "Les Nuits fauves" (Wild Nights), which was written and directed by an HIV-positive man, Cyril Collard, who himself played the film's leading role and later died of the disease. In Québec, one could also cite Anne Claire Poirier's "Tu as crié 'Let me Go' " (You Screamed 'Let me go') (1997), a film that deals with her daughter's drug addiction and murder in part through interviews with other parents whose children have died in a similar fashion.

3. Besides *Aporias*, see also Derrida's *Adieu à Emmanuel Lévinas* (*A Farewell to Emmanuel Lévinas*) (Paris, Galilée, 1997), and "Donner la mort" ("To Give Death") in *L'Ethique du don* (*The Ethics of the Gift*), Jean-Michel Rabaté and Michael Wetzel, eds. (Paris, Transition, 1992).

4. See also "Madeleine Gagnon: Les constantes d'une écriture" (The Constants of Writing), where Boulanger first advances the idea that: "LA PENSÉE DE LA MORT A PROBABLEMENT ÉTÉ LE PREMIER DÉCLENCHEUR DE L'ÉCRITURE DE MADELEINE GAGNON" (49, *sic*) [the thought of death was probably the first trigger of Madeleine Gagnon's writing].

5. This is the title of one of the chapters in Gagnon's *Les Cathédrales sauvages*.

6. "Coming to writing" is the English translation of *La Venue à l'écriture*, the collaborative book Gagnon wrote with Hélène Cixous and Annie Leclerc. The citations come from Gagnon's contribution, "Mon corps dans l'écriture," 113 and 107, respectively.

7. For a more extensive analysis of the ways in which writing embodies both life and death drives, see my forthcoming study "Menaces de mort, pulsions d'écrits dans l'oeuvre hyvrardienne" ("Death Threats and Writing Drives in the Works of Jeanne Hyvrard").

8. It should also be noted that Marie, like the girl who dies in the fire, is never heard. Both are innocent victims of fires (real and libidinal) that they do not originate but that consume them utterly. After the fire, no remains of the little girl can be found in the burned-out house, just as there is no sign of Marie when the narrator returns to the scene of the molestation. Both girls simply disappear without a trace.

9. In "Les Trois coffrets" ("The Three Caskets") (CS 110), there is a suggestion that the narrator identifies Marie with the woman in this vision, but because she recalls this in a remark about a dream of Marie dying in a different way, the reader remains free to interpret her original vision in all its symbolic dimensions.

10. The chapter "Post-scriptum" seems to pick up this autobiographical thread when the narrator recounts a meeting with a professor, Madame Fa, with whom she discusses how to reconcile poetry and psychoanalysis in her thesis, using a concept she calls "imagination transcendantale" (CS 151–57) (transcendental imagination).

11. The one time when all the previous chapters' characters seem to be united is in "Les Trois coffrets," where the dead and the living, the perpetrators of violence and their victims all recount their lives and deaths in an oneiric accumulation of narrative fragments. Their mysterious stories (CS 107–14) do resolve some ambiguities from the preceding chapters, but overall leave an impression of unreality and incoherence, despite the relief some readers may feel at finding, united in one place, several recognizable narrative voices.

12. For an analysis of embedding, *mise en abyme,* and self-referentiality as characteristic of postmodern textual poetics, see Janet Paterson, 9–39.

13. Is it this book to which she refers? The narrator of "Le Livre rêvé" says that she plans a chapter intitled "Qui" and "un dernier chapitre, témoin et orphelin du livre rêvé" (CS 123) [a last chapter, witness and orphan of the ideal book], which may be Gagnon's "Post-scriptum."

14. The only identifiable male voices appear in direct speech: the father speaks in "Histoire vraie," and, in "Les Trois coffrets," we briefly hear the voices of Maurice, Alice's partner, and Samuel, whose daughter narrates the third chapter (CS 111–12).

15. Gagnon herself reveals a source of this ambiguity when she admits in *Le Deuil du soleil* to having modeled the character of Joseph on her late artist friend Lucie Laporte (DS 24).

16. In *Le Deuil du soleil,* Gagnon calls "Requiem pour une abeille" ("Requiem for a Bee") her first "TOMBEAU écrit" (DS 14–15, sic) (written ELEGY) and, in the chapter "Cimetière aux oeillets" ("Carnation-filled Cemetery"), she visits the grave of Baudelaire among other writers she admires. She is thus clearly situating her text in this French literary tradition of the elegy.

Works Cited

Boulanger, Madeleine. "Madeleine Gagnon: Les constantes d'une écriture." *Voix et Images* 8, no. 1 (1982): 45–51.

———. "Madeleine Gagnon: Words of Women, Words of Life." *Ellipse* 33, no. 34 (1985): 32–37.

Comte-Sponville, André. "Vivre, c'est perdre." *Autrement* 128 (1992): 14–23.

Derrida, Jacques. *Aporias: Dying—Awaiting (One Another at) the "Limits of Truth."* Translated by Thomas Dutoit. Stanford, Calif.: Stanford University Press, 1993.

Gagnon, Madeleine. *Les Cathédrales sauvages.* Montreal: VLB, 1994.

———. *Le Deuil du soleil.* Montréal: VLB, 1998.

———. "Prétexte." ts. MSS-285. Fonds Gagnon of the Bibliothèque nationale of Québec, Montréal.

———. *Le Vent majeur.* Montréal: VLB, 1995.

Gagnon, Madeleine, et al. *La Venue à l'écriture.* Paris: Union Générale d'Éditions, 1977.

Paterson, Janet. *Moments postmodernes dans le roman québécois.* Ottawa: Ottawa University Press, 1993.

Phelan, Peggy. *Mourning Sex: Performing Public Memories.* New York: Routledge, 1997.

Santoro, Miléna. "Feminist Translation: Writing and Transmission among Women in Nicole Brossard's *Le Désert mauve* and Madeleine Gagnon's *Lueur*." In *Women by Women: The Treatment of Female Characters by Women Writers of Fiction in Québec since 1980*, edited by Roseanna Dufault, 147–68. Madison, N.J.: Fairleigh Dickinson University Press, 1997.

———. "Menaces de mort, pulsions d'écrits dans l'oeuvre hyvrardienne." In *Ut philosophia poesis: Études sur l'oeuvre de Jeanne Hyvrard,* edited by Jean-François Kosta-Théfaine. Amsterdam: Rodopi (forthcoming).

Rewriting Women into Historical Struggle as Transformative and Transformed Grace: Madeleine Ouellette-Michalska's *L'Été de l'Île de Grâce*

MAUREEN F. O'MEARA

L'ÉTÉ DE L'ÎLE DE GRÂCE (THE SUMMER OF GRACE ISLAND) ADDRESSES A significant gap in the recorded history of Québec and Canada, in telling the story of what took place on Grosse Île. This island in the Saint Lawrence, located only thirty miles below Québec City, served as a quarantine station from 1832 to 1937. Madeleine Ouellette-Michalska's novel recounts a battle between life and death, between meaningful life and the absurd, waged there in the summer of 1847 by the medical director of the station, his staff, his housekeeper, and the Irish immigrants in their care.

This is important because, as James Mangan remarked in his forword to Marianna O'Gallagher's *Gateway to Grosse Île*, the island "has passed through a period of almost complete oblivion dating back to the early years of the twentieth century"(Mangan, in O'Gallagher 1984, 11). This trend continues even in recent general histories of Québec, which focus only upon the thousands who died that summer. For example, in Young and Dickinson's *A Short History of Québec*, the drama of the summer of 1847 is reduced to a single sentence emphasizing the indignity of death and misidentifying the epidemic: "In 1847, about a third of the 60 000 immigrants quarantined at Grosse Île died of cholera; gravediggers on the island were paid $4 a day and used hooks to drag the dead to open graves"(174). Similarly, Jacques Lacoursière in his *Histoire populaire du Québec*, entitles his brief treatment of Grosse Île in 1847 "Des Milliers de morts" ("Thousands of Dead"); it consists of three paragraphs dealing with the unhealthful conditions on board the coffin ships, the insufficiency of funds devoted to the quarantine station and to other relief efforts, and the numbers of dead (III, 1996, 36). The title of another recent history *The Untold Story: The*

Irish in Canada (Toronto: Celtic Arts of Canada, 1988) indicates that this silenced episode forms part of a larger gap in Canadian history. Yet, the very historians devoted to recounting the untold story, Sheelagh Conway reminds us, continue to exclude women from it (85).

Ouellette-Michalska numbers among the "people of Québec, people of both Irish and French Canadian descent, [who] did not let the story of the island die out in their memory" (Mangan in O'Gallagher 1984, 11). Moreover, her novel addresses the erasure of women from the story of the island, in accordance with her general preoccupation regarding the holes in women's collective memories:[2] "La femme—comme groupe social—a une mémoire altérée, pleine de trous, une mémoire incertaine et une conscience parfois absente"(Ouellette-Michalska in Paterson 1997, 19) [Woman—as a social group—has a falsified memory, full of holes, an uncertain memory and a consciousness that is sometimes absent]. Once again, her response to this blank in women's collective consciousness has been to create an alternative history within fiction: "Comme d'autres écrivaines, j'ai senti le besoin d'être à l'écoute de cette mémoire et d'en restituer une partie dans mes fictions" (Ouellette-Michalska in Paterson 1997, 19) [Like other women writers, I felt the need to keep my ears open for this memory and to restore a part of it in my fiction].

To retell the story of the summer of 1847, Ouellette-Michalska does not need completely to imagine her male protagonist, Dr. Milroy. The annals of history provide her with a model, Dr. George Douglas, who served as the medical director of Grosse Île from 1836 to 1847. The introduction of a fictional woman character—his housekeeper Persévérance—however, brings into focus the hidden role of French-Canadian working-class women in the incorporation of the Irish immigrants into a Québec society under British rule. In focusing on this woman rather than on the nameless nurses found in the historical records of Grosse Île (Charbonneau and Sévigny 1997, 3, 17), Ouellette-Michalska writes a significant, everyday woman's role into this human drama. As Marilyn Randall concludes in her article "Histoire, roman et texte national: Comment lire *L'Été de l'Île de Grace*" ("History, Novel and the National Text: How to Read *The Summer of Grace Island*"), it is the creation of the strong fictional character Persévérance that helps to make the forgotten struggle for life of Irish immigrants in the summer of 1847 live in the memory of Québecers (Randall 1997, 82). At the end of the novel, Persévérance's move from the island to the Richelieu Street orphanage in Québec City places her at the moment in history when the adopted Irish orphans will enter Québec society, reminding us of the false simplicity of the French/English dichotomy frequently used to tell the history of Québec.

Writing within the context of history, within the historical conditions of the typhus epidemic on Grosse Île, imposes limits on the form that the creativity of both the author and her imagined character Persévérance may take. As Ouellette-Michalska recounts in her interview with Janet Paterson, the magnitude of the human tragedy at Grosse-Île, erased from Canadian history books until recently, completely overwhelmed her, and forced her to renounce her desire to create another postmodernist novel blending history and the present, following in the line of her previous work *La Maison Trestler* (*The Trestler House*). In order to put into words a human crisis of exile and death that concerned several thousand people, she found herself forced to return to a simpler form, that of the more traditional third-person novel. She characterizes *L'Été de l'Île de Grâce* (*The Summer of Grace Island*) as "le livre de l'impuissance" (the book of powerlessness) (Ouellette-Michalska interviewed in Paterson 1997, 17) but also as "mon livre le plus humble et le plus généreux" (Ouellette-Michalska interviewed in Paterson 1997, 16) [my most humble and most generous book].

As Ouellette-Michalska reminds her readers and critics in this interview, the subversive, transformative power of this book is not in its form but in its characters and its use of the imaginary (Paterson 1997, 17). Historical conditions do not allow Persévérance to be the first-person narrator. As a nineteenth-century domestic servant, she cannot write herself into history: "Puisqu'elle n'a ni profession ni scolarisation, cela n'aurait pas été simple de la laisser assumer le récit" (Ouellette-Michalska in Paterson 1997, 17) [because she has neither a profession nor an education, it would not have been natural to allow her to assume responsibility for the telling of the story]. Persévérance must use the invisible third-person voice of the twentieth-century narrator to come into being, but once she has done so, she invites her reader to recognize the significance of the imaginary, which disappears in historical accounts.

The Transformative Power of Persévérance

In her article, Randall reminds us of the heroic character of Persévérance, "this phenomenal woman who possesses not only the talents of a remarkable chef and nurse, but who is an historian, a doctor, an educator, a botanist, a poet and a true alchemist" (Randall 1997, 73). However, although Randall speaks of Persévérance's eclipsing Milroy in the story, it is only with the two of them together that a simple history of death on this quarantined island can be transformed into a history of survival. In contrast to the hellish conditions on the island, the overwhelming deaths and absurdity of the epidemic that Milroy encounters in his daily work with the dying, Persévérance both as character and as storyteller points to the possibility of everyday ways to reinscribe life within this tale of death. As the narrator notes, life and death are inextricable one from the other on the Saint Lawrence: "Le fleuve mêlait la vie et la mort en une coulée que rien n'arrêtait" (*EIG* 70) [the river continued to mingle life and death in a flow that nothing could stop].[3]

The novel restores the true stuff of the extraordinary, corporal encounters between men and women, which—as Ouellette-Michalska herself has observed—the annals of history have erased by expunging the body: "L'histoire n'est pas du tout dans le corps à corps, elle est dans le récit des gains et des pertes de pouvoir. Elle ne veut rien savoir du corps. . . . Elle laisse à la fiction le soin d'assumer ses avatars. Elle laisse le roman intégrer les expériences qu'elle ne prend pas en charge ou qu'elle n'a pas pris en charge assez vite" (Ouellette-Michalska in Paterson 22) [History does not consist at all of the bodily combat of individuals, it consists of the story of the gains and the losses of power. It does not concern itself with the body. . . . It leaves to fiction the task of embodying. It leaves it to the novel to integrate the experiences for which it does not take responsibility or does not take responsibility soon enough].

Yet, as the novel demonstrates, these everyday encounters are also encounters of the imaginary, the way in which each person sees and interprets the world and one's place in it. In reintegrating a heroine who searches for subjectivity within a position as a domestic worker, *L'Été de l'Île de Grâce* (*The Summer of Grace Island*) explores not only the material conditions of the life of woman at another time but also the relations between these conditions and her elaboration of her dreams for herself and for humanity.

From the beginning of the novel, Persévérance embodies the incorporation of the imagination and the imaginary into everyday life. Her naive belief in, and hope for, immortality and grace are tied to a simple but rare creature, a blue butterfly that for her represents the miracles perceived from time to time in everyday life: "Elle avait toujours souhaité apercevoir un de ces papillons renommés pour apporter la chance, car semble-t-il qu'ils protégeaient, ou même empêchaient de mourir, ceux qui les apercevaient une seule fois dans leur vie" (*EIG* 18) [She had always hoped to catch a glimpse of one of these butterflies renowned for bringing good luck for it seems that they protected, or even kept from dying, those who caught sight of them once in their lifetime].

By painting the image of this blue butterfly onto the biscuits she serves Milroy and his family during his wife and children's brief visit to the island cut short by the discovery of typhus, Persévérance both demonstrates "plus de fantaisie que n'en laissaient deviner son langage et ses manières" (*EIG* 18) [more imagination than one would guess from her language and her behavior] and provides both material and spiritual nourishment to those around her. In the presence of a pervasive odor of human death on the island that reminds both Milroy and his wife of the 1832 cholera epidemic, she affirms the possibility of eternal life.

Throughout the novel, Persévérance is linked to other empowering objects that represent the saving grace of appreciating everyday beauty. Objects are transformed by her vision and hands into spiritual forces that restore the joy of life, even if only for a moment. After Milroy's encounter with the first coffin ship, the geraniums she places at the windows, as well as the bouquets of medicinal herbs that hang in the kitchen, shield him from the recurring vision of death outside: "Derrière la vitre s'étendait l'île sans passé ni avenir qui ne retenait du passage du temps que son odeur, une odeur de pourriture humaine que l'humidité décuplait" (*EIG* 55) [Behind the windowpane stretched out the island with neither past nor future; all it retained from the passing of time was its odor, an odor of human putrefaction that the humidity increased tenfold]. At various points in the novel, the presence of these geraniums is noted and associated with the saving power of momentary forgetfulness coupled with a life-giving force to continue to face the epidemic.

A birdcage that enigmatically arrives on the island as a gift from the governor serves as another such object. Although Milroy attempts to read a possibly sinister meaning behind the gift, it becomes in Persévérance's eyes only an object of true beauty: "Pourquoi vous préoccupez-vous du gouverneur? répondit-elle. La volière est un objet de beauté. Ces objets-là servent à faire oublier la laideur, il ne faut rien leur demander de plus" (*EIG*, 267) [Why are you preoccupied with the governor? she answered. The birdcage is an object of beauty. Such objects are useful for forgetting ugliness, one must ask nothing further of them]. Once she coaxes domestic finches to take up residence there, the birdcage becomes an element of joy and wonder for the personnel of the island. And for the sick being transported to the hospital, it restores briefly what their ocean voyage had taken from them: "le souvenir de ce qu'ils avaient été, ce qu'ils avaient souhaité être avant d'aboutir là-bas" (*EIG* 266) [the memory of what they had been, of what they had hoped to be before having ended up there].

Moreover, Persévérance herself, her body, and her stories bring the presence of grace to the individuals and the community around her. Through her experience as told in this novel, grace is no longer a supernatural intervention coming from a divine power that excludes any mention of a link to the body, but rather a gift brought by this simple woman and her commitment to the transformation of the material. Nor is it the social grace of an elegantly costumed body. It is simply the gift of life in moments of crisis.

In the context of her daily work Persévérance is both storyteller and herbalist who transforms the local plants into preparations that bring great comfort to the sick and to the medical director of the station. These two works merge, reincorporating the magic of language into the body from which it comes: "L'alchimie des plantes et la magie des mots devenaient une seule et même chose. Tout cela participait du même prodige: la langue et les doigts créaient quelque chose qui possédait le pouvoir de se précipiter dans des formes ou des textures nouvelles" (*EIG* 87) [Plant alchemy and the magic of words became one and the same thing. It all formed part of the same wondrous ability: language and the fingers created something that could crystallize into new forms and textures]. The forehead of each of Persévérance's assistants, Berthe and Angélique, is "couvert de la buée chaude indissociable désormais du fond sonore sur lequel s'effectuaient les transformations magiques" (*EIG* 96) [covered with hot steam henceforth undistinguishable from the background sounds underlying the magical transformations]. Participating in this work and listening to Persévérance's stories opens for them "des portes d'un univers d'audace et de fantaisie" (*EIG* 96–97) [doors to a daring and fanciful universe]. Through her work and her storytelling, she creates an intergenerational female community, initiating younger women into the possibility of wonder.

The products of these sessions also create an atmosphere that allows the male representatives of the army and of public health, those who will be recorded in the history of the island, to function and not to give in to the forces of despair and death. Early in the novel, Milroy notes the effect of the odors of the kitchen "remplie de vapeurs tièdes et de parfums acidulés qui lui faisaient oublier les effluves pestilentiels qui régnaient au dehors" (*EIG* 97) [filled with lukewarm steam and with slightly acid fragrances that made him forget the foul-smelling exhalations that prevailed outside]. Upon Milroy's return to the island after a short visit to Québec City to secure assistance for the quarantine station, a similar effect is noted by both him and the military officer, Clark; they comment on the enabling power of Persévérance's work and link her kitchen nostalgically to the safe spaces created by other women in their lives.

During her work with Angélique and Berthe, Persévérance tells many stories—those of the local plants used in her culinary creations, that of the cholera epidemic of 1832, and that of the great fire in Québec City. All of these tales link the storyteller and her listeners to a human drama that transcends the language and experience of life's daily necessities. Addressing loss by reconnecting these listeners to their past and their hopes for the future, they present "l'envers de l'histoire officielle, où s'affichent des dates, des guerres, des trafics de territoire, une prétention à régir le monde, l'impuissance à en régir le déclin ou la chute" (Ouellette-Michalska 1984, 110) [the reverse of official history, where dates, wars, the trading of territories, a claim to rule the world, and the powerlessness to control its decline or collapse are displayed]. Unlike official history, they momentarily reconnect listeners to life through the theater of the storyteller's body as well as her words. Persévérance's voice, similar to the voice described by Madeleine Ouellette-Michalska in *La Tentation de dire (Tempted to Tell)*, links her body to her magical storytelling: "La voix, c'est le temps traversant le corps. . . . Portée par la bouche, l'écriture perd sa froideur et sa linéarité. Elle restitue l'épaisseur de désir qui va dans tous les sens, par tous les sens, suivant la dissémination des cellules, canaux et tissus inaptes à se satisfaire d'une mémoire cérébrale, mémoire de tête qui serait pur constat du passage de l'instant" (1985, 45) [Voice is time traveling through the body. . . . Carried by mouth, writing loses its coldness and its linearity. It restores the depth of desire, which goes in all directions, through all the senses, following the dissemination of a body's cells, canals, and tissues unsuited to be satisfied with a merely cerebral memory, memory limited to the brain that would be a simple recording of the moment's passing]. Yet, the stories told by such women, so essential to the transmission of life and culture, disappear unless they are transformed into writing by authors such as Ouellette-Michalska.[4]

Persévérance's imaginative storytelling offers a potential for transforming the larger community that is suffering from the effects of the typhus epidemic: "Ces ruses de l'imaginaire, qui invitaient à l'optimisme et à la détente, transformaient le monde en une fiction sympathique à laquelle le réel se voyait ensuite forcé de ressembler. Il [Milroy] pensa alors que la station de quarantaine pourrait profiter de cette puissance d'imagination trahissant une générosité du coeur non moins grande" (*EIG* 88) [These ruses of the imagination, which induced optimism and relaxation, transformed the world into a pleasant fiction to which the real found itself obliged to resemble. He (Milroy) thought therefore that the quarantine station could profit from this powerful imagination that revealed an equally big heart]. Recognizing her power, Milroy asks Persévérance to accompany him in his visits to the immigrants in the tent camps established for those free from the visible symptoms of typhus. Whereas the life of these immigrants is not threatened immediately, they are living spiritually between life and death, as they exist severed from the life-giving forces of family, friends, and homeland.

Lacking a common language with these immigrants, but believing that people in general "parlaient à peu près tous le même langage puisqu'ils partageaient les mêmes rêves, les mêmes misères, les mêmes faiblesses" (*EIG* 89) [almost all spoke the same language because they shared the same dreams, the same miseries, the same weaknesses], Persévérance begins her session with the learned Latin prayers of her childhood in order to establish their commonality. Suddenly, after the prayers are said and Milroy departs, she finds herself alone, left to her own resources. Struck by the demoralization of those around her, she recognizes that "pour augmenter en eux l'énergie vitale qui leur permettrait de se rétablir, il fallait les faire bouger" (*EIG* 81) [to increase in them the life force that would allow them to recover, it was necessary to make them stir]. Grace here operates through a salvation that stresses a resurrection before, rather than after death, by inviting the immigrants to repossess their bodies. Persévérance precedes her stories by a rhythmic dance that also resurrects the energizing force of the earth and the island: "Tous ces mouvements créaient un rythme dont la cadence arrachait une poussière orange à la terre qui paraissait s'éveiller " (*EIG* 90) [All these movements created a rhythm whose cadence lifted an orange dust from the earth that seemed to awaken].

In their dance, the immigrants momentarily forget their exile on this island, the presence of the British soldiers, and their separation from their beloved, both sick and dead. However, during her second encounter with the immigrants that begins with an Ave Maria, their common prayer to another handmaiden full of grace, Persévérance endeavors to go beyond simple exercise, and to provide a link to something greater, a universal, creative force and spirit. For the immigrants, it is not what she says, the secrets that she reveals about the native plants, but the theater of her body telling the story that transforms the "island of death" into a blessed place, a threshold to the New World and to hope: "Ils la suivaient, moins avides de percer le secret des plantes que d'assister à ce théâtre de gestes et de mots qui rendait l'île un peu plus proche du Nouveau Monde dont il leur tardait de franchir le seuil. L'île devenait un lieu béni des dieux" (*EIG* 100) [They followed her, less anxious to penetrate the secret of the plants than to witness this theater of gestures and words which brought the island a little closer to the New World whose threshhold they were longing to cross. The island became a place blessed by the gods].

Thus, in contrast to history denounced by the narrator of *La Maison Trestler* (*The Trestler House*) as "le théâtre des mots" (the theater of mere words) (239), the living theater that Perséveránce presents to the immigrants in the *Camps de santé* (Health Camps) features her sacred body. It reconnects them to the energy of life, saves them from despair, and draws forth their voices to tell their story and to speak of their pain. Persévérance also demonstrates an ability to appreciate these voices raised in the traditional folk songs she teaches them, rather than to find fault with their accents. Their dance and song integrate them into a new cultural heritage and give them a new homeland: "Venus de l'autre bout du monde, ils dansaient et chantaient comme s'ils avaient vécu là depuis toujours" (*EIG* 93) [Having come from the other side of the world, they danced and sang as if they had lived there forever].

In the scenes at these camps, the nineteenth-century Persévérance also prefigures the inscription of the feminine in twentieth-century writing that Ouellette-Michalska examined in her master's thesis. Both she and this type of writing represent "une réceptivité dynamique qui est d'abord prise de contact avec son propre corps, ses sensations, ses douleurs et ses joies avant de devenir relation au monde et à autrui" (Ouellette-Michalska 1978, cited by Green 86) [a dynamic receptivity, which means first entering into contact with one's own body, sensations, suffering, and joys before relating to the world and to others]. Following her discovery and acceptance of the gifts of her own body, in a subsequent session, she links the isolated island to the universe:

> Cette portion de terre, disait-elle en levant une main généreuse sur l'ensemble de l'île, était voisine de toute autre portion de terre visible ou invisible de l'univers. Élargissant davantage la main, elle expliquait que la multitude de plateaux, de vallées, de plaines, de fleuves, de col-

lines et d'archipels répandus à travers le monde formaient un seul et même monde. (*EIG* 103)

[This plot of land, said she sweeping her hand over the entire island, was contiguous to all other plots of land visible or invisible in the universe. Stretching out her hand farther, she explained that the numerous plateaus, valleys, plains, rivers, hills, and archipelagos spread across the globe formed one and the same world.]

This seamless world also makes no distinction between historical tragedies and personal disappointments; they are both made of the same human fabric.

In a nineteenth century that prides itself on its scientific approach to medicine and knowledge, Persévérance—the embodiment of a folk medicine that combines passion and belief—also represents the validity of hope, even in the form of illusory cures, in a time of crisis. Folk remedies and the comfort they offer here become life-giving rather than life-threatening; the power of medicine that divorces itself from the bodies it seeks to treat is, on the other hand, put into question by Doctor Milroy himself: "L'épidémie avait au moins ça de bon: elle lui rappelait que le corps reste le meilleur guide de la médecine" (*EIG* 75) [At least, the epidemic was good for reminding him that the body remains the best guide for the medical profession]. Furthermore, in Milroy's triumph over typhus when he himself becomes ill, which is staged as a combat between sickness and the body, it becomes difficult for Persévérance to distinguish whether his cure results from her herbal remedy or simply from his will to live: "elle se demandait si cette guérison était due à la volonté du docteur Milroy, ou au traitement d'herbes à dindes qu'elle lui avait administré" (*EIG* 143) [she wondered if this cure was to be credited to Dr. Milroy's will, or to the yarrow treatment that she had administered to him].

The Transformation of Persévérance

However, Persévérance not only transforms others but also experiences transformation. Reflecting on the creation of her herbal remedies, she concludes that it represents almost a mystical celebration, one that she later admits would probably not have been possible in the ordinary married life of her time. It provides her a link to the natural world around her, gives her a personal space for dreams and for delving into life's significance. It also serves to awaken her powers of transformation and to bring her infinite joy. Moreover, her storytelling bestows upon her a sense of accomplishment, not available to her otherwise: "Ces constructions mentales ajoutaient du poids à sa vie, lui donnant l'impression d'atteindre l'accomplissement" (*EIG* 89–90) [These cerebral constructions added weight to her life, giving her the impression of achieving fulfillment].

On the first trip to the camps, Persévérance assumes a proud public demeanor, buoyed by Milroy's recognition of her gift of storytelling and honored by her official association with him: "En passant devant la guérite de contrôle, elle salua le garde avec fierté. C'était le premier déplacement qu'elle effectuait en si bonne compagnie [celle de Milroy] depuis son arrivée sur l'île" (*EIG* 88) [Passing in front of the guardhouse, she proudly saluted the guard. This was the first trip that she took in such good company (i.e., Milroy's) since her arrival on the island].

As the novel progresses, in addition to public recognition, the personal recognition both of the convalescing immigrants in the camps and of Doctor Milroy become essential to Persévérance. Both furnish the love that previously seemed impossible to her. Yet, whereas her relationship with the immigrants of these camps will soon provide unambiguous fulfillment, her emotions regarding her relationship with Milroy remain far more complex.

Persévérance's work in the camps rapidly effects a physical transformation in her. During the first session, in response to the rhythm she creates in the dance with the immigrants, she begins to resemble the graceful women at a wedding that she previously only envied. Like them, she now participates in an enchanting dance: "Ensuite, elle bombait le torse, empruntant cette pose à la danse dont elle avait été témoin autrefois, lors d'un mariage, assise, enviant les femmes aux reins parfaitement cambrés qui tournoyaient au milieu de la pièce, lascives et fières, capables d'envoûter le plus endurci des célibataires" (*EIG* 90) [Next, she stuck out her torso, borrowing this position from a dance she had formerly witnessed, at the time of a marriage; seated, she had envied the women with their lower backs perfectly arched who were whirling in the center of the room, lustful and proud, capable of charming the most hardened of bachelors].

It is the circle of the immigrants surrounding her that transforms Persévérance and erases her wish to be someone else. An ensuing sense of responsibility toward them leads her to lay claim to the title of Madame, fills her with pride, and obliges her to surpass herself. Her botanical lessons in the camps ultimately result in the circle of immigrants singing the words of *À la claire fontaine* (*At the Clear Fountain*), encircling her with their love.

In the course of their reciprocal project of bringing the immigrants back to life, it is recognition by Milroy that becomes the primary force of a more complex and threatening transformation for Persévérance. Upon her first return from the camps, Milroy utters a brief declaration that transforms her existence: "Sans vous, cette île sera un enfer. Vous m'aidez à tenir. Vous m'aidez à continuer de croire en l'impossible" (*EIG* 87) [Without you, this island would be hell. You help me to stand it. You help me to continue to believe in the impossible]. After blushing, she will react with both joy and terror; for these words move her into the universe of desire. They invite her to believe in a different impossibility, that of an individual man recognizing her value. Milroy's words will echo in her dreams more and more joyfully, but in her waking hours the differences between her and his young and elegant wife Agnès Frémont will haunt her. When Milroy later is forced to announce the dismantlement of the camps, Persévérance will recognize the personal void that this loss represents. For he is separating her from the satisfaction and recognition derived from the community she has drawn together to celebrate the beauty of the universe: "personne ne l'appelerait par son nom, et elle n'aurait plus personne à qui parler de la grandeur de l'univers, de l'énergie vitale contenue dans le moindre pétale, la moindre tige ou la moindre racine" (*EIG* 110) [No longer would anybody call her by her name, and she would no longer have anyone with whom to speak of the grandeur of the universe, of the life energy contained in the smallest petal, stem, or root].

Looking at the traces of her botanical pursuits that previously provided a sense of self-attainment, she realizes that "tout cela ne suffirait peut-être plus à remplir ses journées" (*EIG* 111) [all this would perhaps no longer be sufficient to fill her days]. Communion with the universe through her culinary herbal creations now demands a complementary human union that will enable her to recognize the personal dreams that constitute her own life force. In these circumstances, only Milroy's recognition of her pain, which results in his agreeing to use one of her botanical remedies, can ease the loss of community. Together with his previous confession of her importance to him, this represents for her "l'unique déclaration d'amour jamais entendue" (*EIG* 105) [the only declaration of love that she had ever heard]. Her love for Dr. Milroy, although it can never be fully acknowledged, leads her to a new audacious move—a direct intervention to save him during his own bout with typhus— and to a dream fantasy of exploring a transformed Grace Island with him after his cure.

Later, at a final celebration of rebirth on the island, a celebration for the baptism of a child who survived the coffin ships, she will discover the joy of an intimate dance with him: "elle même le regardait comme elle ne l'avait encore jamais regardé . . . . elle se tut, et son corps parut s'affiner. Sans doute attendait-elle cet instant depuis longtemps, depuis des mois ou des semaines, peut-être même depuis toujours" (*EIG* 348) [she herself looked at him as she had never looked at him before . . . she became silent and her body seemed to become more refined. No doubt she had been waiting for this moment for a long time, for months or weeks, perhaps even forever]. However, as she recognizes her own desire, she must also leave her dancing partner, to protect "le bonheur secret de ceux qui aiment aimer" (*EIG* 348) [the secret happiness of those who love being in love] (*EIG* 348).

In addition to the immigrants and to Milroy, there is a third important agent in Persévérance's self-transformation. The arrival of the French chemist Lechaunay, the inventor of a fluid that the authorities hope will eradicate the typhus epidemic, creates some of her greatest challenges and opportunities for growth. Their first meeting establishes a conflict that provides a total contrast to the reciprocity of her other two previously described relationships. First, Lechaunay overlooks the beauty of the birdcage and her efforts to provide a dinner that would make a special occasion of his arrival. For Persévérance, his incapability to recognize the domestic creativity inherent in her "seaweed and cabbage soup" constitutes a threat to her importance in the household. In addition, when she attempts to offer her finest dessert "la gelée d'églantier . . . [à laquelle] elle tenait comme aux prunelles de ses yeux" (*EIG* 287) [her treasured wild rose jelly], he makes a point of calling it by its proper technical French name "la gelée des cynorrhodons" (*EIG* 287) [cynorrhodon jelly]. She experiences this insistence on correcting her French as not only an insult to her, but to all her people: "comment pouvait-il vouloir leur en remontrer à propos d'une langue née d'une même souche, nourrie d'un même sang, qu'ils avaient toujours défendue avec ardeur?"(*EIG* 287) [how could he want to prove his superiority in regard to a language that shared a common origin, that was nurtured by the same blood, that they (in Québec) had always ardently defended?].

After Lechaunay himself falls victim to the illness his fluid was supposed to cure, Persévérance first grasps the relationship between his incurable illness and her hard-heartedness to the suffering of another: "Pour la première fois, elle saisissait dans le regard de l'autre le reflet de sa propre dureté. . . . Elle restait donc face à une contradiction insoluble; elle avait préparé des remèdes capables de guérir des centaines de malades, mais elle ne pouvait rien pour celui-là [Lechaunay]" (*EIG* 307–308) [For the first time she saw in the look of the other the reflection of her own hard-heartedness; she remained, therefore, faced with an insoluble contradiction; she had prepared remedies capable of curing hundreds of sick people, but she could do nothing for him]. As a result, she experiences remorse as incurable and life-draining as Lechaunay's typhus. She comes to understand that her redemption must come both from herself and from Lechaunay, rather than from a supernatural force. To renounce her anger against him, she performs a purification ritual, washing in the fluid he had invented to cure the typhus epidemic: "Elle . . . versa lentement quelques gouttes dans le bassin d'eau tiède posé sur la table de chevet. Puis elle y trempa ses mains comme pour indiquer qu'elle se purifiait de ses anciennes colères et l'acceptait dans ce qu'il avait de plus cher, ce fluide qui lui avait fait traverser les mers" (*EIG* 309) [She slowly poured a few drops into the bowl of lukewarm water that stood on the nightstand. Then she dipped her hands into it as if to indicate that she was purifying herself from her former anger and that she was accepting him in what he treasured most, this fluid which had made him cross the ocean]. Only once she has accepted what he values most can he begin to heal, to appreciate her creations, and finally even to participate in the preparation of her herbal remedies. During this process, Lechaunay realizes that Persévérance "était plus attirée par la profondeur des choses que par leur surface" (*EIG* 315) [was more attracted by the depth of things than by their surface]. Accordingly, he introduces her to a scientific instrument, a microscope that will change her vision of the world, first terrifying her and then finally bringing her the joys of childhood she has never experienced.

Symbolically, near the end of the novel, it is Lechaunay and Persévérance who will serve as the godparents for a miraculous child. The mother of this child had lost her husband during the crossing from Ireland but believed him to be buried on Grosse-Île; she, therefore, returned to have her child baptized there. This child represents the miracle of life, triumphing over an environment of death. As the narrator remarks, he is ultimate grace, calling all around him back to life after the summer of 1847: "Cet enfant qui avait triomphé de la fièvre des navires, n'était pas un enfant comme les autres; il était la fleur fragile, surgie d'un monceau de cadavres, qui incarnait une miraculeuse vitalité" (*EIG* 335) [This child who had triumphed over the fever of the coffin ships was not like other children; he was a fragile flower, sprung from a pile of cadavers, that embodied miraculous vitality]. To celebrate his baptism, both Persévérance and Lechaunay join together in the serving of what they had jointly created during the months of Lechaunay's convalescence; they are equally proud of this "mead of the ancients" that Lechaunay proclaims to be the "drink of the gods." The elegant table setting also incorporates elements from Persévérance's wedding trousseau. Looking with equal satisfaction at the table and at the child wrapped in her wedding shawl, Persévérance sees the reincarnation of her lost hopes and ambitions.

A Departure for a New World

Yet, as the summer comes to an end, faced with separation from those who contributed to her transformation, looking around to see that she has not forgotten to pack something, Persévérance can no longer obtain grace from the material objects that she used earlier to transform the life of others: "Tout était là, mais elle ne s'était jamais sentie, aussi dépossédée de tout" (*EIG* 347) [It was all there, but she had never felt as totally dispossessed]. Nor can she feel "solidaire de l'amour universel porté à la beauté du monde" (*EIG* 347) [in solidarity with a universal love for the beauty of the world]. Looking at her, Milroy is struck by the difference between his own return to his wife and family and Persévérance's departure without a destination. Recognizing her need to work within a structure that will encourage her creativity and autonomy, he finally envisages the idea of a position for her at the orphanage, established on the Rue Richelieu by *La Société Charitable des Dames Catholiques de Québec* (*The Catholic Ladies of Québec Charitable Society*).[5]

Paradoxically, the Franco-Canadian Persévérance, by interacting with the "sadness of 1847 [which] belongs to the Irish" (O'Gallagher 1984, 47) and by providing compassion and life within an atmosphere of death, finds her own personal salvation and grace. She recognizes that "il lui avait fallu s'éloigner de la maison paternelle pour découvrir la richesse du monde, son langage, son ampleur" (*EIG* 328) [it had been necessary for her to leave her father's house to discover the richness of the world, its language, and its scope]. She compares her summer to the new discoveries she has made under Lechaunay's microscope: "Ainsi avait été son été: tout avait été amplifié, vu sous un autre angle, vécu avec plus d'intensité. Dans cette maison, sur cette île, elle avait risqué plus d'audaces et éprouvé plus de joie que pendant le reste de sa vie" (*EIG* 328) [Her whole summer had been similar: everything had been magnified, seen from another angle, lived more intensely. In this house, on this island, she had dared to act more audaciously and had felt more joy than at any other time during her life]. Yet, after her discoveries in Milroy's house, and under his protection, she must also depart from there and from the isolation of the island.

To overcome the profound loss she feels, to continue without those who have become a part of her, she has the prospect of a new community that resembles her godchild, that of the Irish orphans of the Rue Richelieu. Armed with Lechaunay's gift of a microscope and a new vision of the material world, she leaves the island to enter, albeit anonymously, into the history of the city of Québec and the intertwining of two cultures. Milroy's story and the novel end in what the narrator characterizes as an image from a serialized novel—the same image of his young wife that he had seen at the beginning of the story. This image bestows on him the grace that allows him to forget that "pour eux aussi le temps passait " (*EIG* 351) [that time was passing for them as well]. On the other hand, a transformed Persévérance goes forward, like the Irish immigrants, to create a new community for herself, to search for her own New World dream on the mainland, "le continent du rêve, espace dont les frontières fuient dès l'instant où on croit les toucher" (*EIG* 67) [the continent of dreams, a space whose borders recede as soon as you think you have reached them].

Notes

1. This translation and all others in this essay are my own.

2. Laure Neuville in "Écrire pour 'vivre le temps à l'envers,' " ("Writing as a Means of Living Time Backwards") analyzes in detail the role of the narrator of *La Maison Trestler (The Trestler House)* in challenging these gaps in official history by presenting "a new way of writing history, based on corporal memory and on empathy" (Neuville, in Pascal 1995, 34).

3. All quotations from this novel are from the 1993 first edition. In the interest of simplicity, future quotations from this work will be identified in the body of the essay by *EIG* and the page reference. All translations of this novel are my own.

4. Functioning in the oral mode, Persévérance is the foremother of the contemporary woman writer described by Ouellette-Michalska in her master's thesis *Le Féminin comme lieu d'inscription scripturale*. She has "une oreille à l'écoute de son corps de chair et l'autre ouverte sur le grand monde" (Ouellette-Michalska

1978, cited in Green, 1997, 94) [one ear listening to her flesh-and-blood body and the other opened to the entire world].

5. In this turn of the plot, the fictional figure of Persévérance departs for one of the rare places where women recorded nineteenth-century Québec history. For as Marianna O'Gallagher points out, the links between the surviving children of the typhus epidemic and the Canadian families who adopted them are provided by the information in the registers of this orphanage on the Rue Richelieu. These registers both provide full information on the 619 children cared for in 1847 and 1848 and serve as an important reminder of the hidden role of Québec women such as Persévérance in this historical crisis.

Works Cited

Charbonneau, André, and André Sévigny. *1847 Grosse Île: Au fil des jours*. Ottawa: Ministre des Travaux Publics et Services Gouvernementaux Canada, 1997.

Conway, Sheelagh. *The Faraway Hills Are Green: Voices of Irish Women in Canada*. Toronto: Women's Press, 1992.

Dickinson, John A., and Brian Young. *A Short History of Québec*. 2d ed. Toronto: Copp Clark Pitman, 1993.

Green, Mary Jean. "L'Itinéraire d'une écriture au féminin: Une lecture féministe de Madeleine Ouellette-Michalska," *Voix et images* 67 (Autumn 1997): 84–99.

Lacoursière, Jacques. *Histoire populaire du Québec*. Tome III, 1841–1896. Sillery: Septentrion, 1996.

Neuville, Laure. "Écrire pour 'vivre le temps à l'envers': Madeleine Ouellette-Michalska et Francine Noël." In *Le Roman québécois au féminin (1980–1995)*, edited by Gabrielle Pascal, 33–45. Montréal: Triptyque, 1995.

O'Driscoll, Robert, and Lorna Reynolds. *The Untold Story: The Irish in Canada*. Vol. 1. Toronto: Celtic Arts of Canada, 1988.

O'Gallagher, Marianna. *Grosse Île: Gateway to Canada, 1832–1937*. St. Foy: Livres Carraig Books, 1984.

Ouellette-Michalska, Madeleine. *L'Été de l'Île de Grâce*. Montréal: Éditions Québec/Amérique (Collection Deux-Continents), 1993.

———. *Le Féminin comme lieu d'inscription scripturale*. Montréal: Université du Québec à Montréal, Mémoire de maîtrise, 1978.

———. *La Maison Trestler ou le 8e jour d'Amérique*. Montréal: Éditions Québec/Amérique, 1984.

———. *La Tentation de dire*. Montréal: Éditions Québec/Amérique, 1985.

Paterson, Janet M. "L'Écriture du désir: Entretien avec Madeleine Ouellette-Michalska." *Voix et images* 67 (Autumn 1997): 11–24.

Randall, Marilyn. "Histoire, roman et texte national: Comment lire *L'Été de l'Île de Grâce*." *Voix et images* (Autumn 1997): 65–83.

Vigneault, Robert. "Madeleine Ouellette-Michalska, essayiste: Une écriture qui se cherche." *Voix et images* (Autumn 1997): 26–38.

Gendered Migrations: History, Women, Class, and Urbanity in France Théoret's *Laurence*

KAREN L. GOULD

MODERNITY IN QUÉBEC LETTERS HAS EMERGED OUT OF AND IN REsponse to the urban Montreal experience. According to Québec critics Pierre Nepveu and Gilles Marcotte, "a city exists, literarily speaking, when it becomes a question, when it *raises questions*" (Nepveu and Marcotte 1992, 8, my translation). In their insightful introduction to the collection *Montréal imaginaire* (*Imaginary Montreal*), they note as well that, since World War II, the city of Montreal has been textually represented as an increasingly complex and contradictory space marked by all of the problems and questions of modern collective life. Indeed, for Nepveu, Marcotte, and many of their contributors, Montreal has become the primary literary site for the most urgent and hotly contested political, cultural, and artistic debates in modern Québec history (Nepveu and Marcotte 1992, 9).

Although France Théoret's works were not the subject of study in any of the essays presented in *Montréal imaginaire*, her writings could easily have served to enrich a number of the analyses appearing in this influential volume. More recently, in an essay focusing on the characteristics and meanings of feminist geography in Québec women's writing, Rosemary Chapman has examined notions of urban space in Théoret's innovative metropolitan novel, *Nous parlerons comme on écrit* (1982) (*We Shall Speak As One Writes*).[1] Indeed, since the appearance of her first experimental text, *Bloody Mary* (1977), Théoret's writings have revealed an ongoing preoccupation with modernity, feminism, and women's experience in the urban sphere. Most, if not all, of her narrators and principal characters are, in fact, *des Montréalaises*. Moreover, in one way or another, all of Théoret's works have emphasized the interconnectedness of Québec's most important city, with issues of modernization, female subjugation and independence, and changing notions of gender identity, particularly among younger women. Of her relationship to Montreal and to the notion of urbanity, France Théoret writes in a 1991 journal entry: "I was born in Montreal, urbanity concerns me, as does solitude. The city is the space where pluralism is possible. My imagination has multiplied all of the eccentric and marginal forms of expressions that I have witnessed there" (*Journal* 207, my translation).

Already a major urban center of nearly a million inhabitants by 1930, the city of Montreal is represented as an enticing, yet intimidating cultural space in Théoret's most recent novel, *Laurence*, which appeared in 1996. Foregrounding critical moments in Québec history and especially the rapid development of Montreal from the late 1920s to the 1940s, *Laurence* chronicles, among other things, the socioeconomic and political significance of the substantial demographic shift toward urban centers in general, and toward Montreal in particular, during the first half of the twentieth century. In so doing, the novel explores the impact of Québec's urban migration on the traditional (i.e., patriarchal, Catholic, and rural) francophone family as well as on the social construction of gender roles in the city.

A more accessible and direct work than many of Théoret's highly "experimental" texts that appeared in the 1970s and 1980s,[2] *Laurence* is also, and most importantly, the story of a young woman's battle against the stultifying weight of tradition and gender inequality. As noted in Théoret's theoretical essays in *Entre raison et déraison* (1987) (*Between Reason and Folly*), in the stories found in *L'Homme qui peignait Staline* (1989) (*The Man Who Painted Stalin*), and in the blending of history and autobiography in Théoret's literary and cultural daybook, *Journal pour mémoire* (1993) (*Diary for Memory*), *Laurence* is grounded in both the personal and the historical. Moreover, as Janet Paterson has remarked of Madeleine Ouellette-Michalska's postmodern historical novel, *La Maison Trestler (The Trestler House)*, *Laurence* is likewise a text "no longer bound by previous authority, be it the classical novel or traditional historical discourse.... By fragmenting the enunciative acts, which are written in the feminine, the text rejects the terror of unitary discourse in which a single voice, generally the father's, is heard" (Paterson 1994, 66).

Théoret's latest novel echoes earlier works in its preoccupation with issues of gender, language, and familial relations—particularly with respect to women's *speechlessness* in patriarchal discourse. As I have already remarked elsewhere with respect to the final story in *L'Homme qui peignait Staline*, "the family is a place where communication and self-disclosure are impossible" in Théoret's writing

(Gould 1993, 403). Furthermore, in a 1988 essay published in the collective work, *La Théorie, un dimanche (What We Talk About on Sundays)*, the author herself acknowledges that "everyday I write my life. I am inescapably alone facing the adolescent" ("Eloge," 191, my translation). As is frequently the case in Théoret's writing—whether fiction, theory, or autobiography—the narrative that unfolds in *Laurence* offers a portrait of adolescent revolt and cultural resistance that Laurence Naud and subsequently her younger sister, Odette, express silently through their respective actions of leaving home for the city. Reminiscent of adolescent protagonists in *Une voix pour Odile* (1978) (*A Voice for Odile*), *Nous parlerons comme on écrit* (1982), and *L'Homme qui peignait Staline* (1989), Théoret's central protagonist in *Laurence* is unable to *speak* her mind, articulate the nature of her feelings, or verbalize the reasons for her "mute" revolt. With fragmentary utterances and limited gestures, Laurence reveals both excitement and uneasiness about a train ride that will lead toward self-determination and independence:

> Tassée dans le fauteuil, longtemps elle ne bougea pas, minuscule, perdue dans la révolte muette. La servitude aurait une fin, la dépendance aussi. Elle scanda les deux syllabes du verbe partir, les yeux immobiles sur la manette de cuivre de la fênetre. L'incantation dura. Les deux syllabes se détachèrent, le mot devint insignifiant. (*Laurence* 1996, 39)

> [She sat bunched up in her seat, motionless, tiny, dazed by her quiet gesture of rebellion. Her servitude was over, her dependence on them, as well. She chanted the two syllables of the verb go-ing, staring at the window's copper handle. The chant became pure sound. The syllables separated, making the word meaningless.] (*Laurence* 1998, 26)

Laurence's initial departure for Québec City and the convent hospital that provides her with nursing training and shelter marks the first phase of the daughter's revolt against the traditional patriarchal family, a moment underscored by the insistent noting of the date: July 2, 1923. Moreover, Théoret's narrator will stress the importance of other significant historical dates and personal events as well. In so doing, the narrative connects the chronology of Laurence's private journey away from the rigid conventions of rural life and toward self-reliance in the city with momentous historical events that influenced the social conditions and cultural outlook of Québec society from the mid-1920s to the mid-1940s. Thus, Théoret's narrative voice makes note of:

1929: the Stock Market Crash, with its effects felt as far away as the small Québec village of Beaupré

January 1930: the bankruptcy and closing of the lumber mill in Beaupré and the ensuing unemployment of many of the local workers, including Laurence's fiancé

The summer of 1932: a period when Laurence is in Montreal and is increasingly cognizant of the many unemployed people wandering the city streets

January 1937: a month when Laurence's overworked younger sister, Odette, falls ill from factory work and two young women from Le Gaspé move into their apartment building, taking up work in a textile manufacturing plant

The Normandy invasion, 1945, and the end of World War II, and the postwar summer of 1945: when Laurence discovers that the salaries and working conditions for Montreal nurses are improving modestly, while she is promoted to chief nurse at a Montreal hospital

In *Laurence*, representations of the city illustrate elements crucial to the advent of modernity in pre-World War II and wartime Québec. Thus, Théoret's narrative reminds the reader of significant historical changes in pre-1945 Québec society, such as the increasing laicisation of the public sphere; the accompanying decrease in Church authority; the growing financial independence of urban workers, including female workers; the decreasing size of the urban family as compared with the traditionally large, rural family; greater opportunities for women and men to socialize outside the family unit or marriage; the visibility of work and class distinctions separating anglophones from francophones and immigrant allophones; the increased visibility of the unemployed and poor; and the rise in urban violence.

For Théoret's protagonist, Laurence, the relative poverty of her agrarian family and, in particular, the controlling nature of her father, Léon Naud, leads to her removal from school at age 11 in order to help with the farm work. Laurence's eldest sister, Amanda, is sent off to the convent to earn spiritual credit for the family with Church officials. Two other sisters follow in Amanda's footsteps. Exhausted by the many babies she has borne and by the difficult physical challenges of farm life, Laurence's ailing mother, Rosalie, weakens rapidly after witnessing the shooting of the injured family horse that is no longer domestically useful. In fact, the analogy constructed between the faithful beast's grim fate after years of dutiful service and the farm mother's own life of sacrifice is a compelling, if troubling one for Laurence.

Even more than farm life and tradition-bound villages that populate rural Québec in the early part of the century, however, representations of the convent and the convent hospital stand in stern opposition in Théoret's novel to the changing cultural values, economic relations, and new gender roles that Laurence and her younger sister Odette encounter once they move to Montreal. A commanding space for the perpetuation of social and moral conformity, the convent also mirrors the father's own dualistic view of rural and city life, which he transposes onto Amanda, the dedicated nun, and Laurence, the inquisitive, unmarried nonconformist:

> L'odieuse comparaison que le père établit entre Amanda et Laurence engendra la figure de soeurs ennemies. Léon vit la seconde si différente de la première qu'il amplifia leurs dissemblances. . . . A la grâce d'Amanda, il opposait la joie de vivre de Laurence. Sa pétulance et sa vivacité le perturbaient, il y percevait de l'excès insupportable. La figure angélique de l'aînée le rassura sur son salut. Il ne prêta pas des traits diaboliques à l'autre, une crainte du châtiment éternel le freinait. Le monde satanique et pervers existait hors de sa maison, il veillait à ce qu'il n'y pénètre pas. Léon Naud pensait constamment au mal, à son emprise. La fille blonde fut la gardienne du bien. Il le voulut ainsi et cultiva sa préférence pour ne pas errer devant le mal. (*Laurence* 1996, 173)

> [The father's appalling way of comparing Laurence and Amanda made enemies of the sisters. Léon thought the second daughter so unlike the first that he exaggerated their differences. . . . He contrasted Amanda's grace to Laurence's joy in life. He took the latter's troubling curiosity and liveliness as manifestations of an unacceptable penchant for excess. The angelic face of his eldest reassured him of his salvation. He refrained from calling the other's traits diabolical out of fear of punishment in the great hereafter. The devil's world, its perversions, existed beyond the walls of his household, and he made sure they didn't enter. Léon Naud thought endlessly of evil, and its hold on people. The blond daughter was the repository of good. Thus he wished it, cultivating a preference for her to keep him from erring in the face of evil.] (*Laurence* 1998, 112)

In a chastising letter sent to Laurence after his younger daughter Odette has secretly departed for Montreal, Léon Naud elaborates on the reasons for his paternal fears and moral condemnation of urban women. According to the distrustful and unyielding patriarch, the city is the site of corruption and lawlessness, "où tant de femmes tournaient mal, où il existait des lieux de débauche et se commettait plus de crimes que partout ailleurs au pays. Il poursuivait son discours, hanté par la progression du mal partout où l'on s'éloignait des moeurs rurales" (*Laurence* 1996, 198) [where so many women went wrong, where there were dens of iniquity and where more crimes were committed than anywhere else in the country. He went on, haunted by the idea that evil was progressing in every place that had left behind rural moral standards] (*Laurence* 1998 129).

Toward the end of Théoret's novel, Laurence's mother, Rosalie, journeys alone to Montreal to visit her youngest daughter and nun, Cécile. In juxtaposition to an urban geography of densely populated streets, strange and stimulating odors, and competing noises, Laurence's mother is descriptively linked to the quiet, cloistered space of the convent and the rigidity of rural, conservative values. Although less judgmental of her daughters than her husband, Rosalie is nonetheless resigned to a way of life that resists difference or change. Her physical demeanor and self-effacing mannerisms are more closely aligned with the attitudes and comportment of the three daughters who have taken religious vows than with the self-assertiveness and progressive beliefs of Odette and Laurence:

> Rosalie portait une robe noire sans ornement qui tombait aux chevilles, des chaussures noires lacées, entre une religieuse et elle, la différence tenait à la coiffure. La femme aux cheveux blancs noués s'effaçait. Elle fut indifférente au milieu urbain, ne porta pas de jugement sur les maisons en rangées et les rues asphaltées, promena un regard étranger autour d'elle. La multiplicité des odeurs, les bruits inconnus, la vision entravée par les logements d'en face rendaient sa respiration à l'étroit. Une surcharge de sensations et d'impressions noyait la réalité de la ville. Inutilement Odette tenta de la convaincre des bienfaits du progrès. Rosalie ne verrait pas de son vivant sa maison électrifiée. (*Laurence* 1996, 278–79)

> [Rosalie wore a plain black dress that fell to her ankles, black lace shoes, and, apart from the bare head, there was nothing to distinguish her from a nun. The woman with her hair in a knot made herself unobtrusive. She was indifferent to the urban surroundings, made no comment on the houses in rows and the paved streets, looked around her with the air of an outsider. She found the different smells, unknown noises, the view limited by the flats opposite, a little suffocating. Whatever the city really was was drowned in an overload of impressions and sensations. Odette tried to convince her about the advantages of progress. Rosalie would not see electricity in her house in her lifetime.] (*Laurence* 1998, 182–83)

As Patricia Smart noted a decade ago in *Writing in the Father's House*, "to be born a girl and to grow into womanhood in the crushing poverty of a pre-Quiet Revolution French-Canadian village is to be taught submission and silence in face of an intolerable reality" (Smart 1991, 251). In *Laurence*, the authorized teaching of submission and silence takes place within convent walls, where rural values are reinforced daily and where the city is overtly demonized as the preeminent site of modern moral corruption and disorder. Although Laurence's father and most of the farm families and villagers of the period view advanced education with suspicion, the convent school along with the convent hospital are generally considered appropriate sites of instruction and service for young women who do not marry or who are deemed too homely to attract a husband. In the Québec countryside of the early 1900s, the acceptability of religious education for young women is directly tied to the perceived need to instruct and enact the perpetuation of tradition. Both the convent and the convent hospital constitute highly disciplined, restrictive spaces ordered by notions of duty, sacrifice, and punishment for those who stray from Church dogma. As Théoret's narrator indicates, the young women's daily schedules are tightly organized, and rules of conduct are stringently applied, resulting in an environment that stresses order and obedience above all else.

Having struggled to overcome the negative aspects of her own convent education, Laurence laments the crippling effect of religious instruction on her younger, less inquiring sister who has come to live with her in Montreal. Upon her arrival, Odette views all that transpires in the city in light of the simple convent discourse that she has dutifully assimilated, a discourse of "ordre et désordre, le premier enseignement de l'institution" (*Laurence* 1996, 220) [order and disorder, the first things she learned at the institution] (*Laurence* 1998, 143). Through these and other key descriptions of Odette's naive perceptions and provincial schooling, Théoret's highly analytical narrative voice underscores how and why traditional Catholic convent instruction educates young girls to grow up thinking like children and to remain entirely dependent upon Church dogma to explain human experience as well as the culture it produces. Théoret has disclosed her own feelings of linguistic inadequacy and isolation in the urban environment as a result of strict religious training, noting that "I was filled with anguish, the only words I had to describe it came from a religious education. But I had no one to talk to" ("Eloge" 180).

In addition to the institutionalized rigidity of the convent and the harsh worldview projected by Church teaching, Laurence witnesses a shocking lack of compassion and a desire to inflict pain among the Catholic medical staff. In the convent hospital, for example, she considers how the nuns mistreat unwed mothers by separating them from expectant married women, refusing them the right to see visitors, and rejecting their need for anesthetics during childbirth in an effort to impose a warranted punishment: "Les religieuses justifiaient l'absence d'anesthésie et de calmants lors de l'accouchement par la nécessité d'éprouver et de se remémorer la douleur. Les femmes attendaient l'enfant du péché, il paraissait juste qu'elles souffrent des conséquences du plaisir illicite" (*Laurence* 1996, 133) [The nuns refused to administer anaesthesia and sedatives during labour because they must feel, and never forget their pain. The women were expecting children begotten in sin and it was only right they should suffer the consequences of illicit pleasure] (*Laurence* 1998, 86).

Laurence comes to realize, moreover, that the convent nursing education she received provided no understanding whatsoever of the financial realities or political issues facing Québec society and North America as well in the 1930s and 1940s. As a result, women like Théoret's determined, if nonetheless naive protagonist, who left the protected space of the convent for city life, were ill-prepared to function in a modernizing Québec economy, and they knew nothing about the major sociopolitical issues of the time. For Laurence, who has had to educate herself about virtually everything unrelated to the medical care of others, the unquestioning collective identity, which results from authoritarian convent teaching, eventually becomes the target of her strong anticlerical critique:

> Son itinéraire dans les institutions dirigées par des femmes lui avait donné la certitude que les religieuses cultivaient une grande ignorance quant à la réalité économique. Elle n'avait rien appris auprès d'elles qui dépassât la nécessité d'une sécurité austère et paisible. La vie recluse tendait vers des habitudes surprotégées, muselait l'esprit d'initiative. Elle qui ne s'était jamais perçue comme un homme désirait une honnête aisance, celle qu'on acquiert par des initiatives personnelles, des activités immobilières, à titre d'exemple. Elle y pensait depuis une décennie, les lois et les conventions sociales allaient à l'encontre de sa volonté. (*Laurence* 1996, 285–86)

[Nuns excelled in gross ignorance when it came to economic realities, wanting only to have a safe, simple, peaceful life. A recluse was overprotected, was rarely required to take initiative. She never thought of herself as a man, but she desired a comfortable, honest lifestyle, the kind you win through your own efforts, through property speculation, for example. These thoughts had been on her mind for a decade, though law and social conventions were against her.] (*Laurence* 1998, 187)

One of the most painful aspects of Laurence's ignorance of urban life is her realization that the world of the convent is a repressive space in which women teach other women to be silent and to remain unschooled in the ways of the outside world. In *Laurence*, the most perverse nuns are those who believe that the way to protect young women from the ills of the world is by making a virtue of ignorance. In addition to the weaknesses in her general education, Laurence is self-conscious about speaking and writing, and especially about her lack of mastery over the basic rules of grammar and style. As noted in many of Théoret's earlier writings, this double dispossession of oral and written language becomes a leitmotiv in *Laurence*.[3] In the convent hospital where Laurence initially trains for certification, her language deficiency is a constant source of embarrassment in front of other students and the nuns. Even after passing her nursing examinations at the end of six years of study and after many years of acquired expertise as a medical attendant, Laurence does not actively seek a promotion to head nurse, fearing ridicule when writing out schedules for others to read. Yet, despite strong feelings of inadequacy, Laurence does eventually receive the promotion.

Over the years, France Théoret has expressed a keen interest in the subject of women's education in her writing. In *Journal pour mémoire*, which appeared in 1993, she writes of her own experience growing up in a Catholic educational system that dismissed the intellectual training and social development of young women as unimportant in a man's world. Her journal entry of 13 February 1989, reads:

> L'éducation des filles et la lutte dans la vie. La vie exige de nous une capacité d'être en lutte. Pourquoi l'éducation ne nous met-elle pas en face de cette réalité? Il y a la compétition, si peu dans l'éducation des filles. (*Journal* 51)

> [The education of young girls and the struggle of life. Life demands of us the capacity for struggle. Why doesn't education place us face to face with this reality? There is competition, which is rare in the education of young girls.] (my translation)

In the poetry of Jacques Godbout, Jean-Guy Pilon, and Alain Grandbois, Pierre Nepveu has noted how the city generates "images of destiny and lived or remembered journeys. The subject-walking-the-sidewalk contrasts with the subject-outside-the-city or . . . the subject-dreaming-the city ('*le sujet-rêvant-la-ville*')" (Nepveu 1992, 332, my translation). In the case of Théoret's *Laurence*, the parallels with Nepveu's observation are striking. Both the positive and negative destinies of Laurence and her younger sister Odette are undeniably forged by and in response to the city and its evolving urban culture. Far more than a spatial backdrop for Théoret's narrative explorations, Montreal is repeatedly personified as an agent of substantial change in the lives of Québec women and men.

In *Laurence*, urbanity elicits the circulation of female desire beyond the strict boundaries of a conventionally sanctioned marital union. During her maturing years in Montreal, Laurence establishes a number of close male friendships and has several affairs. Female desire in the city is thus acknowledged through Laurence's sexual liaisons, but her independence is never compromised. On the contrary, it seems that with each new affair and its subsequent termination, Laurence grows more self-sufficient and less anxious about her solitude.

On the other hand, Odette's desire for a marital union of her own choosing does not guarantee happiness in her new urban setting. Odette's marriage to a self-absorbed city drifter, who, even after three children and mounting debts, wanders city streets looking for the ideal card game and the money that will help him open a bar, proves disastrous. Alone and increasingly fretful, Odette fears leaving the apartment, worries about the safety and cleanliness of her children on city streets, and waits sadly every evening for her husband's return. For Odette, who is unable to construct an independent identity as Laurence does, her marriage becomes an alienating and degrading experience for which she holds the city and all of its temptations responsible.

Regrettably, Léon Naud is correct in one sense about the threat to women in the city. Montreal, like other large urban centers then and now, is indeed a place of potential danger for the women in Théoret's novel—as Laurence discovers when she is manipulated and raped by two men in an unfamiliar part of the city. Yet, Laurence does not allow this single incident, however demeaning and hurtful, to thwart her ambition to control her own life. Thus, although Laurence's resistance to the weight of Québec tradition is not a painless gesture, she succeeds nonetheless in countering the constraints of rural conservatism with an urban optimism grounded in the belief that women can define the future through projects of their own choosing. Literally and figuratively speaking, then, her desire at the close of the novel to build two lakeside chalets as a long-term financial investment signals Laurence's need to construct a new foundation on which to stake her future. Despite criticisms from friends and family that this construction project is inappropriate for a single woman, Laurence will not be dissuaded.

In examining the works of Montreal's contemporary immigrant writers such as Nadine Ltaif, Gérard Etienne, and Régine Robin, Québec cultural critic Simon Harel has stressed the importance of "rupture"—*rupture* with the perceived "home" country or place; *rupture* as well with common cultural references; and most profoundly, *rupture* with a former sense of personal identity. Harel concludes, "[E]very territorial rupture (exile or immigration) is full of consequences" (Harel 1992, 394, my translation). In *Laurence*, the female protagonist and her sister Odette do not migrate from one country to another. Yet, in many ways their respective efforts to flee the rigid and unequal gendered roles of rural life, the nostalgic orientation of traditional Québec culture, and the inadequacy of convent teaching for the modern world do constitute significant forms of rupture. Indeed, the radical break with rural tradition and institutionalized forms of female dependency produces a destabilization of identity—personal, social, cultural—with which many of Théoret's female protagonists have repeatedly struggled.

A historical novel written on the verge of a new millenium, Théoret's *Laurence* is the story of a woman who refuses to submit to the tradition-bound culture into which she has been born and about which she is rigidly instructed. Even so, as a feminist critic, Théoret has underscored the challenge of such a rebellious stance for women today, as well as in earlier decades. She has also recognized the special challenge for women who lack the financial means or educational access needed to make their way and develop their identity independently: "For every woman, individuality is a difficult struggle. When a woman is not born into a middle-class family, individuality is an even greater struggle" (*Théorie* 189, my translation). In *Laurence*, issues of gender, class, and urbanity converge in ways that will continue to provoke both contemporary and historical reflections.

Notes

1. Several essays in the collection on *Montréal, 1642–1992: Le grand passage* also discuss the interconnectedness of modernity and urbanity. Both this volume

and *Montréal imaginaire* were published in connection with the observance of the 300-year anniversary of the city of Montreal.

2. See Chapman's discussion of *Nous parlerons comme on écrit* in her essay "L'écriture de l'espace au féminin: Géographie féministe et textes littéraires québécois" (21–23). In an essay entitled "Ecrire (dans) la ville: La *Métropolis* au féminin," Claudine Potvin discusses the representation of the city in Théoret's opening novella from *L'Homme qui peignait Staline*.

3. Although women's problematic relationship to language has been the central theme in much of Théoret's writing, many of the author's earlier texts have approached the issue of women and language in a highly theoretical (as well as personal) manner, offering a conscious critique of the place of women and women's experience in a language that is primarily male-oriented and "man-made." In fact, critics have sometimes reproached Théoret for constructing a visibly halting language in which her female characters endeavor to express themselves. However, Théoret's objective has always been clear in this regard. Whereas women's needs to vocalize themselves, their lived reality, and their hope for a better life are undeniable, their attempts to do so are, in her view, especially challenging and often painful. For a discussion of Théoret's experimental practice of "writing in the feminine/écriture au féminin," see Louise Dupré, *Stratégies du vertige (Strategies of Vertigo)*, and Karen Gould, *Writing in the Feminine: Feminism and Experimental Writing in Québec*.

Works Cited

Chapman, Rosemary. "L'Écriture de l'espace au féminin: Géographie féministe et textes littéraires québécois." *Recherches Féministes: Territoires* 10, no. 2 (1997): 13–26.

Dupré, Louise. *Stratégies du vertige*. Montreal: Remue-ménage, 1989.

Gould, Karen. "Autobiographical History and the Lure of the Recent Past: *L'Homme qui peignait Staline*," *L'Esprit créateur* 33.2 (Summer 1993): 83–93. Special issue: "Postcolonial Women's Writing."

———. *Writing in the Feminine: Feminism and Experimental Writing in Québec*. Carbondale: Southern Illinois University Press, 1990.

Harel, Simon. "La Parole orpheline de l'écrivain migrant." In *Montréal imaginaire*. Edited by Pierre Nepveu and Gilles Marcotte. Montreal: Fides, 1992: 373–418.

Melançon, Benoît, and Pierre Popovic, eds. *Montréal, 1642–1992: Le grand passage*. Montreal: XYZ, 1994.

Nepveu, Pierre, and Gilles Marcotte, eds. *Montréal Imaginaire: Ville et littérature*. Montreal: Fides, 1992.

Paterson, Janet M. *Postmodernism and the Québec Novel*. Translated by David Homel and Charles Phillips. Toronto: University of Toronto Press, 1994.

Potvin, Claudine. "Ecrire (dans) la ville: La *Métropolis* au féminin," *Tangence* 48 (October 1995): 84–96.

Smart, Patricia. *Writing in the Father's House: The Emergence of the Feminine in the Québec Literary Tradition*. Toronto: University of Toronto Press, 1991.

Théoret, France. *Bloody Mary*. Montreal: Les Herbes Rouges, 1977.

———. "Eloge de la mémoire des femmes." In *La Théorie, un dimanche*. Montreal: Remue-ménage, 1988: 175–91.

———. *Journal pour mémoire*. Montreal: L'Hexagone, 1993.

———. *Laurence*. Montreal: Les Herbes Rouges, 1996. Translated by Gail Scott under the title *Laurence* (Toronto: Mercury Press, 1998).

———. *L'Homme qui peignait Staline*. Montreal: Montreal: Les Herbes Rouges, 1989. Translated by Luise Von Flotow under the title *The Man Who Painted Stalin* (Toronto: Mercury Press, 1991).

———. *Nous parlerons comme on écrit*. Montreal: Les Herbes Rouges, 1982.

———. *Une voix pour Odile*. Montreal: Les Herbes Rouges, 1978.

Passionate Postmortems: Couples Plays by Women Dramatists

JANE MOSS

THE "PASSIONATE POSTMORTEMS" OF MY TITLE REFERS NOT ONLY TO plays that perform autopsies on dead love affairs, but also to the demise of a theatrical movement. Sadly, we must acknowledge the end of feminist theater as a collective project whose aims were to promote positive changes in the lives of Québec women, replace negative representations of women with more empowering models, and problematize socially constructed gender roles. Playwrights and critics agree that most feminist theater had disappeared by the mid 1980s (Burgoyne 1990, 1992; Fréchette 1991; Godard 1992; Lafon 1992; Larrue 1991; Noiseux 1990; P. Pelletier 1995), killed off by internal conflicts, cutbacks in government arts funding, and hostile critics. Yet, although some still lament the unfulfilled promise of feminist theater, one can take solace in recognizing the indelible mark that feminism left on Québec drama. Were it not for Marie Savard's "Marquise," the witches of *La Nef des sorcières* (*A Clash of Symbols*), Denise Boucher's "Fairies," Jovette Marchessault's "wet hens," the rebellious women of the Théâtre expérimental des femmes, and other self-dramatizing women who dared to transgress codes of behavior and modes of speech, one would not have the honest expressions of sexuality that are heard today in plays by women and men.

The feminist plays of the 1970s denounced the sexual exploitation and repression of women by the patriarchal establishment of conservative Catholic Québec and spoke openly about all aspects of female sexuality, including masturbation, maternal *jouissance* (pleasure), menopause, and lesbian eroticism. Overcoming the shame that Jansenist doctrine attached to the body and the censorship that silenced them, women playwrights found the words to talk about their sexuality. For the most part, this body talk was heard in monologues or among women because they seemed to need the safe space of female intimacy while making the transition from sexual objects to desiring subjects. Since sex, procreation, and motherhood had always gone together for heterosexual women, they could think about their sexuality differently once the availability of contraception and abortion made childbearing a choice. In numerous works during the 1980s, women playwrights took on the issue of maternity in their continuing examination of the key issues in women's lives.[1] Only when sex and pregnancy were separated was it possible for women to explore their erotic potential fully and to consider the role of sexuality in their amorous relationships. It is important to point out that, whereas lesbian rights and erotics were integral aspects of early feminist theater, these issues had faded from the scene by the end of the 1980s, even while homosexual men were creating a vibrant gay theater that blurred binary gender identities and celebrated homoeroticism.[2]

Lesbianism was not the only thing that disappeared from the stage; feminist politics also vanished. At the same time that women were assuming leadership roles in institutional theaters and scoring hits as directors,[3] many women who had participated in the creation of women's theater—women such as Carole Fréchette (Théâtre des Cuisines), Pol Pelletier, and Ginette Noiseux (Théâtre expérimental des femmes), Marie Laberge, and Jovette Marchessault—either ceased identifying with feminist theater practice or simply stopped working in the theater. Whether one blames antifeminist backlash or internal divisions, clearly the feminist political agenda was no longer considered urgent by theater women. One could suggest that because Québec society was quick to respond to feminist calls for change, it was not long before the political impulse gave way to more personal issues. Beginning in the 1980s and continuing in the 1990s, a significant number of plays by women took up the subject of "la vie du couple" (the couple's life). Exploring the difficulty of living together on equal terms, these works focus on the quest for individual fulfillment and happiness, a key component of which is sexuality.

As I claimed earlier, the continuing interest in dramatizing the liberated discourse of female sexuality points to the continuing influence of feminism on Québec drama. That the right to sexual equality and pleasure is no longer contested leads me to suggest that one can talk about a *post*-feminist theater. While acknowledging that this term troubles many feminists, I use it to refer to women's plays that begin with the assumption of women's independence. The authors of these postfeminist plays no longer feel obliged to denounce patriarchal oppression, lament victimization, or make political demands. Having achieved material comfort, reconciled with their mothers, redefined their roles within the family, and reinvented motherhood on their own terms, postfeminist playwrights are free to work on issues of emotional and sensual satisfaction. In numerous plays, therefore, one hears women characters talk about their quests for happiness as they analyze their amorous relationships. Because female sexuality is no longer repressed, there is no more need for the hysterical acting out that characterized feminist theater in the 1970s.

One should not assume that postfeminist theater signals a return to conventional dramatic forms or old-fashioned models of femininity. Most of the couples plays centered on analyzing ended affairs are not staged in the usual sites of bourgeois realist drama. They no longer take place in the kitchens or living rooms of the Québec family home, the traditional social space that used to define and restrict women. They take place in a cloister (*Pierre, ou la Consolation* [*Pierre, or Consolation*]), an empty theater (*Double Mélodie* [*Double Melody*]), a futuristic apartment (*L'Ombre de toi* [*The Shadow of You*]), the streets of Brussels (*La Peau d'Élisa* [*Elisa's Skin*]), or a Japanese media space (*Un Samouraï amoureux* [*A Samurai in Love*]).[4] In other words, these postfeminist plays are also post-*Québécois* in the way that they transcend nationalist concerns and alter realism. There are no parents or children to distract the former lovers with talk of familial duties. More often, the dialogue or parallel monologues take place in closed, liminal, or nonreal spaces that point to a conscious choice to isolate the couple from everyday life to ensure privacy for the expression of intimate feelings. The women characters in these plays never question femininity or gender identity, but their sexual behavior is never restrained by old notions of female passivity. These are passionate women not afraid to express desire or to eroticize the male body. This postfeminist theater is still transgressive and subversive in that it rejects gendered eroticism and celebrates women as desiring subjects.

Contemporary plays by women also use language in ways not possible twenty years ago: sometimes poetic, sometimes vulgar, always explicit, the new discourse of female desire has a vocabulary unavailable to women characters of the past. Not used as a cry of revolt or as a hysterical expression of alienation, the discourse of female desire still makes men uncomfortable. It is often troubling because it de-romanticizes the language of love and signals a role reversal, a shift in the balance of erotic power. Whereas women used to associate sex and love, this is not always the case in contemporary women's drama. It is the question of the relation between physical and emotional satisfaction that is raised constantly by what I am calling postfeminist theater. Whether they belong to the generation that began writing in the 1970s or are members of *la relève* (the next generation), contemporary women dramatists analyze what went wrong in "la vie du couple" in order to focus on issues of identity and happiness.

Dramatizing "la vie du couple" poses a number of difficulties. On the one hand, it is hard to avoid the clichés of domestic tragedy, melodrama, or farce that cast women as victims, hysterics, or sluts. On the other hand, the representation of sexuality can tip over into an eroticism (or pornography) that forces spectators to become voyeurs, as when the Théâtre expérimental des femmes staged the explicit scenes of *La Soirée des murmures* (*The Evening of Murmurs*) (1987) or Anne-Marie Cadieux performed the crude sex acts of *La Nuit* (*The Night*) (1996). Carole Fréchette has said, "On fait des films d'amour, mais on ne fait pas des pièces d'amour" (1991, 28) [They make films about love, but they don't make plays about love]. In a discussion among men and women dramatists chaired and edited by Gilbert Turp for the Centre des auteurs dramatiques, Fréchette reiterated her belief that it is difficult to write about sexual love for the theater: "Il me semble que la sexualité au théâtre n'a pas d'autre choix que d'être métaphorisée" (10) [It seems to me that sexuality in the theater has no choice but to be made into a metaphor]. In the same discussion, Élizabeth Bourget noted that, unlike film, eroticism is hardly ever present in the theater because it is a communal art form. She also revealed that she wanted to write more about sexuality in *Appelle-moi* (*Call Me*), but she censored herself for fear of making the audience ill at ease (10). The plays under discussion here "narrativize" rather than perform sexuality; they talk about it in the past tense so that what is being dramatized is the discourse about sexuality more than sexuality itself. Temporal distance not only allows the female character to analyze and verbalize more clearly, it also reduces the erotic charge emitted by the couple and relieves the audience's sexual anxiety. Because the relationship has ended, the woman can separate desire, passion, and sexual satisfaction from love and happiness. In some instances, career and independence issues are also balanced against emotional attachment.

The work of Élizabeth Bourget illustrates the evolution from feminist to postfeminist theater. *Bernadette et Juliette, ou la vie, c'est comme la vaisselle, c'est toujours à recommencer (Bernadette and Juliette, or Life Is Like Doing the Dishes, You Are Always Starting Over)* (1978) carries the political charge of 1970s feminism as it shows two young women living out their dreams of sexual freedom, educational advancement, and career opportunities. Because Bernadette and Juliette assume that liberation includes sexual activity, they have a hard time reconciling their desire for independence with their need for male partners. When they talk about sex, it is more sexual banter and innuendo than erotic dialogue. Juliette, for example, seduces Pierre, saying: "Bon ben veux-tu on va baiser pis après ça, on parlera?" (41) [Okay, do you wanna fuck and then afterwards we'll talk?]. Although she may feel free to initiate sex, her ability to verbalize her desire is decidedly unsubtle. Recognizing that she does not know how to express her sexuality, Juliette writes a letter to her mother in which she laments the impoverished and vulgar vocabulary that prevented them from discussing sex: "Tu savais que j'f'rais l'amour, mais tu savais pas comment m'dire que j'aimerais ça. . . . T'aurais voulu m'en parler, mais t'attendais après moi pour que j'te donne les mots" (108) [You knew that I'd make love, but you didn't know how to tell me that I'd like it . . . You would've liked to talk to me about it, but you were waiting for me to give you the words].

Eighteen years after *Bernadette et Juliette*, Bourget is still interested in the problems faced by couples as they try to fulfill their sexual and emotional needs. In *Appelle-moi* (1995), she stages the parallel monologues of "Elle et Lui" (Her and Him)—thirty-something Montrealers who broke up six months ago following a six-month affair. After a chance encounter at the cinema, they each reflect on the relationship, wanting to understand why it did not last. Because the original title of this "pièce intime" (intimate play) was *Une histoire de cul* (*A Sex Story*), it comes as no surprise that one of the main topics is sex. More precisely, the two each question how sexual compatibility relates to love, if it is necessary to be in love to continue having sex with someone. Whereas the critics saw *Appelle-moi* as an ably constructed (if somewhat clichéd) study of the miscommunication, insecurities, and fear of commitment that condemns many people to loneliness (Bérard 1997, 37–38; O'Neill-Karch 1997–98, 396), I think that one needs to take a closer look at the language of the play. What one hears is a woman speaking freely about sex, creating an erotic discourse to accompany her female gaze.

Marie-Andrée Roy ("Elle") is a college-educated advertising copywriter who owns her own home and seems very comfortable with her sexuality. In fact, after meeting Réjean ("Lui") through the personal ads, she was the one who de-romanticized the affair and wanted to see it simply as filling important physical needs:

"C'était juste une histoire de cul. . . . J'avais envie de baiser, y baisait bien, ça fait qu'on a baisé pendant six mois. C'est tout" (20) [It was just a sexual affair . . . I felt like fucking, he fucked well, so we fucked for six months. That's all]. When she describes their lovemaking, he becomes the object of her desire, her fantasies:

On était en début d'après-midi.
La lumière de la journée entrait par la fenêtre.
Je me suis mise à regarder ses cuisses . . . pis j'ai trouvé qu'il avait des ben belles cuisses. On aurait dit que c'était la première fois que je les voyais.
Vraiment des belles cuisses. Longues, mais pas trop. Fermes. Avec ben du poil.
J'ai eu envie de les caresser . . .
Mais au lieu de le faire, je l'ai dit.
On était couchés un à côté de l'autre, on se touchait . . .
Pas vraiment, on se frôlait.
Je lui ai dit que j'avais envie de caresser ses cuisses. Il a voulu se tourner vers moi, je lui ai dit de pas bouger, de me laisser parler.
J'ai continué.
Je lui ai dit ce que je ferais après avoir caressé ses cuisses, ce que lui, j'aimerais qu'il m'fasse, pis ce que moi, je ferais ensuite, pis ce que lui ferait ensuite . . . (Un temps.)
Pis quand j'ai arrêté de parler, on a fait tout ce que j'avais dit. (Un temps.)
C'était bien, cette fois-là. (45)

[It was early afternoon.
Daylight was coming in through the window.
I started looking at his thighs . . . and I thought he had very good-looking
thighs. One would've thought it was the first time I was seeing them.
Really beautiful thighs. Long, but not too long. Firm. With lots of hair.
I wanted to stroke them . . .
But instead of doing it, I said it.
We were lying next to each other, our bodies touching . . .
Not really, just barely touching.
I told him that I wanted to caress his thighs. He started to turn toward me,
I told him not to move, to let me talk.
I continued.
I told him what I'd do after stroking his thighs, what I wanted him to do
to me, and what I'd do next, and then what he'd do after that . . . (Pause.)
And when I stopped talking, we did everything I'd said. (Pause.)
It was good, that time.]

While admiring the nostalgic and poetic tone of this sensual memory, one should also note that she becomes the sexual aggressor in the erotic scenario that she scripts for them.

Traditional gender roles seem to be reversed throughout *Appelle-moi*. He admits repeatedly that he was puzzled and overwhelmed by her sexuality. Proud to have given her such pleasure, he also complains that her expectations made him feel like a sexual object (75). He feels insecure because she is socially and culturally superior to him; he complains that she never introduced him to her friends or talked about herself; he wants to hear her say that she loves him; he initiates the breakup because he cannot imagine a future with her (47, 57, 61, 70, 79, 88). Uninhibited female sexuality and the liberated discourse of female desire are unsettling to Bourget's male protagonist. Women may have learned to express their eroticism freely, but men are still adjusting their response to this discourse that destabilizes old gender roles.

In *Appelle-moi*, pride, insecurities, and lack of communication lead inevitably to the end of the affair. What one has left is the postmortem analysis that questions the relationship between de-romanticized sex and love. The advertising woman who uses love to sell products admits that she no longer knows what the term means:

> Moi, mon problème, c'est que je sais plus trop c'est quoi l'amour. (67)
> [Me, my problem is that I don't know what love is anymore.]

> On aurait pu se dire qu'on était bien ensemble pis qu'on avait envie de continuer . . .
> Est-ce que c'est ça l'amour? C'est quoi, l'amour? (72)
> [We could've said we were good together and that we wanted to go on . . .
> Is that love? What is love?]

> C'est fou c'que j'vas te dire, mais j't'aime . . . même si je sais plus c'est quoi l'amour. (87)
> [It's crazy what I'm going to say to you, but I love you . . . even if I don't know what love is anymore.]

The sex may be better in the guilt-free, gender-equal world of postfeminist theater, but happy endings aren't guaranteed.

Bourget's male protagonist has much in common with the former husbands and lovers of many postfeminist plays. Unlike the sexist, violent, exploitative male characters of the past, they are basically nice. Yet, even though they try to be passionate lovers, sensitive and supportive partners, they somehow fail to make women happy. Some have egos too fragile to deal with an independent and successful woman; some do not have the courage to resist societal pressures; some cannot commit to a permanent relationship. Whatever the case, they exhibit weaknesses and flaws that make them seem unworthy of the strong female protagonists often seen in postfeminist plays. It is also true that many of these postfeminist plays express a skeptical attitude toward love, the inevitable result of having accepted sexual liberation but rejected romanticism. Happiness based on the couple's relationship seems to be an illusion; solitude is the (existential?) reality.

Maryse Pelletier's 1985 *Duo pour voix obstinées* (*Duo for Obstinate Voices*) is an early version of the couple's postmortem play that shows a woman, Catherine, who learns to express herself during her five-year relationship with Philippe. Through the use of direct address to the audience accentuated by lighting changes, Pelletier subverts the conventions of realism and makes it clear that the relationship has already ended before the play begins. The scenes one sees are flashbacks tracing their amorous history from the initial encounter, when he was a thirty-three-year-old television journalist and she a twenty-three-year-old dance student, through the breakup brought on by career jealousies and emotional insecurities. In the end, they acknowledge their unhappiness and part more out of sorrow than bitterness. When they meet again in the last scene, a year after the breakup, they are able to look back on their affair with tenderness. Pelletier's heroine has found herself and learned that she can be happy without having to depend on a man.

The playwright undercuts her own love story with some ironic observations made by the facetiously named Valentino, an Italo-Québécois waiter who reappears over the five-year duration of the affair in the minor role of witness and commentator. At the beginning of the play, Valentino watches the lovers seduce each other and then addresses this comment directly to the audience:

L'amour, y a rien comme ça. Moi, j'aime toutes les femmes. Mais j'aime pas ça quand c'est compliqué. Ah lala! Quand c'est compliqué, moi, je suis plus là. Je comprends rien à ça, moi, ce qu'on lit dans les journaux, les gens qui se tuent ou s'étranglent par amour. L'amour, c'est simple. Quand c'est fini, tu t'en vas. C'est tout! (18)

[*L'amore, l'amore!* There is nothing like it. Me, I love the women. But I don't like it when it gets too complicated. *Mamma mia*, when it gets that way, I am gone! I don't understand that stuff in the papers, some people they go crazy, they kill and strangle for love. Love is simple. When it is finished, you leave, and that is it! (*L'amore è semplice. Quando è finito, te ne vai. Tutto qua!*)] (20)

After Catherine and Philippe say a final farewell in the play's last scene, this latter day Cupid says to the audience:

> L'amour, finalement, c'est pas grand'chose. Ça passe, ça passe. Y a rien qu'une chose qui reste, c'est la famille. Ça, ils en parlent pas dans les journaux. Ils aiment mieux raconter des drames d'amour. Moi, ça, les drames d'amour, ça m'intéresse plus, alors je lis plus les journaux. Ça m'arrivera pas, ces histoires-là, alors pourquoi je m'en occuperais, hein, pourquoi? (114)

> [Love is not such a big deal after all! It passes away. The only thing that lasts is the family. They don't talk about that in the papers, though. They'd rather talk about tragic love stories. Personally, I don't care for tragic love stories anymore, so I don't read the papers. Things like that are not going to happen to me, anyway. So tell me, why should I bother?] (146–47)

Valentino may deny his interest in love stories, but the playwright continues to write them.

In *Un Samouraï amoureux* (1991), Pelletier pursues her exploration of contemporary sexual relations by analyzing three failed couples. The dramatic technique is again nonrealistic, with staging that includes video clips and slides projected on a stylized Japanese stage. The three couples represent different affairs of the female protagonist, Victorine, as reenacted by six other characters and reviewed in conversations with her talking, humanoid dog, Victor. These six characters are recognizable personality types and facilitate the analysis of amorous failures. Critic Jean-Marc Larrue found the male types ("seducer-heartbreaker-liar") offensive and condemned the play as banal and immature (51). Patricia Belzil (72) and Louise Vigeant (158) were also disappointed by the superficiality of Pelletier's treatment of romantic difficulties.

Although I agree with these critical assessments of the play's weaknesses, I would suggest that Pelletier's skeptical view of romantic love makes it difficult for her to write convincingly on the subject—difficult, but not impossible, because *Un Samouraï amoureux* shows that she has learned to describe desire in moving poetic language. Interestingly, she attributes this newfound passionate discourse to the Japanese characters, as if to suggest that it is still impossible for Québécois to express desire in their own idiom. Whereas the two Québécois couples (Aurélien-Amélie, Étienne-Élizabeth) seduce each other with lines like "Je te veux aussi" (48) (I want you, too) and "Je t'invite" (52) (How about it?) and make love playfully (57), Yukiko and the Samouraï go through a serious, elaborate seduction scene that begins with her dancing for him. To emphasize the foreignness of this passionate discourse, Pelletier's script indicates that Yukiko speaks French with a Japanese accent (2).

The two lovers wax poetic describing the power of desire, which they compare to constantly changing running water—sometimes a stream singing softly and melting into the forest, sometimes a raging flood destroying everything in its path.

>Yukiko: Le désir transforme. Celui [qui] s'y laisse aller ne se reconnaît plus. Il est bouleversé, déséquilibré, tremblant, dépendant.
>Samouraï: Celui qui suit son désir est nourri, heureux, puissant. Comme le conquérant d'une terre nouvelle, le paysan engrangeant sa récolte. Tout ici part du désir et aboutit au désir.
>Yukiko: Celui qui cède au désir est triste.
>Samouraï: Non, transfiguré. La vie ne se laisse pas endiguer par nos pauvres barrages. La femme qui résiste à son désir est une terre épuisée, une rizière sans eau. (54)

>[Yukiko: Desire transforms. He who gives in to it no longer recognizes himself. He is overwhelmed, unbalanced, trembling, dependent.
>Samouraï: He who follows his desire is nourished, happy, powerful. Like the conqueror of a new land, the peasant bringing in his harvest. Everything starts from desire and ends with desire.
>Yukiko: He who gives in to desire is sad.
>Samouraï: No, transfigured. Life cannot be held back by our poor dams. The woman who fights her desire is an exhausted field, a rice paddy without water.]

Whereas the two Québécois couples make no declarations of love and no promises beyond immediate sexual gratification, the Japanese lovers foresee their lovemaking as the prelude to a physical and emotional union that portends both exquisite pleasure and suffering (55).

The second act of *Un Samouraï amoureux* analyzes the breakup of the three couples formed in the first act. Here again, the playwright resorts to facile pop psychology and ordinary language, except in the case of Yukiko, who alone seems capable of the total self-abandonment required by love. Her desperate plea to the lover who is leaving her is a true *cri de coeur* (cry from the heart) from an impassioned, desiring woman:

> J'ai regardé, touché, étudié avec amour et désir chaque parcelle de ton corps; chaque cellule de ta peau, je la connais par coeur, je connais ses odeurs, sa soie, son velouté, ses traces profondes, jusqu'à ce sexe dont je me réjouissais et m'étonnais qu'il se cabre, qu'il s'enfle, qu'il grandisse, qu'il bouge sous mes doigts, dans ma bouche, dans mon ventre pendant que je ruisselais et que je m'abandonnais, que je pleurais et que je riais, enfin vivante, enfin donnée, enfin prise. Il n'y aura jamais personne d'autre. Jamais. Tue-moi! (88)

> [I looked at, touched, studied with love and desire every fragment of your body; I know by heart each cell of your skin, I know its scent, silkiness, velvet, and deep lines, right down to your member which delighted and surprised me when it rose, swelled, grew big, moved beneath my fingers, in my mouth, inside me as I flowed and surrendered myself, and I laughed and cried, finally alive, finally possessed. There will never be anyone else. Never. Kill me!]

With the notable exception of Yukiko's erotic lament, *Un Samouraï amoureux* fails as a passionate postmortem and falls back on talking dog humor to undercut the seriousness of its subject matter. Yet, if this 1990s vision of male-female relations seems depressingly negative, it must be said that Maryse Pelletier is overcoming the inhibitions that previously blocked her female protagonists from talking about their sexual desire.

Sylvie Provost's *L'Ombre de toi* (1994) follows a scenario similar to that of *Duo pour voix obstinées,* also using nonrealistic dramatic techniques. This time, one sees a couple reliving a ten-year relationship that has just ended in divorce in fifty-five brief scenes alternating between the past and the present. Further undermining temporal realism is the fact that the past is the actual time of the performance and the present is ten years in the future. Julie Loiselle was a seventeen-year-old aspiring painter, and Jean-Philippe Blondin was a twenty-one-year-old architecture student when they met and fell in love. After they married, she abandoned her studies to support his professional career until, sensing her unhappiness, he encouraged her to take art courses. When her career starts to take off, he resents the fact that she is pursuing her artistic dreams while he has sacrificed his for commercial success. His ambivalence about her career and his fear of losing her result in bitter arguments that lead to divorce. After the divorce, he shows up at her apartment to plead for a reconciliation, threatening her with a gun when she insists that the marriage is over. As was the case in *Duo pour voix obstinées*, *L'Ombre de toi* ends with a plea to remember the relationship without regrets, to accept the breakup and move on. Jean-Philippe's gun was not loaded, so the melodramatic gesture gives way to tears and consoling hugs.

Reviewing *L'Ombre de toi*, Sylvie Bérard astutely points out the crisis of contemporary values that underlies Julie and Jean-Philippe's drama, what she calls the "contemporary values of me-myself-I" (1995, 41). In addition to narcissism, the play also points to divorce and the exploded nuclear family as sources of psychological problems. Because both main characters come from broken homes, they fear abandonment and invest heavy emotional capital in the marriage. Because of the multiple conjugal failures that marred his childhood, Jean-Philippe expresses a somewhat confused view of romantic love and its relationship to sex: "Y a tellement de monde qui mélange le sexe avec l'amour" (39) [There are so many people who confuse sex with love]. Later in the play (scene 36), one hears a television show on the topic "l'amour en l'an 2002" (love in the year 2002), during which a "model" couple talks about careers and marriage. After the wife declares that the true work of love begins when the passion starts to fade, the husband adds that people are willing to work on their careers but assume that love takes care of itself (87). Yet, having raised a number of issues related to the pursuit of individual happiness at the expense of others, Provost opts for what now seems to pass for a happy ending: an amicable separation.

Sylvie Provost's decision to focus on the generation after feminist activism clearly places her in the postfeminist category for which I have been arguing. Her female protagonist is the daughter of a committed 1970s feminist, a television journalist who hosts a weekly segment entitled "Le féminisme, d'hier à aujourd'hui" (29) (Feminism, from yesterday to today). While accepting sexual freedom, Julie rejects sexual politics. She claims that her mother bears a grudge against all men (29) and is quick to dissociate herself from feminism: "J'ai-tu l'air d'une féministe?" (30) (Do I look like a feminist to you?). In *L'Ombre de toi*, there is no power struggle between the sexes, no patriarchy, no villain—just two people trying to find happiness through professional and emotional satisfaction.

The couples plays examined thus far have focused on the difficulty of negotiating careers, equality, and personal fulfillment. Bourget, Pelletier, and Provost assume the libidinal rights of their female protagonists, but they do not endow them all with the eroticized language necessary to express their sexuality. Personal identity issues and gender politics still distract women from more intimate feelings. In recent plays by Carole Fréchette and Marie Laberge, however, one does hear a more liberated, poetic discourse of desire that could be labeled *neo*-romantic.

Fréchette, who began her theatrical career with the radical feminist collective Le Théâtre des cuisines, may have declared her break with feminist theater, but she is still writing "au féminin" (1991, 27) (in the feminine). Her recent work, *La Peau d'Élisa* (1998), is a nonlinear dramatic narrative that concentrates on the expression of passion to the exclusion of other themes. The play performs postmortems on multiple love affairs, seducing the audience into a vicarious erotic experience with its sensual detail. As the title suggests, this play is all about the body—about smelling, touching, and getting into the skin of various lovers. Fréchette tells the reader that one needs desire, passion, physical contact, and sexual intimacy to stay alive; without it, the skin grows as the flesh shrinks. If there is not enough passion in one's life, one can appropriate the erotic energy one needs by telling (and hearing) other people's love stories (19–20).

The narrativized language of desire replaces action in *La Peau d'Élisa*. A middle-aged woman, seated alone on the stage, recounts the love affairs of numerous people—male and female—whose identities she assumes as she recalls intimate details. Élisa becomes an eighteen-year-old schoolgirl describing her madcap adventures with Sigfried (7–8, 11, 21–22); a woman who works on film crews talking about her handsome lover Jan (8–9, 22); a male university student recalling his desire for Ginette (9); a foreign woman obsessed with the man in the apartment upstairs (10–11); a twenty-year-old worker who falls in love with a married immigrant woman named Anna (12, 21); a lesbian journalist remembering the risks she took with her lover Marguerite (14–15); and a bored housewife telling about her affair with Edmond (15). Élisa's polyvocal monologue is interrupted by the appearances of Le jeune homme (The young man), who tells Élisa first about his wild passion for an exotic fellow student named Sarah (13–14), then reappears to talk about his love affair with Louise (16).

Although he does not appear until Élisa is well into her storytelling, Le jeune homme holds the key to the play. She met him one day in a café when she was depressed and crying. Rather than consoling her or asking about her problems, he started talking about his past love affairs, insisting that Élisa relive his passion with him, visualizing the details of his lover's body, feeling his emotion in her presence, and experiencing the pleasure of their kiss (13–14, 16).

Although the sexual encounters are recalled in the past tense rather than played out in the present, Fréchette's text creates a body language that metaphorizes sexuality. Élisa is constantly examining various parts of her body—her face, mouth, neck, hands, elbows, cheek, stomach, knees—as if to monitor the corporeality that affirms her existence. To maintain this physical presence, she must continue to talk about the passionate experiences of others, so she invites the audience to share their erotic memories with her (23–24). As Le jeune homme told her:

> ... les souvenirs amoureux, quand ils montent de l'intérieur, quand ils passent dans la gorge et dans la bouche, ils dégagent une espèce de substance qui se répand dans la peau et l'empêche de pousser. ... Il faut raconter avec beaucoup de précision, décrire les lieux, l'ambiance, il faut faire surgir des images; il faut que ceux qui écoutent aient des frissons. Puis il faut insister sur les petites choses du corps, la sueur, le frémissement, le sang qui bat. Ce sont ces détails-là qui activent la substance. (19)

> [... memories of love, when they rise up from deep within, when they pass from the throat and into the mouth, they give off a kind of substance that spreads through the skin and prevents it from growing. ... One must recount them very precisely, describe places, the ambiance, one must make the images come to life so that the listeners shiver. Then one must insist on the bodily details, the sweat, the trembling, the throbbing blood. These are the details that activate the substance.]

The rich erotic detail of the play proves that Élisa has heeded Le jeune homme's advice. It also proves that Fréchette has overcome all inhibitions in talking about sexuality and transcended social concerns.

Marie Laberge has likewise moved beyond nationalist and gender issues. The strong female protagonists of her later plays are no longer victims of the conservative, patriarchal Catholic ideology that affected the raped maid of *C'était avant la guerre à l'Anse-à-Gilles* (*Before the War, Down at l'Anse à Gilles*) (1981); the frustrated housewife of *Avec l'hiver qui s'en vient* (*With Winter Coming*) (1980); the sterile woman of *Ils étaient venus pour* ... (*They Came to* ...) (1981); the suicidal daughter of *Jocelyne Trudelle trouvée morte dans ses larmes* (*Jocelyne Trudelle Found Dead in her Tears*) (1982); the depressed wife of *Deux Tangos pour toute une vie* (*Two Tangos for a Whole Life*) (1985); and the abused anorexic of *L'Homme gris* (*Night*) (1986), to name a few. I have argued elsewhere[5] that as long as Laberge's women defined themselves in the context of the traditional Québec family, their sexuality would be limited to procreation and repressed by misogyny. Only when Labergian women began to violate "la loi du père" (the law of the father), to question the roles and duties assigned to them, and to reject the stigma of sin attached to sex would they be free. In Laberge's dramatic universe, liberation started with la Chatte (The Cat), the exuberant young woman of *Aurélie, ma soeur* (*Aurélie, My Sister*) (1989) who spoke of the object of her desire, Pierre-Louis, with unabashed erotic enthusiasm, recounting the details of their love affair to her aunt/sister Aurélie (22–23, 32–35). Unfortunately, Pierre-Louis was a serial adulterer, too weak to act honestly and not worthy of la Chatte. When they finally broke up, she suffered what Aurélie called "l'apprentissage de la douleur" (90) (the apprenticeship of suffering), the inevitable pain that comes with the knowledge that men are imperfect and love is not eternal.

The emotions and physical pleasure that accompany passion, however, counterbalance the pain of a couple's separation. In the two last plays that Laberge wrote before quitting drama for fiction, she concentrates on the expression of female sexuality, as if to give voice to all the sensual women silenced for centuries. *Pierre, ou la Consolation* (1992) and *Double Mélodie* (1990)[6] are both passionate postmortems in which an extraordinary woman looks back on lost love with lucidity and emotion, asserting the right to sexual pleasure and celebrating passion as a cherished malady. Both plays are spectacles of desire in which the main dramatic action is the theatricalization of passion. With great emotion, but without sentimentality, Laberge examines the psychology and metaphysics of passion in language remarkable for its poetic and erotic charge.

Pierre, ou la Consolation revives the legend of Héloïse and Pierre Abélard, twelfth-century lovers cruelly separated and punished by a religion that denigrates carnal love. In a prefatory note to the published text, Laberge clearly states that this is not an historical play and that her goal is to evoke the poetic music of medieval French rather than to reproduce it accurately. The play imagines the lovers' reunion—a poignant moment that occurs only after twenty years of forced separation and the death of Abélard. When the corpse of her castrated husband is brought to her convent, Héloïse is overwhelmed by memories that reignite her passion for Pierre and her anger at those who caused so much suffering. As the sun rises after her night of mourning, she finds a way to accept her destiny and to reconcile herself with God and divine love without diminishing herself or human love.

In the first part of the play, Héloïse whispers to her dead lover, pouring out all the passion she has contained for years:

> Ainsi donc voici ce corps qui tant a brûlé ma souvenance
> qui tant a hanté le repos de mes nuits
> qui tant a brisé l'abandonement de mes jours
> ce corps tant aimé, tant enchéri
> que pas un seul de mes doigts, jamais,
>   n'a renié
>   ni oublié
> Tu es là, mon unique.
> Tu es là. (23)

> [Thus then here is this body that so burned in my memory
> that so haunted the repose of my nights
> that so shattered the abandon of my days
> this body so beloved, so cherished
> that not one of my fingers, ever,
>   has denied
>   nor forgotten
> You are here, my one and only.
> You are here.]

This moving testament to her enduring love for Pierre is filled with corporeal memories—of their mutual desire, of feverish bodies touching and making love for the first time when she was sixteen (32–33), of nights spent in her convent cell consumed by sensuality (31). Even now, standing before his earthly remains, she admits that she is devoured by desire:

> Et tout maintenant, devant ce corps
>   Que ravage la mort,
> désirance me mord (32)

> [And even now, before this body
>   Ravaged by death,
> Desire consumes me]

The passage of time has not dulled her body's memories of love nor her spirit's defiance of the Church's injunction to mortify the flesh. Temporal distance has allowed her to understand, to theorize, the role of passion in human life.

Her conversation with Pierre le Vénérable, the Cluny abbot who escorts Abélard's body, turns into a debate about the conflict between carnal desire and spiritual purity, earthly happiness and eternal salvation. Through Héloïse, Laberge expresses her own belief that, although love often seems like "poison" (59), "folie et desraison" (82) (madness and unreason), to deny sexuality is to mutilate human beings just as Abélard was mutilated. To remain true to herself and to preserve her spirituality, Héloïse must reaffirm her passion even while acknowledging that Abélard proved himself unworthy by submitting to the Church's punishment (37–38). Endowed with lucidity and strength, tested by adversity and the passage of time, Héloïse can look back on her love and appreciate the true value of sexuality. The intellectual force and emotional charge of Héloïse/Marie Laberge's words make *Pierre, ou la Consolation* what critic Réjean Bergeron called a beautiful text "on love and on the deep and sometimes unfathomable impression that this emotion leaves on each one of us" (147).

Rendered impossible by forced separation, misunderstanding, the silencing of women, or male inadequacy, male-female dialogue does seems absent from Laberge's theater, as critic Lucie Robert has noted (49). This fact makes it all the more lamentable that Laberge's last play, *La Double Mélodie* (1990), was never staged because here, finally, a man and a woman speak honestly to each other about sexual desire and love. In *Double Mélodie*, Lili and Thomas, actors who have not seen each other since their seven-year-long love affair ended thirteen years earlier, come together to perform a play about a couple (Hélène and Charles) who separate after one night of torrid lovemaking and then meet again a few years later. The *mise-en-abyme* plot structure enables Laberge to double the dialogue on past love and to (re-)enact erotic moments in a play focused entirely on passion. No social, political, or religious issues interfere with the exploration of sexuality; finally, women and men talk to each other as equals.

The décor, an empty stage where Lili and Thomas reminisce and rehearse, underscores the point Laberge wants to make about theater as a site of seduction. The playwright scripts the scenario of passion, the director interprets and casts it, and then the actors seduce one another and the audience in a controlled performance of desire. From the moment Lili and Thomas meet again, the sexual tension is palpable, and it increases as they work together until the fourth part, in which we see that they have given in to their mutual attraction one final time (33–34). The seduction is both verbal and physical: he first fell in love with her watching her act when they were students at the Conservatory (12), and he falls in love again hearing her talk about desire.

As they rehearse the seduction scene they will perform together, they relive their own erotic attraction—a guilt-free, uninhibited, playful coming together. While he was aroused by her long legs, she was mesmerized by his buttocks:

> Les plus belles fesses que j'ai rencontrées dans ma vie. . . .
> J'te voyais sur scène des années après, pis j'avais encore envie d'les prendre, les caresser, les mordre. . . .
> Y a pas un corps qui m'a troublée autant que le tien dans ma vie. . . .(15)

> [The most beautiful ass that I've seen in my life . . .
> I saw you on stage years later, and I still wanted to grab it, caress it, bite into it . . .
> In my whole life, no body ever aroused me as much as yours. . . .]

Lili talks about lovers she had before and after Thomas, but she leaves no doubt that he was the standard by which she judges them all:

> T'avais une façon d'embrasser mes paupières la nuit. . . . Personne sait embrasser comme toi, personne, jamais, m'a tenue comme toi dans ses bras aussi fort, aussi totalement que toi. Thomas, des fois la nuit, j'me réveille encore en cherchant tes baisers sur mes paupières. La paix de ta bouche sur mes yeux fermés. (17)

> [You had a way of kissing my eyelids at night . . . Nobody knows how to kiss like you do, nobody, ever, held me in his arms as firmly, as completely as you did. Thomas, sometimes at night, I still wake up seeking your kisses on my eyelids. The peace of your lips touching my closed eyes.]

Like la Chatte and Héloïse, Lili is not afraid to articulate her desire. She is a true Labergian woman: troubled and troubling, but also intelligent, honest, lively, and sensuous.

Memory alone does not bring Lili and Thomas together again; in the thirteen years since they parted, they have both had time to analyze their relationship in particular and love in the abstract. They now have the experience and self-knowledge necessary to perform a joint amorous autopsy. In describing passion, Laberge's protagonists use many of the pathological comparisons of conventional love poetry. It is difficult to separate the words of the female author of the play-within-the-play, the thoughts of the male director, and the opinions of the actors from those of Laberge. For all, passion is "égoïste" (selfish), "une obsession" (18) (an obsession), "une marque ineffaçable" (22) (an indelible mark), "un pacte d'esclavage" (24) (a pact of enslavement), a "dépossession" (24) (dispossession), "un cadeau empoisonné" (29) (a poisoned gift), "une maladie mortelle" (30) (a mortal malady). It is an addictive drug and a disruptive need; it provokes ferocious jealousy, making the lover lose control while craving total control over the beloved (27). *Double Mélodie* draws a distinction between passion and love:

> La passion respecte rien, mettez-vous ça dans tête. L'amour, oui. L'amour cultive l'autre, son respect, ses libertés. Pas la passion. La passion, c'est l'enfermement, l'aveuglement, le dépassement par le beau ou le laid. Y a rien qui entraîne aussi haut ni aussi bas que la passion. (27)

> [Passion respects nothing, get that in your head. Love, yes. Love nurtures the other, his respect, his freedoms. Not passion. Passion is imprisonment, blindness, being overwhelmed by the beautiful or ugly. Nothing moves us to such heights or to such depths as passion.]

Yet, if love seems to bring calm happiness and reasoned contentment, it can also be an illusion. A passage of the play-within-the-play repeated at the beginning and end of the frame play suggests that happiness is "une sorte de brume sur le paysage; juste assez opaque pour masquer les contours, les lignes trop dures et juste assez légère pour permettre de percevoir les couleurs" (9, 36) [a sort of mist covering the countryside, just opaque enough to hide the contours, the hard lines, and just light enough to let colors show through]. Whereas Lili and Hélène both abandoned their lovers because they wanted passion rather than tranquil love and because love threatened their autonomy (26), years later they both still wonder if it was cowardice or courage that made them leave (38). Having analyzed their affairs with honesty and lucidity, both pairs of lovers can embrace their shared past and welcome the feelings of tenderness that have replaced erotic passion (38).

Whether they look back on past love affairs with the poetic neo-romanticism of Laberge and Fréchette or the skeptical nostalgia of Bourget, Pelletier, and Provost, Québec women playwrights of the 1990s are creating a liberated discourse on female sexuality.[7] As they move beyond the politicized gender issues that characterized the collective feminist theater movement of the 1970s and 1980s, they explore the personal question of happiness and two of its key components—sexuality and intimate relationships. By creating narratives of desire, they can theatricalize female eroticism without turning their spectators into voyeurs. By focusing on relationships that have ended, they give their female protagonists the temporal distance necessary for reflection and understanding. The passionate postmortems performed on the stage most often lead to a new kind of self-awareness, acceptance, or reconciliation—a healthy sign for women on both sides of the footlights. In this postfeminist Québec theater, women are now free to express themselves in sexually liberated language, but they must recognize that they are now responsible for their own happiness.

Notes

1. I have explored how feminist theater focused on the female body, sexuality, mother-daughter relations, and maternity in a series of articles. See Moss 1986, 1989, 1992, 1995, 1997.
2. One must be careful not to conflate feminist and lesbian theater. I have argued that while a cultural feminist lesbian such as Jovette Marchessault does not question traditional notions of femininity, more radical lesbians do question gender construction and roles. See Moss 1992–93. On gay theater, see Moss 1987 and Lafon.
3. In addition to Yvette Brind'Amour at the Théâtre du Rideau Vert and Nicole Filion at the Théâtre Populaire du Québec, Marie Laberge was in charge of the Théâtre du Trident, Michelle Rossignol directs the Théâtre d'Aujourd'hui, Maryse Pelletier headed the Théâtre Populaire du Québec, Brigitte Haentjens was artistic director of the Nouvelle Compagnie Théâtrale, and Lorraine Pintal took over at the Théâtre du Nouveau Monde. Directors Martine Beaulne, Alice Ronfard, Lise Vaillancourt, and Gisèle Sallin have also gained power through their successes.
4. Unless the English version has been published, all translations are my own.
5. See my "Family Histories: Marie Laberge and Women's Theater in Québec," "Dramatizing the Discourse of Female Desire," and "Québécois Theatre: Michel Tremblay and Marie Laberge."
6. *Pierre* was written in 1989 and performed in 1992; *Double Mélodie* was written in 1990, given a public reading at the Centre des auteurs dramatiques in 1995, but never performed. In a personal conversation on 4 November 1998, Laberge explained that she did not publish *Double Mélodie* because it had not been produced and the only possibility of production at the time was by an amateur group that she did not trust to do justice to her work.
7. This liberated discourse is heterosexual only. I have already pointed out the disappearance of overt lesbian themes from the contemporary Québec stage. See Lynda Burgoyne 1990.

Works Cited

Belzil, Patricia. "Dans l'intimité des petites salles: l'attente . . ." In *Veilleurs de nuit 3: Bilan de la saison théâtrale 1990–1991,* edited by Gilbert David, Liette Fortin, Gilles Deschâtelets, Yves Jubinville, and Jeanne Painchaud, 66–77. Montréal: Les Herbes rouges, 1991.

Bérard, Sylvie. "Hiatus." *Lettres québécoises* 87 (1997): 37–38.

———. "Quelques époques épiques." *Lettres québécoises* 77 (1995): 40–41.

———. "Trop." *Lettres québécoises* 80 (1995): 39–40.

Bergeron, Réjean. Compte-rendu de *Pierre, ou la Consolation*. *Jeu* 64 (1992): 145–47.

Boucher, Denise. *Les Fées ont soif.* Montréal: Intermède, 1978. Translated by Alan Brown under the title *The Fairies Are Thirsty*. Vancouver: Talonbooks, 1982.

Bourget, Élizabeth. *Appelle-moi*. Montréal: VLB éditeur, 1996.

———. *Bernadette et Juliette, ou la vie, c'est comme la vaisselle, c'est toujours à recommencer*. Montréal: VLB éditeur, 1979.

Burgoyne, Lynda. "Des dragons, de l'absurde ... et des femmes." *Veilleurs de nuit 4 : Bilan de la saison théâtrale 1991–1992*, edited by Gilbert David, Gilles Deschâtelets, Hélène Beauchamp, Hélène Boivin, Yves Jubinville, and Jeanne Painchaud, 27–37. Montréal: Les Herbes rouges, 1992.

———. "Théâtre et homosexualité féminine: Un continent invisible." *Jeu* 54 (1990): 114–18.

Collectif. *La Nef des sorcières*. Montréal: Quinze, 1976. Translated by Linda Gaboriau under the title *A Clash of Symbols*. Toronto: Coach House Press, 1977.

Fréchette, Carole. *La Peau d'Élisa*. Montréal/Paris: Leméac/Actes Sud, 1998.

———. "Questions et confidences." *Jeu* 61 (1991): 27–28.

Godard, Barbara. "Between Repetition and Rehearsal: Conditions of (Women's) Theatre in Canada in a Space of Reproduction." *Theatre Research in Canada* 13, no. 1–2 (1992): 18–33.

Laberge, Marie. *Aurélie, ma soeur*. Montréal: VLB éditeur, 1988. [rpt. 1992 Boréal]

———. *Avec l'hiver qui s'en vient*. Montréal: VLB éditeur, 1980.

———. *C'était avant la guerre à l'Anse-à-Gilles*. Montréal: VLB éditeur, 1981.

———. *Deux tangos pour toute une vie*. Montréal: VLB éditeur, 1985. [rpt. 1993 Boréal]

———. *Double Mélodie*. Unpublished ms. Centre des auteurs dramatiques, 1990.

———. *Jocelyne Trudelle, trouvée morte dans ses larmes*. Montréal: VLB éditeur, 1983. [rpt. 1992 Boréal]

———. *L'Homme gris*. Montréal: VLB éditeur, 1986. Translated by Rina Fraticelli under the title *Night*. Toronto: Methuen, 1988.

———. *Pierre, ou la Consolation*. Montréal: Boréal, 1992.

———. Telephone conversation with Jane Moss, 4 November 1998.

Lafon, Dominique. "Entre Cassandre et Clytemnestre: Le théâtre québécois, 1970–90." *Theatre Research International* 17, no. 3 (1992): 236–45.

Larrue, Jean-Marc. "Une saison déroutante." *Veilleurs de nuit 3: Bilan de la saison théâtrale 1990–1991*, edited by Gilbert David, Liette Fortin, Gilles Deschâtelets, Yves Jubinville, and Jeanne Painchaud, 48–56. Montréal: Les Herbes rouges, 1991.

Marchessault, Jovette. *La Saga des poules mouillées*. Montréal: Les Éditions de la pleine lune, 1981. Translated by Linda Gaboriau under the title *The Saga of the Wet Hens*. Vancouver: Talonbooks, 1983.

Moss, Jane. " 'All in the Family': Québec Family Drama in the 1980s." *Journal of Canadian Studies* 27, no. 2 (Summer 1992): 97–106.

———. "The Body as Spectacle: Women's Theater in Québec." *Women and Performance* 3, no. 1 (1986): 5–16.

———. "Dramatizing the Discourse of Female Desire." In *Women By Women*, edited by Roseanna Lewis Dufault, 17–33. Madison, N.J.: Fairleigh Dickinson University Press, 1997.

———. "Dramatizing Sexual Difference: Gay and Lesbian Theater in Québec." *American Review of Canadian Studies* 22, no. 3 (Winter 1992–93): 489–98.

———. "Family Histories: Marie Laberge and Women's Theater in Québec." In *Postcolonial Subjects: Francophone Women Writers*, edited by Karen Gould, Mary Jean Green, Jack Yeager, Michelle Rice-Maximim, Keith Warner, 79–97. Minneapolis: University of Minnesota Press, 1996.

———. "Fillial (Im)pieties: Mothers and Daughters in Québec Women's Theatre." *American Review of Canadian Studies* 19, no. 2 (Summer 1989): 177–85.

———. "Hysterical Pregnancies and Post-partum Blues: Staging the Maternal Body in Recent Québec Plays." In *Essays on Modern Québec Theater*, edited by Jonathan Weiss and Joseph Donohoe, 47–60. East Lansing: Michigan State University Press, 1995.

———. "Québécois Theatre: Michel Tremblay and Marie Laberge." *Theatre Research International* 21, no. 3 (Fall 1996): 196–207.

———. "Sexual Games: Hypertheatricality and Homosexuality in Recent Québec Plays." *American Review of Canadian Studies* 17, no. 3 (1987): 287–96.

Noiseux, Ginette. "Du théâtre expérimental des femmes à l'espace go: Entretien avec Ginette Noiseux." *Jeu* 57 (1990): 51–62.

O'Neill-Karch, Mariel. "Théâtre: Lettres canadiennes, 1996." *University of Toronto Quarterly* 67, no. 1 (1997–98): 390–99.

Pavlovic, Diane. Compte-rendu de *Duo pour voix obstinées*. *Jeu* 85 (1985): 164–65.

Pelletier, Maryse. *Duo pour voix obstinées*. Montréal: VLB éditeur, 1985. Translated by Louise Ringuet under the title *Duo for Obstinate Voices*. Montréal: Guernica, 1990.

———. *Un Samouraï amoureux*. Staged by the Théâtre de la Manufacture in 1991. Unpublished ms. Centre des auteurs dramatiques.

Pelletier, Pol. *Joie*. Montréal: Les Éditions du remue-ménage, 1995.

Provost, Sylvie. *L'Ombre de toi*. Montréal: VLB éditeur, 1994.

Robert, Lucie. "Changing the Subject: A Reading of Contemporary Québec Feminist Drama." In *Women on the Canadian Stage: The Legacy of Hrotsvit*, edited by Rita Much, 43–55. Winnipeg: Blizzard Publishing, 1992.

Savard, Marie. *Bien à moi*. Montréal: Les Éditions de la pleine lune, 1979.

Turp, Gilbert. "Écrire pour le corps." Entrevue avec Serge Boucher, Élizabeth Bourget, Carole Fréchette, Wajdi Mouawad, Larry Tremblay. *Titre provisoire* 3, no. 2 (1996): 3–16.

Vigeant, Louise. Compte-rendu d'*Un Samouraï amoureux*. *Jeu* 60 (1991): 156–58.

It Takes Two to Tango: Pauline Harvey's *Un Homme est une valse*

KARIN EGLOFF

PAULINE HARVEY DOES NOT MINCE WORDS. *UN HOMME EST UNE VALSE* (*A Man Is a Waltz*),[1] published in 1992, is the story of two characters, Shelling and Rose, who take their relationship on the road. They try their self-(un)declared passion in different settings—rural, urban, foreign, domestic—before the action comes full circle in Montréal and they each go their own way. The text is striking; the novel is teeming with the mind and body games of the two heroes. Even though it is not always the most inviting for the reader who feels slightly "offside" now and then, Pauline Harvey's stylistic art is noteworthy. In the book, imagination is both a male and a female prerogative, insofar as Shelling and Rose share that specific talent in an almost equal way, as they keep "documenting" the different stages of their peregrinations. The prose style is, in turn, proliferating, even showy, or modest and spare. Ellipses are numerous, but, as for the pleasure of the text, these gaps are not at all unwelcome, because they attempt to (de)construct the text and (de/re)construct the subject. The question of representation, the interconnections between the literary text, its cultural context, and the sexual identity of the person who writes make up the essence of Harvey's claim: there should be, in discourse and in reality, within language and within culture, a true dialogue between men and women.

However, the intimate uncertainties of the male and female sex make up the backdrop of the novel, therefore greatly contributing to its many internal paradoxes. These uncertainties emerge in different shapes, obviously in the author's writing style, but also in the characters' particular ways of expressing their thoughts and aspirations. Shelling and Rose give an impression of continual play, for instance, as they both strive to be in control of the gaze, even though the author can, and does, shift the perspective, in order to inscribe the female gaze into the core of her narrative. Consequently, a struggle over meaning emerges, and the events that make up the framework of the story are often arbitrary, although not pointless. They echo the characters' restless wandering, which determines the rhythm of the text and increases with the meandering of the story. It is an eye-opener to observe the continual, seemingly haphazard coming and going of people, cities, situations in which Pauline Harvey mercilessly describes her characters' grappling with the difficulty and challenge of being, which does not keep them from shameless self-promotion, as if theirs was the most essential contribution to the story. The entire novel is a popularity race lacking in basic honesty and lucidity. Between *what* the characters mean and *how* they mean, there is a perpetual struggle for control.

After having depicted the disarray of youth in *Encore une partie pour Berry (One More Game for Berry)*, the author now tackles adult wandering and transgressions, trying to think in new ways about the ideologies that underlie the readers'—and possibly the characters'—assumptions about male and female interaction. The story rests on three protagonists: Valentino Popofski, Shelling, and Rose, the woman whose name, if it really is hers, is mentioned only once in the whole book. Very quickly, Valentino's character disappears, and Shelling and Rose have to share the endless drifting that makes the novel. Rose is the narrator, and, as such, she shakes up and defies "literary conventions" to try to write her own rendition of the furious swirl that will take them both very far from their respective starting points. The contradictions of male and female discourse allow space for disturbances of dominant meaning to occur, with results that signify essential shifts.

At that level of analysis, the text appears to be a search, a disorderly quest for recognition, through a universe whose signs are identified or not by the characters who, in their game of sense and nonsense, repeatedly tend to swing in the direction of appearances. The reader's function, literally, consists in putting aside the writer's fiction to pick up the characters' *authorship*. The narrator, on the fringes of her own life, attempts to play opposite the usurper/ man who tries to impose, with relative subtlety at first, the rigid frame of his own identity. Can a female perspective be produced from the mainstream of the male discourse, and, if so, what will it look like, and look at?

Very swiftly, creative impulse will be coupled, in each of the characters, with their sexual urges. The protagonists will not always know how to fill their space, their discourse, or their writing. They will behave like overgrown, androgynous adolescents looking for a transition between the arbitrary nature of play and the quest for the absolute that is so close to their hearts. One of their most challenging, thankless tasks consists in learning to name, and more than that, to acknowledge their failure, as much emotionally as intellectually speaking. The author's part is to sketch her characters through what they think and live, without revealing too much, however. Harvey is responsible for the physical and emotional geography of her characters, but to a certain extent only.

In *Un Homme est une valse*, it is very clear that space can take precedence over the characters themselves. Space defines the characters, even as far as their sexual identity. In an interview by Jean Royer, Harvey explains that her protagonists "portent la bombe de l'impulsion violente, sexuelle, de la pulsion de vie par rapport à l'inquiétude actuelle. Ils ont aussi la passion de la création, qui est violente et qui peut mener à des délires épouvantables" (Royer 104–5) [carry their violent, sexual drive like a bomb, an impulse for life rather than this ongoing anxiety. They also have a passion for creation, a violent passion that can lead to dreadful excess].

From that point of view, the masculine and feminine "roles" are often reversed in the novel. The male body in representation, when it is subjected to the female gaze, is not necessarily able to bear the kind of objectification women's bodies have borne for so long. In *Un Homme est une valse*, the traditional structure male *looking*/female *to be looked at* is not replicated: the notion of a dominant male gaze becomes an orthodoxy. In her precise, firm, and efficient language, Harvey demonstrates how the art of lying—to oneself and to the other—can become playful, albeit dangerous, (day)dreaming. Tragicomedy stands out as a counterpart to hypocrisy, in a perpetual festival of words, in what Madeleine Ouellette-Michalska calls "un air de liberté ouvert à tous les temps et à tous les ailleurs" (28) [a manner of freedom open to all times and to all faraway places].

Karen Gould, in her article "Writing and Reading 'Otherwise:' Québec Women Writers and the Exploration of Difference," writes about the different forms of sexed writing. She explains how these forms depend, for example, on individual political perspectives, narrative strategies, linguistic forms, thematic lines. With Harvey, the writing is complicated because the author's discourse is only a part of the whole text. As for the characters/writers, the sex difference, which transpires in their writing, is not necessarily a claim to subversion, to gender differentiation. It does not mean total self-effacement or withdrawal either, not on Shelling's part, and not on

Rose's. Rather, it is somewhere halfway in between: it is a hybrid type of writing, made of ellipses, gaps, postponed explanations. The act of writing becomes a way of exploring male *and* female consciousness and sexuality. Even though, clearly, female desire and sexuality occupy the foreground of discourse, the act of individual self-possession is also an act of collective reappropriation. In other words, it includes the male character. Many narratives depend for their specific meaning on the play between masculine and feminine elements, and this play can shift the boundaries of the definitions themselves. There is, however, a danger in privileging gender as a deciding factor: it tends to depoliticize other power relations.

In *Un Homme est une valse*, is there a specificity, if any, of the relation between the woman and language or the writing process? Does Harvey not reverse the established canon by also giving a chance to her male character, as if she were to have him say, "I am neither a male writer, nor a female writer. I am someone who writes?" The shift in the specificity of feminine writing is at best an ambiguous concept because, as Karen Gould reminds us, it is a notion that has to do with theme, stylistics, ideology, in addition to being a gender problem. For Rose, writing might help her break the fatal circle of the paranoia and the depression that seem progressively to take hold of her. The ambivalence, the refusal to systematically make certain denominations more masculine or more feminine, make the strength and the savor of Harvey's and/or her characters' text. The protagonists find themselves in an awkward position; they force the readers to change their perspective on the link between formal strategies and the sexual identity of the person who writes. Writing is on no account neutral, but it is first and foremost an open space for the character's personal freedom. It needs to dissociate itself from the dominant discourse, by using, or not, the complexity of the connections between sex and text. In Harvey's novel, Rose is very capable of writing in terms where her feminine side would never come out. By the same token, Shelling writes letters and poems that undoubtedly carry the mark of the feminine. By game or by strategy, Harvey does her best to cloud the issue, to erase any identifiable signs.

Besides the written discourse, the experience of intimacy makes the difference between Shelling and Rose. The text overlaps with the sex, the fragments with the desire for continuity. The archaeology of the intimate enables the character to set up his or her identity better, to fight against his or her sensation of dispersion. The text begins to look like a spiral inside which the characters try to establish connections between the different strata of memory and of experience with or against the other. Absence and loss create the necessity for self-redefinition. Why not, then, also recount the emergence, in the text, of a male subject?

At the beginning of the novel, the narrator is in control of places and discourse, but only briefly. The male character is already in the wings, ready to take over. The subtext shows magnificent suggestion, among other things, of feminine desire: "Et j'ai voulu cette maison, je l'ai désirée de toutes mes forces. Une semaine plus tard, je la trouvais" (Harvey 10) [And I wanted that house, I wanted it with all my heart. A week later, I found it]. The female character learns that freedom comes through alienation, and the situation undoubtedly suits her at first. A man might be a waltz, but a woman does not survive either if and when she is, literally, getting nowhere: "il faut savoir courir plus vite que les autres afin de pouvoir sortir de la troupe" (12) [you must learn to run faster than others so that you can leave the pack]. The rhythm of the novel is now similar to a staccato dance, sometimes more of a tango than a waltz. In other words, the figures it represents emerge, move, and, eventually, leave. *Contemporary malaise* is a possible catchy phrase to define the fragmentation, eclecticism, and nihilism of *Un Homme est une valse*. The protagonists lead a life that is played out on the surface, without, at first, much depth or meaning, in what Rose at least would like to be an eternal present where her/their fantasies are no longer merely representations, but are themselves reality.

The ushering in of Shelling is revealing. One must appreciate the contrast between his physical appearance, "Un visage brut d'ouvrier. À la barbe forte" (14) [A rough worker's face. A bristly beard], and the way he expresses himself: "Je n'écris pas pour sortir d'ici, ni pour appeler au secours, simplement j'ai envie d'envoyer des lettres à quelqu'un" (14) [I am not writing to get out of here, or to call for help, I simply feel like sending letters to someone]. Rose is waiting for him, like a deus ex machina, someone who showers a woman with a deluge of letters, of words, whereas, later in the text, she is the one who writes and he is the one who plays. In fact, the reader is left with a multitude of shorter narratives, which, logically enough, leave space for interpretation and, eventually, rupture.

Consequently, the mythology surrounding the characters' relationship comes as no surprise. Rose defines the rules of the game, up to the point when Shelling appears. All she does in fact is find herself face to face with her solitude. Harvey is using this ambiguity as a somewhat political strategy, in an attempt to disturb representations and definitions of the feminine and masculine. Each in their own turn, the female and male voices appear to be speaking in a vacuum. By the same token, these voices can transform images into reality for themselves, as if they could afford to dismiss what really stands behind those images.

Along the same lines, whenever it deals with the relationship with Valentino Popofski, the text takes on a quicker pace because Valentino is the one who is physically present, therefore not very interesting or attractive. One might indeed question what Valentino's character brings to the text as a whole, other than the fact that he presents himself as Shelling's foreshadowing, his omen, so to speak. He too is a man whose language and discourse make his charm. Rose will never have a physical relationship with him; she only acts as if she is staging Valentino, pulling his strings, as a man who: "parle d'une voix douce, un peu studieuse, gentiment précieuse" (25) [speaks in a soft voice, slightly studious, playfully affected]. He paves the way for Shelling, the man who is still absent, therefore desirable. Even if matters are bound to change later in the book, it is indeed distance that shapes desire at the beginning. In the same way, it is indifference that allows the intimacy between Rose and Valentino. Because of their common—although different in nature—tie to the female character, Valentino and Shelling's stories are tightly woven, tangled, and for brief moments they even overlap. In those moments, the absolute freedom of the writer is at its best. Under the appearance of anecdote, Harvey touches on issues as grave as the relation between game/art and life or the void of purely aesthetic quarrels. Depth—or lack thereof—does not foreclose, here and there, vivid allusions to real-life events. Furthermore, characters are almost Harvey's thematic, her excuse for real writing, a very personal adventure. Maybe that is why there are no superfluous characters in the novel, no more than there are any truly powerful ones.

The first part of the novel ends on a note of confusion and self-denying despair, and, as one might expect, the second part starts with a letter, written by Rose this time, which signifies a continuation of the relationship. Oddly enough, absence becomes an emptiness, whereas it was not to start with; it was more of a stimulus. Rose wants to win back her control over the circumstances: "Je n'étais plus moi-même pendant quelques jours, j'avais l'impression d'avoir été entraînée dans la grande roue d'un cirque d'où je ne pourrais plus descendre" (40) [I wasn't myself for a few days, I felt like I was caught on a circus Ferris wheel and could not get off]. A fear of the future creeps into Rose, a fear coupled with a need for replacement. Absence is not a pleasure anymore; there is a shift in the feminine discourse, just as there will be one in the masculine discourse, sooner or later. The shock of words, the aggressiveness, the woman's desire come up to the surface of a text filled with strong sexual overtones: "La seule vérité est sexuelle, je n'ai une idée exacte de vous que lorsque je vous désire" (44) [The only truth is sexual, I have an accurate idea of you only when I want you]. As abrupt as her confession to the absent "other" might be, it is honest. The separation, even temporary, makes the woman become more outspoken. When the "other" is not present, there is not much risk involved in her semisexual discourse, at least not in an immediate way.

The body is not the only site where the contradictions of female subjectivity are played out, and yet the waltz resumes with renewed vigor when "Shelling est revenu après que je lui ai envoyé cette dernière lettre" (46) [Shelling came back after I sent him that last letter]. Characters live life at top speed, as if not taking the time to live every instant to its fullest. Their hope is to take advantage of each of the male forays into the female world, as if, literally, there was no tomorrow: "on n'a fait que baiser (46). Nous sommes très polis et plus nous sommes polis, plus nous baisons ensemble" (47) [all we did was fuck. We are very polite, and the more polite we are, the more we fuck]. In those moments, true marathons of physical love, the author uses a vocabulary typically deemed masculine to describe an experience that is first and foremost feminine. Harvey tells the story of a woman who, literally, builds herself throughout the different stages of her amorous escapades. Readers have little access to the male character's thoughts on love and/or lust. However, Shelling's *mind* games are accessible to all, readers and female character alike, although Rose cares little about his scheme. She thinks she knows that, just as *she* had done earlier in the text, it is now *he* who wants to create desire by absence when he claims he wants to leave her.

Personal landmarks become blurred and the ensuing confusion is as attractive as it is puzzling. The text gathers speed; Rose, whose curiosity has been sufficiently aroused, starts deciphering the man in her life. Shelling is an enigma, Rose is the investigator. The city becomes an empty, shallow space when the man is not in it. The fact is that, to a certain extent, the man imposes the city onto the woman: "il est tout le discours montréalais" (56) [he is the entire Montreal discourse]. The rural and potentially idyllic setting of the lake gives way to hotel rooms, conveniently lacking in a common past and, above all, not very conducive to commitment. The city is a sufficiently vast and anonymous setting to include both the masculine and the feminine discourse. Moreover, the city allows Rose to express her voyeuristic cravings in an artistic rather than a personal and/or sexual way.

The attraction to the "other" being much too unbearable, Rose resorts to compromise. In Paris, one can also find the country—that is to say, a way for Rose to tell herself that she is still somewhat in control of what is happening to her, especially as far as responding to the masculine discourse is concerned, which, all of a sudden, finds itself out of reach: "Pourquoi Shelling parle-t-il ainsi?" (59) [Why does Shelling talk like that?]. In Paris, Shelling clearly dominates the discourse; he plays host to Rose on his own territory. Her reaction is instantaneous: "Je ne comprenais pas ce qu'il faisait dans ma vie, une simple colère comme j'en faisais à Valentino" (60) [I could not understand what he was doing in my life, (this was) a simple tantrum, the kind I would have with Valentino]. The sparring match takes shape: "C'est un cauchemar de vivre avec Shelling et c'est très amusant" (60) [It is a nightmare to live with Shelling, and it is very amusing]. The "Vort-Da" game resumes. One more time, the female character, determined to survive the affront, takes an attitude of feigned indifference, which, according to the canon, is masculine. It appears that the identity of each character is jeopardized by the other's gaze and discourse. In this lack of reciprocal understanding, one can only hope that each of the two protagonists will at least comprehend his or her own distress and confusion.

The chapter ends on a language twist, which, ironically enough, represents no more than the *common* discourse for both characters: "la générosité d'un homme, c'est son sperme" (61) [a man's generosity lies in his sperm]. Physical love and sentimental quest are not to be equated. Echoing man's *generosity*, "toute femme sait que l'exhibition de la simple toison pubique suffit à faire venir un homme" (64) [any woman knows that a simple show of pubic hair is enough to have a man come]. If the image is not the most astute or subtle, it certainly helps in showing how the relationship of these characters is above all a conflict, a search for power, contrast, specificity, even after they have attempted physical connivance. Behind the bravado, one can sense a hint of panic: "Pourquoi ne s'en va-t-il pas s'il veut vraiment s'en aller?" (66) [Why doesn't he leave if that's really what he wants?]. Rose dreams up a mythical city in order to grow away from her man before he grows away from her.

About halfway through the book, Rose has a moment of revelation that she does not perceive in terms of discourse, but rather in terms of blunt sexuality: "Un homme ça sert à jouir, s'il y a des amants leur nom est jouissance, sexualité, un homme est une valse" (70) [A man is good for pleasure, if there are lovers, their name is orgasm, sexuality, a man is a waltz]. Sexuality becomes the meta-discourse of the novel. Her choice to connect or not with Shelling gives Rose a great feeling of freedom. Thanks to discourse, Rose stands back and looks objectively at the hold both Shelling and time, another element to get under control, have on her. Her reasonings—"Je n'appelle pas Shelling et j'en jouis" (75) [I am not calling Shelling and it gives me great pleasure]—are amazing, even if they no longer carry the sheen of novelty and originality. Because she gives herself a choice, Rose does not worry about not being fully aware of what is happening to her. Happiness, or illusion, means that, "Loin d'être insupportable, cette minute qui s'éternise se vit dans le plus parfait consentement" (75) [Far from unbearable, that eternal minute goes by in most perfect harmony]. Immediately, the miracle of fiction happens, provided that it is accepted for what it is. Harvey seems to resolve an artistic equation that allows for the metaphorical soaring of fantasy over reality. It was to be predicted; the attempt to freeze time was in fact a way of enduring absence: "Puis c'est le soir et Shelling revient" (76) [then evening comes and Shelling is back]. On with the foolish, absurd games: "je voudrais lui dire que je le quitte, juste pour voir" (76) [I would like to tell him I am leaving him, just to see]. Roles are reversed, but no one is fooled: "Il commençait à voir que je jouais" (77) [He was starting to realize I was playing]. The moves on the chessboard have become very predictable; the waltz is dragging a bit.

Nevertheless, the female character, as if aware of the void left behind by her passionate experience with Shelling, reverts to discourse, the panacea, the sovereign remedy for love wounds: "Etre une femme douce, écrire tous les jours, toute la journée et ne jamais cesser d'écrire" (79) [To be a gentle woman, to write every day, all day and to never stop writing]. Although it might seem as though writing replaces the male character, the reprieve is of short duration. Shelling always comes back and soon, writing, but also the games with Shelling make up Rose's favorite staple. She constantly opens and closes the window, not only of her forlorn writer apartment, but also of her intellect, her heart, her body. The practice is exhausting.

There is an essential change of perspective in the second half of the novel. Why does Rose, who claims to be so independent, constantly come back to the object, the target of her love/desire/game? Her approaches are slightly irritating, and yet, more and more, the rhythm of the text follows the female character's passionate or sometimes doting thoughts. The setting of the relationship changes again, to conclude another rapprochement. The "Dungeons and Dragons" game is a badly veiled metaphor for the war of the sexes present throughout the whole novel. Banality, desire, sexuality, orgasm, and solitude are the ingredients that tie or untie the two characters, neither of whom is ready to admit defeat to the other.

"La Valse Mephisto," the appropriately named third part of the novel, is literally a descent into hell, even if, a priori, it does not look like it at all. The simplicity, the daintiness of the place where the lovers have decided to take their passion seems to be giving the text and the characters' feelings a certain lightness, an ease that had not had the time to bloom earlier in the novel. The content of the discourse changes, as if the character finally realizes that he or she also *is* a discourse: "Je voudrais maintenant faire le tour du monde à la recherche de l'écriture" (99) [I would like now to go around the world, in search of writing]. Rose finds she has a soul, when she has already arrived "au milieu de son âge" (100) [halfway through her life]. The transition is not the simplest. Desire, love, death cannot be set aside; they are constantly implicit within the text, a text which, it seems, becomes more and more profound and gripping. The battle against decline, the failure of will power, the death of the body become the female protagonist's new hobbyhorse: "Il faut donc . . . se mettre dans une situation où la volonté doit s'exercer . . . si le corps ne veut pas mourir" (106) [So . . . you must put yourself in a situation where will power must be exerted . . . so that the body will not die]. Both characters seem finally to have reached a certain balance in their respect for each other's independence, even if, for the reader, it is clear that Shelling is calling the tune.

The stay in Lerici looks like a pilgrimage, but not a religious one: "L'Italie est un coup de foudre" (111) [Italy is love at first sight]. The close connection between the characters and the scenery shadows the intimate rapport that first grows and then comes undone between them. Again, there is a shift, a drift of which the protagonist is completely aware. A character seeking protection from his or her writing and/or discourse can be compared to the octopus hiding behind its own ink. The respite does not last, though: "Il continue de jouer à ce jeu curieux quand il baise, de vérifier à quoi je pense et si je pense bien à lui et non pas à quelqu'un d'autre" (114) [He keeps on playing that weird game when he fucks, he checks what I am thinking about and if I am indeed thinking about him and not somebody else]. Rose finally lets herself be possessed, led by the "valse Mephisto," whether it be out of lust or from sheer weariness. The reader realizes and maybe hopes that, for the last time, Rose and Shelling have played with death, love, and desire. Much before the protagonists, the reader feels a need for closure. The character keeps on believing in his or her pipe dreams for a while.

In chapter 3 of the third part of the book, the sinews of war are finally going to be exposed: "La question est . . . de savoir comment est faite la femme devant qui l'homme s'ouvre" (118). "Un homme qui s'ouvre appelle le ventre" (119) [The point is . . . to find out what the woman, for whom a man opens up, is made of. A man who opens up calls for the vagina]. If characters succeed in finding their authentic self through sex, they will discover trust—that is to say, a promise for upcoming sex, titillating anticipation. The waltz, adequate illustration for sex, ultimate struggle, and power abuse, becomes a hand-to-hand combat, which itself changes into a trance: "Il n'y a rien à craindre des sexes" (122) [There is nothing to fear from the sexes]. After the apocalypse, things calm down, in the comfort of Montréal, the well-known and/or yet to be discovered setting: "Montréal est une fourmilière où l'amour prend peu de place dans les conversations" (125) [Montreal is an anthill where love takes up little room in conversations]. The waltz will go on. If the characters give up, in mid-dance, they have had it, because they fall victims to this constant desire to know what is going to happen "after." In other words, the waltz needs to become perpetual.

Pleasure through writing leads to writing for pleasure; over more than fifteen pages, the waltz becomes intensely erotic. Rose surrenders to the plea of the flesh: "La virilité c'est la chose la plus étrange du monde, la plus excitante certainement" (132) [Manliness is the strangest thing in the world, certainly the most exciting]. As for him, the male sex object makes a spectacle of himself, as if he wanted to finish the waltz in a solo. The game between assertive minds becomes a little bit tedious and can best be summed up in an excellent metaphor, which, on its own, illustrates the entire genesis: "Il dit que je ne peux pas apprendre le fonctionnement du jeu sans d'abord me perdre, c'est un langage" (147) [He says I cannot learn how to play the game without first losing myself, that's a given]. It might be too easy to argue that divergence equals dilution, but to despise and ignore difference is hardly a productive strategy, nor is it a very enjoyable one. Through *Un Homme est une valse*, the reader is better off searching, not for icons, but for inroads to the cultural/sexual/political terrain that constitutes the system of power that shapes and defines the (wrong)doings of both characters.

The last pages of the novel may be the promise of a new waltz. They might also indicate the end of a cycle, as if the male and female characters had, literally, exhausted the question and had nothing more to learn. By leaving the hotel/the woman, Shelling recreates desire through absence and through things unsaid, apparently his only remaining weapon. Harvey's characters desire what they cannot enunciate and, along their journey, they will not have learned to name. Shelling zooms out of Rose's world the same way he came into it: without much ado. Left to her own devices, the narrator goes back to writing, only too anxious to fill up the "blank pages" bequeathed to her by Shelling. There is also a possibility that she might already be thinking about the next dance.

Note

1. Unless otherwise noted, all translations are my own.

Works Cited

Gould, Karen. "Writing and Reading 'Otherwise': Québec Women Writers and the Exploration of Difference." In *Studies in Canadian Literature,* edited by Arnold E. Davidson, 207–25. New York: MLA, 1990.

Harvey, Pauline. *Un Homme est une valse.* Montréal: Les Herbes Rouges, 1992.

Ouellete-Michalska, Madeleine. "Pauline Harvey: Du côté des funambules." *Le Devoir,* 2 octobre 1982: 28.

Royer, Jean. "Pauline Harvey." *Magazine littéraire,* octobre 1986: 104–5.

The Future of Memory in Louise Dupré's *La Memoria*

KAREN MCPHERSON

Language remembers.
—Anne Michaels, "What the Light Teaches"

Remembering our past is crucial for our sense of identity . . . to know what we were confirms that we are.
—David Lowenthal

MEMORY IS EVERYWHERE THESE DAYS. WITNESS THE RECENT POPULARity of the memoir form which journalist Anna Quindlen has called the "oeuvre du jour" (11 May 1997). In a review of Jamaica Kincaid's memoir about her brother's death from AIDS, Quindlen notes that "this is not real life, but real life recollected" and that "what that memoir is about [is] the chasm between the self we might have been and one that we have somehow, often inexplicably, become" (19 October 1997). Louise Dupré's novel *La Memoria* is not a memoir, but it foregrounds the relationship between memory and fiction making in such a way as to raise the question of its own fictional status and, by extension, of the status of fiction in general as "not true."[1] Dupré's novel might most accurately be called a "roman intime" (intimate novel), its first-person narration of a woman's story of loss and recovery incorporating characteristics of both the letter and the *journal intime* (private diary), two generic forms often associated with women's autobiographical writings.[2] Indeed, *La Memoria* appears to be engaged in the same process of exploring female subjectivity and agency that Barbara Havercroft has located as a central problematic in contemporary "autofictions" by women.

La Memoria is also, however, an extraordinarily lyrical work that in many ways resembles the hybrid genre of "poésie en prose" (prose poetry) (although in this case one would have to speak of "prose en poésie" [poetic prose]), a genre that Dupré has elsewhere identified as singularly situated to offer "la possibilité de mettre en scène la complexité de la subjectivité" ("Subjectivité" 6) [the possibility of presenting the complexity of subjectivity].³ As Dupré describes it: "la poésie en prose, au Québec, est marquée par une hybidité qui met en contact la poésie et la réflexion, ou encore la poésie et la narration. Ou encore, le poétique, le réflexif et le narratif" ("Écrire" 6) [prose poetry, in Quebec, is marked by a hybridity that brings together poetry and reflection, or even poetry and narration. Or yet again the poetic, the reflective, and the narrative]. There is no question that Louise Dupré writes as a poet no matter what genre she has chosen to write in, and *La Memoria* engages "le poétique, le réflexif et le narratif" in ways that locate this "roman intime" clearly within poetic space.

Inasmuch as all writing is in the face of death, as both Benjamin and Derrida have suggested,⁴ the poet is, of course, no less concerned with the workings of memory than is the memorialist. In a recent critical article, Dupré has clearly situated the poet in relation to a lost past: "Le poète ne se voit-il pas comme un déraciné, un exilé, un sans-patrie qui essaie de retrouver dans la langue sinon un pays, du moins un paysage familier?"("Racines" 117) [Doesn't the poet see himself as uprooted, exiled, a person without a homeland who is trying to find in language if not a country at least a familiar landscape?]. The poet seeking to survive the melancholy of loss and "déracinement" (uprooting) through a rooting (*enracinement*) in poetic language is necessarily writing *through the memory of that language*. It is this memory writing that makes survival possible. As Dupré puts it so eloquently in her own most recent volume of poetry: "Poème, oui. À chaque fois que je meurs, je survis" ("Tout près" 45) [Poem, yes. Each time I die, I survive].

WOMEN WRITING MEMORY

Memory is an ecosystem.

—Mary Meigs

When Mary Meigs refers to memory as "an ecosystem," she is emphasizing the urgency of not allowing the memories—however small, singular, or apparently insignificant—of "those who have always been silenced by history" (61) to be wiped out. Nicole Brossard likewise sees women's return to and through memory as a global necessity. It is through memory, writes Brossard, that women come to writing and through writing that they may begin to "apprendre à penser l'inimaginable, l'inconcevable" (1985, 82) [to learn to think the unimaginable, the inconceivable] (*Aerial* 1988, 99). Brossard explains that, in a woman's body, "[memory] repeats itself endlessly, same scene, same decor, same people, unless there is narration. Without an internal account, without narrative illumination, without its text, memory is an eater of destiny" ("Memory" 1988, 43). For Brossard, then, writing marks a site where our memories and our desires may actually generate change. She describes this process as memory "work[ing] its own legend," and she calls it "actualizing memory, one that initiates presence in the world" ("Memory" 1988, 43). Brossard's concept of the writing of memory seems to suggest this process as a way for women to heal that chasm between "what they might have been and what they have, inexplicably, become" (Quindlen).

Emma Villeray, the narrator of *La Memoria*, is involved in just such a memory process. Her struggle to survive her losses is a struggle toward self-conception and self-actualization. Her narration marks her evolution from a state of *waiting* (curled up in fetal position in her bed), to the beginnings of movement: "on se remet à bouger" (91) [we get moving again] (87), and finally to full agency and entry into the world: "Je suis entrée dans le temps de la résurrection" (196) [I have entered the time of resurrection] (191); "Je franchis la barrière" (211) [And I go through the gate] (206).[5] This evolution is not strictly linear; memory and mourning "work their legends" through repeated circlings back to the place of loss. Yet, these are not closed, vicious circles—rather they resemble Brossardian spirals, opening onto new futures.[6]

No Blank Slates

After her abandonment by Jérôme, her lover of ten years, Emma cannot conceive of her past ever releasing its hold on her present. The broken relationship is tenaciously reconstituted in both the present and the future in Emma's narration addressed to the absent Jérôme: "Un matin, il faudra bien qu'il y ait une lettre de toi dans la boîte, je m'acharne à me le répéter. On ne peut pas effacer dix ans de cette façon, la vie n'est pas une tablette magique" (17) [There will have to be a letter from you in the mailbox one morning, I stubbornly keep telling myself. One cannot erase ten years just like that, life isn't a magic notepad] (13). Why does Emma hold so firmly to the conviction that there is no such thing as vanishing without a trace? Is it despite or because of her younger sister Noëlle's disappearance some twenty years earlier? You cannot just wipe out ten or twenty years. *La vie n'est pas une tablette magique.*

Yet, even the *tablette magique* is not what it pretends to be. Its magic lies elsewhere than in its ability to make words and images vanish in an instant. The *tablette magique* to which Emma refers is, in fact, none other than Freud's *Wunderblock*, his Mystic Writing-Pad, notable precisely because what is apparently erased is never really gone. Freud saw this child's toy as an ideal metaphor for the structure of "the perceptual apparatus of our mind." As he noted, when the covering sheet is lifted, "the surface of the Mystic Pad is clear of writing and once more capable of receiving impressions. But it is easy to discover that the permanent trace of what was written is retained upon the wax slab itself and is legible in suitable lights" (230). The magic of Freud's Mystic Writing-Pad was, then, not the disappearance but the *permanent* trace, the memory. It is *this* magic that captures Emma's imagination. She recounts:

> Pour Noëlle, je dessinais de grandes maisons, tu sais, avec des fenêtres et puis je décollais la feuille plastifiée et tout disparaissait. Mais j'avais appuyé sur le crayon et la maison restait imprimée sur le canevas en dessous, elle se superposait aux arbres, aux oiseaux, aux chats, aux fillettes qui dansaient à la corde et aux mamans qui les surveillaient. Cela formait un étrange paysage que j'arrivais pourtant à déchiffrer. Aucune image n'était effacée. (17)

> [For Noëlle I used to draw large houses, you know, with windows, then when I lifted up the plastic-coated sheet everything disappeared. But I had pressed hard on the pencil and the house remained imprinted on the slate underneath. It was superimposed on the trees, the birds, the cats, the rope-skipping little girls and the mothers who watched them. It formed a strange landscape, yet I was able to make it out. None of the pictures were erased.] (13)

Yet, if images are never completely erased and there are no clean slates, how, then, does one go on after loss? This is the crux of *La Memoria*: as long as one is looking back, deciphering the "strange landscape" of the past, how can one look, much less move, ahead? Emma at one point notes that "la vraie question [c'est] la question du deuil" (115) [the real question is the question of mourning] (109, translation modified). And it is by no means a simple question in the novel, for mourning encodes memory and functions paradoxically both as an obstacle to living on, to surviving, and as a way—perhaps the only way—to begin to do so.

The Question of Mourning

Chaque chagrin est le seul au monde.
—Dupré, *La Memoria*

There are different kinds of memory and different kinds of mourning in *La Memoria*. At times, memory is figured as a container, a place of safekeeping, a reliquary, for the urge to hold onto the past—to preserve and treasure it—is strong. To erect this kind of memory is to mount a defense against loss. However, a repository of memories can easily become a prison house, and the act of mourning can then be experienced not as a *process* but as an eternal and interminable *state*, an emptying of presence, a death in life. In embracing this kind of memory, the survivor *becomes* (and thus does *not* survive) the loss. A figure emblematizing this kind of memory is evoked by Emma's friend Bénédicte, who advises her to forget about Jérôme: "*Il faut se souvenir de la femme de Loth*" (54) [We must remember Lot's wife] (51). Lot's wife, a woman turned into a pillar of salt for having looked back, stands as a sign of the dangers of trying to hang on to the past. At times Emma seems to be thus transfixed: "Je suis devenue comme Noëlle," she says, "Un corps vidé" (23) [I've become just like Noëlle. An empty shell] (19). Emma's father has also succumbed to this kind of memory. She attributes his death to the fact that he no longer wanted to live, for "la mémoire l'avait rattrapé. Noëlle. . . . Rien ne pouvait le ramener vers nous" (63). [His memory had caught up with him. Noëlle. . . . Nothing could bring him back to us] (59). Indeed, Emma's father's dying words to her express his wish that she might find a way out of this cycle of loss: "Essaie d'oublier, toi" (64) [*You* must try to forget] (60).

Yet, how *can* she forget? His death, compounding her losses, speaks louder than his words, making her even more determined to remember, to keep remembering. Besides, among her carefully preserved memories are other voices, other admonitions, that directly challenge her father's advice. She recalls in particular the words of the policemen who came to the house to question her after Noëlle's disappearance—had she seen something that could help them locate the missing girl? "Essayez de vous souvenir," they told her (45) [Try to remember] (41). She hadn't been able to remember anything, and Noëlle was irretrievably lost. Could memory have been the key? Might a different future have been contained in that lost moment in the past?

So, while Emma has at times attempted to construct retaining walls to hold back the annihilating power of the past, her attempts to build "une mémoire propre . . . une raison aussi solide qu'une patrie" (160) [(an) orderly memory . . . (an) acceptance of things . . . as solid as a native land] (154) are doomed to fail. There is no propriety, there is no reason, there is no homeland because "on ne s'habitue pas à l'idée de la disparition" (39) [we never become accustomed to someone's disappearance] (35). Emma's mother, believing in her own way in "an orderly memory," has had Noëlle's name and birth date carved onto the family tombstone. Although she, like Emma, is in many ways suspended in the limbo of mourning (essentially incapable, since Noëlle's disappearance, of recognizing or being present for her remaining children), she nevertheless holds fast to the idea that one day, when they recover Noëlle's body, they will be able to complete the inscription and find closure. For Emma even this tentative step, this nod toward a possible future, seems impossible, inconceivable: "Dans ma tête il y avait une fosse qui ne se refermerait jamais" (46) [In my mind there was a grave that would never be closed] (44).

With Jérôme's departure, that grave becomes a gaping chasm into which Emma is endlessly falling, for Jérôme's abandonment keeps alive and is kept alive by the unresolved disappearance of Noëlle two decades earlier. Emma's incapacity to get beyond the event of Jérôme's leaving may in part be explained by the fact of this retraumatization. That this is indeed a trauma is further suggested by the fact that it is in many ways the *shock* of Jérôme's leaving that Emma cannot get over. In a repeated phrase that I believe intentionally recalls the traumatic climax of Nicole Brossard's *Mauve Desert*, Emma expresses this shock: "Je n'avais rien vu venir"(18) [I hadn't seen anything coming] (14).[7] Jérôme's departure radically undermines her sense of the meaning and predictability of the world and shakes her belief in her own integrity and identity. What *can* she know if she did not know that this turn of events was possible? Who *was* that person who walked so blindly into disaster? Surely that person will never exist again—then who, if anyone, has survived?

Remaking a Self

How does one remake a self from the scattered shards of disrupted memory?
—Susan Brison

The trauma of multiple losses has produced a dual crisis for Emma: ontological and epistemological. Not only does she no longer know who she is, her sense of *how* she knows—and how she *trusts* her knowledge—has been radically undermined. Contemporary feminist philosopher Susan Brison has described just such an "epistemological crisis" as a characteristic reaction to traumatic events. In the wake of trauma there seems to be no map: the self is fractured, the fabric of time and causality is violently rent. The survivor is left, Brison says, "with virtually no bearings by which to navigate" (21). Emma's description of her own situation is strikingly similar: "Une partie de ma vérité s'est détachée de moi, elle flotte, inaccessible dans l'espace, et je m'acharne à la rattraper. J'ai peur. Voilà ce qu'il me reste. La peur, le vent. Je m'accroche au sol pour ne pas m'envoler" (23) [A part of my reality has split off from me, it's drifting in space, out of reach, and I'm desperately trying to catch hold of it again. I'm filled with fear. That's what I have left. Fear. The wind. I cling to the ground so as not to be blown away] (19).

The question here is clearly one of both identity and survival. On one level Emma believes that it should be possible to fashion "an orderly memory," to put the past neatly away in its proper place. Yet, at the same time she rejects any memorializing reconstruction, because, when carried to its logical conclusion, this kind of memory is precisely what she most fears. This, she imagines, is the way in which Jérôme has remembered, and forgotten, *her*. She senses, in the apparent ease with which he has managed to entomb her memory, that she has left no impression at all. In fighting against this kind of memorializing erasure, Emma is fighting for her life. "Je ne veux rien oublier," she says, "Guérir, oui, mais ne rien oublier" (165) [I don't want to forget anything. Get better, yes, but not forget anything] (159).

Brison stresses the importance of "connectedness" in the process of healing from trauma. It is clear in Dupré's novel that Emma's recovery of her *self* is only possible in the context of her present connections with those around her. In one of the novel's key scenes, Emma and her friend Bénédicte confess to one another that each one's deepest fear is of losing the other. As they talk, it is also evident that in their minds this loss coincides with the fear of being forgotten:

> *J'ai peur de te perdre*. J'ai dit seulement cela, 5 syllabes suspendues au-dessus de moi, dans le vide. . . . j'étais jalouse? J'ai fait signe que non, mais je craignais d'être délaissée. Oubliée.
> Dans ma gorge, la boule dure. Elle est venue avec le mot *oubliée*. Cet aveu m'avait rejetée dans un espace informe, un trou sans fond. (100)

["I'm afraid of losing you." This is all I said, seven syllables suspended above me in empty space. . . . was I jealous? I shook my head, I wasn't, but I feared being abandoned. Forgotten.
  The lump sat in my throat. It came with the word "forgotten." Confessing this had pitched me once more into a void without form, a bottomless pit.] (95)

Emma wants to heal without forgetting—neither to be trapped in the past, nor to lose it—but she also wants not to *be lost* in it. She wants, in other words, also to heal without *being forgotten*. A central component of Emma's healing work thus involves forging and maintaining connections with others that will extend through time. To heal in this way is not simple, because nothing is fixed (in either sense of the word—anchored or repaired). As Emma says of her conversation with Bénédicte: "nous avions affronté aujourd'hui notre peur la plus tenace et nous l'avions vaincue, jusqu'à la prochaine fois" (102) [we had confronted our deepest fear today and conquered it, until the next time] (97). Remembering is an ongoing process of conscious and determined reconnection—which is why many of Emma's most meaningful relationships throughout this period of crisis involve making the shared present memorable and promising and believing that it *will be remembered*.

Making Shared Memories

Bénédicte, immediately following Noëlle's disappearance, made every effort to ground Emma in the present by insisting upon their connectedness and upon the existence of a future. She slipped Emma a note whose second sentence read like a lifeline: "Pas question que tu rates tes examens. *Nous étudierons ensemble*" (54, my emphasis) [There's no question of your failing your exams, *we'll study together*] (52), and she gave her a set of tarot cards, which they ritually used together to look into the future. Now, with Jérôme's departure, Emma feels as if she has lost her "don de voyance" (23) [gift of clairvoyance] (18), and Bénédicte is once again there for her. Significantly, Bénédicte's orientation toward the future does *not* mean a total erasure of the past. For instance, it is Bénédicte who reconnects Emma with Vincent, a man who had been Emma's friend and Bénédicte's lover years earlier. Bénédicte also shares with Emma a kind of repetition that opens up possibilities: "La répétition, c'était aussi ce beau vertige de fin de soirée, cette valse où depuis vingt ans nous pivotons sur nous-mêmes, en agrandissant constamment notre espace" (56–57) [Also repeating itself was that glorious late-night giddiness, the waltz that for the last twenty years had had us swirling around in ever-widening circles] (53). Dancing together, Bénédicte and Emma participate in the conscious creation of shared *future* memories: "Nous chantonnions en comptant les mesures, nous nous enroulions autour de nos pas, nous voulions déposer, dans notre boîte à souvenirs, une scène à conserver toujours" (57) [We hummed along with the music, we twisted around our steps—we wanted to store away in our memory chest a scene to hold on to forever] (54).

Like Bénédicte, Vincent helps Emma to escape the paralyzing embrace of the past. He offers her a future by constructing shared memories, their picture taken by a stranger, for instance: *"Quand nous serons vieux, nous dirons, 'Nous étions là'"* (107) [In our old age we'll say, "We were there."] (103). In addition, as her lover, he finds her and holds her in the present. In Vincent's caresses, Emma recognizes "[son] désir fou de nous faire une place au milieu des ruines" (92) [(his) passionate wish to create a place for us among the ruins] (87). The relationship awakens in Emma her own desires, which ground her in her present body, a grounding that, in turn, gives her a vision of the future and a sense of her own agency: "J'ai aimé cette vision, le désir qui crée un mouvement infini, le cercle du temps qui s'ouvre sans nous broyer. Je suis allée chercher une tablette, une plume et de l'encre mauve . . ." (43) [I liked that vision—desire creating infinite motion, the circle of time opening, and not crushing us. I went to get a writing tablet, a pen, and mauve ink] (39).

Ariadne's Thread

The single most important companion on Emma's journey is Madame Girard, the former inhabitant of the house into which Emma moves after Jérôme's departure. Emma's new house, her attempt at a clean slate, still holds the indelible impression, the memory trace, of Madame Girard's own traumatic history, for it was in the basement of this house that Monsieur Girard committed suicide. When Emma pays a visit to Madame Girard, the older woman offers her a new perspective on the role of memory in mourning. She shows her a collection of beautifully bound books of ancient history, saying *"Voilà le réservoir infini de la mémoire . . . la* memoria" (67) [There you have the infinite reservoir of memory . . . *memoria.*] (63).[8] Unlike Emma's mother, whose mode of memorializing is to cover the place of absence with a tombstone, Madame Girard offers a model of memory that is dynamic, one that strives to open up the past through narrative rather than to fix it, parenthetically, in time (between a birth date and a death date).

Madame Girard has another important lesson for Emma. In answer to Emma's question about whether one can ever understand abandonment, Madame Girard whispers, *"Il faut accepter même si on ne comprend pas"* (66) [We have to accept things even if we can't understand them.] (62). Yet, her acceptance is not blind. When Madame Girard heads off to Greece, she is not going in order to *escape* her past. She is consciously venturing *into* the past (indeed, into ancient history, the past of the human species) in order to be able to get through it. She will return. When Madame Girard makes another statement that serves as a kind of beacon for Emma ("Quand je reviendrai de voyage, je serai capable de retourner dans la cave") [When I return from my trip, I will be able to go down into the basement again], Emma reflects that "Madame Girard essayait de se projeter dans le futur. Peut-être l'avenir fait-il aussi partie de la mémoire. De la *memoria*" (78) [Madame Girard was trying to project herself into the future. Perhaps the future is also part of memory. Of *memoria*] (74). The "memoria" of the book's title is precisely summed up by Madame Girard's two statements to Emma: *memoria* is both the acceptance of loss in all of its incomprehensibility and the belief in a future still connected to that loss, to that past.

Madame Girard sets out on a journey "[au] fond de la mémoire humaine" (205) [(to) the beginning of human memory] (200), and in her first letter to Emma from Crete, she describes her daily "pilgrimage" to Knossos: "elle se promenait dans les ruines, elle imaginait la vie dans ce labyrinthe grandiose, puis la légende, le Minotaure, et Ariane, Ariane et son fil" (130) [She would walk among the ruins, picture life in that great labyrinth, think of the legend of the Minotaur, and Ariadne, Ariadne and her thread] (125, translation modified). In the book's third section, this model of memory introduced by Madame Girard stands in marked contrast to the earlier model represented by Lot's wife. In the story of the Cretan labyrinth, it is Ariadne who gives Theseus a thread to follow in order to *get in* to the center of the labyrinth (where he can slay the Minotaur) and then *get out* again safely. In a sense Madame Girard's own quest serves as Emma's Ariadne's thread. After rereading the letter, Emma goes out walking—"je rejoindrais Madame Girard dans son éblouissement" [I was going to join Madame Girard, be dazzled along with her]—and from the top of the mountain she looks out, letting her mind stretch into the distance "jusqu'à cette force obscure qu'il faut pour recommencer. C'était le balancement vivant de la vie, hors des limites et des frontières, hors de la prison du passé" (131) [all the way to that obscure force that is needed to start over again. I felt the dramatic swaying of life, outside of boundaries and frontiers, beyond the prison of the past] (125, translation modified). Madame Girard's journey and her letter, her daily, repeated imaginings of the past, have taken Emma to a place where she can imagine a future, a place in which life goes on "beyond the prison of the past" and in which there is a way *through* the labyrinth. Upon her return from the mountain, Emma reflects: "Toute la journée, j'avais suivi un fil qui m'avait menée très loin. Vers une porte qui s'ouvrait sur les deux côtés du temps" (132) [All day I had followed a thread that took me a long, long way from here. Right up to a door opening out onto both sides of time] (126). This double door of *la memoria* will be the way out of the labyrinth of mourning that will allow Emma not to have to turn her back on *either* the past *or* the future.

Mourning Work

Seule l'imagination peut contrer l'effritement.
—Dupré, *La Memoria*

When Jérôme left, Emma was in the middle of trying to finish a translation. After his departure, the lack of progress on this project clearly mirrors the lack of movement in her life: "J'attends. Je me retrouve devant une *réalité intraduisible* et j'attends" (48, my emphasis) [I am waiting. Ahead of me looms an *untranslatable reality* and I am waiting] (45, translation modified). Her breakthrough comes when Vincent urges her to work on a piece of writing of her own, a film scenario: "il voudrait un texte de moi, c'est bien ce qu'il veut, un texte qui me ressemble" (41) [He would like a text by me. That's what he really wants, a text that is a reflection of me] (37, translation modified). In offering Emma this possibility, Vincent holds out to her another one of Ariadne's threads, and she takes it, for shortly thereafter she does begin to make notes for the scenario. Furthermore, having that scenario in her imagination, she finds herself able to complete her translation. This represents a crucial stage in the healing process. When she looks at the finished manuscript of the translation, she remarks (addressing herself to the absent Jérôme): "Le manuscrit avait résisté à ton départ. Dans ma serviette, je portais la preuve de ma survie" (120) [The manuscript had withstood your leaving. In my briefcase I was carrying proof of my survival] (114). The finished translation represents her *own* translation from *before* the crisis to *after:* "J'avais reappris à marcher, fièrement . . . à traduire la voix d'une autre femme, bien sûr, mais c'était aussi ma voix que je transportais au milieu de la rumeur, ma voix de rescapée" (120) [I had learned to walk again, proudly . . . to translate the voice of another woman. Yet I wasn't only carrying *her* voice through the din but my own as well, my survivor's voice] (114).

Emma is able to complete the translation because she now has a map for the scenario that will keep her voice alive. Like any map of uncharted territory, hers is, of course, mostly empty, white space. On the first page of her notebook she has written simply three names—her own, Noëlle's, and Jérôme's—and on the last page she has inscribed two words: The end (47, in English in the original). These reference points do not achieve closure or convey any narrative logic; they are merely the roughest sketch of a couple of landmarks in an unknown territory. It is not until Emma is able to look through the door "that opens on both sides of time," not until she has found a way to heal without forgetting, that she will be able to fill in all those intervening pages. She knows from the start what that writing will mean, that it is what some theorists have referred to as "mourning work" (Elsaesser 1989, 242). "Un jour," she thinks, "j'aurais terminé mon scénario. Je ne me sentirais plus obligée de porter du noir" (47) [Some day my script would be finished. I wouldn't feel that I had to wear black any more] (44).

Through her "mourning work," Emma may hope eventually to heal the breach between absence and presence. The work of mourning and the work of writing both involve a transformation, a painstaking process of translation of what *was* into what *can be*. The writer and the mourner—and Emma is both of these—must each confront the evidence of absence and enter that place of loss in order to grasp some piece of what *was* and carry it across into language, where it can tell the stories of both loss and survival.

As Emma moves through the labyrinth of mourning, she often feels that she is merely walking in circles, that "la vie humaine est un scénario qui n'en finit pas de reprendre les mêmes scènes" (136) [Human existence is a screenplay with the same scenes repeating themselves over and over] (130). She sees history repeating itself and her life "comme une civilisation minuscule qui n'arrive pas à sortir de ses cercles" (154) [as a tiny civilization stuck in a circular path] (148). Yet, her writing project offers her occasional glimpses of a world where past and future need *not* be mutually exclusive. One passage in particular shows the extent to which writing and language are fundamental to Emma's acquisition of this vision: "Dans mon cahier, la vie se défait et je la regarde se défaire sans avoir peur, je ressens une sorte de tranquillité dans le mot *douleur*, il s'agit de la faire rimer avec *couleur* pour imaginer, sous son écorce, un début de joie" (144) [In my notebook, life is disintegrating and I watch it disintegrate without being afraid. I feel a kind of serenity in the word grief, all I need do is make it rhyme with leaf to imagine a budding happiness underneath its skin] (138).[9]

The rhyming of despair and hope seems to make possible a transformative act of imagination that can in turn open up the possibility of beginning once again. When she first determines to write the scenario, Emma explains it as a way to "saisir la minute exacte où la vie nous reprend, la perte qui se transforme en fiction" (43) [capture the precise moment when we come back to life, when loss is transformed into fiction] (39).

Mourning the Mother

Comment faire entrer maman dans mon scenario?
                                Dupré, *La Memoria*

Toward the end of the novel's third section, Emma imagines a woman weeping over her husband's casket. The woman slowly rises, leaning on the cold body, pushing herself up, and Emma thinks: "Voilà tout ce que je peux écrire aujourd'hui. Une femme effondrée, mais qui se relève. Une femme qui me précède" (163) [That's all I can write today. A woman who has collapsed but gets up again. A woman who is ahead of me] (157). It is tempting to read this weeping woman as a figurative representation of the two women in mourning whose grieving runs parallel to Emma's: Madame Girard and Rosa, the Spanish neighbor. Just as Emma turns to Madame Girard for understanding, consolation and direction, she also listens each evening for her neighbor's song of grief: "j'entendrai sa voix chaude, veloutée. Et je me laisserai bercer. Dix heures, tous les soirs, la même complainte en espagnol. La tristesse traverse toutes les langues" (27) [I'll hear her warm velvety voice. And I will let myself be rocked and lulled by it. Every evening at ten, the same lament in Spanish. Sadness travels through every language] (23, translation modified). The comfort that Emma derives from her contact with Madame Girard and Rosa recalls the kinds of comfort a child receives from a mother: "Alors Madame Girard s'est approchée et m'a prise dans ses bras. Je suis redevenue une petite fille, je me suis laissé bercer" (66) [Then Madame Girard came over to me and took me in her arms. I became a little girl again, I let myself be rocked and comforted] (62, translation modified). The importance of this "maternal" comfort cannot be overstated, because it could be argued that the original loss in *La Memoria* was the loss of the mother.[10]

Emma expresses on a number of occasions her desire to be mothered. Observing a young girl playing on the sidewalk under the watchful eye of a woman on a nearby balcony, she thinks: "Envie d'avoir son âge, une mère qui m'envelopperait de son regard. Une mère qui ressemblerait à maman, avant le drame" (38) [A sudden longing to be her âge, have a mother who would focus her gaze on me. A mother like Mama before the tragedy] (35). Even when describing Jérôme's departure to Vincent, she seems to be talking about an earlier, more primal loss: "Je dis tout, même la honte, ne plus être aimée, ne plus mériter d'être aimée, *ni être bordée le soir avant de m'endormir*" (33, my emphasis) [I tell Vincent everything, even how ashamed I feel of not being loved any more, of not being worthy of love, *of not being cherished enough to be tucked in at night before I go to sleep*] (29).

Emma seems to want to believe that it was only after Noëlle's departure that her mother retreated into a place of nostalgia from which she could not save her (133). Yet, there are indications that the mother's "absence" predated the crisis of losing Noëlle. When her mother declared, "J'espère que Dieu me pardonnera.... Je ne sais pas garder mes enfants" [I hope God will forgive me.... I don't know how to hold on to my children], Emma tried to remind her that *she* was still there ("Tu as su me garder moi" [You've managed to hold on to *me*]). Her words made no impression. Her mother was "enfermée très loin à l'intérieur d'elle-même. *Là où je n'avais jamais pu la rejoindre*" (95, my emphasis) [shut away in some remote spot deep inside herself. *Where I had never been able to reach her*] (90). It seems as if the mother, once lost, has *always* been lost.

Emma's relationship with her mother throughout the novel is complex and ambivalent. It is from her mother that Emma has inherited her romantic ideals, but while Emma clings to these ideals for herself, she finds them distressing in her mother. Flirting with Monsieur Quintal at the market, her mother "n'était plus notre mère" (30) [wasn't our mother any more] (26). So, whereas Emma insists that she, unlike her mother, will live a life of passion, and will have no children, her feelings about her mother's "renunciation" of the role of desirable woman are very mixed. She finds the transformation above all reassuring ("j'étais tranquille maintenant" [I needn't worry any more]), but there is also a suggestion in her reference to the mother's "coeur endormi" (30) [her sleeping heart] (26) that this withdrawal into "ce bonheur simple qui suit le renoncement" (31) [that simple kind of happiness that follows renunciation] (27) might somehow have made her less capable of loving Emma in the way she needed to be loved. It is impossible for the reader to know, because Emma does not know, why mother and daughter cannot connect. At some point, probably very early, there was a failure in the relationship: "Quelque chose s'est brisé quelque part, je ne sais pas quand. Et je suis semblable à maman, je mets des bornes nettes aux époques, je dis *avant* et *après*, j'associe ces deux mots avec disparition et départ, mais je sais que c'est bien avant" (160) [Somewhere along the way, I don't know when, something was broken. And I am like Mama, I neatly section off time periods. I say "before" and "after," I link these words with disappearance and departure, but I know it happened long before] (154). Part of Emma's mourning work has to do with grieving and trying to make sense of that failure in order to find a way to reconnect with her mother or at least with the mother in her.

All of the returns in the novel prefigure the final return in the last section of the book: the reappearance and definitive disappearance of Noëlle. When news arrives of Noëlle's death in an auto accident in Los Angeles, Emma can only think that this resembles a scenario for a bad film: on her deathbed, her sister's dying wish had been that her four-year-old daughter be cared for by her sister Emma. The daughter is named Emma, too, but her given name is Emmanuelle (a name that significantly combines both Emma and Noëlle). It is she, Emmanuelle, who is finally able to connect Emma simultaneously to both the past and the future. Noëlle's daughter represents a human connection that *embodies* loss. Noëlle, now definitively found, is able both to be lost—and remembered. But not as a name and date inscribed on a tombstone. The living and growing person of Emmanuelle will remind Emma of her sister, and Noëlle will also be remembered by her daughter, who will keep her alive in memory.

After vacillating between anger at the sister who has now twice abandoned her and acceptance of her final gift, Emma is able to make the step of imagination that she could not make earlier, a step that seems to rewrite the story of Lot's wife: "On s'arrête, on se retourne pour regarder les traces de ses pas, puis on se met à chanter, la complainte de Rosa, on bifurque, on avance vers une terre inconnue, on entraîne avec soi une enfant. C'est aimer, dans son état la plus simple" (183) [You stop, you turn around to look at your footprints, then start singing Rosa's lament. You have come to a fork, and you take the road that leads to an unknown land. You are bringing a little girl along with you. This is loving in its simplest form] (178, translation modified). In preparation for Emmanuelle's arrival, Vincent and Emma plan to have the basement renovated, turning it into an office for Vincent and, in the place where Monsieur Girard's blood had splattered the dust, a playroom for Emmanuelle. Emma notes, however, that Monsieur Girard's death will not be forgotten: "elle sera recouverte par des pas d'enfant" (197) [it will be covered over by the footprints of a child] (192). This is a double "recovery," both covering over and recuperation, healing without forgetting.[11]

Stepping in as mother to the motherless child, Emma has chosen to survive in the face of the incomprehensible. She has chosen to affirm and reaffirm the truth of the present in the face of the undeniable evidence of the past. She has found both reason and force of imagination to remake hope each day, to be able to promise her adopted daughter what we all need in part to hear and to believe in order to go on living: *On ne meurt pas ici* [People don't die here]. "Chaque jour, le combat. Chaque jour, répéter, devant une enfant, on ne meurt pas ici" (201) [The fight never ends. Each day one must repeat to a child, "People don't die here"] (196).

Noëlle's death enables Emma finally to stop looking for her mother where she is not and to find her where she is. In this process, Emma becomes, in a sense, her *own* mother. In the closing section of the novel, Emma's mother brings over for the young Emmanuelle's bed a quilt made by *her* mother, and Emma suddenly looks through the double doors of *la memoria*, imagining her mother as her grandmother's daughter and herself as her mother's daughter and the mother of her sister's daughter, seeing the generations of women extending in both directions and finding a place for herself there:

> Alors brusquement les années ont reculé, je l'ai remerciée d'une voix mouillée, ma voix brune de fillette robuste et aussi sa voix à elle quand elle disait merci à sa mère. J'ai eu l'impression de sentir dans ma chair ce que Madame Girard appelle la *memoria*, est-ce cela aussi devenir mère? (202)
>
> [As she did this, the years suddenly fell away. I thanked her in a voice charged with emotion, my dark-and-sturdy-little-girl voice and also *her*

voice when she would say thank you to her own mother. It was as though I could feel in every fibre of my body what Madame Girard calls *memoria*—is that also what it means to become a mother?] (197).

Notes

1. This is not to imply that *La Memoria* could or should be read either as autobiography or as a *roman à clef*, but rather that in raising the question of what makes a fiction (especially through the *mise en abyme* of Emma's scenario) the novel transgresses its own generic limits to suggest along with Anna Quindlen that "fact is different from truth and truth is different from insight" ("How Dark?").

2. Although not epistolary in form, the narration, addressed in the second person to the absent Jérôme, closely resembles that of a personal correspondence. The "impossible dialogue" produced by the absence of the addressee is very similar to that described by Dupré in her article on Geneviève Amyot's *Je t'écrirai encore demain*, a text in which the poet, writing a series of letters to her dead brother, "écrit le deuil" ("Racines" 120) [writes her grieving]. Amyot's prose poetry and Dupré's article set up striking intertextual resonances with *La Memoria*.

3. Unless otherwise noted, translations are my own.

4. "Death is the sanction of everything the storyteller can tell. He has borrowed his authority from death" (Benjamin 1968, 94). "What I call writing, mark, trace, and so on . . . neither lives nor dies; it lives *on (il sur-vit)*" (Derrida 1979, 103).

5. Page numbers refer to *Memoria*, Liedewy Hawke's English translation of Dupré's novel. Where I have modified this translation, I have so indicated.

6. See Nicole Brossard, *The Aerial Letter*: "From excess, from the circle (as the sum of fragments accumulated from having been repeatedly shattered), and from the void, I would then translate the results into the feminine by a shift in meaning going from excess to ecstacy, from circle to spiral, and from void to opening, as a solution for continuity" (71).

7. See *Mauve Desert*, 36, 132, and 202 [*Le Désert mauve*, 51, 141, and 220].

8. Michel Beaujour has written of the term *memoria* in its Renaissance context: "In an instance of fruitful confusion, *memoria* tends to be associated with the work of recuperation from the ancient corpus and, correspondingly, with that of filling in the hiatus between Antiquity and the modern world" (107, my translation).

9. Hawke's pairing of *grief* and *leaf* is a felicitous rendering of Dupré's original rhyming pair, *douleur* (grief) and *couleur* (color). The striking orthographic similarity of the two French words is, however, unavoidably lost in translation.

10. The important role played by the loss of the mother in a woman's quest for her own identity and agency is discussed by both Havercroft and Dupré in the context of their respective readings of Annie Ernaux's *Je ne suis pas sortie de ma nuit* and Genevière Amyot's *Je t'écrirai encore demain*.

11. The text of *La Memoria* is referring only to a literal "recovering," but I believe my double association is valid because the two different verbs in French—*recouvrir* [to cover or cover over] and *recouvrer* [to recover, regain]—are closely related and in fact do share a substantive—*recouvrement* [recovery].

WORKS CITED

Beaujour, Michel. "Une mémoire sans sujet: *Memoria* à la Renaissance." *Corps écrit* 11: 103–10.

Benjamin, Walter. *Illuminations*. Translated by Harry Zohn. New York: Schocken, 1968.

Brison, Susan. "Outliving Oneself: Trauma, Memory, and Personal Identity." In *Feminists Rethink the Self*, edited by Diana T. Meyers, 13–39. Boulder: Westview, 1997.

Brossard, Nicole. *Le Désert mauve*. Montreal: L'Hexagone, 1987. Translated by Susanne de Lotbinière-Harwood as *Mauve Desert*. Toronto: Coach House Press, 1990.

———. *La Lettre aérienne*. Montreal: Les Éditions du remue-ménage, 1985. Translated by Marlene Wildeman as *The Aerial Letter*. Toronto: Women's Press, 1988.

———. "Memory: Hologram of Desire." *Trivia, A Journal of Ideas*. Part I: Memory/Transgression: Women Writing in Québec 13 (Fall 1988): 42–47.

Derrida, Jacques. "Living On: Border Lines." In *Deconstruction and Criticism*, edited by Harold Bloom et al., 75–176. New York: Seabury Press, 1979.

Dupré, Louise. "Écrire est plein de conséquences." Manuscript.

———. *La Memoria*. Montreal: XYZ Éditeur, 1997. Translated by Liedewy Hawke as *Memoria*. Toronto: Dundern Press, 1999.

———. "Racines poétiques, racines maternelles." *Revue des Lettres et de Traduction* 4 (1998): 117–27.

———. "Subjectivité et quête identitaire dans *La dernière femme* de Claudine Bertrand." Manuscript.

———. *Tout près*. Saint-Hippolyte, Que.: Éditions du Noroît, 1998.

Elsaesser, Thomas. *New German Cinema: A History*. Hampshire & London: MacMillan Education Ltd., 1989.

Freud, Sigmund. "A Note upon the 'Mystic Writing-Pad'." *International Journal of Psycho-analysis* 21 (1940): 469–74.

Havercroft, Barbara. "Auto/biographie et agentivité au féminin dans *"Je ne suis pas sortie de ma nuit"* d'Annie Ernaux." Manuscript. Forthcoming in *Femmes de lettres et le français hors frontière*, edited by Lucie Lequin and Catherine Maurikakis. Montreal/Paris: L'Harmattan.

Lowenthal, David. *The Past Is a Foreign Country*. New York: Cambridge University Press, 1985.

Meigs, Mary. "Memories of Age." *Trivia, A Journal of Ideas*. Part I: Memory/Transgression: Women Writing in Québec 13 (Fall 1988): 57–65.

Michaels, Anne. *The Weight of Oranges/Miner's Pond* (poems). Toronto: McClelland & Stewart, 1997.

Quindlen, Anna. "The Past Is Another Country." Review of *My Brother*, by Jamaica Kinkaid. *New York Times Book Review*, 19 October 1997, 7.

———. "How Dark? How Stormy? I Can't Recall." *New York Times Book Review*, 11 May 1997, 35.

The Construction and Deconstruction of Gender in the Novels of Monique Proulx

SANDRA BEYER

IN MONIQUE PROULX'S NOVELS OF THE 1980S, ONE SEES HER ATTEMPTS to identify the feminine and define the role of gender in the creation of her characters. She constructs women from many different walks of life and portrays them in many types of relationships. Some of her female characters are bound by traditional gender roles, whereas others search for new ones. Those who accept traditional roles are failures, and are characterized as either pathetic or ridiculous. Those who attempt to create new roles are defeated, not dramatically, but quietly and passively. Society and their own internal limitations present glass ceilings and brick walls that they cannot break through, even with their energy and many talents. In fact, they see life as a maze in which they lose their way.

Perhaps the most ambitious attempt to construct gender occurs in *Le Sexe des étoiles (The Sex of the Stars)*, a novel published in 1987. One of the main characters is a transsexual in search of the meaning of gender. Besides wearing the outward trappings of pretty dresses and high heels, she/he must find identity as a newly created female while at the same time battling societal prejudices and bureaucratic intransigence. Her quest is not successful, and her final solution is to board a plane for California—one assumes to try her luck in an exile of limitless possibility.

After the failed attempt to construct gender in *Le Sexe des étoiles*, Proulx, in a later novel, *Homme invisible à la fenêtre (Invisible Man at the Window)* (1993), uses her male narrator to deconstruct the idea of gender. Women are reduced to their various components, yet the deconstruction of the feminine when approached in this manner is as inadequate as that generated by previous efforts of construction. This does not mean that the prose writings of Proulx are inadequate or ineffectual—it may simply mean that the definition of gender is elusive, and that it cannot be found in literature. As Julia Kristeva explained: "the feminine in discourse is a very difficult position to specify. As soon as one specifies it, one loses it, seeing that, perhaps the feminine is precisely what escapes nomination and representation" (Guberman 1996, 32).

The narrator of *Homme invisible à la fenêtre* is a male who sees others and the world through the eyes of one of the invisible people in society, for he is a wheelchair-bound paraplegic. Max is a creator, having become a painter since the "Big Bang," his name for the accident that deprived him of the use of the bottom half of his body. He sees himself as a eunuch, the observer who does not act, but only sees and analyses the lives of others. His apartment is the meeting place for his group of friends who come to help him with daily tasks that he cannot manage on his own, but more importantly to seek solace, absolution, or an audience before whom to act out their passions and anguish: "T'es le centre du monde, tu le sais, le seul qui reste là pendant que tout crisse le camp" (229) [You're the center of the world, you know, the only one who stays put while everything else goes to hell].[1] It is thus that Gerald Mortimer, his sculptor friend, characterizes him. Max is well aware of his role of depository of all the chaos that his friends' lives have brought them when he says, "Je suis leur garde-fou de dernière instance" (53) [I'm their guardrail of last resort]. Ironically, his friends come to provide him with food and drink, or to perform various services for him, and to further his career as an artist, but each one brings a burden of angst to lay at his paralyzed feet.

The fact that Proulx has chosen a male narrator is significant. The women in the novel are created by a female author and filtered through the lens of a male narrator. This gives the reader a unique perspective about gender, because what the reader gains from the text is the view of women seen through the eyes of a male—at least, a woman's notion of how men view women. The equivocal nature of the narration is counterweighted by the equivocal nature of gender itself, according to Proulx, whose works, while preoccupied with the idea of being male or female and the consequences thereof, never reach a convincing conclusion about the role of gender in the creation of characters.

Although Max, the narrator, has performed oral sex on two of the women in his life since the accident, he sees himself as, "cette chose sur une chaise qui est moi" (13) [this thing on a chair that is me] and speaks of his impotence. He provides the women in the novel with a male, but a safe one; he cannot beat them, betray them, or be unfaithful to them. What they do not realize is that, while he is incapable of committing those typically male sins, he can deconstruct them, depersonalize them, and in so doing destroy their very essence. At one point in the novel, Maggie, the artists' and photographers' model, asks Max to paint her entire body, not just her "maudite tête blonde" (156) [damned blonde head]. He refuses, saying: "Je ne dessine pas, je ne peins rien, surtout pas son corps qui vit trop fort en ce moment pour l'immobiliser sur une toile" (158) [I don't draw, I paint nothing, especially not her body that is living too intensely at this moment to immobilize on a canvas]. Max, the artist, is not interested in creating a living woman on canvas; he is like the collector who pins beautiful specimens of dead butterflies on a matting. It is only the outward beauty that interests the artist, not the profound self of the model.

This beautiful model, Maggie, is an extreme example of woman as victim. This "paysage de juin" (19) (June landscape), as Max calls her, is from the village of Labelle, where she was married to Gaëtan, whose ambition it was to "éteindre en elle ce qui pouvait devenir incendiaire" (19) [extinguish in her what could catch fire]. She went to Montréal, where, because of her beauty, she found jobs as an artists' and photographers' model, as well as minor roles in film. Her lover and film director, Martin, beats her: "Il veut me tuer il m'a battue c'est horrible Max, il m'aime je l'aime c'est extraordinaire qu'il m'aime" (44) [He wants to kill me he beat me it's horrible Max, he loves me I love him it's extraordinary that he loves me].

Soon after arriving at Max's apartment, Maggie meets Gerald Mortimer, and the two of them become lovers. Her lot in love does not improve, for Mortimer, another artist, treats her as an object. After their first meeting, Mortimer says that beauty is "une maladie métaphysique" (24) (metaphysical disease). His coldness as he attempts to "cure" that malady, drives her to the extreme measure of self-mutilation. She cuts off her hair, her eyelashes and brows, and smears herself with a horrific mixture of paint, ink, glue, and peroxide (198–99). Mortimer's reaction is to tell her to wash it off. When he finds out that Maggie and Max have made love, he suggests that they share her (163). Max has the humanity to suggest that she might have her own ideas about that. She sees herself on film, and says that a woman as beautiful as that must be happy. She ends her tirade about the animal passion her beauty incites in men and the glacial stares it receives from women by saying, "tout cela s'adresse à elle, la belle fille, celle qui est tellement heureuse et qui n'existe pas" (158) [all of that is directed at her, the beautiful girl, who is so happy and who doesn't exist]. Her very beauty has been the cause of her victimization, and eventually leads to the obliteration of the person inside the beautiful body.

Not only has he made study after study of Maggie's magnificent head, but he has deconstructed and objectified other women of his acquaintance. He has painted many times the hands of Julienne, his mother, and the arms of Pauline, one of the habitués of his apartment, but he has never painted the entire woman. When he first sees Lady, his former lover, in the apartment across from his, he describes her: "C'est une femme tout en lignes longues, une architecture pure et dépouillée qui ne laisse rien paraître de ce qui s'officie à l'intérieur" (29) [She is a woman drawn entirely in long lines, a pure stark architecture that shows nothing of what is going on inside]. He says this with the admiration of a painter interested only in the exterior aspects of his model. At the end of the novel, when he paints a self-portrait, he paints himself with Maggie's head, Pauline's arms, and Julienne's hands. By so doing, he steals their bodies, but is indifferent to their souls. This depersonalization of women and the destruction of their essence are consonant with a leitmotiv that runs through Québécois novels: "Feeling mutilated, impotent, unsure of his identity, and ill at ease in his body, [the male] dreams of a woman in whose embrace he can allow his identity to dissolve, and yet at the same time whom he can dominate using her submission and humiliation as a proof of his power" (Smart 1991, 192). Of course, Max has an even greater need to humiliate women, because his mutilation and impotence are not only metaphysical, but also physical.

Max does paint the entire body of his fellow artist and the friend, Gerald Mortimer, who secretly buys all of Max's work, and who is identified as the driver of the truck in which Max was riding at the time of the accident. Mortimer is an artist of genius, according to Max, as well as the paraplegic's anonymous benefactor. Max says, "je te veux nu, rugissant et infernal car il faut bien que je te vole ton âme" (235) [I want you naked, roaring and infernal for I must steal your soul from you]. He envies the passion, both aesthetic and carnal that animates Mortimer, and wishes to make it his own. There is nothing in Maggie, Pauline, or Julienne that Max wishes to possess, other than certain body parts.

The two women in the novel who are of the greatest importance to Max are his mother (Julienne) and Lady. The way these two women—the only ones in the novel who knew him before the accident—are introduced provides a clear indication of how the narrator deconstructs women. Julienne, Max's mother, is first presented as a voice on the telephone answering machine. She leaves several messages, none of them revealing any emotional content whatsoever: "Bonjour, Max, c'est moi, c'est maman. A plus tard . . ." (31) [Hello, Max, it's me, it's mom. Later . . .]. Yet, Max's reaction is

"Maman, mot presque exécré, si j'avais des forces pour haïr, maman, c'est maman. Comment les éliminer tout à fait, ces témoins gênants d'avant le Big Bang, comment transformer sa vie en film de gangsters" (31) [Mom, an almost hateful word, if I had the strength to hate, mom, it's mom. How can I rub them out completely, these troublesome witnesses from before the Big Bang, how can I change my life into a gangster movie]?

Julienne is next introduced to the reader by the two jars of gooseberry jam she leaves outside her son's door. The funereal images evoked by the jam, the berries that are "les cadavres blafards qui tanguent dans le formol du sirop" (40) [the pallid cadavers floating in the syrupy formalin], and "le parfum confit du passé qui se retourne dans sa tombe, le parfum de Julienne" (40) [the preserved perfume of the past turning over in its grave, Julienne's perfume] show that Max associates the idea of mother with death, rather than with life. Julienne next appears at the door, and Max objectifies her. She becomes the odor of wool and old perfume, the cloche hat. He says, "Ça frappe" (54) [It's knocking]. Finally, he concedes her humanity by saying, "elle frappe" (54) [she's knocking].

It would be easy to assume that Julienne had been a difficult mother, or that she had reacted badly to Max's accident. He explains that "ce qu'elle voit, c'est une victime pathétique, une métaphore pitoyable de l'injustice divine" (65) [what she sees is a pathetic victim, a pitiful metaphor of divine injustice]. He fears her pity and her palpable suffering. He also fears her reproaches about his abandonment of her, since he has not seen her for two years. However, when he finally lets her visit him, she talks about the weather, taxes, and her rheumatism. She stays just long enough to be polite, and he wonders, "Je me demande comment j'ai pu avoir peur d'elle, quelle perversité me l'a fait tenir à distance si longtemps" (67) [I wonder how I could have been afraid of her, what perversity made me hold her at a distance for so long]. He invites her to come back, but she says that she does not want to bother him.

Later in the novel, she moves into the apartment next to that of her son, and on one occasion Max visits her. All is as he remembers it in her home. She cooks for him, offers to knit for him, and tricks him into thinking that the two of them are thirty years younger, that he is still a child whose mother can protect him from all of the evils of the world. She calls her apartment an "oasis de souvenirs (124)" [oasis of memory] where all is possible. His reaction is to leave immediately, promising to move as soon as he can. He is in such a rage when he leaves her apartment that he summons Gerald

Mortimer, and the two of them exchange furious blows: "je le frappe je le frappe et je ne sais plus qui de lui ou de moi encaisse les blessures et les inflige" (125) [I hit him and hit him and I no longer know whether he or I receive the wounds or deliver them]. Swigart says that this rage is a son's typical reaction to his mother: "Rage toward those we love, love toward those we hate, whose power we envy; longing for the one who frustrates us: Ambivalence is so painful that children put off feeling it as long as they can, turning maternal images into the 'Good Mother' and 'Bad Witch' of fairy tales" (Swigart 1991, 80).

The reader might reasonably assume that the alienation between mother and son was a result of his accident. It could well be that the tenderness shown by Julienne was a manifestation of pity, something that the artist shuns, while at the same time he uses this same pity to manipulate his friends. However, the relationship between the other mother-son pair in the novel, Pauline and Laurel, makes it clear that this is not the complete explanation. Laurel, a seventeen-year-old, is also fleeing his mother. He comes to Max's apartment to escape his mother, and to try out his new adult persona. He confides in Max about his mistress, a woman much older than he, who opens to him the world of the intellect and the arts. When Laurel stays out all night, Pauline spends the whole night searching for him in bars, and concludes the vigil at Max's apartment, where she pours out her fears for her son. Laurel asks Max's help in dealing with Pauline: "Je peux plus la voir. Le matin, je me lève plus tard pour pas déjeuner avec elle. Je veux plus qu'elle me regarde avec ses yeux cernés . . . pourquoi elle reste là, toujours, comme si rien avait changé" (139) [I can't stand to see her. I get up later in the morning to keep from having breakfast with her. I can't stand for her to look at me with her haggard eyes . . . why does she stand there, always, as if nothing has changed]? There are many recent studies of motherhood, both literary and psychological, and many of them center on the mother-daughter relationship. However, most studies of the mother-son relationship agree on the necessity of the son rebelling against the mother to achieve a virility that is thwarted by "the mythical mother fantasized as overwhelming and 'castrating' by the patriarchal mind" (Smart 1991, 191).

While Julienne, Max's mother, causes her son torment because of her very kindness and passive approach to reconciliation, the other important woman in Max's life, Lady, aggressively attempts to see him and begin again the relationship they had before the Big Bang. Max deconstructs her, just as he has the other women in his life. When he first sees her in the window across from his, he admires the "pure architecture" of the "femme-garçon . . . une tête d'héroïne romantique sur un corps chenu de garçon. Les poignets fins, le cou long, comme un filet" (30) [woman/boy . . . a romantic heroine's head on the aging body of a boy. The slim wrists, the long neck, like a thread].

As in the case of Julienne, Max holds Lady at arm's length by listening to her endless messages on his answering machine and refusing to talk to her. Her many messages run the gamut from anger and frustration to pleading. He considers disconnecting the telephone, but finally she breaks down his resistance by accusing him of base cowardice. He tells her that he has gained twenty pounds, is now blind and deaf, and therefore does not hear her. Max's silence broken, the two former lovers begin an intermittent conversation, partly by telephone, partly nonverbal communication from their respective apartment windows. Lady explains that she has rented the apartment to escape from her normal life and spend the nights writing a play—a love story that takes place over the telephone.

Up to that point, Max has been unable to paint Lady, the "architecture pure" that he sees in the window. However, when she brings her meal to the window and hungrily devours a steak, he says that he can now finally draw her "dans sa grâce féroce de carnivore" (196) [in her fierce carnivorous grace]. He has her do a sort of strip-tease in front of the window, and he says, "je la prends toute ainsi, ma plume comme un sexe dirigeable et ferme, je la dessine les jambes entravées et la tête rejetée vers l'arrière, les mains entre les cuisses et le regard parti loin dans le plaisir tandis que sa voix rauque m'écorche en profondeur et m'arrache des lambeaux et défaille"(197) [I take her like that, my pen like a controllable rigid penis, I draw her with her legs spread and her head rearing back, her hands between her thighs and her gaze lost in pleasure while her hoarse voice chafes me deep within and tears me to shreds and dies away]. Lady, with her persistent messages and pleas, has avoided the fate of the other women in the novel, that of deconstruction to her various body parts, an arm or a blonde head.

The author, however, does not permit the "whole" Lady to reenter Max's life. Lady's pleading for a face-to-face meeting appears to be bearing fruit, and the artist says that he will go to her apartment to see her. After a most painful ride on his "fidèle Rosinante" (faithful Rosinante), as he calls his wheelchair, he arrives at her apartment with help from two strangers who take pity on him, only to find that she has fled, leaving the remains of her meal behind and her door wide open. The one woman whose whole body he has painted has vanished, and with her his only hope of transcending his injury and creating a new relationship with a woman.

There is a certain symmetry in Max's relationships with Julienne and Lady. He flees Julienne and her unconditional love; Lady flees Max and his inconsistent behavior—the act of drawing her, which, in his eyes, and hers, is sexual, followed by silence, followed by his statement that he will go to her apartment. Max runs away from his mother because he cannot stand the flood of emotions that overtakes him when he is with her; Lady runs away because she cannot face the emotions she would feel if she saw him paralyzed and in his wheelchair.

The whole question of gender, and what it means to be female or male, is treated ambiguously in *Homme invisible*. Early in the novel, Max makes a statement in which he decries the current social construction of the battle between the sexes: "Cette époque est idiote, qui n'en finit plus de dresser l'un contre l'autre ce qui est fait pour se mêler, frappant les homme d'incurable culpabilité dont ils émergent en brutes épaisses ou en mollassons racornis, muant les femmes en hypocrites vierges offensées qui affichent des décolletés audacieux pour mieux émasculer la main qui osera s'y aventurer" (46) [This is an idiotic age that pits those who are meant to be one against each other, tarring men with insurmountable guilt that makes them into brutal dullards or shriveled wimps, and turns women into offended virginal hypocrites who provocatively display their breasts, all the better to emasculate the hand that dares venture toward them]. He then goes on to say that the only women he could love are strong women who are on an equal footing with men.

Toward the end of the novel, however, he expresses a conflicting point of view. As his mind replays the accident, he says: "le camion amorçait une danse longue longue sur le flanc et sur le dos, le camion pattes en l'air dessus dessous comme savent danser les camions et les femmes qui retournent à l'état sauvage loin des mains directives des hommes" (174) [the truck was starting a long long dance on its side and on its back, the truck its paws in the air upside down like trucks and women can dance when they return to their wild state outside of the controlling hands of men]. Women are meant to be dominated by men or they dance out of control, Max says, and the reader wonders what has occurred in the course of the novel to change his mind from his earlier, almost feminist, stance. He has not yet seen Lady, and the situation with his mother has not yet exploded. It is possible that Proulx is telling the reader that even the men who express feminist views are reciting politically correct speeches, but in the very depths of their consciousness, in the place inhabited by their innermost selves, they feel that women in their natural state are wild and irresponsibly sexual, the perpetrators of original sin, and that men need to control female instincts.

The whole question of gender in Proulx's novels is ambiguous, because the female author is seeing reality through the eyes of a male. There is in the text a vivid indictment of the practice of separating mind and body, a characteristic of Western literature. Christa Wolf, as well as other critics, says that "women, for historical and biological reasons, experience a different reality than men." They are "the objects of objects, second-degree objects, frequently the objects of men who are themselves objects" (Wolf 1984, 259). Is it then possible for a woman to write an authentic work through a man's voice, albeit a man who, because of a physical disability, is himself an "other"? The questions posed by the writings of Monique Proulx are perhaps a result of "writing in such a way that otherness, the real, and the temporal realm speak through the disorganized texture of the text" (Smart 1991, 12). One might add that these contradictory elements speak through the disorganized texture of life itself.

Note

1. Unless otherwise noted, all translations are my own.

Works cited

Guberman, Ross Mitchell, ed. *Julia Kristeva Interviews*. New York: Columbia University Press, 1996.

Proulx, Monique. *Homme invisible à la fenêtre*. Montréal: Boréal/Seuil, 1993.

———. *Le Sexe des étoiles*. Montréal: Québec/Amérique, 1987.

Smart, Patricia. *Writing in the Father's House: The Emergence of the Feminine in the Quebec Literary Tradition*. Toronto: University of Toronto Press, 1991.

Swigart, Jane. *The Myth of the Bad Mother: The Emotional Realities of Mothering*. New York: Doubleday, 1991.

Wolf, Christa. *Cassandra*. New York: Farrar, Straus, Giroux, 1984.

The Other Family Romance: Daughters and Fathers in Québec Women's Fiction of the Nineties

LORI SAINT-MARTIN

WHILE THE MOTHER-DAUGHTER BOND HAS FOR SOME TIME BEEN A nexus of exploration, perhaps even a cultural commonplace, much less has been written about the father-daughter relationship. In an attempt to write their way out of a patriarchal cultural context, where women played at best a supporting role, and to challenge the literary and critical canon's emphasis on male experience (including Oedipal rivalry between fathers and sons), many women writers, theoreticians, and critics worked to develop a female perspective and a woman's culture that emphasized bonds among women, especially the mother-daughter relationship, which came to be seen as the bedrock of female identity. The "other" family romance, the daughter-father relationship, paled in comparison.[1]

The power of pre-Oedipal mothers, as opposed to patriarchal mothers who have only their powerlessness and their fearful acquiescence to pass on, is fantasized as elemental, all-encompassing, tender, benevolent, and nourishing for daughters, whether that symbolic power can be actualized in the world of patriarchy or not. The mother-artist of Gabrielle Roy, identified metaphorically with undulating hills and broad, flowing rivers; the protective female chorus of voices from the sea in Anne Hébert's *Les Fous de Bassan (In the Shadow of the Wind)*; and the fantasized pre-Oedipal and prepatriarchal mother-goddesses of Louky Bersianik, Madeleine Gagnon, and Jovette Marchessault are among these benevolent mother figures. The father, however, is solidly and almost irrevocably linked to patriarchal power, which he at once symbolizes, embodies, and enforces, a power that feminists emphatically reject. Do feminist daughters have to throw out the father with the bathwater of patriarchy? In their struggle to discover the human being behind the patriarchal mother who passed on the culture's taboos and rigid sex roles, have daughters made an effort to discover the real and sometimes vulnerable man behind the figurehead of the patriarchal father?

What Marianne Hirsch calls the "feminist family romance" of the 1970s and what Elaine Showalter calls the "sustained quest" for the mother presupposes "the elimination of fathers" as "either a precondition or an important preoccupation of female plots" (Hirsch 1989, 121) and a fantasized return to the pre-Oedipal realm of mother-daughter union. In Québec, too, much of the experimental feminist writing of the 1970s, and even the mainstream novel of that time, seemed to have given up on the father entirely. Similarly, although mother-daughter relationships in Québec literature have been widely explored (Forsyth, Gould, Saint-Martin, and Smart), the father-daughter bond has been of less interest to critics, with Smart's book being a notable exception. More recently, although the mother-daughter relationship continues to inspire today's writers, the father's role has been attracting much more attention. This renewed interest in fathers began in the 1980s, with Francine Noël's elusive but fascinating Tom (*Maryse* 1983); Jovette Marchessault's humanitarian "Bangor Lion" (*Des Cailloux blancs pour les forêts obscures* [*White Pebbles in the Dark Forests*] 1987); Monique Proulx's seductive transsexual Marie-Pierre (*Le Sexe des étoiles* [*Sex of the Stars*] 1987); Francine d'Amour's dying alcoholic Charles (*Les Dimanches sont mortels* [*Sundays are Deadly*] 1987); and many others. The 1990s have consolidated the trend. A number of women writers of Québec have begun to explore the complex knots, ambivalences, longings, resentments, and gratitude the father-daughter relationship holds. Among them, Lise Lacasse, Ying Chen, and Monique LaRue are noteworthy.

In this paper, I will be studying four other works: "La Gifle" ("The Slap"), a short story by Christiane Teasdale; "Friperie" ("Used Clothing Store"), a short story by Élise Turcotte; *Laurence*, France Théoret's latest novel; and *La Danse juive* (*The Jewish Dance*), just published by Lise Tremblay. These works sketch a wide-ranging variety of bonds, from seduction to rage, from rejection to compassion, and invite us to turn our gaze toward what I call the "other family romance."

Fathers and Daughters: A Story of Oedipal Power

As Linda Boose points out in her introduction to *Daughters and Fathers* (2), of all the parent-child figures analyzed in Western theory and fiction, father and son are the most visible pair, followed by mother and son; feminist theory has emphasized mother-daughter pairs, while the narrative of father and daughter was long shrouded in silence. Theoreticians of literature (who have, until recently, ignored the bulk of women's writing) tell us that Oedipal rivalry between fathers and sons lies at the very heart of plot. As different as they may be, Roland Barthes, Harold Bloom, Peter Brooks, René Girard, Marthe Robert, and countless others, all drawing on Freudian and/or Lacanian theory, see male rivalry, real or symbolic castration, competition for the mother and other females, and parricide as the story of "our" culture. Needless to say, and as many feminist critics, from Virginia Woolf to Luce Irigaray and a host of our contemporaries have pointed out, this story is equally significant in terms of everything it leaves out, most notably women's experience, bonds between women, particularly between mothers and daughters, and female subjectivity. Women's silence and subservience have been essential to this plot, which, although entirely focused on males, is predicated on, and cannot survive without, female presence and compliance. As Luce Irigaray puts it, the eternal tragedy of mothers and daughters is that they have been separated from one another and from their own agency and sense of self by the cultural laws that subordinate them to men: daughters belong to the father until he hands them over to a husband of his choice. Female genealogies have been lost, and women have been forced into an alien symbolic order: "Le complexe d'Oedipe féminin, c'est finalement l'entrée de la femme dans un système de valeurs qui n'est pas le sien, et où elle ne peut 'apparaître' et circuler qu'enveloppée dans les besoins-désirs-fantasmes des autres-hommes" (Irigaray 132) [In the last analysis, the female Oedipus complex is woman's entry into a system of values that is not hers, and in which she can "appear" and circulate only when enveloped in the needs/desires/fantasies of others, namely, men] (134).

For daughters and fathers, the Oedipal rivalry paradigm does not hold, because, culturally speaking, the daughter does not stand to inherit the father's material and spiritual kingdom of symbolic, social, and domestic power: that honor is reserved for the son (since the mother has little or nothing of her own to pass on, the daughter is effectively disinherited). What shape, then, will women's writing about fathers take? What will it substitute for Oedipal rivalry? As many critics, including Marianne Hirsch, have shown, the daughter's story will be a complex one. To the well-known patterns of Oedipal rejection and attraction, ambivalence and oscillation, feminist daughters add other shifts and mixed loyalties: ambivalence about the mother's powerlessness, a move toward the mother to work out a female genealogy, rejection of the father and of the power and social order he represents.

When women write, then, they of necessity tell *another* story, one that has traditionally been seen as marginal, minor, un-great, banal yet threatening. Certainly, if Freud was correct in supposing that plot is a direct outgrowth of each writer's own "family romance," then differences in male and female pre-Oedipal and Oedipal relationships will strongly influence novelistic form and content (Hirsch).

While Irigaray's reading and her call to explore "female genealogies" (cross-generational female relationships and transmission) have struck responsive chords in many women, she sees the father as an all-powerful being, as a disembodied presence, a pure incarnation of the Law. She rarely, if ever, sees him as what he also is for most daughters: a human being who awakens powerful, conflicting emotions in his female children, not just submission or rebellion, and whose own desires, fears, conflicts, and ambivalences profoundly affect them, as well. The awe-inspiring power of the father, so idealized, even when hated, by many male writers—no doubt because the son has no interest in truly challenging a power he hopes one day to claim for his own—is often criticized by women writers who challenge and refigure his "centrality and omnipotence" (Yaeger x). Feminists have long realized that "the father's house" or "the name of the father" refers not only to a literal dwelling and a family structure, but also, metaphorically, to the entire space of Western culture, with its religious, political, social and cultural systems, its myths, its ideology, and its literary forms (Boose, Smart).

However, this conflation of the father with patriarchy does not tell the whole story: the father is always both singular and plural, linked to powerful myths yet rooted in historical reality, synecdoche as much as metaphor, in Beth Kowaleski-Wallace's phrase (Yaeger 296–311). In order to challenge the powers that be, "it is essential not only to explore the father's diverging jural, political, familial, racial, and psychological positions but also to examine these divergences within individual father figures" (Yaeger xiv), while still recalling their links with "the disembodied voice of patriarchal culture—the voice that is amorphous, unlocatable, and hence reverberates everywhere" (Boose 6).

Playing Chess with the Patriarch: Christiane Teasdale's "La gifle" ("The slap")

This short but powerful story opens Christiane Teasdale's ironically titled debut collection, *À propos de l'amour (About Love)*

(1990). It is 1973, and for the first time Marie is playing chess with her father after a crash course on the way the pieces move. Immediately after she captures one of his bishops with a pawn and begins joyfully to anticipate her victory and his humiliation, he triumphantly announces he has checkmated her. Without thinking, she slaps him violently in the face and runs to her room, halfway between laughter and tears.

Early on in the story, we learn that every morning, as he drives her to high school, Marie's father lectures her on male superiority: "Les femmes sont inférieures aux hommes, commence-t-il. Vous êtes inférieures, c'est prouvé" (11) [Women are inferior to men, he begins. You're inferior, it's been proven].[2] He goes on to argue, familiarly, that there have never been any great women writers, painters, musicians, or scientists. Marie is forced to listen calmly and politely; he would not tolerate any signs of resistance or skepticism. The "disembodied voice of patriarchal culture" (Boose 6) takes on a tangible form here. When she mentions Marie Curie, he answers that she was only her husband's assistant. The scene thus becomes a metaphor of the daughter's position within traditional male culture: a prisoner in a confined space where she is subjected to the father's discourse on her natural, eternal inferiority and dares not even show her anger. The power relationship between "the two figures most asymmetrically proportioned in terms of gender, age, authority, and cultural privilege" (Boose 20) could hardly be more unequal. The story charts both the daughter's resistance (she tries not to listen to her father, instead pursuing her own train of thought) and her intimate fear that his view of women is accurate: "Pourtant, lorsqu'elle descend devant la porte du collège, ses livres sous le bras, la nausée est là quand même avec une sorte de lourdeur dans l'esprit. Et un début de panique, aussi, parce qu'il a peut-être raison?" (Teasdale 12) [And yet, when she gets out of the car in front of the high school with her books under her arm, she still has the sick feeling along with a heavy spirit. And the beginnings of panic as well, because he just might be right?].

The two sentences just quoted, with their mingling of physical and spiritual malaise, emphasize the power of the father's apparent lack of body. Marie's father illustrates Jane Gallop's assertion that "By giving up their bodies, men gain power—the power to theorize, to represent themselves, to exchange women, to reproduce themselves and mark their offspring with their name" (67). Whereas Marie's bodily states, her feeling of nausea and physical, even sexual vulnerability (as she leaves the room after slapping her father, she is holding "une main sur le ventre" [a hand on her stomach]) are often described in the text, the father is a disembodied presence, a voice beside her in the car hammering home the litany of male superiority, eyes and brain facing her across the chessboard, not a body at all. He is a male-supremacist crusader with history and the law on his side.

Still, the text suggests a certain vulnerability on the father's part. Before enlisting Marie to play chess, he tries to convince his wife to play cards with him, but she "languit dans leur chambre rose devant des magazines ou une réussite"(10) [languishes in the pink bedroom with magazines or a game of solitaire] and refuses to play. He is bored and "en a marre de jouer seul" (10) [tired of playing alone]; his daughter does him a favor when she tears herself away from *Wuthering Heights*[3] to play with him. In other words, the father's game is predicated on mother and daughter as willing players; their refusal would stalemate him. Similarly, his need to lecture his daughter about male superiority is a sign of weakness rather than strength, a bluster rather than a calm conviction. His words are only "true" insofar as the daughter believes and internalizes them.

As the chess match begins, Marie hopes to beat the father at his own game. Because she knows he has spent evening after evening poring over books of strategy, "le battre par la voie normale est chose impossible" (9) [beating him in the normal way is impossible]. She adopts a different strategy, playing erratically, intuitively, "dans le désordre total" (9) [in total disorder], hoping to stumble upon the chink in his armor or to be visited by a flash of inspiration. Her father, in contrast, is ponderous but methodical and ruthless; he knows the rules and the ropes. The magic Marie was hoping for never materializes; the defeat is, again, a metaphor for the way this daughter has been deprived of her own style, her own approach.

In fact, chess is the father's game par excellence, based as it is on abstract reasoning and strict, unvarying rules, with its emphasis on strategy, its near-elimination of chance, and its vision of the world as a battlefield where opposing forces clash and lock into combat to the death (or at least to a stalemate). Here, the game becomes a war between the generations and the sexes, with the odds stacked against the daughter from the beginning, since she is ignorant of its rules and untrained in its subtleties. Like those who argue that the dearth of great women artists demonstrates male superiority, ignoring social, psychological and family obstacles as well as gender-biased conventions of what greatness really is, Marie's father concludes from his easy victory that his daughter "really" is inferior. The father's game, simply, is power. Under the iron glove is an iron fist. At the same time, however, and precisely because of its emphasis on rules rather than on brute force, chess is at least potentially winnable for the daughter, if, that is, she is willing to play by the rules, perhaps losing as much as she gains in the process. Marie's erratic style condemns her to defeat, but at least it is hers.

How, finally, should one interpret Marie's slapping her father as he gloats over his victory? The gesture is shocking and, at least partially, empowering for the daughter: she has finally broken through her father's armor, reversed the power distribution between them (he is now the one who is surprised and hurt, as she was a moment before), and expressed her own repressed aggression. Slapping her father is also a way of reminding him that he has a body, that he is vulnerable and can, literally and figuratively, be touched by his daughter: she can put her mark on him. He is not likely to forget what she did to him.

At the same time, Marie's violent reaction ironically illustrates her powerlessness and confirms her defeat. Unable to win, she resorts to blind violence. She is, therefore, clearly and ironically, her father's daughter, using physical violence (usually associated with the father rather than the daughter) to fight his symbolic violence. The battle is lost in advance, not only because of the father's greater physical strength, whether he elects to use it or keeps it in check (there is no sign in this text of physical violence on his part), but also because the violence turns against the daughter, who is unable to confront the father verbally or to play by his rules. Her father laughs as he announces he has checkmated her. She laughs after slapping him, but her joy quickly turns into sadness: "de drôles de petits hoquets qui par moments ressemblent à des sanglots" (14) [strange little hiccups that sometimes sound like sobs].

The chess game and the ensuing slap are a powerful metaphor of the daughter's double bind in patriarchy: playing the father's game is self-destructive for her, but it is the only game in town. The silent woman in the pink bedroom who refuses altogether to play the father's game seems, in retrospect, more powerful than she first appeared. Marie's "uncontrollable laughter" shows how the father's culture makes the daughter hysterical and therefore unable to escape the father's rule(s).

A Troubled Alliance: Elise Turcotte's "Friperie" ("Used Clothing Store")

By contrast, the father figure in Élise Turcotte's "Friperie," the first story in her short-story collection (she has also published several books of poetry and two novels), is her ally against her overly glamorous, unloving mother. The story's main action occurs in a secondhand clothing store, the "friperie" of the title. The story describes the narrator's (Marie's) chance encounter with her mother, who left her family years ago and whom Marie barely knows. The mother, still beautiful and sensual, makes Marie feel like "un vieux tas de feuilles mortes" (14) [an old heap of dead leaves]; she quickly makes friends with the saleswoman, and they conspire to make Marie buy a particularly unbecoming black dress. This story is told among flashbacks relating a similar incident in a clothing store when Marie was a preteen, various examples of Marie's mother's indifference and neglect, and the story of the day she left her family and moved away, with another woman helping her carry her belongings to her car.

Marie describes her mother's alluring beauty and her own feelings of inadequacy: she hates her looks and, although she is well educated and successful, she is out of touch with her own desire: "je n'ai jamais su ce que je désirais. Je n'ai jamais su comment m'habiller, comment arranger mes cheveux, comment plaire" (14) [I've never known what I wanted. I've never known how to dress, how to do my hair, how to make myself attractive]. All these problems, she makes abundantly clear, are her mother's fault: her mother has always humiliated her—for example, by loudly insisting, in front of customers and saleswomen, on buying Marie a bra when she was ten and flat-chested, then taking advantage of her shame and confusion to force an ugly outfit upon her. Every time she sees Marie, the mother lets drop a single devastating phrase ("Your skirt is too long"; "Your hair is too short") before floating away again "avec des cheveux légers comme le vent" (15) [with her hair light as the wind]. The fitting room, with its unflattering mirrors, its critical saleswomen, and, just outside, the mother's piercing gaze ("Sortir d'une cabine d'essayage devant elle est la pire chose qui puisse m'arriver" [18] [Coming out of a fitting room in front of her is the worst thing that could happen to me]) is a kind of parody of what the good mother's gaze should be to allow for the child's sense of selfhood to develop, according to psychoanalysts like D. W. Winnicott.

What recourse, then, does this damaged daughter have? To whom can she turn when her mother turns her attention elsewhere, particularly to the little dogs she is inordinately fond of? When one of these dogs bites Marie as a child, the mother laughs and rushes off to Mass, while her father bandages her hand and takes her to the Dairy Queen. Eating ice cream becomes a weekly ritual for father and daughter: the father becomes symbolically far more cherishing and nourishing than the mother, intent mostly on making her escape. In this sense, the father replaces the mother as mother figure (the mother is in no sense maternal) even before she leaves. The daughter turns away from the mother's beauty and seduction, preferring her father as he seems to prefer her. Interestingly enough, although the mother's power game with its devastating effects on Marie is described in detail, the father seems a stranger to manipulation of any kind; he is pure goodness, pure nourishment. The mother is referred to only as "she" until the final lines of the story, keeping her at a distance (it is only gradually that the reader recognizes her as Marie's mother), while the father is consistently referred to as "my father" rather than "he," emphasizing the connection between the two. At the end of the story, after leaving the clothing store, Marie's mother holds out her business card. Marie immediately calls her father and goes to his home, where they add the business card to a box of other objects. The final lines of the story are: "C'est ainsi que nous transformons ma mère en souvenir. Nous l'avons simplifiée" (24) [That's how we turn my mother into a memory. We have simplified her]. This father-daughter alliance against the powerful, seductive mother-wife is their only defense against grief and loss after she leaves them both. It would seem that Marie has indeed "simplified" not only her mother but also her family dynamics: she sees her mother as the source of all her ills and her father as a benevolent, nourishing presence. Although Marie dreams of killing both her mother and her mother's dog, her father is entirely spared.

Here, then, is a young woman who seems to have successfully performed the transfer of allegiance Freud considers necessary to normal femininity, turning away from the mother and toward the father, binding with him against her; and yet she is troubled, narcissistically damaged, half-dead spiritually. An orthodox Freudian might argue that the father is too weak, not phallic enough, to pull the daughter away from the mother; a feminist reading would suggest instead that both father and daughter are refusing here to come to terms with the mother's strength, seduction, and physical presence (or absence), preferring to avert their gaze and "simplify" her. Either way, the story shows how even father-as-ally can be eclipsed by a powerful mother, and how precarious the daughter's alliance with him can be, particularly when he is, like her, a wounded child rather than an adult, let alone a god.

Beyond the Name of the Father: France Théoret's *Laurence*

France Théoret is one of the best-known of a group of Québec feminist writers who began their careers in the 1970s by breaking with traditional language, plot, and narrative structure in an attempt to forge a politically aware, gender-marked "writing in the feminine" (*écriture au féminin*). More recently, she has written a realistic work of fiction, *Laurence* (1996), a historical novel about a young woman who, between 1928 and 1945, when the novel ends, leaves her impoverished rural family of fifteen and moves to the city, becomes a nurse, falls in and out of love, makes friends, and gradually becomes a free woman. One of the most serious obstacles to her freedom is her compassion for her ailing mother and her sense of obligation to her father, a cold, severe figure, the law incarnate. Despite the financial difficulties that make him dependent on his children—Laurence will continue to send him a large chunk of her salary for most of her adult life—the father remains as authoritarian as ever and insists on their debt to him. He clings to all his privileges, including violence (he once beat Laurence so badly that she spent four days in bed), convinces himself that he is all-seeing (he believes, wrongly, that none of his children have ever lied to him), and orders his adult daughter to change out of a skirt that reveals an inch of kneecap. A first-class manipulator, he knows how to awaken her pity and compassion with his hard-luck stories. His ability to convert his need into her debt is impressive. Laurence loves him, loves to listen to him talk, longs to escape him, longs to help him. His words have marked her, and one of her tasks in life will be to separate her view of the world, her language, from his, and to leave his house figuratively as well as literally.

This task is complicated by the fact that, whereas she refuses to become a nun or to marry and have children, the typical fates of women in Québec at that time, Laurence believes that overt rebellion would damage her as well as her family. She begins looking for ways to reconcile her sense of family solidarity and her need to break free. The novel compellingly dramatizes the ways in which fathers (and weak, needy mothers) force or seduce daughters into becoming symbolic mothers, like Laurence's sister Rosalie, who gives her life up to run the father's home after the mother takes to her bed, or Laurence herself, who, in addition to taking care of her sister Odette, who comes to live with her in Montreal, provides for other children in the family, thus becoming a symbolic father as well. As the novel progresses, Laurence gradually frees herself: elegant clothes, paid work, female friendships, love affairs, time to walk alone and to think things through—all are at once the means she uses to assert her agency and the concrete signs of her success. Later on, and against the active opposition of family members, she works to ensure her financial security by having several rental units built, thereby finding her own house, her own space, to replace the father's. At the same time, she continues to help family members and friends, paying for her sisters to enter a convent; covering the costs of an illegal abortion for a classmate; buying skis, pretty dresses; and music lessons for Odette in addition to the necessities of life. Laurence seems to have struck a fine balance between the need for closeness and the need for autonomy, which many psychologists and psychoanalysts have identified as a serious problem for women.

Laurence's success would seem to come to a large extent from her serene, patient approach to life. Although she refuses to follow her society's gender expectations, she is not openly violent or defiant as an adult, as she was as a young girl; she simply goes her own way. Between her mother's self-annihilating abnegation and Odette's sterile egotism; between her father, who taught her to "put duty first" (Scott 54); and her own emerging desire, Laurence finds a middle ground that allows her to come to terms with her father's wild claims on her and to move beyond them without sacrificing either her principles or her family's very real financial needs. She is able to give up her fantasy of paternal approval: "Elle aurait aimé se raconter à son père comme une femme libre. Il le lui refusait" (172) [She would have liked to talk of herself, a free woman, to her father. He wasn't interested] (112). She finds confirmation for her actions in her own satisfaction: "le bonheur confirmait sa décision" (172) [her happiness proved her right] (my translation).

Because the myth of romantic love "is entangled with the question of woman's complicity: it may be the bribe that has persuaded her to agree to her own exclusion" (Gallop 1982, 79). Laurence, in refusing to allow her father or another man to own her, turns away from the father and toward herself. In her quest for self-realization, Laurence manages, in her quiet way, to subvert the name of the father. The name, Naud (pronounced "no" in French), recalls the father's attitude, a violent negation, a stubborn refusal of life itself. Yet, Laurence, who never marries, and therefore keeps her father's name, will say "no" to her father; she uses his name to escape him, turning his word into her ultimate means of escape. The "nom-du-père" (Name of the Father) becomes a "non au père" (No to the Father), a woman's move toward independence and agency.

Finishing off the Father: Lise Tremblay's *La Danse juive* (*The Jewish Dance*)

The narrator of Lise Tremblay's third novel, *La Danse juive*, an aging, obese woman who works as an accompanist at a ballet school, is obsessed with her slim, conventional mother and especially with her father, whom she closely resembles. Throughout the novel, although they seldom meet or even talk on the telephone, they influence each other's lives.

Patricia Yaeger has written that "if *somatophobia*, or fear of the body's fleshliness and mutability, characterizes our conflict with women's bodies, then *asomia*, or bodilessness, characterizes our way of describing and thinking about the father" (Yeager 1989, 9, her italics). Feminist analyses need, in her opinion, to "give the father a body" (9), to locate his "vulnerability, his desire and his libidinal body" (19). Lise Tremblay's novel, with its emphasis on the daughter's and the father's bodies, invites such a reading.

Bodies are all, it would seem, in *La Danse juive*. Lise Tremblay's narrator is surrounded by thin, beautiful dancers who sometimes faint from hunger, but their bodies are described only briefly, as a kind of foil to her own. Similarly, her mother's thin body is barely mentioned. The narrator's body, by contrast, is constantly before our eyes: its weight, its curves, its folds of fat, its premature aging, are all described in detail, as are the narrator's slow gait, breathlessness, pounding heart, and chronic exhaustion. She also describes bathtubs she cannot fit into, the trouble she has finding suitable clothes, the effects of heat on her skin, sex with her obese lover, Mel. Her relationship with her own body is a mixture of loathing, scorn, and tender caring.

Interestingly, the other body the novel refers to continually is the narrator's father's. He is a small-town boy who succeeded in Montreal in the cutthroat world of writing and producing for television, and the narrator regularly sees his picture, with his slim, young new girlfriend, on the cover of popular magazines. The narrator is obsessed with his body and the possible changes in it: "J'allonge le bras, prends le magazine, regarde la photo en détail. Mon père a recommencé à grossir, beaucoup; il va redevenir comme ses frères, comme moi, un bel obèse bien rose. Il doit mourir de peur. C'était le seul de sa famille qui avait réussi à se débarrasser de sa graisse, au prix d'efforts immenses. Sa greffe de cheveux n'est pas très réussie" (13) [I reach for the magazine and scrutinize the photograph. My father has started putting on weight again, a lot of weight; he's going to be like his brothers again, like me, a lovely pink obese person. He must be terrified. He was the only one in his family who had managed to get rid of his fat through tremendous effort. His hair transplant is not a big success]. The father's public status has turned him into a kind of cultural icon, but also into an object (body, hair . . .) to be contemplated and criticized, as a woman would be under similar circumstances. The daughter's lucidity encompasses not only her father's incipient return to obesity, which she longs for and perhaps also dreads, but his inner terror. Because the father's entire family is obese, he is the only one who has escaped, at least temporarily, from the prison of fat, just as he escaped from the small town to become rich and famous while they all remained in undistinguished jobs. Still, he craves their approval, which is not forthcoming, and is terrified at the idea of looking like them once again. For the narrator, and for the father as well, the body is a hereditary problem, a dead weight from which there is no escape.

Throughout the novel, the narrator explores her father's influence on her and discovers several personality and behavior traits they share. The most damaging of all is his contempt for others, which barely masks his own deep shame about his origins, his poverty, his fat. No amount of worldly success will ever fill the void in him. The narrator, too, alternates between contempt and shame; whereas contempt dominates in her more successful father, shame is her most common emotion. Although she revels in public occasions where her father is ill at ease to have people seeing his fat daughter, she is ashamed of her father's neediness, his showing off, his pathetic attempts to seem young. When he calls her for reassurance, she carefully avoids offering it. But the daughter's lucidity, her scorn for her father, her ironic remarks about his hairpiece barely mask the fact that loathing for him is a form of self-loathing: "Je suis le châtiment de mon père; il a engendré un monstre" (57), she says. "La honte ne guérit jamais, elle est éternelle" (131) [I am my father's punishment. He fathered a monster. Shame never heals, it's eternal].

The narrator often says that her feelings are buried in her fat; she rarely expresses her emotions, and especially not her anger: "Ma graisse renferme aussi toutes les histoires que je n'ai pas pu raconter" (105) [My fat also holds all the stories I haven't been able to tell]. Reading about her father in magazines, she longs for "la faille qui le propulsera dans l'opprobre, dans l'échec, dans les mauvais sentiments" (117) [the crack through which he will fall into public dishonor, failure, bad feelings]. During the final pages of the novel, she reveals that she never wanted to be a pianist; her father chose the conservatory for her because of its social prestige. Yet, she has never rebelled or confronted her father: "la révolte est emprisonnée avec le reste, dans ma graisse" (141) [rebellion is locked up with everything else, in my fat]. Almost immediately afterward, she stabs her father with a Swiss army knife and watches him bleed to death.

While murder is of course always shocking, the daughter's gesture here is doubly so because it is so unexpected and seems so out of character. Does she kill him simply because of the recent crises in her own personal and professional life, described at length in her narrative? Or because he has succeeded where she has not, because he has abandoned her to her fat and her obscurity? Because he is ashamed of her? Because she is ashamed of him? Or, returning to Yaeger's concerns about the father's asomia, because he has a body and has forced it upon her, not through incest, but through his genes? Despite his success, the father is not so much an incarnation of patriarchal law here as a vulnerable body, a needy spirit. His body is present as the mother's is not, and it is through him, through his body, that the daughter inherits her own body. By plunging her knife into his "fat neck" (142) in a transparently phallic gesture, the daughter punishes him for his pretensions and for his contempt for her, but she destroys herself in the attempt. Here, the father's embodiment is a catastrophe, not a blessing.

Conclusion: Daughters Writing Back

Revolt, rebellion, seduction, or murder are only a few of the paths daughters may take as they comply, resist, equivocate, or strike out on their own. All the writers studied here insist on the father's law, or at least on his seduction (Turcotte) but also, varyingly, on his vulnerability and on his need for his daughter: "The father's power is never whole or unified—its manifestations are splintered, divisive, in crisis, shot through with disorder and desire" (Yaeger and Kowaleski-Wallace 1989, xii). As Linda Boose points out, daughters' freedom violates the existing social order: "When the threat of insurrection comes from the son, it fits into the authorized structure of patriarchy. When it comes from the detached daughter, it engenders a vision of social inversion that must be vehemently quashed within the fiction, if allowed to enter the cultural canon at all" (Boose 1989, 34).

Women's fiction of the 1990s tells new stories of "detached daughters" working, sometimes painfully and problematically, toward new visions of the family, new solutions to old problems, even, perhaps, a new cultural canon. If "being the father's daughter is a symbolic position rather than an actual relationship" (Haney-Peritz 1989, 203), a careful reading of the "other family romance" in Québec women's writing should speak volumes about women's language, body image, self-worth, agency, and ability to face the future undamaged, or at least alive and writing.

NOTES

This article is part of a series made possible by a research grant from the Social Sciences and Humanities Research Council of Canada (SSHRC), "La Question du père dans la littérature québécoise: Analyse féministe comparative de la production féminine et masculine, 1975–2000" ("The Question of the Father in Quebec Literature: A Comparative Feminist Analysis of Women's and Men's Fiction, 1975–2000").

1. Borrowed from Freud, the term "family romance" refers to the fantasy, or story, each individual invents to account for his or her own origins and to cope with early disappointments and desires in the parent-child relationship.

2. All translations from the works of fiction discussed in this paper, except for passages from *Laurence*, translated by Gail Scott, are my own.

3. The choice of this strange family romance is no doubt significant.

WORKS CITED

Barthes, Roland. *Le Plaisir du texte*. Paris: Seuil, 1973.

Bloom, Harold. *The Anxiety of Influence*. New York: Oxford University Press, 1973.

Boose, Linda. "The Father's House and the Daughter in It." In *Daughters and Fathers*, edited by Linda Boose and Betty S. Flowers, 19–74. Baltimore: Johns Hopkins University Press, 1989.

Boose, Linda, and Betty S. Flowers. "Introduction." In *Daughters and Fathers*, edited by Linda Boose and Betty S. Flowers, 1–14. Baltimore: Johns Hopkins University Press, 1989.

Brooks, Peter. *Reading for the Plot: Design and Intention in Narrative*. New York: Knopf, 1976.

Chen, Ying. *L'Ingratitude*. Montréal/Arles: Leméac/Actes Sud, 1995.

Croft, Esther. *Au commencement était le froid*. Montréal: Boréal, 1993.

D'Amour, Francine. *Les Dimances sont mortels*. Montréal: Guérin, 1987.

Freud, Sigmund. "The Family Romance." *The Standard Edition of the Complete*

Psychological Works of Sigmund Freud, ed. James Strachey. vol. 9, 237–41. London: Hogarth Press, 1953–74.

Forsyth, Louise H. "The Radical Transformation of the Mother-Daughter Relationship in Some Women Writers of Québec." *Frontiers* 7, no. 1 (1981): 44–50.

Gallop, Jane. *The Father's Seduction: Feminism and Psychoanalysis*. Ithaca: Cornell University Press, 1982.

Girard, René. *Deceit, Desire, and the Novel: Self and Other in Literary Structure*. Translated by Yvonne Freccero. Baltimore: Johns Hopkins University Press, 1965.

Gould, Karen. "Refiguring the Mother: Québec Women Writers in the '80s." *Revue internationale d'études canadiennes* 6 (Fall 1992): 113–25.

Haney-Peritz, Janice. "Engendering the Exemplary Daughter: The Deployment of Sexuality in Richardson's *Clarissa*." In *Daughters and Fathers*, edited by Linda Boose and Betty S. Flowers, 181–207. Baltimore: Johns Hopkins University Press, 1989.

Hébert, Anne. *Les Fous de Bassan*. Paris: Seuil, 1982. Translated by Sheila Fischman as *In the Shadow of the Wind*. Toronto: New Canadian Library, 1994.

Hirsch, Marianne. *The Mother/Daughter Plot: Narrative, Psychoanalysis, Feminism*. Bloomington: University of Indiana Press, 1989.

Irigaray, Luce. *Ce sexe qui n'en est pas un*. Paris: Minuit, 1977. Translated by Catherine Porter (with Carolyn Burke) as *This Sex Which Is Not One*. Ithaca: Cornell University Press, 1996.

Kowaleski-Wallace, Beth. "Reading the Father Metaphorically." In *Refiguring the Father: New Feminist Readings of Patriarchy*, edited by Patricia Yaeger and Beth Kowaleski-Wallace, 296–311. Carbondale: Southern Illinois University Press, 1989.

Lacasse, Lise. *Avant d'oublier*. Montréal: Trois, 1992.

LaRue, Monique. *La Démarche du crabe*. Montréal: Boréal, 1995.

Noël, Francine. *Maryse*. Montréal: VLB, 1983.

Marchessault, Jovette. *Des Cailloux blancs pour les forêts obscures*. Montréal: Leméac, 1987. Translated by Yvonne M. Klein as *White Pebbles in the Dark Forests*. Toronto: Talonbooks, 1990.

Proulx, Monique. *Le Sexe des étoiles*. Montréal: Québec/Amérique, 1987. Translated by Matt Cohen as *Sex of the Stars*. Vancouver: Douglas & McIntyre, 1987.

Robert, Marthe. *Roman des origines et origines du roman*. Paris: Gallimard, 1972.

Saint-Martin, Lori. *Le Nom de la mère: Mères, filles et écriture dans la littérature québécoise au féminin*. Québec: Nota Bene, 1999.

Showalter, Elaine. "Toward a Feminist Poetics." In *The New Feminist Criticism: Essays on Women, Literature, Theory*, edited by Elaine Showalter, 125–43. New York: Pantheon, 1985.

Smart, Patricia. *Écrire dans la maison du père: L'Emergence du féminin dans la tradition littéraire du Québec*. Montréal, Québec/Amérique, 1988.

Teasdale, Christine. *À propos de l'amour*. Montréal: Boréal, 1990.

Théoret, France. *Laurence*. Montréal: Herbes Rouges, 1996. Translated by Gail Scott as *Laurence*. Toronto: Mercury Press, 1998.

Tremblay, Lise. *La Danse juive*. Montréal: Leméac, 1999.

Turcotte, Élise. *Caravane*. Montréal: Leméac, 1994.

Yaeger, Patricia. "The Father's Breasts." In *Refiguring the Father: New Feminist Readings of Patriarchy*, edited by Patricia Yaeger and Beth Kowaleski-Wallace, 3–21. Carbondale: Southern Illinois University Press, 1989.

Yaeger, Patricia, and Beth Kowaleski-Wallace. "Introduction." In *Refiguring the Father: New Feminist Readings of Patriarchy*, edited by Patricia Yaeger and Beth Kowaleski-Wallace, ix–xxiii. Carbondale: Southern Illinois University Press, 1989.

The Daughter's Revenge: Father-Daughter Incest in Gabrielle Gourdeau's *L'Écho du silence*

SUSAN IRELAND

THE PAST DECADE HAS SEEN THE EMERGENCE OF A GROWING BODY OF texts on the subject of sexual abuse, ranging from psychological and sociological studies to self-help manuals and first-person narratives written by survivors of incest. Historically, social norms have dictated that what happens in the home is a private matter, but today the increasing number of media reports, specialist studies, and autobiographical accounts have begun to break the rule of silence surrounding incest and have made it a public issue. In particular, the feminist emphasis on finding a voice has provided the impetus for many women to speak out about their experience of father-daughter incest. Gabrielle Gourdeau's 1997 novel, *L'Écho du silence* (*The Echo of Silence*), explores the physical and psychological effects of father-daughter incest on three generations of women in a middle-class family: the mother, the four daughters, and the child born of one of the incestuous relationships. The five interlocking narratives that form the novel present the emotional reactions of the mother and of the daughters, whose ages range from five to the early twenties. Gourdeau's use of a different narrative format and a distinct set of images for each woman's account creates the impression of five individual voices relating a shared trauma. Likewise, the varied narrative styles, which include black humor, social satire, intertextuality, and ludic wordplay,[1] reflect both the diverse effects of incest on the women's self-image[2] and their individual strategies for survival.

The title of the novel and the epigraph from Alfred de Vigny—"On étouffe les clameurs, mais comment se venger du silence" [one can smother the cries, but how can one avenge oneself for the silence][3]—draw attention from the outset to the two central themes of silencing and the concomitant desire for revenge. Throughout the novel, the emphasis on silence underscores the notion of incest as an unspeakable act and suggests the inarticulable suffering of those subjected to it: "le silence qui depuis toujours écrase les mots dans ma bouche" (30) [the silence that has crushed the words in my mouth for as long as I can remember]. At the same time, the word "échos" (echoes) refers not only to the dynamics of incest and secrecy operating over several generations, but also to the experiences and themes common to the five separate yet similar narratives. In each case, the theme of voicelessness draws attention to the alternative means the daughters use to communicate their pain, thereby raising the question of how the ineffable is textualized.

Gourdeau takes as her point of departure one of the most typical situations in which incest occurs, that of an apparently respectable middle-class family, "une famille à l'aise" [a comfortably off family], whose children appear on the surface to be well provided for: "Ecole privée. Vêtements griffés. Hygiène dentaire. Saine alimentation" (51) [Private school. Brand-name clothes. Dental hygiene. Healthy food]. Viewed from the outside, "la maison Desmarais" (the Desmarais house) is a solid old house in an affluent neighborhood that attests to the social and professional success of engineer Jean-Louis Desmarais, father of seven and "citoyen respectable et contribuable sans reproche" (58) [respectable citizen and faithful taxpayer]. However, the name "Desmarais" suggests the murky waters and unstable foundations that threaten the equilibrium of the family, and it evokes the unhealthy atmosphere hidden behind the lavishly furnished interior—"du silence malsain qui suinte de tous les murs" (32) [an unhealthy silence that oozes from all the walls]. In this sense, the Father's House[4] stands for the traditional authority-obedience model of power that reigns in the household, a model in which father-daughter incest appears as an extreme manifestation of absolute paternal rule. The embodiment of the "grand méchant loup" [the big bad wolf] little girls are warned about (57), the father is represented above all by his sexual organ, which is clearly equated with paternal authority and, from the daughters' perspective, with the abuse of power that has destroyed their lives—"vies défoncées par le phallus paternel" (56) [lives battered by the father's phallus]. As such, the Desmarais House, in which the father's phallus literally inscribes its law on the daughters' bodies, reflects in microcosm the broader societal structures of which the patriarchal family unit forms the base. The image of "une enfance trouée à grands coups de verge paternelle" (54) [a childhood lacerated by great lashes of the paternal rod], with its play on the two meanings of the word "verge" ("penis" and "cane"), thus illustrates Michel de Certeau's observation that "there is no law that is not inscribed on bodies" (139). As a tool of inscription[5] and the primary symbol of the patriarchal order, the father's phallus underscores the relationship between the body and the law in *L'Écho du silence*. Other passages establish a parallel between paternal authority and the various institutions that fail to provide adequate support for the daughters—especially the male-dominated legal, medical, and psychiatric professions, thereby emphasizing the links between the concepts of care, justice, and the law.

The opening narrative, which adopts the form of an epistolary novel, portrays the perspective of the eldest daughter through the letters she writes to her lesbian lover. Intimate and highly personal in nature, the letters convey Nathalie's struggle against the "spectres du passé" (33) [ghosts from the past] that haunt her nightmares, cause her depression, and constantly threaten to disrupt her life. The impressionistic, telegraphic style of Nathalie's self-description, with its catalog of nouns evoking the classic symptoms of trauma, suggests the magnitude of her efforts to survive: "Courroux. Crises de nerfs. Idées noires. Cauchemars. Déchaînements. Explosions. Automutilations. Somnifères. Antidépresseurs. Stabilisateurs" (Gourdeau 34) [Anger. Hysteria. Suicidal thoughts. Nightmares. Fits of rage. Explosions. Self-mutilation. Sleeping pills. Anti-depressants. Sedatives]. Throughout the letters, medical images related to surgery and illness suggest the "body in pain"[6] and the amputation of the self-esteem of the incest victim. At the same time, Nathalie's profession as a nurse symbolizes her commitment to healing and survival, and her desire to protect her younger sisters. The frequent juxtaposition of descriptions of suffering in the hospital with passages in which Nathalie declares her love for Emilie highlights the two poles of her life, the past represented by her father and the future symbolized by her lover. In these passages, the often graphic terms used to describe injury, illness, and pain contrast with the calming rhythms created by the sentence structures and the repetition of certain nouns chosen by Nathalie to express her feelings for Emilie: "Emilie, mon amante, ma douce, ma vie" (11) [Emily, my love, my sweet, my life], "Emilie, ma grande, ma douce, ma vie, ma reine" (34) [Emily, my dear, my sweet, my life, my queen]. Likewise, the sudden transitions between past and present, and the House and the hospital, reinforce the parallel between the patients' fears the night before surgery and the daughters' terror at the thought of their father's nightly visits: "Les futurs opérés crèvent de peur sous leur drap glacé. Comme les petites filles la nuit, quand la mère dort son soûl et que le papa rôde" (14) [Those waiting to be operated on lie petrified under their icy sheets. Like little girls at night when their mother is sleeping soundly and their father is on the prowl]. In this fashion, Gourdeau emphasizes the link between "le corps mutilé" (24) [the mutilated body]—the body in pain—and the ensuing psychological trauma, and the comparison between incest and surgery suggests that the father has cut off his daughters' lives, paralyzing their emotions and turning them into living dead—"les tuer . . . en prenant bien soin de les laisser pour vivantes" (26) [killing them while taking great care to leave them alive].

Intertextual references to Baudelaire's "La Chevelure" ("Hair") make Nathalie's hair the symbol of the femininity her father has amputated. In her nightmares, her cousin's golden locks contrast with her own short hair, the "cheveux à la garçonne" (18) [boyish haircut] that symbolize her rejection of her female body. Whereas the memories Baudelaire associates with his lover's hair suggest desire, sensuality, and voluptuousness, Nathalie's hair conjures up images of an unwanted abusive relationship with a man who still tortures her in her dreams, "ses longs doigts crapuleux s'ouvrant et se refermant, comme pour saisir ma féminité" (29) [his long slimy fingers opening and closing as if to grab hold of my femininity]. These memories, unlike those described in "La Chevelure," bring back Nathalie's depression and are equated with "le spleen" (spleen) rather than "l'idéal" (the ideal) (*Les Fleurs du mal* [*Flowers of Evil*]); the atmosphere associated with them is "Bas et lourd" [stifling and sultry] and "pèse comme un couvercle" (22) [as oppressive as a lid],[7] and they thus lack the warmth and hope suggested in "La Chevelure."

In contrast, a second set of images linked to recovery and survival suggests a voyage into the future rather than the past. In this journey, Emilie takes on the role of lover previously assumed by the father and embodies the same positive qualities as Baudelaire's mistress. In her role as "déesse des Méditerranées" (18) [goddess of the Mediterranean], Emilie has enabled Nathalie to rediscover her femininity symbolized by "le goût des cheveux longs" (27) [a taste for long hair], and the passionate letters written by "Nathalie reféminisée" (27) [a refeminized Nathalie] attest to her newly found sensuality and desire. Her relationship with Emilie thus holds the promise of a return to the "idéal" of "La Chevelure," to a "paradis qui sera loin d'être artificiel" (22) [a paradise which is in no way artificial], and the allusion to Baudelaire's "Paradis artificiels" ("Artificial Paradise") suggests that Nathalie's life, like Baudelaire's poems, can be rewritten.

The second narrative, a soliloquy addressed to an imaginary audience, reveals the self-destructive tendencies of the seventeen-year-old daughter who has carried her father's child. Whereas Nathalie voices her pain in her letters, Isabelle, who is "condamnée au monologue intérieur" (42) [condemned to using interior monologue], inscribes it on her body: her antisocial behavior, which takes the form of drug addiction, alcoholism, and prostitution, reflects the shame and lack of self-esteem caused by her "delinquent" relationship with her father.[8] Her description of herself illustrates both the nature of her rebellion and the defiance with which she expresses it: "Je suis la belle, la rebelle de la famille. . . . Je suis Isabelle, la délinquante. Source intéressante de création d'emplois pour les travailleurs sociaux . . . Je suis la belle, la rebelle. Je suis tordue, foutue, infectée, droguée et alcolo" (66) [I am the beauty, the rebel in the family. I am Isabelle, the delinquent. An interesting source of new jobs for social workers. . . . I'm the beauty, the rebel. I'm twisted, messed up, infected, addicted to drugs and alcohol].

In her monologue, recurrent references to nineteenth-century poetry underscore her need to "s'envoyer aux paradis artificiels" [send herself to an artificial paradise] as a means of surviving her ordeal (54). She turns to poetry in general and to the "poètes maudits" (the damned poets) in particular in search of compassionate figures who give voice to suffering and despair similar to her own.[9] In some cases, the intertextual allusions woven into the soliloquy directly mirror her own emotions: on her seventeenth birthday, for example, her world-weariness is expressed through a quotation from Baudelaire—"*J'ai plus de souvenirs que si j'avais mille ans*" (70) [*I have more memories than if I were a hundred years old*]— while a well-known line from Verlaine conveys her depression: "*il pleure dans mon coeur comme il pleut sur la ville*" (50) [*it weeps in my heart as it rains on the town*]. On other occasions, references to poets such as Eluard and Apollinaire are recontextualized, and in this sense rewritten, in light of Isabelle's experiences: " '*La terre est bleue comme une orange.*' Fruit pourri dans la corbeille de notre galaxie" (55) ["*The earth is blue like an orange.*" A rotten fruit in the basket of our galaxy]; "Bourreau-mec machin étouffait bébé sous l'eau glacée du robinet parce que bébé avait la diarrhée. '*La colombe poignardée et le jet d'eau douces figures poignardées chères lèvres fleuries.*' " (64) [Executioner-guy thing was smothering baby under the icy tap-water because baby had diarrhea. "*The wounded dove and the fountain, sweet wounded faces, dear lips in flower*"].

Unlike Nathalie, for whom Emilie represents the ideal, Isabelle sees only "spleen" and "le mal" (evil): even the flowers she alludes to, the "oreillers fleuris" [flowery pillowcases] that camouflage blood stains on the daughters' beds, and the "fleurs pleinement épanouies" (60) [flowers in full bloom] of her shame, all have negative connotations.

Of all the forms of "mal" evoked in the monologue, prostitution in particular is used to characterize Isabelle's self-destructive behavior. Recurrent corporeal images underscore her negative feelings about her own body,[10] while grotesque descriptions of her father's and other men's bodies suggest the disgust the incestuous relationship inspires in her: "Il bave la plupart du temps. De l'alcool en trop. Du jus de couilles en trop. Du gaz digestif en trop. Tout ça gicle sur moi entre deux rots écoeurants quand le bonhomme vient me dire bonsoir" (45) [He drools most of the time. Too much alcohol. Too much semen. Too much wind. It all squirts out onto me between two disgusting burps when the old man comes to wish me good night]. Taken together, the bodily images highlight the downward spiral of self-hatred that characterizes Isabelle's transformation from incest victim to "pute officielle" (49) [official whore]: "faire le trottoir pour se haïr davantage et justifier sa haine de soi" (54) [walking the streets in order to hate oneself more and to justify one's self-hatred]. Other references to prostitution specifically designate the father as the cause of her self-abuse—"Le bonhomme a fait de moi une pute . . . Le bonhomme. Mon premier pimp" (53) [The old man has turned me into a whore . . . The old man. My first pimp], and her evolution from his secret mistress to prostitute on the street publicly proclaims her sense of worthlessness. Lacking an audience in the traditional sense, she communicates her suffering by writing it on her body in the form of a profession society associates with the "moins que rien"(49) [completely worthless].

Isabelle's repugnance for men's bodies is reflected in her contempt for male psychoanalysts. Equating men with the cause of her problems rather than their cure, she associates her "petit père psy" (53) [little father shrink] with both her father and the theme of prostitution. Furthermore, as a disciple of the father of psychoanalysis, her "petit Freud" (53) [little Freud] recalls the fact that Freud, who at first drew attention to father-daughter incest in *The Aetiology of Hysteria*, later abandoned this "literal" interpretation of his patients' symptoms in favor of a more symbolic reading.[11] For Isabelle, the ticking of the clock counting out the minutes on the analyst's desk represents not the promise of a cure, but her lost childhood and the sizable income the therapist is earning for treating her problems. In this fashion, she suggests a form of complicity between the paternal order and the psychiatric profession, and the analyst's inability to help her leads to the condemnation contained in the parallel between her profession and his, a comparison in which Isabelle for once portrays herself in the more positive light: "Au fond, vous et moi, m'sieur psy, on fait le même travail de putes: on avale le trop-plein de saloperies de nos clients. Mais, moi, au moins, je les fais jouir mes clients" (52) [Basically, Mr. Shrink, you and I both work as whores: we swallow our clients' load of drivel. But at least I make my clients come].

Isabelle's anger leads to a general denunciation of "la justice des hommes" (61) [men's justice]. Her parodic version of the "Our Father," for example, with its blurring of the distinction between God and her father, constitutes a scathing indictment of the latter while at the same time condemning the violence committed on the familial and societal levels in the name of paternal law: "Notre père qui est odieux, si vous nous aviez donné notre pain quotidien sans nous le faire payer au centuple en hypothéquant nos joies enfantines et nos rêves adolescents, nous n'aurions rien à pardonner à celui qui nous a offensés" (60) [Our father who art hateful, if you had given us our daily bread without making us pay for it a hundred times over by mortgaging our childhood pleasures and adolescent dreams, we would have nothing to forgive the one who has trespassed against us].

In contrast, the form of justice Isabelle envisages—"impregnating" her father with the AIDS virus—calls for a reversal of the process by which he made her pregnant, and constitutes a kind of murder-suicide inspired by the prostitute-pimp relationship. Couched in religious terms, it casts her as a Christ figure: "Ceci est mon corps. Ceci est mon sang. Que vous avez empoisonné. Reprenez-le. Avec ses fatales impuretés. . . . Je vais te planter la mort dans le ventre comme tu as planté le mal dans le mien" (68–69) [This is my body. This is my blood. That you have poisoned. Take it back. With its fatal impurities. . . . I'm going to plant death in your stomach just as you planted evil in mine]. All the descriptions of her imagined form of revenge use similar allusions and reversals to emphasize the father's role as the giver of death rather than life: "Je l'aurai mon sida. Tu l'auras mon sida. Il l'aura. Nous l'aurons. C'est toi, bonhomme, qui m'as appris a conjuger le verbe de la mort. Un verbe intransigeant" (68) [I'll get it, my AIDS. You'll get it, my AIDS. He'll get it. We'll get it. It's you, my old man, who taught me how to conjugate the verb of death. An intransigent verb]. Here, as in the rest of the monologue, the wordplay and intertextual allusions create the black humor and idiosyncratic style of Isabelle's speech. Throughout the chapter, the constant juxtaposition of different registers and the use of colloquial expressions powerfully convey the intensity of the rage expressed in her drug-inspired "délires verbaux" [verbal delirium] during which "sa bouche éjecte des mots dans tous les sens, mitraille des murs invisibles de silence épais" (26) [her mouth spits out words in every direction, bombards invisible walls with heavy silence]. The unconventional, irreverent style thus makes language itself part of her rebellion, and her taunting manner, along with her self-derision, constitutes another means of communicating her pain.

In contrast, thirteen-year-old Véronique uses twentieth-century references and identifies with Anne Frank when she describes her experiences in a diary. Like Isabelle's soliloquy delivered to an imaginary audience, Véronique's diary constitutes a kind of safe space in which she can combat silence and recount her story. The diary's role as confidant and interlocutor is emphasized by her giving it a name (Fosco), just as Anne Frank did, thereby making it her "ami de papier" (77) [paper friend]. In the diary, her reactions to sexual abuse are displaced onto the events of World War II. By transposing her own experiences into a different context, she displays the distancing that is a common survival strategy in victims of incest, and the choice of warfare as a metaphor, like the eldest daughter's use of medical images, highlights the themes of survival, mutilation, and trauma. Torn between the desire to repress her traumatic memories—"non, ce n'est pas ma guerre" (118) [this isn't my war]—and the equally strong need to proclaim them to the world, she constantly relives and recounts them through the filter of war. For this reason, vocabulary related to World War II recurs throughout the diary as her memories are formulated in terms of the occupied zone, resistance, collaboration, sabotage, air raids, prisoners of war, execution squads, and the role of the Allies (her sisters). In this fashion, the wounded soldiers on the battlefield serve as a metaphor for Véronique's own physical and psychological trauma—her mind and body under siege as she struggles to retain her selfhood: "Je suis un soldat mort de trouille dans son trou bourbeux. Je suis un peleton sacrifié en tête de pont au jour. Je suis un bataillon largué sur un océan grouillant de sous-marins ennemis. . . . Je suis un million de prisonniers de guerre, hâves, émaciés, pouilleux, apeurés, affamés, affaiblis, hagards, derrière les barbelés" (87) [I'm a soldier scared to death in my muddy hole. I'm a platoon sacrificed on the bridge at daybreak. I'm a battalion adrift on an ocean swarming with enemy submarines. I'm a million prisoners of war behind barbed-wire fences—gaunt, emaciated, filthy, frightened, hungry, weak, haggard]. In the elaborate scenario she constructs in order to banish thoughts of incest from her conscious memory, her father's attack becomes "une Blitzkrieg" (119), while the "trou antinazis" (118) [anti-Nazi hole] she builds as a hiding place at the bottom of the garden stands for her psychological defenses and her desire to escape her father's advances. In this sense, the bunker represents the protective shell she has built around her psyche to block out traumatic memories, a survival strategy underscored in her portrayal of the enemy as a kind of vampire that sucks the life out of its victims: "Empêcher quelque barbare de percer ma pauvre coquille pour sucer, après, ma substance vitale, comme on faisait avec les oeufs de Pâques peinturlurés, à la maternelle" (96) [To prevent some barbarian from piercing my shell in order to suck out my life blood just as we did with painted Easter eggs at kindergarten].

The notion of the disintegration of the self is reinforced through Véronique's simulated "amputation" of various body parts. Her selective removal of a different sense or limb each week, as she makes herself alternately blind, deaf, dumb, armless or unable to walk, constitutes a form of bodily inscription of her pain, an inscription that progresses from imaginary to real self-mutilation when she stabs herself in the arm. Although her preoccupation with physical suffering helps her repress the corresponding emotional pain, her "wounds" nonetheless speak eloquently of her trauma and call out for healing.

A different type of amputation Véronique envisages involves her refusal to become a woman. Whereas Nathalie cuts her hair to indicate her rejection of femininity, Véronique attempts to remove all signs of the female nature of her body by binding her breasts and planning the surgery she intends to undergo at age eighteen: "On videra mon abdomen de l'affreux sac où sont complotés les enfants. On sectionnera les oeufs. Plus d'ovaire. Plus d'ovules. Plus de vagin. Plus de vulve. Plus de lèvres" (114) [The hideous sack where children are hatched will be removed from my abdomen. The eggs will be cut out. No more ovary. No more ova. No more vagina. No more vulva. No more lips]. She thus associates survival with becoming asexual—"asexuée comme un ange" (95) [asexual like an angel], and the repetition of the negative "plus de" (no more) underscores the parallel between her denial of her sexuality and her desire for the bodily equivalent of a "pays neutre" (119) (neutral country) where she will be safe from further attack—"un esprit libre dans un corps neutre" (115) [a free mind in a neutral body].

Véronique's treatment by the same psychoanalyst as Isabelle reinforces the notion that the Freudian "psy-mec" (99) (shrink-guy) is ill-equipped to deal with the aftereffects of incest.[12] While Isabelle symbolically destroys the therapist's clocks, Véronique makes a pact with him according to which she and he both read a book while a prerecorded cassette creates the illusion that she is confiding in him. Like Isabelle's monologue, Véronique's cassette provides an outlet and an audience for her anger, and her playful recording of a stream of insults arranged in alphabetical order foregrounds both the therapist's inability to listen and his complicity in silencing Véronique. Whereas Isabelle turns to poetry when psychoanalysis fails her, Véronique rejects fiction in favor of fact-based disciplines that are grounded in reality, especially science and history. In particular, her emphasis on proof, logic, and rational explanation reveals her preoccupation with finding the truth and alerting others to what really happens in the Father's House—"Des faits. Des données. Du solide. Des preuves. Des noms. Des dates. Des adresses. Qu'on m'explique, ça presse" (82) [Facts. Data. Tangible evidence. Proof. Names. Dates. Addresses. I need explanations, quickly]. Likewise, her proposed career as a "biologiste spécialisée en génétique psychique" (80) [biologist specializing in psychological genetics] is linked to her attempts to find a logical explanation for her psychological problems. The complex mock-scientific genetic theories she develops to account for her sense of kinship with the injured soldiers create a coherent system of meaning which hinges upon her grandfather's participation in World War II and his transmission of his memories from one generation to another through recessive "chromosomes de guerre" (84) [war chromosomes]. By focusing on her grandfather rather than her father as the source of her symptoms, her theory constitutes yet another form of displacement and reinforces the complex web of denial and repression she has created.

The youngest daughter's experiences, which are conveyed through her conversations with her doll, focus on the physical pain of being raped and the psychological distress caused by the father's imposition of "un secret d'amoureux" (142) [lover's secret], a form of silencing that renders her "muette comme une tombe" (33) [as silent as the grave]. Here, the naive perspective of the five-year-old child, with her rudimentary vocabulary and comprehension, foregrounds the notion of searching for the words with which to describe the unspeakable. Throughout the narrative, realistic descriptions of the forms the abuse has taken are juxtaposed with Julie's attempts to understand "adult" issues and to explain away the discrepancy between what she has been told at school and what she experiences at home. The fact that the most explicit references to sexual acts appear in the youngest daughter's account emphasizes the enormity of the father's actions: the recurrent allusions to the father's body and bodily fluids, and to the daughter's bleeding as a result of his actions, forcefully convey Julie's feelings of abjection and disgust as well as her vulnerability and terror. At the same time, the numerous descriptions of various forms of invasion—oral, vaginal, and anal—draw attention to the many boundaries that have been violated, thus highlighting the link between bodily integrity and psychological wholeness: "Je suis déjà morte, là, dans toutes mes bouches" (168) [I'm already dead there, in all my mouths].

Julie's rag doll, which serves as her confidante and her double, plays the same role of interlocutor as Isabelle's imaginary audience and Véronique's diary. As a kind of alter ego, the doll is sometimes made to resemble Julie, while on other occasions Julie imitates the doll. When the father is abusing her, for example, Julie makes her body limp like her doll's—"je fais la poupée de guenille" (127) [I pretend to be a rag doll], her lack of movement reflecting her powerless surrender and her attempt to distance herself from the situation. At other times, however, she inscribes her fate and her pain onto the doll's body, covering it with clothes to protect it and finally killing it to put it out of its misery. Her inscription, which again contains echoes of *Les Fleurs du mal,* reinforces the association between "fleurs" (flowers) and "mal" (evil) (she draws flowers of blood around the doll's three "mouths") and foregrounds the contrast between the flowers on the daughters' sheets, a symbol of childhood innocence, and the "fleur de trop" (134) [flower too many], the blood stain that symbolizes incest and lost virginity. Like Véronique's simulated wounds, then, the text written on the doll's body communicates Julie's call for help and her fear of speaking out.

The intertextual allusions to *Le Petit Prince* play a similar role as Julie tries to read her experience of incest through a story appropriate for her age. Because of her traumatic experiences, she identifies most closely with the character in *Le Petit Prince* who must constantly light street lamps, a gesture she associates with warding off night and its terrors, and her portrayal of herself as "désespérée comme le monsieur allumeur de réverbères" (159) [as desperate as the lamplighter] forms a leitmotiv in her narrative. In similar fashion, her fantasy of putting an end to the abuse by dismembering her father is expressed through a comparison with the little prince, who saves his planet from destruction by uprooting all the baobab trees: "j'aimerais donc ça, arracher le gros doigt-champignon de papa comme le Petit Prince qui arrache les baobabs de sa planète" (Gourdeau 166) [that's what I'd like to do, to uproot papa's big mushroom-finger just like the Little Prince who pulls up all the baobab trees on his planet]. Her actual attempt at putting her father out of action involves the same childlike form of logic: concluding that her father is a type of vermin, she puts rat poison in his drink.

The final narrative, a short autobiographical "confession" recounted by the mother from her hospital bed, provides another perspective on the daughters' lives by revealing the origin of the "terrible loi du silence" (177) [the terrible law of silence]. In particular, the revelation that the mother too is a victim of sexual abuse sheds a different light on the daughters' portrayal of her as the father's accomplice—"Maman se bouchait les oreilles. Elle couvrait papa" (157) [Mama put her fingers in her ears. She covered for papa]. Orphaned at age three, the mother was abused by her adoptive father George-Albert Desmarais (her future husband's father), quickly learned the rule of silence when her distress signals to her stepmother went unheard, and has suffered ever since from aftereffects that include depression, alcoholism, and repeated suicide attempts.[13] The inclusion of the mother's perspective thus introduces the irony that, unbeknown to Véronique, the grandfather's genetic legacy is not his experience of suffering as a war hero but rather the abusive tendencies he has transmitted to his son. In this sense, the mother stands at the center of the various echoes that resonate throughout the text and between the two generations, a pivotal position suggested by the title of the chapter, "Échos de la mère morte" (169) ("Echoes of the Dead Mother"). Her own experience of incest, which establishes her as a mirror image of her daughters, also presents her as a link in a larger chain that extends beyond the individual family and that hands down a deadly legacy: "Je vous ai passé, sans dire un mot, le témoin empoisonné d'une odieuse course à relais de laquelle les femmes sortent perdantes depuis la nuit des temps" (183) [Without saying a word, I have passed down to you the poisoned witness of a hateful relay race which women have been losing since the beginning of time]. This broader perspective makes the mother a kind of echo chamber in which the sounds of silence—the stifled cries of abused women—reverberate endlessly, creating "un concert infernal de silences insoutenables" (172) [an infernal chorus of unbearable silence].

The coma in which the mother finds herself at the end of the novel is both literal and figurative, and serves as an image of her life as a victim of father-daughter incest. Throughout her narrative, images suggesting blindness and deafness underscore her inability to help her daughters because of her own past. Like Véronique, she has "amputated" certain senses in order to survive her ordeal, and her "état de mort-vivance chronique" (171) [chronic state of living deadness] is thus passed on to her daughters. Likewise, her flight into alcohol metaphorically reflects her desire to "drown out" her experiences and those of her daughters, thereby reinforcing the reign of violence and silence in the home. Although the mother's narrative goes unheard because she is now literally unable to speak, it marks a shift from silence to voice. In it, the mother clearly articulates her desire to speak out, and the final words of the chapter, which portray her as a Christ-like figure ready to take on the suffering of others, promise that the legacy of silence will be broken and the abuse avenged: "je veillerai à ce que vos hurlements étouffés fassent éclater leur coquille et retentissent comme autant de sonneries d'alarme dans les oreilles des mères autruches, partout dans l'univers" (190) [I'll make sure that your stifled screams shatter their shells and set off alarm bells in the ears of mothers who have buried their heads in the sand, where ever they are in the universe].

The daughters' actual revenge, their removal of the "phallus paternel" (56) [father's phallus] in a surgical operation that resembles a ritual sacrifice, finally reverses the pattern of mutilation and silencing, and symbolically inflicts on the father a punishment that fits his crime. Failed by paternal law, "la justice des bonshommes" (69) [guys' justice], the daughters literally take the law into their own hands and create an alternative form of "légitime défense à rebours" (187) [self-defense in reverse]. Their chosen form of revenge is prefigured in Julie's reading of *Le Petit Prince* and in Isabelle's delirious reaction to an article describing another abused woman's retaliation: "Une bonnefemme a sectionné l'engin de son petit copain.... Zoom sur le zizi zozo zigouillé pour zizanie. Zut! un zélé l'a recousu au mec méchant. Mais zizi zozo pas revenu. Zizi zombi. Tant mieux.... Bonnesfemmes du monde entier, allez-vous vous unir à la fin? A vos couteaux!" (65–66) [A woman severed her boyfriend's thing.... Zoomed in on his silly willy, did it in because of the ill-will it caused. Darn it! Some overzealous person sewed it back on for the nasty guy. But silly willy doesn't work. Willy's a zombi. Good. Women of the whole world, are you finally going to unite? Get your knives!].[14] Isabelle's carnivalesque response, with its subversive laughter and wordplay, anticipates the liberating nature of the daughters' transgressive act, and the cathartic aspect of freeing themselves from the specter of the phallus—an act that Jane Gallop in a different context calls "dephallicizing the father" (xv)—is underscored by Véronique's planting an "arbre de la libération" [tree of freedom] over the spot where "les restes de la mâlitude paternelle" (184) [the remains of paternal virility] are buried.

While each daughter had previously harbored her own revenge fantasy, the dismemberment unites them in a common project designed to place the father in the position of "lack" and powerlessness traditionally assigned to women. In this sense, he, rather than Véronique, is amputated and "neutralized," and the operation, with its macabre echoes of horror movies (*The Revenge of the Living Dead*), reverses the earlier situation by making the father a "mort vivant" (187) [one of the living dead] in his turn.[15] The ritualistic aspects of the sacrificial scene suggest the enactment of a revenge fantasy common to incest survivors: "The revenge fantasy is often a mirror image of the traumatic memory in which the roles of perpetrator and victim are reversed" (Herman 1992, 189). In this ritual, the daughters take on the traditionally negative role of castrating women in order to put an end to the rule of the phallus in both the literal and figurative senses—as a weapon of sexual abuse and as the signifier of paternal law. The dismemberment thus designates the father rather than the daughters as the one in need of treatment, and suggests the parallel dismantling of the paternal order. In this sense, the knife wielded by the daughters, a symbol of agency and inscription, writes a new daughter-oriented script on the father's body. The combination of the theme of surgery with that of inscription reinforces the notion of writing a new law: by usurping the role of surgeon traditionally associated with men—"ces messieurs les docteurs" (15) [their Lordships the doctors]—the daughters appropriate the means to shape their own recovery and, by extension, to reconfigure the social body.[16]

The epilogue suggests the nature of the new order by presenting a utopian vision of a community of women caring for the "fille-petite-fille" (193) [daughter-grand-daughter] born of the father-daughter incest. Here, the brightly colored house owned by the women replaces the Father's House and constitutes a safe space in which to heal and grow. Vocabulary related to healing, along with the use of the future tense, highlights the themes of recovery and reconstruction, of rebuilding body and mind, the "corps défoncés" [battered bodies] and the "âmes pillées" [plundered souls]: "nous irons panser les blessures.... Nous cautériserons les amputations de l'enfance. Nous ressouderons les os brisés de l'adolescence. Nous laverons les plaies de la honte. Nous remplacerons les organes vitaux de l'âme" (11) [We will bind the wounds. We will cauterize the limbs amputated during childhood. We will mend the bones broken in adolescence. We will wash the wounds of shame. We will replace the vital organs of the soul]. In this fashion, the daughters' gradual re-memberment contrasts with, and is dependent on, the parallel dismemberment of the Father. The symbolically named Eva in particular represents rebirth and hope for the future, "la promesse de tous les recommencements possibles" (195) [the promise of all the new beginnings possible]. The child of incest, she will not be subjected to it in her turn, thereby breaking the chain of abuse, and suggesting that in the new environment, and with a different family structure ("elle a cinq mamans" [195] [she has five mothers]), the daughters can be "newly born" in Cixous's sense of the term.

A powerful parable of what may happen when the "couvercle de silence a sauté" (35) [the lid of silence has blown off], *L'Écho du silence* forcefully conveys the message that those who abuse women will not go unpunished. Although not a survivor narrative in the usual sense,[17] the novel illustrates Judith Herman's contention that "[the survivor] must be the author and arbiter of her own recovery (1992, 139), and it presents in allegorical form the transition from the position of powerless victim to that of active survivor. In Gourdeau's new community, then, the replacement of the father, the symbol of sovereign patriarchal authority, with the "reine soleil" (30) [the sun queen] and a benevolent, caring sisterhood represents the end of the father-daughter, obedience-authority model. For this reason, the women's move to their new House coincides with their rejection of the psychoanalysts and doctors who were unable or unwilling to listen to their stories, and who reproduced in a different context the father's abusive relationship with his daughters. Throughout the text, the nonlinear structure and the extensive use of intertextual allusions reinforce the theme of disrupting the old order and breaking the chain handed down from one generation to the next. The echoes of earlier texts that run through *L'Écho du silence* mirror the ghosts from the past that haunt the daughters' lives, and by incorporating these intertextual traces into the novel, Gourdeau emphasizes the need to reread and to rewrite old scripts in order to produce new possibilities for the future. Only by adopting such a subversive, irreverent attitude, she suggests, will women ultimately be able to heal the wounds inflicted by the Father.

Notes

1. These traits, which are the hallmarks of Gourdeau's style, also characterize all her earlier fictional works: *La Ballade des tendus* (*The Ballad of the Tense*) (short stories, 1991), *Maria Chapdelaine ou le paradis retrouvé* (*Maria Chapdelaine or Paradise Regained*) (novel, 1992), and *L'Âge dur* (*The Difficult Age*) (short stories, 1996).

2. The effects of incest have been documented in many studies. They include mental illness, alienation, loss of sense of self, self-destructive behavior, negative feelings about one's body, nightmares, depression, insomnia, feelings of guilt, and antisocial behavior. For a discussion of these symptoms, see, for example, Judith Lewis Herman's *Father-Daughter Incest* and E. Sue Blume's *Secret Survivors: Uncovering Incest and its Aftereffects in Women*.

3. All translations are my own.

4. The expression "the Father's House" is from the title of Patricia Smart's *Writing in the Father's House: the Emergence of the Feminine in the Québec Literary Tradition*.

5. See de Certeau's discussion of the role tools play in creating the social body: "Tools work on the body . . . the apparatus of tools retains the function of marking or shaping bodies in the name of a law" (141, 143).

6. *The Body in Pain* is the title of Elaine Scarry's study of language, torture, and power.

7. The quotations are from a Baudelaire poem entitled "Spleen."

8. Isabelle thus illustrates Blume's observation that incest survivors may try to be "perfect" or "perfectly bad"—rebellious and defiant (116–17).

9. The poets she refers to range from Villon and Ronsard to Eluard, Apollinaire and Québec poet Emile Nelligan, who shares with her the somber memory of "un père qui a saccagé le jardin de notre enfance" (71) [a father who trampled our childhood garden].

10. Typical examples include the following: "Le corps? Je me sens aussi fraîche et pure qu'une tenancière de bordel même en sortant d'une baignoire remplie d'Ivory liquide" (1997, 48–49) [My body? I feel as fresh and pure as the manager of a brothel, even when I get out of a bath full of Ivory liquid soap].

11. For a discussion of Freud's work on father-daughter incest, see Herman's *Father-Daughter Incest* and Rosaria Champagne's *The Politics of Survivorship: Incest, Women's Literature, and Feminist Theory*.

12. It is interesting to note that the victims of incest and war often display the same psychological symptoms. These were originally described by the separate terms "hysteria" and "shell shock," but both are now generally referred to as "posttraumatic stress disorder."

13. The mother's situation thus illustrates the observation that survivors of incest are less able than other women to protect their children from similar abuse and are likely to attempt suicide.

14. The quotation is from François-René de Chateaubriand's *René*.

15. Gourdeau refers frequently to the awakening of the living dead and the stillborn: "Maintenant, les femmes mort-nées se réveillent d'entre les mortes et se

font justice" (70) [Now, stillborn women are awakening from the dead and are taking revenge]; "Un jour, on entendra l'appel des mortes vivantes" (190) [One day, the call of the living dead will be heard].

16. For de Certeau, the surgeon forms part of the machinery "that transforms individual bodies into a body politic" (142): the surgeon's tools, his knives and scalpels, work on the body in the name of the law and have the power to reconfigure it (143).

17. The term "survivor narrative" generally applies to an autobiographical account of incest.

Works Cited

Blume, E. Sue. *Secret Survivors: Uncovering Incest and its Aftereffects in Women*. New York: Wiley, 1990.

Certeau, Michel de. *The Practice of Everyday Life*. Translated by Steven F. Rendall. Berkeley: University of California Press, 1984.

Champagne, Rosaria. *The Politics of Survivorship: Incest, Women's Literature, and Feminist Theory*. New York: New York University Press, 1996.

Cixous, Hélène, and Catherine Clément. *The Newly Born Woman*. Translated by Betty Wing. Minneapolis: University of Minnesota Press, 1986.

Gallop, Jane. *The Daughter's Seduction: Feminism and Psychoanalysis*. Ithaca: University of Cornell Press, 1982.

Gourdeau, Gabrielle. *La Ballade des tendus*. Montreal: VLB, 1991.

———. *Maria Chapdelaine ou le paradis retrouvé*. Montreal: Editions Quinze, 1992.

———. *L'Âge dur*. Trois Pistoles: Editions Trois Pistoles, 1996.

———. *L'Écho du silence*. Trois Pistoles: Editions Trois Pistoles, 1997.

Herman, Judith Lewis. *Trauma and Recovery*. New York: Basic Books, 1992.

Herman, Judith Lewis, and Lisa Hirschman. *Father-Daughter Incest*. Cambridge: Harvard University Press, 1981.

Scarry, Elaine. *The Body in Pain*. Oxford: Oxford University Press, 1985.

Smart, Patricia. *Writing in the Father's House*. Toronto: University of Toronto Press, 1991.

The Legacy of Words : Mothers as Agents of Cultural Subterfuge and Subversion

LUCIE LEQUIN

FOR THOUSANDS OF YEARS, MOTHERS HAVE HANDED DOWN AND PERpetuated tradition. In the early 1970s, some writers—Nicole Brossard, Louky Bersianik, in particular—discerned the dominant transmission of overt patriarchal values, because mothers had difficulty extricating themselves from the false roles dictated by the voices of authority, such as education and economics, spheres dominated chiefly by men. More recent works reveal that tradition also includes a particular version of women's history and the values that are intrinsic to such a view.[1] In fact, at the very heart of tradition, breaking existing rules is ever at work, new questions and issues are raised, images are fashioned and constructed, inspired by autonomous, independent women. Yet, a daughter's emancipation is never an easy process, for it evolves in the mainstream of established values but is also influenced and diverted by the strong undercurrents of limitless potential and possibilities. Thus, the cultural legacy handed down from mother to daughter includes feelings of anguish and doubt, but it is also blessed with a zest for life and the promise of pleasure.

In this article, I would like to outline cultural heritage as it manifests itself in women's lineage as described in three novels: *La Dot de Sara* (*Sara's Dowry*) by Marie-Célie Agnant, *L'Ingratitude* (*Ingratitude*) by Ying Chen, and *Le Bonheur a la queue glissante* (*Dounia: A World*) by Abla Farhoud. This transmission of cultural values is not presented in a single, straightforward way in these three works, because each treatment of this concept varies somewhat and may take a divergent path. The novels I have chosen to discuss are only "des terrains de culture" (lands of culture), an array of "paysages privés" (private sceneries)—expressions borrowed from Jean-Pierre Richard—that set about to explore the world rather than to simply define it. Therefore, a dowry seen from a woman's point of view is not a single, clear-cut concept, but rather a source of deep reflection. When this legacy is complicated by the whole problem of life in exile, the accompanying anguish is tenfold, for mother and daughter undertake the process in a blind zone where the issue of nationality also enters into play.

THE CONFUSING CONTEXT OF LIFE IN EXILE

Before dealing with the issue of cultural fil(l)iation,[2] it is important to first define it within the context of exile, whether it be linked to legal immigration or a feeling of estrangement felt within one's homeland. When cut off from recognizable icons, the person who travels from one country to another tends to approach tradition in a safe and secure framework, often symbolized by the importance given to sensorial memory.

Yet, before living in exile, tradition was perceived as stifling and was no longer even felt since its influence was invisible, especially women's silence as described in *Le Bonheur a la queue glissante*. However, exclusion is not always linked to an actual life of exile. In Ying Chen's novel, for example, a sense of exile is experienced even when living one's life in familiar surroundings. In each of these novels, a character, often a woman, feels incapable of accepting the social or familial status quo and thus interiorly lives on the edge and adopts a marginal stance. Sometimes, this sensitive person feels the burning need for change, at other times he or she seems to live in a serene fashion. Nevertheless, deep, inner suffering is a psychological constant for such a being.

Living in exile forces one to rethink, both superficially and in depth, one's identity, ethnic traditions, and culture, because certainties surrounding these concepts are turned topsy-turvy, and confronting a new culture and its values leads to doubts and soul-searching questions.

In several works written by migrant authors, besides this ambivalent feeling, there is also a strong and pervasive impression of being disconnected, a state that becomes part and parcel of the displaced person's life: "Non seulement lui faut-il faire la part, jour après jour, de ce qui n'est pas tout à fait mort et de ce qui en lui n'est point réellement engendré, mais encore il lui faut faire face comme il peut, ainsi écartelé, à la société qu'il affronte" (Médam 1989, 139) [Because he must not only juggle unceasingly both with that part of himself which is not quite dead and with that other part struggling to be born, he must also, in this still fragmented state, come to terms with his new environment].

Disconnection, discontinuity, anguish, nostalgia, but also the unknown and the unusual are all words that define the journey and outline the territory of these men and women who pull up roots and settle elsewhere, hoping to become rooted in a new land.

So, the whole concept and experience of exile is full of paradoxes: to go without and yet to be blessed, to be there and yet here, to be neither at home here in this land nor in the distant homeland. Invisible and concrete factors both enter into play during the long process of *métissage* of identities and cultures that occurs when various cultural groups meet and rub shoulders. In fact, in such a confusing context, the transmission of cultural values is very complex, due to the pervasive presence of a new culture. In a very broad sense, this role attributed to exile is manifested in most migrant literature.

THE DEEP PLEASURE FLOWING FROM THE SPOKEN WORD

Marie-Célie Agnant was born in Haiti and has lived in Québec for the last thirty years. *La Dot de Sara* is her second book. It describes the daily life of women workers in Haiti and Québec, with a special emphasis on more elderly women. Relationships between the various generations of women are the focal point of the novel. It is the story of a "commune obstination à vouloir envers et contre tout vaincre" (35) [a joint and stubborn determination to overcome by all means].

Men do not play a significant role in the plot. They are described as "papa pitit" [small daddy], that is, as sires, so to speak, of children; they are elusive as "les loups-garous" [werewolves] who have "le don de disparaître quand bon leur sembl[e]" (22) [who have the ability to disappear whimsically], incapable of establishing stable, long-term relationships, either as lovers or as fathers. For example, whether it be the great-grandmother Aïda or Giselle, Sara's mother, the women in this family raise their children on their own and their offspring have only a vague memory of who their fathers are, because they do not know them or hardly knew them at all. Only the elderly Aïda had a solid relationship with her father, whom she knew well, as they were in a mutually loving relationship (15). The narrator Marianna does not really explain why these men are no longer involved with their family; yet, increasingly poor economic conditions and an unstable political situation seem to be linked to men's fickle ways. In fact she refuses to make up a tender "histoire de grand-père"(25) [grandpa's story]. She is really only inspired by her "monde de femmes et de légendes"(67) [world of women and legends], a long love story of bravery and generosity that is, for her, at the heart of human life.

The grandmothers' generation is a courageous one; these women are "guerrières, survivantes" (34) [warriors, survivors], who "peuvent tondre un oeuf ou faire japper un poisson" (84) [who can mow an egg or make a fish bark] and who churn "l'eau pour essayer d'en tirer du beurre" (86) [water so as to make butter]. This poetic idiom, an intricate weaving of Creole imagery and the French language, gives a unique rhythm and tone to the story being told, but it is also a stage in the evolution of a distinct women's language. In fact, Marianna refers to their dual role as breadwinners and mothers when describing moral or psychological issues. The hidden meaning of the many physical tasks that women dealing with all family responsibilities must perform is thus enhanced and enriched. Due to this poetic language, these hardworking women attain a grandeur and a nobility, both in a real and a moral sense, that is the reflection of their very lives.

From beginning to end, the story is told to Sara, who is forever asking Marianna to tell her tales from "là-bas au temps longtemps" (26) [over in the old country, way back when]. One day, Marianna, a seamstress living in Port-au-Prince, gets an emergency call from Montreal; her daughter Giselle asks her to come at once because she is going to give birth to a child. Marianna was supposed to stay in Montreal for a short time, but she ends up living in this city for twenty years, during which time she helps her daughter raise Sara. Three generations of women live together under the same roof. Marianna and Giselle's arguments become less and less frequent over time. On the one hand, the grandmother remains very faithful to her Haitian culture and ways; for example, she needs a special coffee filter that she has sent from Haiti. On the other hand, Giselle, who is a teacher, says that she will be staying in Québec, and, although she does not abandon her native culture, she is not really set on transmitting these traditions to Sara; she lives in the present moment. These two women represent two ways of raising children and two different ways of living in exile. Giselle states that she cannot live in two worlds at the same time, whereas Marianna can only live her life with both worlds as reference points. So, they wrangle about their relationship with Sara, and it is only because Giselle is growing older herself that, after a few years, she also appreciates and cherishes her mother's memories.

Marianna's stories often entail three aspects: women's lineage, popular oral culture, and sensorial memory. Thus Sara discovers in turn the life of her great-grandmother Aïda, Marianna's youth, Giselle's childhood, Marianna's initial upheaval when she came to settle in the city, her humiliation when she would go to her daughter's boarding school there facing the nuns' disdain, and later Giselle's emancipation. Due to Sara's persistent questions, Marianna tries to better grasp the meaning of her own life, yet cannot quite do so: "Cette image de ma vie, telle une anguille que je m'acharnais à vouloir guider mais qui s'en allait de tous côtés. Ma vie, girouette au gré des tempêtes, ballot de vieilles hardes mille fois reprisées" (23) [This image of my life, like an eel which, though I tried to guide it, would wander everywhere, changing directions as would a weather vane; my life, like a bundle of rags, a thousand times mended].

The story of Sara's genealogy also includes the opportunity to tell of the work of women workers as a whole: seamstresses, merchants, for instance. It also describes children's games, legends they were told, and life in the country. The grandmother adds many and myriad details to her stories so as to familiarize Sara with Haitian culture that is her legacy, for, in Marianna's view, the past plays a crucial role. Moreover, she often compares Sara and Aïda, the young girl being the "réincarnation" (reincarnation) (14) of her great-grandmother. This resemblance between the two creates a sort of time warp. In fact, the past shapes the present, just as it opens the path to the future. Marianna feels that Sara's future was already being formed and forged in Aïda's time, since the young descendant has inherited her ancestor's strengths. Marianna's stories also deal with the senses; she describes clothing, houses and landscapes, for instance, in great detail, while referring to a whole array of colors, she describes the texture of things and makes special mention of smells and scents. This rich and varied sensorial memory is handed down via words and is often referred to because something in daily life is missing. The smell of coffee is a perfect example:

> Du bon café! Il était beaucoup plus parfumé que celui-ci et son arôme emplissait tout le voisinage. . . . J'essaie bien des méthodes pour en améliorer le goût et le parfum, rien n'y fait. C'est l'air du pays, on dirait; la façon et le moment choisi pour le griller aussi. Ici tout se fait tellement vite. (49)

> [So good was the coffee. It's aroma was a lot finer than this one's, you could smell it blocks away. . . . I have tried many methods to make it taste and smell better, to no avail. It's something in the country's air it

seems; in the way they roast it, the moment they choose to do so. Here everything is done so quickly.]

Marianna's stories also help her to be closer to the abandoned homeland, for she feels lonesome and isolated. She does not have any friends anymore, and, worst of all, she often used to spend time outdoors, so she suffers from being cooped up in an apartment. She is afraid of the city; the cold becomes a symbol of her acute uneasiness in such a strange setting. She perceives that people look sad and unfriendly. The sheer abundance of merchandise in the stores overwhelms her and only makes her state of confusion worse. Only the open-air market, in warm weather, gives her some pleasure with its pungent smells, but she also seems somewhat lonesome, since these are not the same smells as in her native country. So her stories help her to overcome her loneliness. Her homeland is far away, yet she is reassured when telling of people and things from her former life and, strangely enough, they do indeed become part and parcel of daily life in Montreal.

Over the years, Marianna's life gradually changes. The spoken word remains essential in moments shared with Sara, but her stories now have a broader scope and include the life of other elderly Haitian women who also came to Montreal to join their beloved families. Marianna happens to run into Chimène, an old friend, who invites her to participate and get more involved in the community. These outings will allow her to add several accounts told by grandmothers, nannies who sometimes have to obey their own children, having become "pareil[les] à un enfant chez son enfant" (77) [having become a child in her child's home]: one woman does not have a bedroom of her own, another lives in poverty ever since she had to leave her daughter's home, yet another was abandoned by her husband, and another is learning how to read even though she is over 70 years old.

All these mini-stories throw light on the plight of these women living in Québec, who are more or less under their children's wing or whose "misère est restée collée à elles comme une seconde identité" (160) [misery stuck to them, as a second identity]. These characters are only sketchy silhouettes, but they play an important role. Details are never presented in a neutral fashion and sometimes instigate changes and help understand the meaning behind them (Schor 1987, 20–25). For a brief moment, the stories of Ita, Marcelle, and others create, in fact, a renewed complicity among Marianna, Sara, and Giselle, who finally begins to appreciate the importance of Marianna's accounts that communicate a sharpened sense of what life is all about. The three women become aware of the need to get involved in protecting these defenseless women. Therefore, the mother and daughter begin to share the same concerns in a world that is changing at a breathtaking pace; together they do things to assist these ill-loved women.

Marianna, at the age of 75, decides to return to her native land. Soon after her arrival, she starts remembering the street where she and Sara walked when she used to accompany her to school, the street that did not recognize her steps (170). Each day, to feel closer to her loved ones, she speaks of them to her neighbor; Sara and Giselle are now the main characters of her stories. She no longer recognizes the streets of Port-au-Prince. This land too, she says, "a peut-être perdu toute trace de [s]on souvenir" (170) [this land too, she says, might have lost all traces of her past]. Is this a country or a tomb, she wonders. Yet, she is happy to live in her house and hopes that Sara will come to visit her. She is no longer quite the same; her sojourn in Québec has transformed her in subtle ways, and she will no doubt always feel torn between the place where she is and that faraway land, between the two places on earth where she feels and knows love. The feeling of being split in two, of being in two places at once, becomes her own personal territory.

What dowry did Marianna leave for Sara? What tradition did she give her as a legacy? Her main gift was the strength of robust, fighting, and struggling women, more particularly Aïda and Chimène's resilience. She also instilled a critical point of view. She initiated her to a certain wisdom that is the fruit of a long life of labor and love, yet without any trace of docility and blind passivity. Sara can already have her own viewpoint on things and can say what she thinks to her mother. She can also choose her own cultural community. Will she be Québecois, Haitian, or both at once? No one really knows; her country will be the land that recognizes her step and where she feels the most at home (165). The very sound of her name in French evokes the future that lies ahead—Sara, saura, sera. [Sara will learn. Sara will be.]

Finally, Marianna the storyteller has introduced her to the artist's world; she enticed her to explore the world of the imagination, yet without neglecting the demands of daily life. In fact, shortly before the grandmother's departure, Sara tells her about her "vie au dehors" (14) (life outside the house), outside the family home, her life as a determined young woman who is well integrated in Québécois society; she speaks to her of her friends, her studies, and her thoughts on marriage, for instance. She even likes the idea of being "mère" (mother) to her own mother (140) and shares this imaginary tale with her grandmother; she would thus have spared Giselle and helped her be aware of her own worth. Like her grandmother, Sara chooses words as her means of expression and is conscious of their power. Words received as a legacy have given her a lineage, traditions, the ability to live daily life to the fullest, to fashion and foresee what lies ahead.

Words That Wreak Death

Ying Chen, born in Shanghai in 1961, has lived in Québec for the last few years. Her third novel *L'Ingratitude* describes a whole other lineage of women. Three generations live together but their lives do not connect at all. Yan-Zi, the granddaughter, has just died. She jumped in front of a truck in order to escape her mother's grip on her life. Before her soul disappears altogether, she observes her own funeral rituals, the feelings of her loved ones, and she recounts the revolt that led her to commit suicide. Yan-Zi's story, all of which occurs during the hours following her death, is, in fact, the journal of a suicide; thus it has the characteristic feel of a posthumous autobiography.

Yan-Zi's conflictual relationship with her mother is the main element of her story, and other characters play only a minor role, but these characters do shed light on this central relationship that is one chiefly of obedience: "Quelquefois, elle [la mère] m'obligeait à m'asseoir auprès d'elle et à lui parler. Pourtant, elle se taisait. Elle ne me regardait pas. Elle se tenait droite sur sa chaise. Le dos de maman ne devait pas s'incliner. En attendant mes paroles, elle tricotait. . . . Les nerfs tendus, nous écoutions le frottement des aiguilles" (33) [Sometimes she would force me to sit next to her and talk. Yet she wouldn't say anything. She wouldn't look at me. She would sit up straight in her chair. Mother's back never bent. She would knit while waiting my words. . . . We would listen to the clicking of the needles, our nerves tensed] (32).

The mother's stiff and strict attitude prevents the daughter from speaking up, so she remains imprisoned in silence, while dreaming of words and affection being exchanged between herself and her mother. The mother only knows how to give orders when dealing with her daughter's future. She even chooses her fiancé. Her love is similar to that "d'une araignée dominant son territoire" (48) [a spider presiding over its web] (50). Yan-Zi is stifled and smothered by this life from which there is no escape, and this feeling leads to her revolt. How is she to live this rebellion? Against whom is she to fight? How is she to become fully free? "Être dépourvu de parents" (21) [To be deprived of parents] could very well be, as Julia Kristeva suggests, the first step toward achieving this inner freedom. Exile itself "n'est-il d'abord qu'un défi à la prégnance parentale. Qui n'a pas vécu l'audace quasi hallucinatoire de se penser sans parents— exempt de dettes et de devoirs—ne comprend pas la folie de l'étranger, ce qu'elle procure comme plaisir ("Je suis mon seul maître"), ce qu'elle contient d'homicide rageur ("Ni père ni mère, ni Dieu ni maître") (35) [is at first no more than a challenge to parental overbearance. Those who have not experienced the near-hallucinatory daring of imagining themselves without parents— free of debt and duties—cannot understand the foreigner's folly, what it provides in the way of pleasure ("I am my sole master"), what it comprises in the way of angry homicide ("Neither father nor mother, neither God nor master . . .")] (21).

Yan-Zi's suicide is meant to be an ultimate act of vengeance against the mother. It is closely linked to the desire "rageur" (angry) of matricide, to borrow Kristeva's expression. One kills oneself in order to kill the mother. Yet, the mother gets over it, and so matricide is a failure.

In the novel *L'Ingratitude*, Yan-Zi sees her mother in a rigid and relentlessly hard light. This much-disparaged woman is the very incarnation of the tradition that forbids individualism in any shape or form. Yan-Zi wants to lead her life independently from her mother and free from the social norms that prevail at work, in the cafés and in the streets, because of the political regime and the pervasive atmosphere of mistrust. She feels spied upon everywhere she goes. The mother becomes the scapegoat of all her inner frustration.

To achieve self-fulfillment, Yan-Zi fights this solitary battle, but to free herself from these shackles, there are no precedents or models to guide her. She cannot, for example, take refuge in her father's world, for the father, an intellectual suffering from poor health, no longer speaks; he lives like a hermit and is not interested in his wife or daughter. He is already "derrière la vie" (35) [trailing behind in life] (35), whereas Yan-Zi wants to ask questions and share her dreams. Yan-Zi's coworkers are afraid of her rebellious attitude; they do not realize why she is rejecting all of her bosses' intransigence and why she is questioning the firmly entrenched social norms of her society. In fact, they are afraid of the whole idea of insubordination and do not offer her any support whatsoever.

She has no allies to help her come up with strategies, either in the real world or in a Utopian one, so in all inevitability she simply attacks her mother blindly, without perceiving her as a victim of an oppressive society, a woman who is, in fact, very much like herself.

Toward the end of the novel, as her spirit and spunk falter, she discovers too late that there is no Paradise after death. She hurtles against a total void. Only at this moment does she realize the narcissistic impasse that her desire to be herself and to be different have thrown her: "Mais les traîtres à leur mère continueront, morts comme vivants, à vagabonder, à se voir exclus du cycle de la vie, à être partout et nulle part. À ne pas être" (129) [But traitors to their mothers will continue to be vagabonds, whether dead or alive, to be excluded from the cycle of life, to be everywhere and nowhere. To not be] (149). The last word, "maman" (mother), the "cri d'un nourisson peut-être"(133) [the cry of an infant] (154), suggests that the only battlefield where the war of liberty is waged is within the mother's sphere, a territory she has denied and rebelled against for years: "On ne peut pas se détourner de sa mère sans se détourner de soi-même" (129) [You can't turn away from your mother without turning away from yourself] (149), nor "éprouver la joie glaciale de l'étranger sans avoir déjà eu une patrie"(132) [feel the glacial joy of the foreign without having once had a homeland] (153), something she will realize on the very threshold of nothingness, at the moment when she is already dead.

In this case, what is the cultural dowry handed down by women? In *L'Ingratitude*, it is not a critical sort of wisdom that the mother transmits nor one that is open to cultural blending, but a too prudent and prudish wisdom that is imprisoned in the mire of passivity and serenity. Therefore, in such a context, dealing with the familiar and the unfamiliar and trying to come up with reasonable compromises simply is not an option. A heavy and dismal dowry of submission and subordination, especially in regard to women, and that eventually leads to death, either by renouncing one's own uniqueness (the mother), or by rebelling in a violent way that is totally futile (Yan-Zi). Women here have no sense of history or notion of a collective memory; they only have to follow rules laid out by an inflexible power that, of course, also defines men's lives.

The mother has prepared a dowry for the daughter's marriage and this dowry has "enchaîné" (chained) Yan-Zi to her mother in a "manière presque humiliante" (114) [manner that was almost humiliating] (130). The young woman must hand over her total salary to her mother, like a child, in spite of holding a job; she has no money of her own. For Yan-Zi, a dowry "préparée avant l'arrivée d'un amour était aussi nécessaire qu'un cercueil construit avant les premiers signes de la mort" (115) [prepared before love arrived was as necessary as a coffin assembled before the first signs of death] (130). Even more important, the mother does not believe in the notion of love. She quotes numerous proverbs for her daughter's benefit, to discourage her from entertaining any illusions. "Deux êtres unis dans un même lit ne se disent pas leurs rêves"(50) [Two people together in a single bed don't tell each other their dreams] (53), she repeats. For her, marriage is just a convenient arrangement, a tradition to respect. Contrary to the approach in *La Dot de Sara*, where the youngest receives her legacy with joy, reassured that she is free to choose, in *L'Ingratitude*, the inheritance is seen as sterile and destructive. Above all, there is no room for the imagination or for dreaming; these are totally and utterly taboo. Unlike Sara, Yan-Zi is never encouraged to become independent and lead her own life. She wants to break the rules and even face danger, if need be. She wants to move forward and build a life of her own, but what she inherits is immobility as if time were passing, yet life was caught up in a timeless framework where no movement is possible: "Je me voyais morte au milieu de la vie"(35) [I saw myself dead in the midst of life] (35). Instead of nurturing a stimulating complicity and closeness, the mother's words, these ready-made formulas from ancient wisdom, bring the dark side of life in their wake and death. In this case, the legacy of mother-daughter relations kills life.

Words within Gestures and Deeds

Abla Farhoud, in *Le Bonheur a la queue glissante*, her first novel, explores another form of language—that is, deeds and gestures. Dounia, the main character, whose name means "le monde" (the world) in Arabic, has crossed several borders. During the period described by the novel, Dounia, a Lebanese native, is 75 years old and is living in Québec. A family gathering is the event that inspires her to speak up; she almost never speaks. So, she begins to go over her life, to see it with new eyes in order to discern its meaning and, at the same time, to come to terms with death that will soon, she feels, snatch her away.

As a woman, it is when Dounia begins her adult life that she finds that the exterior scope of her existence is suddenly and dramatically limited, a loss that leads her to fall into a silent way of life and to no longer feel confident in herself. Silence is imposed by customs not of her choosing; journeys too, imposed by her husband who does not even consult her. Neither the father nor the husband, who took it upon themselves to become the guardians of traditional customs, ever helped her to understand by offering her opportunities to learn more about her culture and about life. The father was well educated, but he told her to learn how to read by herself. In Québec, the issue of Dounia's taking French courses was never even discussed.

In her new homeland, Dounia stays at home and is the perfect mother and wife. Yet, she learns by observing children, neighbors, customers at her husband's store; she discovers the cold climate, the way households are run, and new kinds of human relationships, for example. She often feels a bit removed from life, caught between two worlds. Her only knowledge is within the sphere of popular Lebanese culture and its many proverbs; here, she seeks the strength to live and to be detached from her unhappiness. Her journey is a solitary one. It is in this detached and solitary state that she learns how to savor the freshness of a simple glass of water (47). Like Marianna in *La Dot de Sara*, Dounia sees life in a positive rather than in a negative way, refusing to be squelched by a feeling of resentment even if sometimes she may have been "cass[ée] bien des fois. En mille morceaux"(58) [bent and broken over and over. In a thousand pieces]. She transforms this limited body of knowledge into a sort of hybrid personal wisdom, by adding elements borrowed from the Québécois culture.

Simultaneously, and quite unconsciously, in spite of doubts about the model she is projecting for her daughters, she prepares them to speak up and constantly acquire new knowledge. She is silent, but her actions speak reams: "Mes mots sont les branches de persil que je lave. . . . J'améliore les plats. . . . Je me demande s'il y a autant de différence dans les mots. . . . C'est ma façon de leur faire du bien, je ne peux pas grand-chose, mais ça, je le peux. . . . Quelquefois j'aimerais pouvoir parler avec des mots. J'ai oublié avec le temps (15) [My words are sprigs of parsley that I wash. . . . I improve the dishes. . . . I wonder if words are that different. . . . This is how I can be good for them. I can't do much else, but I know how to do that. . . . Sometimes I would like to be able to speak, with words. As time went by I forgot how].

The daughters knew how to decipher their mother's actions; thus they learned the ways of strength, tenderness, and dignity. Each one found her own way (voice): one daughter teaches, another is a writer, and the third is a businesswoman. She intuitively encouraged them to broaden the interior and exterior scope of their lives; her daughters are spiritually strong and leave their mark in the public realm. Besides, they are open to the world and its ways, as their choice of companions proves; they do not feel obliged to share their life with a Lebanese man. Dounia never made her own personal choices, but she gave them the legacy of being able to freely choose the life they would lead. By her very deeds, she has given them a curiosity and openness to the world, the meaning of her first name, even if she herself was unable to live it to the fullest.

The cultural dowry handed down from grandmother to daughter, then to granddaughter, brings either sensual pleasure or death. Mothers and grandmothers who are open to life bestow culture and freedom as a legacy, but those women who do not dare question the status quo hand down a legacy that leads to death. The ability to come up with a personal construct and identity, either by interiorizing various cultures, or by legitimizing different values, even those that conflict with the status quo, is not a solitary skill, but one that is nurtured within the family on the one hand, and within society on the other. Without this room to breathe and stretch, the legacy can be too heavy a burden and can lead to death, as in Yan-Zi's case. However, if there is scope to grow, the fiber of one's identity can be knit together in an atmosphere of healthy doubt and freedom, as in the case of Sara and the three daughters of Dounia. In such a milieu, cultural blending can blossom and grow, one can create one's personal journey and history, an ethnogenesis,[3] an innovative way of spreading one's wings, while simultaneously accepting one's familial cultural legacy. In short, women are *passeures de culture* (agents of culture), true agents of social subterfuge and cultural movement.

NOTES

Translated by Rachelle Renaud.

1. See articles by Susan Ireland and Roseanna Lewis Dufault in *Women by Women. The Treatment of Female Characters by Women Writers of Fiction in Québec since 1980,* edited by Roseanna Lewis Dufault, 34–53; 181–94. Madison, N.J.: Fairleigh Dickinson University Press, 1997.

2. The word fil(l)iation is borrowed from the feminist Gabrielle Frémont. It plays on the word "fille" (daughter).

3. This is Winfried Siemerling's expression for the emergence of a cultural identity that is derived from one's native culture, but that is also dramatically different from it because it implies cross-cultural elements, hybridity, and invention.

Works Cited

Agnant, Marie-Célie. *La Dot de Sara*. Montréal: Remue-ménage, 1995. Translated by Marie-Célie Agnant as *Sara's Dowry*.

Chen, Ying. *L'Ingratitude*. Montréal: Leméac/Actes sud, 1995. Translated by Carol Volk as *Ingratitude*. Berkeley: University of California Press, 1999.

Dufault, Roseanna Lewis. "Acting Mothers: The Maternal Role in Recent Novels by Marie-Claire Blais and Anne Hébert." In *Women by Women: The Treatment of Female Characters by Women Writers of Fiction in Québec since 1980*, edited by Roseanna Lewis Dufault, 181–94. Madison, N.J.: Fairleigh Dickinson University Press, 1997.

Farhoud, Abla. *Le Bonheur a la queue glissante*. Montréal: L'Hexagone, 1998. Translated by Jill Mac Dougall as *Dounia: A World*. Publication pending.

Frémont, Gabrielle. "Petite histoire d'un grand mouvement. L'écriture des femmes." In *Identités féminines: mémoire et création*, 176–82. Québec: IQRC, 1986.

Ireland, Susan. "The Figure of the Mother in the Novels of Monique LaRue." In *Women by Women: The Treatment of Female Characters by Women Writers of Fiction in Québec since 1980*, edited by Roseanna Lewis Dufault, 34–53. Madison, N.J.: Fairleigh Dickinson University Press, 1997.

Kristeva, Julia. *Étrangers à nous-mêmes*. Paris: Fayard, 1988. Translated by Leon S. Roudiez as *Strangers to Ourselves*. New York: Columbia University Press, 1991.

Médam, Alain. "Ethnos et polis: À propos du cosmopolitisme montréalais." *Revue internationale d'action communautaire* (1989): 137–53. The quotation is translated by Maïr Verthuy.

Richard, Jean-Pierre. *Terrains de lecture*. Paris: Gallimard, 1996.

Schor, Naomi. *Reading in Details: Aesthetics and the Feminine*. New York: Methuen, 1987.

Siermerling, Winfried. "Writing Ethnicity: Introduction." *Essays in Canadian Writing* 57 (1995):1–32.

Ying Chen's *Les Lettres chinoises* and Epistolary Identity

EILEEN SIVERT

"*La littérature migrante*," (migrant literature) situated as it is between cultures and communities, has often been called a multi-voiced literature. The 1993 novel *Les Lettres chinoises* (*Chinese Letters*) is no exception. What is remarkable in this novel is the very visible way in which multiplicity is produced. *Les Lettres chinoises*, written by Ying Chen, born in Shanghai—now living in Montreal—is a working through in epistolary form of the immigrant experience. Here, four interwoven voices, two male and two female, allow the reader to follow the transformation not only of voluntary exile, but also of those who remain in the country of origin. Through letters, the novel first follows the immigration of Yuan, who chooses to leave Shanghai to begin a new life in Montreal. His correspondents are his father and his fiancée, Sassa, both remaining in Shanghai. Yuan's letters are filled with requests for Sassa to join him, but, by the end of the novel, her health has deteriorated and she is near death. These letters are soon joined by those from and to Da Li, a young woman from Shanghai and Sassa's good friend, who also comes to Montreal as an immigrant, looks to Yuan for help in getting settled, and falls in love with him.

As one might expect in an epistolary novel, writing itself is central to what the text is all about, and the letters elicit an interplay of cultural discourses. The four separate first-person narrations leave no space for an omniscient voice, instead they produce voices of complementarity and confrontation as each narrator controls, to some extent, the telling of his or her own story. This novel, however, is more than four separate viewpoints on the immigrant experience. The four narrators offer their different, yet ever changing, perspectives, not only to the reader, but to each other, and each narrator reacts to, and affects, the remaining three narrations. Interaction between narrator and reader is thus complicated by exchange between narrators, whose voices are given almost equal weight in a text that takes the form of multiple dialogues. More provocatively (as each voice speaks from one continent to another), each letter inhabits the space of both the country of origin and the host country; every letter, then, is informed by the space of its writer as well as that of the person for whom it is written. Indeed, the notion of the letter as a bridge appears to be embodied in the act of writing for Sassa, who remarks: "Mon stylo bouge sur les formulaires. J'ai l'impression que c'est mon corps qui traverse ces lignes à la fois précises et déroutantes pour s'approcher de toi" (52) [My pen moves over the forms. I feel that it is my body crossing these at once precise and disconcerting lines to draw near to you].[1]

My intent, however, is to show that the form goes beyond dialogue, that the narrators write as much to themselves as to their correspondents, and that in doing so they construct reality as much as they depict it. Those arriving in a new country are engaged in an act not so much of observing a culture, or a system of meaning, but of deciphering, transforming, and refining this system as they represent it. The host culture is not alone in being decoded and constructed in writing as it is transmitted from one continent to the other. Some of the writers are also engaged in the process of reconstructing themselves through confrontation with a number of others: the "other" who is a foreigner to them, the "other" from their country of origin, as well as the gendered "other."

Indeed, to some extent, though subtly, the difference in the migratory experience in this novel can itself be read as linked to gender rather than to a split between those who leave and those who stay behind. There is a noticeable tendency on the part of the male letter writers, Yuan in Québec, his father in China, to feel caught between two cultures or in the turmoil of a changing culture and to feel a need to maintain or reestablish roots. The women, on the other hand, in an opposition one might not expect to be gender-defined in this way, are both more rootless and nomadic—homeless even in the homeland. Never represented in unidimensional terms, Sassa and Da Li are in some ways as traditional as they are modern. Yet, although on occasion she is pulled back by the *esprit asiatique* (Asian mind-set) she mocks, Da Li consistently cuts her ties to the past, insisting, "Je n'aime pas les racines. Je les trouve les unes comme les autres laides, têtues, à l'origine des préjugés, coupables de conflits douloureux, destructeurs et vains" (83) [I dislike roots. I find them all ugly, stubborn, at the base of prejudice, to blame for painful, destructive and futile conflicts]. Sassa is the stay-at-home wanderer, floating aimlessly while she remains in a community from which she feels increasingly detached.

Yuan claims to be reborn in the intersection of cultures. Because he lacks the shared history of the Québécois, one could say that he reads his new surroundings from the unsettled and unsettling point of view of a stranger. Yet, he does not lack a history; his reading is informed by a past that never leaves him, and his newly forming identity is born of the cultural juncture. "Pour pouvoir vivre dans un monde civilisé, il faut s'identifier, c'est cela" (10) [In order to live in a civilized world, you have to identify yourself, that's the thing], Yuan writes to his skeptical fiancée Sassa. *Les Lettres chinoises* takes this process a step further. Change brought about by a meeting of two cultures does not remain on one continent; letters transport that meeting, and with it the questioning and transformation going on in the receiving community, to the community of origin.

Although this novel does not investigate the beleaguered immigrant, and offers no examples of violent or aggressive racism, the text is clearly interested in difference. Worried about reports of the effects of prejudice against a Chinese friend in Japan, where he is less visibly different, Yuan's father fears for his son "parmi les gens d'une race complètement différente" (96) [among people of a completely different race]. Although he takes his examples of human nature from his country of origin, from the history he knows, Yuan describes, without saying so, the situation of the host country, of the immigrant as minority in French-speaking Québec, itself the minority in Anglophone North America. "On est toujours un peu méprisé et méprisant à la fois" (97) [We are always a little bit scorned and scornful at the same time].

It is Da Li, however, recently arrived in Montreal, who best perceives the complex and shifting layers of prejudgment when she responds to her friend Sassa's letter that asks if the man she loves is a foreigner: "Quand tu dis 'étranger,' Sassa, je sais qu'il ne s'agit pas des Africains ni des Chinois d'outre-mer. Depuis la guerre de l'Opium, les Chinois ont l'habitude de ne considérer comme étrangers que ceux de race blanche. Un étranger, c'est quelqu'un qui inspire chez nous la peur, l'admiration et la rancune" (82) [When you say "foreigner," Sassa, I know you're not referring to Africans or to Chinese living abroad. Ever since the Opium War, Chinese have tended to consider only whites to be foreigners. A foreigner is someone who arouses in us fear, admiration, and rancor]. Her letter asks the reader to consider perspective. Aware that what Sassa really wants to know is whether or not the man is Chinese, Da Li turns the question upside down, telling Sassa that she should have asked, "Ce quelqu'un est-il un non-étranger?" (82) [Is this someone a nonforeigner?]. Sassa has forgotten the space traversed by the letters and that, in Québec, it is Da Li who is the foreigner, the stranger. Da Li moves beyond Yuan's notion of the nonessential quality of minority and majority, as she suggests that one is central or marginal depending on the direction of one's gaze. For Da Li, spatial displacement changes the meaning of the word "foreigner," as well as her own position in the system, and causes her to question the very notion of a stable identity.

Da Li's obligatory shift in perspective is caused by contact with another cultural community. Yet, her explanation of the shift suggests that geographic movement may be helpful, but not necessary, to an understanding of the shifting concept of alterity. Pierre L'Hérault's discussion of cultural heterogeneity speaks of "displacements not only from the self to the other, but within one's own cultural, identity, and memory complex" (75). In a similar fashion Da Li broadens the question to include gender when, after defining a foreigner/stranger as one who inspires fear, submission, admiration, and rancor, she adds, "Ces sentiments, je les éprouve chaque fois que je me crois en amour avec un garçon" (82) [I experience these feelings every time I think I'm in love with a boy]. She is afraid of what is not her, what is not female, what is other. "Native or foreigner" evolves into a division between the self and the other: between the West and China, between China and a coastal city like Shanghai, perhaps between the city and one's own neighborhood, or between the street and one's home and family, and, within that family, between man and woman.

Not even sisters bridge the abyss: witness Sassa's sister, who tells her not once, but several times: "tu es devenue étrangère" (37) [You have become a stranger/foreigner]. The status of foreigner in this novel does not belong exclusively to the immigrant, and *Les Lettres chinoises* devotes extensive space to the contradictory position of Sassa. Although more closely tied to family and tradition than are the others, Sassa feels detached, a stranger in her own land, a status she finds more problematic than that of being an immigrant in a foreign land. Exiled, one can reinvent the country of origin, purify it, and make it a thing it never was. One can blame feelings of uneasiness, of being out of place, on exile itself, and one can imagine for oneself a home country in which one finds the fit that was never there before departure. Those who stay behind, however, yet who remain foreigners in their own country, have nothing on which to blame their status as outsider. Their life is a daily experience of exile within the familiar, surrounded by the material world that reminds them of their loss.

What can be read in Sassa's refusal to leave a country in which she does not really belong is perhaps a better understanding of immigration than what we see in Yuan's writing. She claims to live in a time of exile: "On vagabonde sans cesse d'un endroit à l'autre. Et on va de plus en plus loin. On parle plusieurs langues, moins pour s'enrichir que pour s'effacer. On veut disparaître" (51) [People wander endlessly from one place to another. And they go farther and farther away. They speak a number of languages, less to enrich than to efface themselves. They want to disappear]. Just as she is torn between ties to cultural tradition and family on the one hand and a sense of rootlessness on the other, Sassa seems continually caught between a desire for, and a fear of, losing her identity, losing herself. On the most concrete level, she desires, above all, not to be visible. She wants to be able to melt into a crowd of people on the street who resemble her. The loss of self that melts into sameness is peaceful and attractive.

Letters from Yuan in Montreal, however, suggest a very different kind of loss because it is a loss with a gain, with new roots to replace the old. Yuan's experience has nothing to do with disappearance, but everything to do with becoming more than what he was. If being adrift in her own culture gives Sassa some kind of pleasure, if for her "rien ne vaut plus que le bonheur d'une disparition complète de soi" (51) [nothing equals the happiness of a complete disappearance of the self], she will not risk immigration and its resultant transformation that is an addition, that adds linguistically and culturally to one's identity while effacing parts of one's linguistic and cultural past.[2]

If Sassa can consider herself "étrangère chez elle" (a foreigner in her own land), the question that arises is whether her feelings of foreignness in her own country are individual, are specific to her culture, or are more universal. Because the novel operates on two continents, can one read a similar issue in Québec? It must first be understood that those who speak in this text are not long-term Québécois. The reader sees Québec through the optic of two newcomers, Yuan and Da Li, and their view is complicated because the two Chinese immigrants sometimes write of culture and community in reference to Québec (and more specifically, Montreal), while at other times the referent is the much larger, and more vague, North America, or even, simply, the West. There are also moments when the spaces are conflated or the reference is unclear.

In many ways, of course, Québec, the host community, is very much like its immigrants. The poetic imagination of Québec has been that of an alienated people, a people in exile. Pierre Nepveu reminds us that "Since the sixties, the Québec imaginary itself has been widely defined as being dominated by exile (psychic, fictive), by lack, by the absent or incomplete nation, and from the very center of this negativity a migrant, plural, and often cosmopolitan imaginary has been constituted" (200–201). One could say that the Québécois have been, until recently, *étrangers chez eux*, exiled without ever having left their land. There has been something unfinished about the status of Québec and the Québécois, a sense that, whatever their position, it was impermanent, a kind of passage between a longed-for past that could no longer exist and a hoped-for future.

Even the history of Québec's language problem provides familiarity for the immigrant and an ease of movement into the host society. The effort of Québécois francophones to sustain their embattled language, always threatened with the overwhelming force of the surrounding English, is a battle for a language whose fragility offers, perhaps, less of an obstacle than do other host languages to the immigrant struggling with his own linguistic vulnerability. Although the comparison of the Québécois to the immigrant is never explicit in this novel, it is suggested by Da Li when she describes songs of Québec: "Il s'agissait toujours, dans ces chansons pleines de conditionnels passés, d'un départ involontaire, d'une infidelité qu'on voulait vainement réparer, d'un appel sans réponse, d'une vie morte mais jamais oubliée, d'un exil sans abri, d'un voyage sans but . . ." (126) [These songs, full of the past conditional, have always dealt with an involuntary departure, with an infidelity one wished in vain to patch up, with an unanswered appeal, with a life that is dead but not forgotten, with an exile without shelter, an aimless voyage . . .].

The novel's decoding of the host community, however, reveals a somewhat more complicated perception. The Québécois are also North Americans, and Yuan's reading of North Americans is that they can never be true exiles, either in their home country or abroad, because their home country is not really home (and by this reasoning, neither can Da Li nor Sassa). In a sense they cannot be exiles because they are forever exiled. If one is, by nature, exiled from everything and everyplace, then the word *exile* loses its meaning. Yuan understands existential anguish in everyday terms, equating metaphysical disconnectedness with physical displacements. North Americans, he feels, have no stable, permanent surroundings: "Les Nord-Américains, eux, ne connaissent pas ce genre de malaises, j'imagine, puisqu'ils restent rarement dans leur foyer. Ils mangent dans les restaurants, voyagent à l'étranger, changent d'emploi et déménagent à une fréquence surprenante" (78) [North Americans do not suffer this kind of malaise, I suppose, because they rarely stay home. They eat in restaurants and travel abroad, they change jobs and residences with a surprising frequency]. One must remember that Yuan is constructing his own identity in letters as he processes the effect of cultural contact. If there is constant movement, there is no *chez soi*, and this immigrant may well find the place he seeks in the open community.

The questions that arise for the reader of these letters are the following: If exile is a part of the very nature of the Westerner (particularly the North American), so much so that it almost ceases to be exile, what, then, is the relation between the non-Western immigrant and the West? Does the immigrant from Asia become Western by the simple act of displacement? By a separation from his or her origins? By moving away from his or her past? Does the difference in perception of Da Li and Yuan complicate the question and indicate that the experience differs depending on one's gender? A fruitful way to approach this question would be to look at the particular societies (host and birth), as well as at the individual letter writers, in terms of their conception of movement and also of time, closely linked to movement and space in this novel. As usual, it is the patterns of everyday life, rather than broad philosophical views held by each community, that emphasize difference.

Yuan's first reaction to Québec is astonishment that daily life moves so quickly, that people pass by on the street with such a serious and hurried look, tapping their heels in an exaggerated cadence. Da Li seems to welcome the rapidity of public life but is surprised that it is replicated in private existence: "Je sais bien que les gens de ce pays marchent vite dans la rue. Mais je ne m'attendais pas à ce qu'on marche aussi vite à la maison" (33) [I am well aware that people in this country walk quickly in the street. But I didn't expect them to walk just as quickly at home]. She notes the lack of difference between public and private space, perhaps indirectly offering an explanation for the fact that North Americans travel so much and eat so often in restaurants. For them, the text suggests, there really is no spatial distinction between public and private. Da Li quickly accepts the notion that houses provide lodging and shelter from the elements, not protective walls and seclusion (and certainly not intimacy), and questions of identity are not expressed in terms of private and public space.

Because of the novel's many conflicting perspectives, what is difficult to determine is whether Yuan and Da Li are transformed by the practices of the host culture, or whether they are, as voluntary exiles, already different from their own culture, already to some degree "Western" or "North American" in their outlook, and to what extent their different reaction to immigration might be associated with gender. Yuan himself is in awe of, but also fears, the rapidity of life in the West, claiming that, in Montreal, "les choses vont à un tel train que je trouve ma vie peu normale" (17) [Things move at such a pace here, that my life does not seem normal]. Sassa, however, reading letters from Québec while remaining in Shanghai, observes in his letters a transformation already in progress, undergoing the influence of life at a faster pace. She surmises that he will have lost the kind of patience he exhibited previously by delicately wiping the sweat from her brow on a hot evening: "Maintenant que tu as appris à balayer la neige à l'autre bout du monde, aurais-tu encore cette manière délicate d'essuyer la sueur au visage d'une fille avec un léger mouchoir brodé de fleurs? Serais-tu capable de faire tout cela lentement, avec patience, en te retirant de la course infinie qui t'entraîne aujourd'hui comme une rafale vers les choses hors de ma portée . . . ?" (115) [Now that you have learned to shovel snow on the other side of the world, will you still retain your delicate manner of wiping beads of sweat from a young girl's face with a fine handkerchief embroidered with flowers? Will you be able to do all that slowly, patiently, withdrawing from the endless race that carries you along like a gust of wind toward things that are beyond my reach?]. Sassa understands, perhaps better than Yuan, the loss that is involved in immigration, the loss one must suffer in order to gain.

Da Li, for her part, goes beyond admiration of the host culture to a desire to live her perception of life in North America, but unlike Yuan, she does so lucidly. "Je me préférais très occidentale, forte, insensible, pratique, voyant dans l'activité sexuelle non pas un rituel mais une tendresse facile qui implique le divertissement, le cadeau, le 'voyage,' la consommation, l'exercise physique et le rapide oubli. Mais je n'y arrive pas" (140) [I preferred to see myself as very Western, strong, insensitive, practical, seeing in sexual activity not a rite, but a facile tenderness that entails amusement, gifts, travel, eating and drinking, physical exercise and swift oblivion. But I never attain this state]. While Da Li claims failure in this desire, Sassa again reads her friend's letters, and her friend, otherwise. "Tu n'es plus une vraie Chinoise . . . ," she tells Da Li, "Tu es devenue comme les Occidentaux: ils perdent leurs bonheurs potentiels ou se créent des malheurs futurs à cause de leur impatience" (107) [You are no longer truly Chinese. . . . You have become like

Westerners: they jeopardize their potential happiness or create future hardship for themselves because of their impatience].

She reminds Da Li as well of the Confucian saying that those who hurry never arrive at their goal. Yet, what is the goal? Need there be one? Could the goal of the "Occidentaux" be, like that of an immigrant such as Da Li, movement itself? Or like Sassa, whose ambivalent words are more a description than a condemnation? The very mobility she claimed could jeopardize the future is, to Sassa as well as to Da Li, an attractive quality in Westerners, but one feared by both Yuan and his father. Admitting the discouragement and paralysis of her own culture that prides itself on its wisdom and careful choice, Sassa admires North Americans who begin a journey even if they do not know where they are going or why, or what awaits them. They simply go. It is the movement itself that counts. Through this frenzied activity, Westerners, especially in North America, begin to come to a self-realization. Yet if the movement itself is the crux of the matter, then there can never be a complete realization of the self, only a constant process, and those who engage in it must be ready for subsequent change when movement carries them to a new space.

Yuan, on the other hand, is sometimes more shaken by, than drawn to, culturally different perceptions of past, present, and future. A particularly apt illustration is provided by an invitation to dinner from his Québécois friend, Nicolas. Yuan is astounded to see on the table an open book of recipes and exclaims, "Tu cuisines donc en suivant un livre!" (106) [You mean you need a cookbook to cook!]. With a ready supply of books, there is no longer a need to learn from one's ancestors. It is not that Nicolas has no parents; he hasn't forgotten his mother who, he claims, is a better cook than he is. Instead, he does not need her. There is no need to rely on family members in order to prepare meals handed down through the generations. Cooking is severed from the oral tradition and so from the family tradition. The recipe, written down and prepared as if it were in a chemistry laboratory instead of a kitchen, will always remain in the present. It will not be affected by variations, alterations, or mistakes made by those who teach by example or by the spoken word. This form of cooking also invites distance from cultural as well as family tradition. If one's source is a cookbook, it does not matter whose book (and whose culture) one uses—Québécois, French, American, Chinese, Brazilian....

Perhaps this break with the family and with tradition is the key to understanding differing concepts of time. Modern life may be nomadic life, but not the life of nomads traveling in family or clan groups. It is a life of solitary wandering. The isolation of the contemporary world appears to be more acutely felt in North America, where many people are descendants of immigrants and are themselves cut off from their traditions and their ancestors. If an immigrant is, as Sassa claims, an orphan, are North Americans inherently orphans? (Of course one must not forget that the same image has often described Québec, cut off from the mother country and obliged to survive in an alien—anglophone—culture.) One need not take Sassa's comparison literally to understand a culture, or perhaps a culture at a specific point in time, whose members live as orphans, voluntarily loosening ties with family. If Da Li describes the life of the modern urban North American in all its starkness, perhaps it is because she is so much like them, a modern urban figure, moving often and cutting herself off repeatedly from those close to her. She sees "des milliers et des milliers d'enfants sans parents, de parents sans enfants, de maris sans femme, de femmes sans mari, d'individus seuls avec chien ou chat. Ce phénomène, encore curieux en Chine, est devenu ici un mode de vie" (143) [Thousands and thousands of children without parents, parents without children, husbands without wives, wives without husbands, solitary people with a dog or a cat. This phenomenon, still strange in China, has become the fashion here]. We will see that, for Da Li, the only way to survive is to live like those she describes, on the surface, in the present, purposely removed from any ties with the past because there is no way to maintain these ties. "J'ai quitté ma ville natale," she writes, "surtout pour quitter ma mère" (71) [I left my home town primarily to get away from my mother].

While Da Li wanders willingly into the benefits and losses of rootless modernity, and Sassa wishes that she could do the same ("Je regrette beaucoup de ne pas être orpheline" [108] [I am very sorry not to be an orphan]), what separates Yuan from the same experience is that the past for him, as for many new arrivals, consists of more than a series of incidents and scenes in memory; it composes identity itself. Yuan may move away from the past, but to cut himself off completely, as does Da Li, would amount to self-annihilation, for, like many recent immigrants, his past is such a large part of the present. Yuan, more than Da Li, is representative of the immigrant caught between two cultures, benefiting and suffering from the pressures of both, and feeling that he belongs incompletely to each, while Da Li feels she belongs to neither. "The migrant imaginary presents itself essentially as indistinct, torn between contradictions that are impossible to resolve . . . ," Pierre Nepveu tells us, "in fact, it is the very categories of near and far, familiar and foreign, similar and different that are mingled" (200). Yuan cannot divorce himself from his past, which is embodied by Sassa.[3] At the same time, he chooses not to return to Shanghai, knowing that by staying in Montreal he will lose Sassa. He cannot rid himself of what he was, because it is still a part of what he is. His past is also his present.

Nepveu could be describing Yuan's letters to Sassa when he says "The migrant text remembers, believes it remembers, is haunted by the original and the authentic, but must at the same time take note that in some way this obsession has no object. . . ." (200). This nostalgia for which there is no "real" object is well illustrated in an exchange of letters between Yuan and Sassa, which begins when Sassa recounts a visit to *la rue Si-Nan* (meaning, not so coincidentally, nostalgia for the south), a street filled with memories of time the two spent there as a couple. Yuan's response is a nostalgic remembrance of a particular restaurant on that street, which Sassa says is to be modernized. He rhapsodizes over the wonderful soup served there, using it as a pretext to praise the culture he has left behind: "pourtant qu'est-ce qu'il y a dans la soupe? Presque rien! . . . Ce qui me rend toujours fier de notre culture, c'est bien cette simplicité dans la façon d'aborder les choses, cette capacité de faire des goûters délicieux à partir de presque rien, ce courage de survivre et même de bien vivre dans le désert du destin, cette quête jamais relâchée de la beauté de la vie, cette délicatesse toujours présente malgré la misère quotidienne" (105) [And yet what is in the soup? Almost nothing! . . . What always makes me proud of our culture is this simplicity with which we approach things, this capacity to create such delicious treats from almost nothing, this courage to survive and even to live well in destiny's wilderness, this relentless pursuit of the beauty of life, this refinement that is always there despite the misery of everyday life]. Sassa, skeptical of this idealization of the past, brings him up short, informing him that the restaurant is as banal as ever and that it was Yuan himself who complained in the past that its soups lacked nourishment and that the bowls were dirty. She accuses Yuan of being blinded by distance from the restaurant and inventing qualities it never had, just as one does, she adds significantly, for a failed love.

Yet, it is not past *reality* that Yuan describes. He is fashioning a past in his letter, just as he has been constructing a present, and maybe a future, in all his writing. Yuan manipulates the past, using it to help him cope with the present. He alters his past life in order to bring it into the life he now lives and to make it work for him in that life. Sassa does not believe in lost, idealized origins, and when she counsels Yuan to live in the present, to keep his life from slipping away in an imaginary past, Yuan replies that the past is always transformed by what is interposed between the moment and the memory. Shanghai will always make up a part of what Yuan is: "Les rues de Shanghai sont devenues quelques lignes gravées sur mes mains par le temps" (112) [The streets of Shanghai have become just a few lines etched by time on my hands]. Yet, even if the restaurant has changed, says Yuan, "elle est déjà défigurée dans ma tête. . . . Le passé est une chose. Le passé ressuscité en est une autre. Donc, il est toujours là, notre passé, mort dans nos mains, insaisissable mais indélébile, utile seulement quand on y lit notre destin" (112–13) [It is already distorted in my mind . . . the past is one thing. The resurrected past is something else. Thus it is always there, our past, lifeless in our hands, elusive, but indelible, useful only when we have our fortune read].

Yuan's letters capture well the process of recall and transformation that Nepveu reveals as a more general component of immigrant writing: "Nostalgia, mourning: one of the greatest contributions of migrant writing is that it has signaled the end of an amnesic modernity, centered on the undiluted present and the cult of the new. . . . Nostalgia without any hope of return" (203). Time functions for Yuan the way culture and geography do. Never content to live in the past, or in a society he finds stifling, or in a country he claims limits him, he will nevertheless recognize that his past coexists with the present, that while he lives physically in Québec, he will never completely remove himself from Shanghai. As the immigrant "pollutes" (to use Nepveu's terminology) and enlivens the host country with what he brings with him, Yuan will do the same to his new life with traces of the old, an old life that may, in fact, never quite have existed. He will construct a present out of his self-fashioned past, and most of this construction will be produced in and by his letters. Yuan may live in Montreal, but if he writes of Shanghai, of la rue Si-Nan, he will not lose them completely. There may be no origins to go back to, but in his writing he is able to represent the past or, in a sense, give birth to it as he does to himself upon his arrival in Montreal.

Through these letters, Chen reveals the process of experiencing both cultures at once, a kind of collaboration of cultures. More than any other character, Yuan finds himself in a hybrid place and time, in a kind of *entre-deux* (in between), where he is nothing but process, passage, and movement, both unstable and unformed, but always moving toward something. His ability to read the new culture through the old makes of him someone who is not exactly a foreigner nor quite integrated into the host society. This is not to say that Yuan is aware of his state. From within the process itself he cannot see either end, and he is less aware of the transformation in his own identity than are others. He no longer perceives the growing space between himself and Sassa because he comprehends it only geographically. He attempts to convince his fiancée that the rue Si-Nan and the rue Saint-Denis are really not so far apart, missing the figurative meaning of Sassa's lament: "Mais je savais qu'en suivant la rue Si-Nan, je n'arriverais jamais à la rue Saint-Denis" (133) [But I knew that I would never get to Saint-Denis Street by going down Si-Nan Street]. Yuan responds in terms of nations and laws. "Les frontières ne peuvent pas nous séparer. Elles nous demandent un passeport, c'est tout" (134) [Borders cannot separate us. We need a passport, that's all]. What he fails to comprehend is that the *frontière* to which Sassa refers exists in experience rather than in geographic space and that she is correct in assuming that, for them, the rue Si-Nan and the rue Saint-Denis will never meet. They have met only within Yuan in a process that Sassa has not undergone.

Rather than treat only the effect of the immigrant on the host country, to treat the ways in which the new collides with the existing to transform it, to enliven it, Ying Chen is also interested in a reverse transculturation. What I refer to here is a process carried out by the exchange of letters that "pollutes" and vivifies not the host country but the country of origin, which cannot remain stable when words, customs, and everyday practices come pouring out of envelopes to collide with the culture that surrounds the letter reader. Male and female reactions differ in reading as they do in writing. Sassa and Yuan's father are both affected by the correspondence they receive, but the father's response is to bury himself uncritically in reinforced principles of his cultural tradition, avoiding risk and attempting to provide his son with the same armor against the new culture, perhaps in order to protect himself from further "contamination."

Both Yuan's father and Sassa acknowledge that China has become more modern through contact with the West. Yet, the father's resistance to change stands in sharp contrast to the reaction of Sassa, who is herself transformed by Yuan's transformation and whose letters begin to accept the kind of modern relationship between two people that she will, however, not agree to experience. She has learned much from her friends' letters and has revised her opinion, if not her practice, about love, condoning the very kind of behavior for which she earlier condemned her sister. She has become aware of the changeability of what she had previously considered to be immutable truth. Sensing the impossibility as well as the undesirability of Yuan's conception of love, "solide comme une prison" (129) [solid as a prison], she now perceives it the way she does the rest of her life, as a "jouet du hasard" (142) [a plaything of destiny]. Much of what she says has as its purpose to facilitate the unacknowledged but obvious relationship between Da Li and Yuan. Wondering at her own early belief in a unique and supernatural love, she now concludes: "Nous avons vieilli maintenant. Nous ne pouvons pas rester aussi naïves qu'autrefois, puisque nous vivons dans une époque plus moderne" (141) [We've grown older now. We can't remain as naive as in the past, since we live in more modern times].

The transformation and its effect on others is not completely lost on the immigrant whose letters initiated it. Yuan senses a change in Sassa's view of the other. "Tu me donnes l'impression que tu n'aimes pas les étrangers. Tu les adores dans les films ou dans les livres. Tu ne veux pas vivre avec eux. Dès que tu sens chez moi une certain odeur "étrangère" tu m'abandonnes (164) [I get the feeling that you don't like foreigners. You love them in films or books. You don't want to live with them. As soon as you sense in me a certain "foreign" scent, you desert me]. What he has not understood is that his letters have more than an "odeur étrangère," they reek of it. He pours himself into his letters, and he is in a state of flux. He can no longer be the man who begged her to come to Canada with him, and she cannot leave to join someone who is already a "foreigner." The letters from Québec have shaken not only her confidence in the identity of her fiancé, but have confirmed her doubts about the notion of stable identity, even her own.

It is the precarious nature of identity in general that the text weaves through the letters of these four writers, using the movement of immigration and the passage of letters in space and time to suggest different views of the constant flow and the always unfinished process of self-construction. Chen's novel about identity and community represents two ways of living the migratory experience. One is that of Da Li, who is called by the ever-perceptive Sassa a "petite boule de verre qui roule facilement. Elle avance, elle glisse, elle saute parfois, et elle s'arrête rarement en chemin" (24) [a little glass ball that rolls easily. It moves forward, it glides, it sometimes jumps, and it rarely stops on its way].

Contrary to the stereotype, it is the men, Yuan and his father, who seek to maintain or reestablish roots. Da Li mistakenly calls Yuan "une plante sans racines" (83) [a plant without roots]; the words more accurately describe Da Li herself as well as the more lucid Sassa, who admits, "Je me sens aussi déracinée que toi, même si je reste encore sur cette terre où je suis née" (84) [I feel myself to be as rootless as you, even though I still remain in this land where I was born].

The term *entre-deux*, which describes Yuan's position, may denote being pulled in two directions, but it also suggests that something substantial exists at either end. It is worthwhile to ask whether the effect of being *entre-deux* is somehow different for women, who might never have felt themselves to be full participants in the community of origin. I have concentrated for the most part on Da Li's new life, but what of the life she left behind? It appears to have none of Yuan's "amour . . . solide" (129) [steadfast love], or his "travail solide comme du fer" (13) [a rock-solid job], but the opposite of substance or solidity. "Toute ma vie, j'ai senti cette inexistence" [All my life I've felt this nonexistence], she writes, and adds that her employment in Shanghai was in a job "où je n'étais pas nécessaire" (91) [where I was not needed]. Sassa's existence is not much different, living exiled "dans des abîmes pourtant familiers" (37) [in abysses that are, nevertheless, familiar]. Their life in Shanghai is represented by Da Li as a perpetual suspension in nothingness. It is therefore no surprise that Da Li leaves Montreal for Paris, just as she left Shanghai for Beijing and later for Montreal. She does not retain traces of one culture, nor does she assimilate another. Clearly differences of place are not strong enough to retain this mobile woman, who tells Sassa: "Naître ou mourir dans un endroit au lieu d'un autre n'est pas important" (91) [To be born or to die in one place instead of another is not important].

The experience of immigration is handled differently by Yuan, whose letters give no indication of living on the surface, of refusing to plan more than three days in the future, of observing life in a new culture from a distance while separating himself from the old, as does Da Li. He is also unlike Sassa, who, in speaking of the culture in which she grew up, which formed her, claims: "Je ne m'accroche plus très bien à mon quotidien. Je glisse" (37) [I don't hold on very well to everyday life. I slip]. Yuan, by contrast will put down roots, will work himself into the daily life of the space in which he finds himself. A sunny apartment, the neighbor's dog who is no longer afraid of him, the neighborhood shop, a few friends like Nicolas, "tout cela commence déjà à m'attacher à cette ville," he writes. "Quand notre vie quotidienne se déroule dans un endroit, cela suffit à le rendre unique à nous yeux" (78) [All that is beginning to tie me to this town. When daily life is played out in one place, that's enough to make it unique in our eyes]. What we love about Shanghai, he adds, is not the city, but its smaller components (a favorite restaurant, for example) that make up our daily life. For that reason, he claims, Montreal has become unique for him, as was Shanghai. Crucial for the success of Yuan's project is that each community remain unique, not melt into the other, but be grafted, one on to the other, taking up more or less space in the construction of his own identity. His move is clear from the beginning when he expresses himself through the prefix "re," or "ra:" "La curiosité, disparue peu à peu avec ma jeunesse, a *ressucité* en moi. J'ai l'impression d'avoir *rajeuni*. Je vis comme un noueau-né. Y a-t-il pour nous, les mortels, rien de plus intéressant que de *renaître*?" (18, emphasis mine) [Curiosity, which disappeared little by little along with my youth, has been revived in me. I seem to be young again. I live like a newborn. Is there anything more important for us mortals than rebirth?]. The prefix reveals that what is important is that what he does, he is doing again. This time, having chosen exile, he is giving birth to himself, but he does so recognizing that there was a previous act of birth, that the life he builds is in addition to the one his parents gave him. The culture he embraces will be an acquisition of layers, slipped into little by little, that fit more or less well on top of that in which he grew up.

We could add to those prefixed words the word *rattacher* (to connect, to link up), which is the function of Yuan's father and Sassa, whose letters maintain his link with home and past. It is Sassa who reaffirms Yuan's need for links to tradition when she gently reminds him that he has forgotten *la fête du printemps* (the festival of spring): "Quand on n'a plus de fêtes, on commence à glisser. Toi et moi, nous avons trop tendance à glisser, alors nous avons besoin des fêtes pour nous accrocher quelque part" (42) [When people no longer celebrate their customary holidays, they begin to float. You and I tend to float away too readily, so we need holidays to keep us attached], even though her own need must be questioned since she refers to this very fête as "une routine vulgaire" (42) [a commonplace routine]. Even a new fête, in Yuan's new life, will do, because he clearly needs something to remind him of the old and could not live the nomadic life of a Da Li. Yuan tells his father that he is what he is due to the influence of both his new life and his old: "Je l'ai appris non seulement de vous, mon père, mais aussi de Nicolas et de Marguerite" (151) [I've learned this not only from you, my father, but also from Nicolas and Marguerite]. Although he seems to write letters to his father in order to strengthen his defenses against modern North American urban life, those he writes to his fiancée suggest participation in it. He is Asian and Western at the same time, adding one cultural attribute to the other and attempting to balance them. Sassa, noting that lovers express themselves physically in the West, but pour their love into letters in China, realizes that "il fait l'amour à Montréal et envoie des lettres à Shanghai, car il vit dans deux mondes et il aime de deux façons" (161) [he makes love in Montreal and sends letters to Shanghai, because he lives in two worlds and loves in two ways].

My study of *Les Lettres chinoises*, like the novel itself, would seem to suggest that one of the four narrating voices is more "equal" than others. Yuan's experience and his letters take up more textual space than do those of his father, Da Li, and Sassa. And yet, the near-equal weight Chen gives the other narrative voices has the effect of undermining any stability afforded to the reader who might identify one character, Yuan, as the protagonist. If the cultural transition for Yuan seems to have been effected somewhat painlessly, one wonders if it is because he represents only one dimension of the immigrant experience, an experience that can be more completely grasped by piecing together the perceptions and reactions of others who are touched by this experience. Whereas Yuan appears to have made a successful cultural transition, the novel leaves us with some very disturbing questions about his status both in the new community and in the novel. Is the transition too easy for Yuan? Is he too eager and accepting? Are the experiences of Sassa and Da Li more uneven because the two women are less oblivious to rupture and more attuned to loss? The novel's form invites us to question Yuan's centrality because it is Sassa whose questioning voice runs through that of all the others; she is the contact among the other three. Consequently her imminent death at what is a very open ending raises still more and very different questions. At one point Yuan compares himself to a kite whose string is held by Sassa. In that case, what will become of him after her death? The transformation seen in Yuan's writing of himself is still in process, but there is a direction. How far will it go? The end of the novel leaves the reader wondering if the multicultural society many seem to seek in the modern world risks evolving from a vivifying heterogeneous mix to a homogeneous blend when the different, the inassimilable die off (Sassa) or move on (Da Li). Yuan has resisted the blend, or the bland, by constructing a self made up of two cultures. Without Sassa we are left wondering if he can keep his balance.

Notes

1. All translations of primary and critical texts are my own.
2. Linguistic, national, and gendered difference become less visible only in Sassa's (sometimes disturbing) dreams, in which passports are indistinguishable from bodies as they melt into puddles of blood, national borders blur and disappear, languages lose their meaning, and a sex-change operation makes of Sassa a person "à l'identitié confuse" (95) [with a confused identity].
3. Lucie Lequin rightly, in my view, sees Sassa's break with Yuan as a refusal "to play the role of guardian of the past which he gives to her little by little, a role that many cultures have traditionally assigned to women" (204).

Works Cited

Chen, Ying. *Les Lettres chinoises*. Montréal: Leméac, 1993.

Harel, Simon. *L'Etranger dans tous ses états: enjeux culturels et littéraires*. Montréal: XYZ, 1992.

Lequin, Lucie. "Entre la mémoire et l'oublie: *Les Lettres chinoises* de Ying Chen." *Neue Romania* 18 (1997): 199–206.

L'Hérault, Pierre. "Pour une cartographie de l'hétérogène: dérives identitaires des années 1980." In *Fictions de l'identitaire au Québec*, edited by Sherry Simon, Pierre L'Hérault, Robert Schwartzwald, and Alexis Nouss, 53–113. Montréal: XYZ, 1991.

Nepveu, Pierre. *L'Ecologie du réel*. Montréal: Boréal, 1988.

Feminine References and Feminine Space in *Entre les fleuves* by Nadine Ltaif

PEGGY DEVAUX

Nadine Ltaif's writing is a significant representative of the work of Québec women writers in the 1990s. As a woman and an immigrant (she was born in Cairo of Lebanese origin and now lives in Montreal), her contribution to Québec literary life participates in both "feminine writing" and "ethnic" writing. An increasing interest in immigrant writing is noticeable in Canada (maybe emphasized by the open multicultural policy in this country), especially since the 1980s, and literary scholars have been drawn to the study of these emerging voices, which particularly reflect the notions of identity, exile and alienation. Montreal seems to have been the center of such literary activity and new development in French-Canadian literature since it is a multicultural space located at the crossroads of linguistic and cultural realities.

Although Ltaif's work has attracted interest, its intrinsic qualities have been studied in a relatively small number of articles. Moreover, Ltaif's voice embodies that of Arab-Canadian (women) writers, an "ethnic" group that has been contributing to the Canadian literary scene, yet has been rarely acknowledged in academic circles. *Entre les fleuves* (*Between/Enter the Rivers*), a long narrative poem published in 1991, presents issues that are still extremely relevant today in the work of other immigrant writers. Her poem echoes the voices of many Québec women who have to find an equilibrium between the fact of being a woman, an immigrant, and a Québécois/Canadian. Ltaif explores her roots and her identity from an inner perspective as well as a geographical and cultural one. On the one hand, the female character is *between* two realities and identities; on the other, she is *entering* both as her identity. Ltaif is on a quest to decipher who she is and where she belongs. Feminine references in addition to a feminization of space seem to be at the core of Ltaif's writing process. Indeed, this type of writing is the main tool in her quest for self-definition and location of her self. Feminine names and nouns pervade the text, and several feminine voices are heard in it. Furthermore, these names allude to mythological, literary, and religious figures among others, which build the feminine character and personality of the writer/narrator. The geographical references such as the island, the mountain, or Egypt (all feminine in French), depict the narrator's attempt to grasp her identity between the Orient and the Occident.

This study of *Entre les fleuves* will aim at deciphering Ltaif's organization of such devices in the assertion of the narrator's identity and its fluid presence in space. The definitions of place and space as exposed by Michel de Certeau will enlighten our discussion, particularly regarding the element of movement present in space. It is precisely this movement "between," back and forth, that creates and/or asserts the identity of the feminine narrator. In that sense, "entering the rivers" could be regarded as moving toward the recognition of Ltaif's self. The following study is not an exhaustive one of Ltaif's text, because the latter offers various possibilities for interpretations and many themes to reflect upon.

According to de Certeau, a place is characterized by the order (whatever it may be) of the coexisting elements; hence a place is a momentary configuration of positions, one that indicates stability (172). Conversely, one should employ the word *space* when factors such as direction, speed, and time are taken into account. Space is therefore a crossroads of moving bodies or objects. De Certeau suggests that the rapport between place and space is similar to the one between the word and the spoken word: in other words, space is an experienced place (173). Hence, space and place are primarily divided by the notion of movement, which is part of space. These definitions will account for our use of space regarding Ltaif's work.

The title is in itself an indication of a double movement, for it is possible to interpret it as follows. On the most obvious level it refers to a space in between, "between the rivers." The three words that compose the title portray this very notion as the article "les" (the) is between the two other words, hence visually representing this concept. Moreover, the structure of the book echoes the same pattern because it is divided into three sections. "With the title of her book of poetry, *Entre les fleuves*, Ltaif represents the superposition of images and meanings; the Nile and the Saint Lawrence, two rivers, two distant histories that are separated" (Lequin 1995, 134). Another possible meaning is related to the exchange, the flow between the reader and the writer.

Yet, it can also be interpreted as "entering the rivers," (in that case the word "entre" [between/enter] is not considered as a preposition but as a form of the verb "entrer" [to enter]), which alludes to an act of penetration, of becoming part of another entity while remaining distinct. Consequently, the word "entre" encapsulates the two (apparently paradoxical) notions of distinct zones and contact. The act of writing for Ltaif could therefore be compared to Daphne Marlatt's experience (an immigrant writer herself, although she arrived in Canada at an early age), who explains that: "looking back, I think that most of my writing has been a vehicle for entry into what was for me the new place, the new world" (219). Writing enables Ltaif to exteriorize her feelings and concerns (about her belonging, her history, dealing with the experience of exile). It becomes a necessary action, as well as a link between her past and her present, her Canadian self and her Arab one; she is able to enter, in other words to exist, by acknowledging her own space.

The text oscillates between separate realities, sometimes opposite ones, and spaces where they meet. The notions of duality as well as plurality, which appear in the title as "fleuves" (rivers) in the plural form, are recurring elements throughout the text. Ltaif has to face two cultures colliding, two histories, two languages, which sometimes imply coming to terms with many more important issues such as languages. The notion of the double also seems to be a dimension of the issue of exile. On the one hand, the concept of madness embodies the fact of being exiled from one's own body and soul (which is a double perspective). On the other, Lequin remarks that exile is always twofold, because there is an "exil vécu" (experienced exile) and an "exil imaginaire" (imaginary exile) (1995, 141). Indeed, throughout the poem, Ltaif (the "je" [I] in the text is evidently as autobiographical as fictional) shifts from one space to the other, from the imaginary to the real, from one voice to the other. The latter fact becomes tangible in the text as two typographies are used, one part of the text appearing in italics. It is interesting to notice that this particular font waves on the page as water does.

The isotopy of water, which pervades the poem, can also be noticed in the title ("fleuves" [rivers]). In addition, the element of the double occurs in the text when Ltaif repeats the same phrase or word ("Parce qu'Elle est fatiguée. Fatiguée" [14] [Because She is tired. Tired.]). "Double" can be understood as a binary opposition ("Gardien ou meurtrier" [42] [Protector or murderer]), such as the Orient versus the Occident, or as an action that has a double impact. For instance, Ltaif writes: "me voilà renaître à nouveau entre ses doigts . . . je décidais qu'Elle allait naître de moi aussi" (7)

[Here I am being born again between her fingers . . . I decided She would be born from me as well]. This movement back and forth in space, which goes hand in hand with any text dealing with exile, is echoed by Ltaif's constant shift from Reason to Madness in her text, which has been paralleled to a schizophrenic space: "Ltaif reconstructs her space and provokes a re-creation of the latter by placing her female narrators in a space of schizophrenia, this territory between two histories/stories" (Lequin 1993, 316). The "double" motif always implies multiple spaces, whether geographical, cultural or other. The most vivid instance is the use, throughout *Entre les fleuves*, of the pronoun "Elle" (She), which takes the double meaning of Lebanon and, through personification, of a female voice. The pronoun reflects ambiguity, that space in-between, as well as the difficulty of naming (we understand that naming results from the assertion of one's identity, for which Ltaif struggles). "Elle" (She) also suggests movement in space through its homonym "aile" in French (wing): it therefore evokes the notion of traveling and the air as one of the major elements in which humans move.

Ltaif focuses on the motifs of air and water throughout her poem. She usually refers implicitly to both using elements that suggest movement, a translation (it emphasizes her will to decipher her own self, to "translate" what she is). Ltaif first mentions the words "tornade" (9) (tornado) and "tempête" (9) (tempest), as well as "Ariel. Du vent. Du vent." (9) [Ariel. Wind. Wind.]. "Ariel" is also a reference to Shakespeare's *The Tempest*, in which Ariel is the "airy spirit." The name also connotes the creative imagination (i.e., there is a movement in the literary space here, or intertext). The wind, as the river, are elements/spaces for which movement is an intrinsic part of their nature.

Ltaif further declares, "J'étais un oiseau" (13) [I was a bird], and later she deals with "les ailes transparentes des abeilles et des libellules" (16) [the bees' and dragonflies' transparent wings] and "hyménoptères" (16) [Hymenoptera], thus using the metaphor of insects and animals to suggest the displacement from one space to the other as well as the change of perspective (from above, corresponding to her quest and questioning). A metaphor is based on a movement, which is echoed by today's use of the Greek word "metaphorai" to refer to public transportation in Athens (de Certeau 1990, 170); a metaphor enables a displacement in space. The other images Ltaif resorts to allude to the conquest of space: "une fusée, j'étais" (15) [a spaceship I was] as well as "voie lactée" (16) [milky way], which emphasize her own quest. In addition, one could perceive the narrator's partner, "R," as a reference to "air" (air) (same pronunciation in French). In that sense, Ltaif would use the metaphor of being associated with continuous movement, a long-lasting exile. Thereby she is implying that once the process of exile has been undertaken, there is always the presence of movement, whether it is a reflection on the past or a movement forward.

The last sentence of *Entre les fleuves* exemplifies the equation of exile and movement: "Mais rompre enfin et libre reprendre mes ailes, l'envol, reprendre l'exil, le souffle interrompu, et la traversée renouvelée de l'éternelle histoire" (51) [To break away at last, and free, regain my wings, taking flight again, and with a halted breath, to be in exile again and to resume yet a new crossing of eternal history]. From minute elements (insects) to gigantic spaces around us, Ltaif embraces the whole universe in her attempt to fit in. Her travel through space seems unlimited, which is already an assertion of her freedom and a way to appropriate her own space, a feminine one.

The next important motif that permeates the whole poem is obviously the one of water. This dominant image, first present in the title, acts as the most powerful space throughout the text. Ltaif is sometimes floating, sometimes drowning, or traveling through it; the water, the river, the sea are anchored in her imagination and reality. Characteristically, the water facilitates movement and is a link between one point and another, one space and another. Water also expresses power, both the power to give birth and to kill. Because Ltaif searches for a compromise in her text, she has to find the strength to use her history to grow instead of continuing on living in a state of chaos where realities conflict without making sense. Referring to "Elle" (She/Her), Ltaif first writes: "j'ai cherché à . . . la noyer de lettres" (7) [I attempted at . . . drowning her in letters], which may express both the desire to "write" her (the country of origin) extensively (one way to overcome the missing), as well as to "awash" her with letters or mail. In any case (another instance of a double meaning), there seems to be an urge for contact, even though there are hints of loss and death.

The next reference is also steeped in the sentiment of death and solitude: two components of exile: "je cherchai une île, l'île du Naufragé" (8) [I searched for an island, the island of the Castaway]. The island, a feminine word in French, is perceived as a place in which things would be stable and settled, as well as a space in-between, which reflects exile and loss of landmarks. The notion of island mainly implies that it is surrounded by a sea or an ocean, yet as Ltaif is narrowing down her identity and resolving some of her dilemmas, the text later moves to smaller watery spaces: "Pour Elle, le lac. Pour moi, l'Euphrate" (12–13) [For Her, the lake. For me, the Euphrates]. The two images of a closed space ("lac" [lake], linked to the country of origin here through "Elle" [Her]) and an open one (the river) are superimposed in order to convey the movement/displacement that occurs in Ltaif's perception (she is related to the space that allows for motion). There is an obvious comparison of the Orient to the Occident, although Ltaif associates herself with the Middle Eastern river: at this point in the poem, she is still embedded in her place of origin. Furthermore, Ltaif's powerful text combines both the motif of air and water in words such as "ois/eau" (13) ["oiseau" means bird and "eau" means water]. Ltaif further returns to the notion of "noyer" (to drown) when she declares: "je me suis noyée" (16) [I drowned (myself)]. Once again, Ltaif's vivid images describe the loss of self and landmarks and represents the "death" that accompanies any exile.

The next pages of *Entre les fleuves* provide further examples of the water motif, all related to "Elle," the former country of residence. First, one reads: "Son corps était de glace" (17) [her body was as cold as ice], which translates the idea of a closed space referred to earlier ("lac" [lake]), in the sense that it is frozen here and therefore cannot change. It also conveys the fact that there is no warm feeling coming from "Elle"; a clear sentiment of rejection overwhelms the narrator. Then, "Elle" is compared to an "anguille" (18) (eel), to portray her rapid movement away from Ltaif, and the fact that she constantly evades contact. Therefore, through the wavering depictions of "Elle," the reader is faced with a movement back and forth, in-between, that characterizes Ltaif's approach to her situation on several levels. In the end of that particular section, we are presented with the following image: "Elle dégouline" (19) [She is trickling]; the latter emphasizes the melting, the transformation, and the inability to grasp it all. The next striking images used by Ltaif deal with "barque" (29) (small boat), as well as "fleuve" (30) (river) and "rivière" (30) (smaller river). The image of a small boat is obviously an allusion to travel, which refers to the voyage into history, memory, and dream, as well as the travel Ltaif embarked upon when she moved from the Middle East to Canada. The Euphrates is further mentioned in the poem, along with the Tigris, which is an interesting combination. Indeed, both Middle Eastern rivers unite before flowing into the Persian Gulf: could it then suggest that it is possible for two different entities to connect?

The last section of the poem, entitled "Le Langage des Sirènes" (44) (The Language of Sirens), alludes to the water motif through the mythological reference to the Sirens. The use of such a reference combines several crucial elements and themes of the text. First, it is a feminine reference, therefore building up a female context in which the assertion of a woman's identity will be easier to achieve. Moreover, Sirens were said to have female body parts but forms of birds: the notions of moving, traveling through water and air, is then present here as well, emphasizing the motif of motion in space. Finally, Ltaif highlights the link between the Sirens and language: Sirens were believed to lure mariners with their sweet singing (which is one way of using the voice). By referring to language at the end of *Entre les fleuves*, Ltaif suggests that she has found her voice, a language that enables her to assert her identity. The following image of the fountain in that section could be regarded as standing for rebirth.

However, to come to that final phase where she is able to find an equilibrium, not only has she had to undergo changes or metamorphoses, but she is compelled to, metaphorically speaking, "kill," or to establish a different hierarchy, in order to reach a more stable situation. Hence comes Ltaif's declaration: "Je suis Méduse quand je veux" (46) [I am Medusa whenever I want]: Medusa was a Greek mythological figure as well, who was usually represented as a winged female (air motif). Medusa was a monster whose appearance could turn the beholder into stone. The Greek poet Hesiod turned Medusa into the daughter of the sea god Phorcys (water motif). As Medusa was the only mortal amongst the Gorgons, Ltaif associates herself with this powerful creature (Ltaif needs powers to undertake and complete her task), who shares the mortal aspect with the human kind.

In addition to the above-mentioned aspects, the water motif establishes a connection with the mother, and hence with the mother/daughter relationship, which is a decisive theme in *Entre les fleuves*. The water alludes to the amniotic liquid present in the womb of the mother, the first space in which humans move. Therefore, the fact of describing motion in water (in rivers, lakes, etc.) symbolizes the phase before birth. Furthermore, Ltaif acknowledges that she, in fact, has several mothers (her real mother, Egypt, Lebanon, and Québec/Montreal), diversifying the "coming into the world." In that sense the pronoun "Elle" used in the narrative embodies the multiple faces of the signified. The French noun "mère" (mother) also has "mer" (sea) for a homonym, creating another semantic link between the motifs of the mother and water. The latter association is emphasized by Verduyn in one of her articles on Ltaif: "the theme of the mother/sea is thoroughly developed in

Entre les fleuves, wherein Ltaif further explores language and insists on two questions raised by migrant writing: Who am I, and where am I?" (44). The questions of identity and place/space are not fragments of a more general issue, but the very heart of Ltaif's writing.

As early as the first section of *Entre les fleuves*, the reader can sense the presence of another female character, highlighting the notion of love (thus it could be the "mother"), yet unrequited love, because the section is entitled "À la belle dame sans merci" (7). The obvious literary reference to the poem by Keats also goes back to Alain Chartier (1385–1433; he was a French poet who entitled one of his poems as such), both of whom attempted to portray an idyllic view of love. Throughout the first part of her poem, Ltaif seems to be aiming at such a love from her mother(s), that could provide her with a feeling of security and reassurance. The preposition "à" (to) suggests that she dedicates her writing to that female character, hence presenting a movement "between." This section can also be regarded as a reflection upon and rewriting of the previous poems published under the same names: a symbolic act of rewriting while Ltaif is rewriting her self. Ltaif further expresses in that section that she was in love with "Elle": passion permeates Ltaif's writing, taking the reader to other dimensions and unexplored spaces.

One of the first explicit references to the mother/child link is expressed as follows: "J'attendais longtemps. Comme une mère veillant sur l'évolution de son enfant. Comme un enfant sur la métamorphose de sa mère" (11–12) [I was waiting for a long time. Like a mother taking care of her child. Like a child witnessing his mother's metamorphosis]. Ltaif thus presents herself as both the mother and the child, another space in-between that conjugates two realities. Later in the poem, Ltaif refines her description of the mother/child relationship: "entre mère et fille, Elle et moi on baigne dans une eau trouble" (16) [between mother and daugther, She and I bathe in turbid water]. The turbid water stands for the ambiguous space in which Ltaif "evolves," the water being itself in-between—that is, between clear and dark. The "entre" alludes to both the connection between the mother and the daughter and the disparity between them. The mother/water motif can also be noticed in the third main section of the poem: "Deux mers entourant le berceau initial" (35) [Two seas surrounding the first cradle]. The latter sentence tackles both issues at once: on the one hand, Ltaif refers to space (birthplace) surrounded by two seas (*between*)—the reference to the cradle in French alludes to water (berc/eau) and to the sea movement as well since "bercer" means "to rock;" and on the other, the phrase evokes two mothers leaning over the cradle ("berceau"). There is an obvious parallel between the mother and the mother country, because both are places of origin.

Ltaif underlines that "sans cette M. [elle] serai[t] morte" (26) [without this female M. she would be dead], where the "M" has a potential of several interpretations: it could stand for "Melaina" (a name she uses and that we shall analyze further later in this study), for "Montreal," or for "mère" (mother) (it also sounds like "aime," [love] a notion that leads back to the need for love expressed by the narrator).

The last element that pervades Ltaif's writing with regard to the mother/water motif is the notion of the womb. Throughout the first sections of *Entre les fleuves*, Ltaif uses the image of being drowned, which can be regarded as expressing her confusion, as well as symbolizing her search for giving birth to her self as being in the womb of the mother. Although she acknowledges that one does not really choose one's "cradle" (45), Ltaif's urge for self-definition demands that she finds her own "cradle"/space to give birth to her self: "J'ai élu pour terre son corps à Elle. Elu pour territoire d'où naître une deuxième fois" (26) [I decided Her body would be my native land. I chose this territory to be born a second time]. The female body becomes the gendered space that will enable Ltaif to assert her identity, in recognizing the female link that ties her to the world. That female territory is mapped throughout the book by going back and forth between the mother country and Québec and through the diverse female spaces alluded to. Ltaif further explains: "Me voilà plongée dans le ventre de la nature canadienne" (27) [I am immersed in Canadian nature's womb], where Canada is personified, and where the mother is traditionally associated with nature. The latter image wittily reaffirms the idea that she has yet to be born in Canada, because it is the space she is unable to feel part of, and she is still metaphorically placed in an enclosed space. Toward the end of the book, Ltaif describes herself getting out of the water, in that sense gradually achieving that second birth, which will provide her with an identity.

The mother motif, without being tied to the water one, is also noticeable in *Entre les fleuves* through the image of the devouring mother (10). There are instances throughout the poem of eating up and swallowing, and food images, which stand for Ltaif's desire to appropriate her histories and assert her identity, as well as the fact that she is first "eaten up" by contradictions and sentiments in-between.

The movement "between" is characterized by a recurring vertical displacement throughout *Entre les fleuves*, which is noticeable in various instances. Both the fact of swallowing and of drowning explore that vertical space, the latter also alluding to the idea of roots, origins, and moving away from them. Other elements referring to verticality appear in the text, among which the wall (12), the comparison tall/small ("Je serai très grande au-dessus d'Elle et Elle sera toute petite" [13] [I will be very tall leaning over and above Her]), the mountain (40), cardinal points ("Elle le Nord, moi le Sud" [41] [She would be the North, I the South]), or through lineage ("[les pays arabes] D'où je descends" [45] [the Arab countries I come from]). The vertical displacement echoes the horizontal/linear one, both reinforcing the notion of exile and the lack of a central landmark.

Ltaif does not simply employ spatial references, she "feminizes" the space, either through the usage of a feminine noun in French, or through her association with female attributes (see above the example of cardinal points). The very beginning of the book exemplifies such an assertion, as Ltaif entitles the first main section "À l'ombre d'Hécate" ("In Hecate's Shade"). The shade, "une ombre" in French, represents a dark space that is hers. Throughout *Entre les fleuves*, a movement between darkness ("mes ténèbres à moi" [7] [my shades of death]) and light occurs ("Elle tient mille torches" [7] [She is holding a thousand torches]), which echoes the process of moving toward an understanding of her own identity. The imbalance between two spaces creates a third space, that which lies in-between. Therefore, the apparent oppositions present in the book conceal the space where opposites meet, a space pregnant with numerous possibilities. Ltaif further mentions "Raison et Folie" (8) [Reason and Lunacy], two divergent notions between which she can create her own space. Another example of such a technique is her explicit description of that space in-between: "Tout autour, des vents contradictoires. Et moi." (9) [All around, contradictory winds. And me]. The writing itself is perceived, along with the shift in perspective, as a way to fill in the gap, to create a dialogue, an exchange, in order for these connections to ground her in the place where she now lives. "L'écriture des femmes migrantes ressort du mouvement et de la capacité d'appréhender un espace particulier mais toujours ouvert à la gestation de nouvelles images d'elles et de nous" (141) [Migrant women's writing emerges from movement and from the ability to deal with a particular space but one that is always open to new images of them and us].

The search for that space in-between can also be regarded as the desire to find the center, or in other words to go back to the origins (alluded to earlier through the reference to the cradle). The act of writing enables Ltaif to reach that goal: "Quand j'écris je rejoins cette vie antérieure d'où je viens" (37) [When I write I connect with this former life I come from]. As the text develops, Ltaif succeeds in identifying the space of origins and to see more clearly through it. Language takes her to the center as well, "la langue me ravale" (42) [the language/tongue swallows me], to the origins ("C'est le magma fécond des Origines. Je suis aux origines: perdue, retrouvée, perdue encore" [42] [It is the fecund magma of the origins of life. I am there: lost, found, lost again]). The desire to achieve a central position is not limited to the outer space (physical, geographical); it is obviously an inner quest as well. However, the quest for her space infers that Ltaif has to first come to terms with her origins, and then put aside some aspects in order to reach an equilibrium. The struggle Ltaif has undertaken leads her to face the "demon inside": "Cet être que je combats. En moi. Hors de moi. En moi à nouveau. Mon démon. Mon ange" (42) [I am fighting this creature inside of me, outside of me. Inside of me again. My demon. My angel]. Ltaif acknowledges that she is inhabited by two cultures, and she decides to gradually distance herself from her "Orient intérieur" (30–31) [inner Orient].

Another interesting aspect in the process of going back to the origins is undertaken through the references to feminine mythological or literary figures. As already mentioned, the first section of *Entre les fleuves* is entitled "À l'ombre d'Hécate," introducing the goddess (which one usually finds in the work of Shakespeare and Milton) who is said to preside over magic and spells, to bestow wealth and all the blessings of daily life. Moreover, it is important to underline that pillars called "hecataea" stood at crossroads and doorways; therefore the use of such a reference in Ltaif's text implies the recurring motif of being in-between.

Some of these characters allow Ltaif to enter a magical, unreal space. For instance, she refers to Myrrha and Morgana (12), both feminine figures pertaining to myths and legends. Furthermore, Ltaif includes figures of various traditions and civilizations (Morgana alludes to "Morgane la fée," a character present in tales from Brittany), such as Hathor. The latter was an Egyptian goddess who symbolized the home of the god Horus. Hathor is an emblematic character inasmuch as she represents a space and she is a woman. Ltaif further refers to Lilith, a female demon of Jewish folklore (whose name is apparently derived from the Babylonian-Assyrian demon called Lilit or Lilu), who has often been regarded as a feminist symbol in the twentieth century due to her refusal to couple with Adam, hence rebelling against patriarchal society.

As Ltaif struggles to identify who she is, not only does she resort to a body of literary and mythological figures, but she also creates her own representations. In the middle of *Entre les fleuves*, Ltaif names herself (her "double" as she puts it), under the patronym of "Melaina Kole" (26). Verduyn associates this name with "mélancolie" (44) (melancholy), which adds to the feeling of loss as well as to lack of equilibrium. Moreover, "Kole" sounds like "coule" (flows) in French, which adds to the references to water and fluidity (emphasizing the fact that she is still "between," moving away). "Kole" could also be regarded as an implicit reference to the verb "to eat" in Arabic, which would then reinforce the idea that she is literally eating up her history to assert her identity. While naming herself "Melaina Kole," she writes: "Vous auriez pu me nommer Kora. Mais mon vrai nom est Melaina Kole" (26) [You could have called me Kora. But my real name is Melaina Kole]. On the one hand, this sentence underlines the conflict arising from being named and naming oneself; on the other, Ltaif employs a symbolic name, "Kora." The latter alludes to several feminine spaces as well as to feminine representations: it sounds like the name of a city in the north of Lebanon; "Koré" is a Greek statue portraying a young woman; and it has been used by Irigaray ("khora") meaning a cave or the womb, as well as by Kristeva ("chora") for the womb (Sellers 1991, 8). Because she refuses to adhere to the name of "Kora," it seems that she therefore avoids the traditional representations of women as womb/men. Ltaif gives birth to her self through (re)writing, seeking, and thinking.

The confusion linked to the fact of being in-between gradually decreases as Ltaif explores several spaces and moves toward accepting and dealing with her origins. Referring to female characters as well as gendered spaces, she asserts the characteristics of her identity and uniqueness of her experience. In so doing, her voice echoes the work of other exiled women writers in Québec, and reinforces the richness of its culture. Ltaif's writing is therefore a significant example of the contemporary Canadian literary scene and the importance of ethnic writers' contribution to it because many of us undergo the feeling of being *between*.

Notes

All translations are my own.

I would like to express my gratitude to Marielle Mencé, my colleague from the Université de Sherbrooke, who not only shared her material on Nadine Ltaif, including personal correspondence with the author, but also provided valuable insights pertaining to my discussion. In addition, I am appreciative of the support from Dr. Nasrin Rahimieh, my supervisor at the University of Alberta, who read the first draft of my article and made valuable suggestions for its improvement.

Works Cited

Brunel, Pierre, ed. *Dictionnaire des mythes littéraires*. Paris: Editions du Rocher, 1988.

Certeau, Michel de. *L'Invention du quotidien*. Paris: Gallimard, 1990.

Lequin, Lucie. "Elles disent leur dépaysement et bâtissent leur repaysement." *Les Bâtisseuses de la cité/Les Cahiers scientifiques* 79 (1993): 306–18.

———. "Quelques mouvements de la transculture." *Essays on Canadian Writing* 57 (Winter 1995): 128–44.

Ltaif, Nadine. *Entre les fleuves*. Montreal: Guernica, 1991.

Marlatt, Daphne. "Entering In." *Canadian Literature* 100 (Spring 1984): 219–23.

Robin, Régine. *La Québécoite*. Montreal: Editions Typo, 1993.

Sellers, Susan. *Language and Sexual Difference*. New York: St. Martin's Press, 1991.

Verduyn, Christl. "Nouvelles voies/voix: L'écriture de Nadine Ltaif." *Québec Studies* 14 (1992): 41–48.

France Daigle's Postmodern Acadian Voice in the Context of Franco-Canadian Lesbian Voices

JANINE RICOUART

FRANCO-CANADIAN LESBIAN WRITERS PUBLISHED MANY EXCELLENT novels in the 1990s. These novels have several characteristics in common, such as the recurrence of multiple narratives contained within the text itself or the reframing of the narrator's gender identity. For example, Nicole Brossard's *Baroque d'aube* (1995) (*Baroque at Dawn*, 1997) takes the reader on a modern scientific expedition with multiple places, voices, and characters. Similarly, in Marie-Claire Blais's *Soifs* (1995) (*These Festive Nights*, 1997), a number of narrative threads underline the multiplicity of narrative voices as well as various positions for the reader. Anne-Marie Alonzo's *Galia qu'elle nommait amour* (1992) (*Galia Whom She Named Love*)[1] and Hélène Harbec's *L'Orgueilleuse* (1998) (*The Proud One*) also use narrative voices giving women a central position. These texts present lesbian relationships in the context of postmodernity and suggest an exploration of identity through writing. Since "the concept of identity lies at the center of all feminist literary criticism" (Mauguière 1997, 55), my exploration of France Daigle's work will focus on expressions of identity (of narrators and characters within stories that reveal their self-consciousness as works of fiction dealing with issues of gender).[2] Although I focus on gender in this essay, I also analyze the construction of a text that conceals or reveals gender issues.

France Daigle's publications have all been reviewed in Canada but have attracted relatively little attention from literary critics, who have "paid little attention to the odd books of the young compatriot of the already standard and reassuring Antonine Maillet,"[3] according to Gabrielle Poulin (18).[4] The reviewers rarely deal with the ambiguity implied by the narrative voices' gender, and their reactions to this issue often contradict each other. For example, in commenting on *Film d'amour et de dépendance* (*Film about Love and Dependency*), Jeannette Gaudet alludes to "an ambiguity concerning the partners' sexual identity" (158), on the one hand, and Michel Beaulieu states that the film director is male, while Stéphane Lépine mentions that "a dialogue starts . . . between man and woman" (20), on the other hand, whereas Daigle talks about a male *or* female voice. However, when she reviews this text, Sally Ross states that "the future film and the dialogue are bathed in a sort of androgynous twilight" (1985, 13). Lise Ouellet, for her part, wonders whether we are dealing with "Feminine or androgynous writing" (1984, 18). On another level, in her review of *L'Été avant la mort* (*The Summer Before Death*), Ross negates Hélène Harbec's voice when she states that the text is definitely in France Daigle's style. The only exception is Suzanne Côté who clearly reads *L'Été avant la mort* as a lesbian text. Although most interpretations usually silence the lesbian voice altogether, ambiguity concerning sexual identity should not be ignored when dealing with Daigle's work.

In the four texts published in the 1990s—*La Beauté de l'affaire. Fiction autobiographique à plusieurs voix sur son rapport tortueux au langage* (1991) (*The Beauty of the Thing: A Multi-voiced Autobiographical Fiction about its Difficult Relationship to Language*); *La Vraie vie* (1993) (*Real Life*, 1995); *1953, Chronique d'une naissance annoncée* (1995)[5] (*1953, Chronicle of a Birth Foretold, 1997*); and *Pas pire* (1998) (*Just Fine*, 1999)—France Daigle explores the role of narrative voices and the importance of language.[6] However, despite Daigle's growing recognition, only four critical essays have been published on her work, and all within Canada.[7]

In her text entitled *1953*, France Daigle refers to Roland Barthes's publication of *Le Degré zéro de l'écriture* (*Writing Degree Zero*, 1977), as one of the year's major events. Following this idea, I am reading Daigle's works in the context of *Le Plaisir du texte* (*The Pleasure of the Text*) where Barthes states: "Pleasure is continually disappointed, reduced, deflated, in favor of strong, noble values: Truth, Death, Progress, Struggle, Joy, etc. Its victorious rival is Desire: we are always being told about Desire, never about Pleasure" (411).[8] When Nicole Brossard talks about "une écriture de *dérive*" (writing adrift) in *La Lettre aérienne* (*The Aerial Letter*, 1988), she suggests that desire can also mean silence: "*Désir de dérive*: désir qui dévie du sens qu'on aurait cru que le texte prendrait—censure quant à une première intention du texte, parfois censure intégrale: silence" (53) [*Elusion desire*: desire which deviates from the sense one would have expected the text to take—censure with respect to the text's primary intention, at times complete censure: silence] (76). I also use Barthes's notion of the "grain" of writing—that is, "the sound of speech *close up*" as it is captured by cinema (413) to analyze the "pleasure of the text" experienced when reading Daigle's works. The reader's pleasure is produced by the complexity of Daigle's narrative based on past events and postmodern notions of fragmentation of identity. By examining the complex structure of Daigle's texts, I present this modern Acadian voice and her subversion of "identity" in the context of the 1990s lesbian literary production. However, to understand Daigle's evolution as a writer, I begin by exploring her previous publications.

France Daigle published her first three texts within three years, and they should be read as a trilogy, as she suggests in her essay entitled "En me rapprochant sans cesse du texte"[9] ("Getting Ever Closer to the Text"). The trilogy includes (1) *Sans jamais parler du vent: Roman de crainte et d'espoir que la mort arrive à temps* (1983) (*Without Ever Talking about the Wind: A Novel about the Fear and Hope that Death Will Come on Time*), (2) *Film d'amour et de dépendance: Chef-d'œuvre obscur* (1984) (*Film About Love and Dependency: An Obscure Work of Art*), and (3) *Histoire de la maison qui brûle, Vaguement suivi d'un dernier regard sur la maison qui brûle* (1985) (*Story of the Burning House, Vaguely Followed by a Last Look at the Burning House*).

In the essay mentioned above, "En me rapprochant sans cesse du texte," Daigle describes the six various stages of writing that one of her texts underwent, and in the process she presents some of her theories about writing that she will use again in her following books. She admits that "Sans être théoricienne de l'écriture, je crois que c'est dans cette admission de et ce recours direct à la confusion que réside le côté essentiellement moderne de cette entreprise littéraire" (44) [Without being a theorist about writing, I believe that it is in the admission of—and the direct recourse to—confusion that the essentially modern aspect of this literary endeavor lies]. In these comments, Daigle also explains why in her writing "se trouve un lien de parenté avec la modernité" [a relationship with modernity can be found]:

> Vivant dans un contexte où la tradition littéraire est à peu près inexistante, je n'avais pas de modèle contre lequel mesurer mon ambition de vouloir "écrire le livre de la mer sans jamais parler du vent." La mer était alors synonyme de liberté, et le vent représentait tout ce qui aurait pu venir troubler cette liberté. L'écriture elle-même se voulait aussi sans attaches.... C'est sans doute cet aspect *dénudé* de la langue et de

l'expression acadienne qui a fait en sorte que ce sentier s'avère finalement voie directe, pour ne pas dire voie rapide, vers la modernité. (44)

[Living in an environment in which literary tradition barely exists, I had no model against which I could measure my ambition to want to "write a book on the sea without ever talking about the wind." The sea was then synonymous with freedom, and the wind meant anything that could have disturbed that freedom. The act of writing itself needed to be without any ties. . . . It is undoubtedly this *bare* aspect of Acadian language and expression that allowed this path to be a direct way, if not an express way, to modernity.]

Daigle suggests that "ce questionnement sur la personnalité et la place incalculables de l'écrivain/e se trouve reflété par le contexte duquel a été extraite la version publiée du passage" (44–45) [this questioning on the invaluable personality and position of the writer is reflected by the context from which the published version of the passage came], and she also defines the mission of the modern writer: "Vivre là exactement où les autres sont de passage. Vivre de passage là où les autres ont une histoire qu'ils qu'elles revendiquent. Notre histoire qui ne compte pas l'écrire. Ne plus se demander à la fin du conte si les choses se suivent. Arriver à conter ou à faire compter, tout simplement" (45) [To live precisely where others only come to visit. To live as if one was just passing through where others have a history to which they lay claim. To write our story that does not matter. Not to wonder at the end whether things are connected with each other. Simply being able to recount or to make it count]. The modern writer must take risks and live and write apart from the general trends, according to her statement and because "la [*sic*] langage inventé par l'homme est pure aliénation" [language as created by man is pure alienation], and "therefore, we must destroy . . . the discourse of patriarchal society," as Josette Déléas-Matthews suggests (123).

In their study entitled "Symétries et réflexivité dans la trilogie de France Daigle" ("Symmetry and Reflexivity in France Daigle's Trilogy"), Raoul Boudreau and Anne-Marie Robichaud stress the symmetry of structure in the first three texts published by Daigle and indicate the relationship among them to suggest that "the trilogy . . . departs from the structure of the traditional novel by denouncing its main circular structure" (147). They also mention a "metaphorical contamination" (150) in reference to recurrent images. These two aspects of Daigle's work—structure of the text and metaphors—are indeed essential. Another important aspect of

Daigle's work is her belief that writing can express everything: "[à cette époque] où je crois encore qu'un jour j'y arriverai au bout de l'écriture et qu'alors je saurai comment vivre. Comme si l'écriture ne serait [sic] qu'un apprentissage, une manière de se rapprocher d'une sorte d'absolu" ("Autoportrait" 40) [(at this time) when I still believe that one day I'll be able to reach the end of writing and that by then I'll know how to live. As if writing were only an apprenticeship, a way to get closer to a kind of absolute].

René Plantier's study of France Daigle included in *Le Corps du déduit* (1996) (*The Inferred Body*) deals mainly with "l'ubiquité vitale" (vital ubiquity) in *Sans jamais parler du vent* and also with the "presence of the body" in the trilogy.[10] Plantier's analysis includes a study of structural symmetry similar to Boudreau and Robichaud's comments as presented in their essay published eight years earlier (1988). Plantier does mention the similarity of his position with theirs, however. As Boudreau and Robichaud indicate, "Once again, the first novel serves to initiate the decoding of these privileged metaphors which can be recognized immediately when they reappear in the following novels" (149, quoted by Plantier 1996, 119–20).

A brief study of the texts Daigle published in the 1980s provides a better understanding of her subsequent production. However, in the 1990s Daigle's horizon has widened, and although we can recognize some of her previous preoccupations with language, structures, and images, her situations, characters, perspectives, and style have evolved.

La Beauté de l'affaire (1991)

The construction of *La Beauté de l'affaire* is as rigorous as Daigle's previous texts, but the structure is more complex.[11] In his examination of the structure of this book (137–51), Plantier mentions that it contains at least two story lines: the story of the architect and his wife who pray in a church and the story of artistic creation, the role of art, writing, and reading, or, as Plantier states, "a meditation on art" and "the meditation of a Christian man facing his civic duty" (138). Martine Jacquot refers to this structure as "a parallel between the story of creation and the act of writing" (38), and Alain Rasson stresses the image of building or construction and the concept of inhabiting one's culture (40). These two levels of narration suggest that if the human story—the architect and his dealings with his wife or with his job—is important, any aspect dealing with art is also essential and creates a double plot or "a novel about trifling things and a novel about sublime inventions" (Plantier 1996, 139), where the small facts of life count as much as works of creation, invention, imagination, or the reshaping of history. The reader must also play the part of a creator to make sense out of these various story lines, "wondering about the relationships between sensations and means of expressing them" (Plantier 1996, 139–40). In her review, Robichaud states that "the most interesting aspect (of her texts) lies in the way they are staged, and not in the plot" (82).

The main "characters" are the architect and his wife, but there is also a "third" person who might in fact be the "I" of an androgynous narrator telling/creating the story. When Plantier asks "Where is the author?" he suggests, "He is . . . there in the 'possessive' form, but he is not confessing in the autobiographical mode" (140). Yet, the author/narrator is not alone, and the naming of other authors connects Daigle's narrative with their voices, suggesting a link with her own texts: "Sa dette à Duras. Comme tout le monde elle a joué, une fois, à *India Song*, répétant nombre de demi-phrases avec cette ardeur monotone en posant son regard translucide ici et là sur les fissures des murs, les bras des fauteuils, les ferrures vieillotes de la chambre de pension surchauffée mais mal éclairée" (*Beauté* 10) [Her debt to Duras. Like everyone else, she acted out *India Song* once, repeating many half-sentences with a monotonous ardor while gazing here and there in a translucid manner at the cracks in the walls, the arms of the armchairs, the old-fashioned ironwork of the overheated but poorly lit rented room]. Daigle mentions "les trous du langage" (39) [the holes in language], which are also reminiscent of Duras. She adds further: "Encore ce jeu d'assemblage et de construction. Elle dit qu'elle peut seulement croire à ce qui éclate dans tous les sens, ou à ce qui ne bouge pas, à une certaine fixité" (*Beauté* 13) [Once again dealing with assembling and constructing. She says that she can only believe in what explodes in every direction, or in what does not move, a certain steadiness]. This "éclatement dans tous les sens" [explosion in every direction] indicates either a fragmentation of meaning or an explosion of all the senses or passions.

This postmodern fragmentation is typical of the structure of the text itself because the story is also fragmented to a point where it needs to be recovered or reconstructed. This "explosion" also suggests a desire to please the modern reader, to suggest a new definition of "beauty" in literature and to expose the reader to a new sense of "pleasure of the text." However, the narrator also believes in "ce qui ne bouge pas" [that which does not move], something fixed and stable, such as the beauty created by the architect of the text, the eternal quest for beauty experienced by all artists, although their definition of beauty may be different at various times. However, "Elle dit tout cela mais en retenant quelque chose" (14) [She says all this while withholding something]; therefore, she does not reveal everything at once. It takes time for this new sense of beauty to be accepted: "Puis . . . cela prend une forme de permanence, cela devient elle" (14) [Then . . . this becomes more permanent, this becomes part of her]. This break from the past suggests a new beginning. The old words assembled in a new fashion, in a new project, eventually become permanent.

Plantier examines the complex structure of *La Beauté* and states that the even-numbered pages contain one text whereas the odd-numbered pages contain two texts, and all the texts are short. Therefore, by following the narrative that the reader can reconstruct from reading only the even-numbered pages, Plantier establishes the story of a man, "l'homme à la chaloupe" (144) [the man in a rowboat], but some even-numbered pages also include a different narrative (141). Plantier explains that the narrative on page 14, for example, is in fact about a critical reflection on writing itself, which follows directly the statement made on the previous page where the narrator states her beliefs regarding literature (Plantier 1996, 141): "Encore ce jeu d'assemblage . . ." (13) [once again this toying with construction . . .]. Plantier gives other examples dealing with writing. On page 20, for example, he states that "on the contrary, the text . . . breaks away from the distance of writing" (142).

Direct references to daily life also recall Duras: "Her sister writes to her from Paris that she is reading *La Vie matérielle*" (Plantier 1996, 142). Plantier fails to note that *La Vie matérielle* is another title by Duras, which complements the reference made earlier and which suggests that "Sa dette à Duras" (10) [Her debt to Duras] is not just about *India Song*. Plantier mentions "the material aspect of any creation" and adds that "the craftsman creates his own edification" (142), but fails to mention this other debt to Duras. In fact, the whole book owes something to Duras: its characters, tone, and images, the importance of houses or stones (or Stein and p/ Pierre in Duras's work), and the style of "half-sentences," as well as the role of God and the Church—all have parallels in Duras's work. However, Plantier explains that "between the believer and the writer there are similarities in the composition of the place of meeting and of exchange" (151). For both the believer and the writer the book plays an essential role: both need faith to read or to write the book on an every day basis.

Later on, Plantier also examines the odd numbered pages, the story of the architect per se, and calls this part "the architect's novel" (144–45). He further notes that "[t]he story of the man in a rowboat parallels the story of writing, which parallels the story of the architect and his wife which parallels a story about a construction site" (145). The complex structure of this text parallels the complex position of an author from Acadia trying to write in French in a mainly anglophone country under the influence of such a famous Acadian figure as Antonine Maillet. This position is complicated by the presence of English invading everything. In such an environment, one can only be schizophrenic, if not have multiple personalities.

The subtitle of *La Beauté de l'affaire* is *Fiction autobiographique à plusieurs voix sur son rapport tortueux au langage*, which suggests several contradictions: "fiction" and "autobiography" are usually separate genres. However, in *Amantes* (1980) (*Lovhers*, 1986), Nicole Brossard defines autobiography as 'l'apparence des faits" (37) [the appearance of facts], which suggests fiction. Furthermore, an "autobiography" is usually written by a single voice and not several, as Daigle's title suggests. The key to the whole book might be found in "son rapport tortueux au langage" [its difficult relationship to language] which stresses the complexity of the relationship between the genre used and language itself. Another aspect of this "fiction autobiographique" (autobiographical fiction) is the silencing of the lesbian narrator in the text: "Les mots comme support de la réalité et, de toute façon, le silence qui fait déjà partie du langage" (43) [Words used to support reality and in any case, silence which is already part of language]. We examine in the next texts how this silence gives the lesbian voice/body a new dimension, because, as Brossard stated in *La Lettre aérienne*, "Toute écriture de fiction est une stratégie pour affronter le réel, pour transformer la réalité, pour en inventer une autre" (72) [All writing of fiction is a strategy for confronting what is real, for transforming this reality, for inventing another one] (92).

La Vraie vie (1993)

In *La Vraie vie* (*Real Life*), the construction of the text is once again central. In her "Découpages et dérapages" ("Cuts and Slips"), Lucie Joubert explains that this text "is divided into one hundred paragraphs properly numbered and titled; and divided into five equal chapters, themselves subdivided into symmetrical parts of two . . . each part . . . presenting alternatively two of the novel's six characters" (4). Each one of these five chapters has a symbolic title such as (1) "L'Aléatoire ordonné" ("Ordered Random"), (2) "Le plus facile" ("The Easier Way"), (3) "Sans trop croire et pourtant sur le qui-vive de croire" ("Without Really Believing but Ready to Believe"), (4) "La Vraie histoire" ("The Real Story"), and (5) "Une si courte éternité" ("Such a Short Eternity"). Each "chapter" is divided into two parts and each one of these parts is itself divided into ten "fragments," each one with its own title.

According to Joubert, *La Vraie vie* provides "a reflection on life, the *real* and *ordinary* life lived by quite ordinary-looking characters," and "the characters . . . destroy the old cliches and suggest new ways to see human destiny" (4). In her "Reality Bites," Eileen Manion further explains that "Although Daigle provides scant plot, her prose has a cinematic quality; the reader can admire her well-composed scenes as they slip past with the ease and speed of a film" (37).[12] Manion also suggests that "we meet characters in constant movement, either oscillating between Montreal and Moncton, or driving around one city or the other" (37), and she indicates the diversity of personalities that Daigle has conceived. "Real life," for these characters, is "A prolonged effort to avoid tension and anxiety. . . . The only energy they exhibit is intellectual, as they 'struggle with their paradoxes' " (Manion 1995, 38).

On the other hand, Frédérick Martin's "L'Envers du décor et le décor du réel" ("Underneath the Decor and the Decor of Reality") suggests a more negative reading of *La Vraie vie*. Martin calls this text "a fragmented novel" or "a pure exercise of style" (18). He states that the six characters seem to be "looking for meaning" (18), and that Daigle "gives the impression that she is engaging in a meditation on existence rather than setting up a fiction" (18). However, Martin seems to forget that modern fiction is different and that readers cannot expect to find the same old familiar characteristics anymore, as Daigle herself explained in her essay on *Sans jamais parler du vent*.[13]

La Vraie vie is easy to read at first, but to understand it well can take time, as Daigle wrote to me in a personal correspondence (28 May 1998): "Ce livre qui a mijoté pendant 4 ans, et nécessité 3 mois d'écriture, n'exige que 2 heures de lecture . . . sans parler des relectures" [This book, which simmered for 4 years and took 3 months to write, takes only 2 hours to read . . . and this does not include rereadings]. To be reconstructed, the complexity of the story lines demands an active participation on the part of the reader, and a cursory reading cannot provide the full depth of the characters' situations.

The six characters seem to be all alone at first, and their own contradictions underline their pain and suffering: Élizabeth, who is a doctor specializing in cancer treatment, is not happy with her life, as she states at the beginning of the book: "elle aimerait avoir une vie" (9) [she'd like to have a life] (3). She explains that she says this "comme d'autres glissent dans la conversation qu'ils rêvent d'écrire un livre" (9) [in the same way that other people mention casually that they'd like to write a book] (3). Her unhappiness is not due to her work but rather stems from her emotional state, as Manion suggests. This parallel between having a life and writing a book is obviously significant. She distinguishes between "être en vie" (being alive), more or less by chance, and having a life: "Comme si la vie était une chose que l'on pouvait réussir à posséder vraiment" (9) [As if life were a thing one could really possess] (3). She is convinced that "les humains . . . portent tous en eux une connaissance absolue de la vraie vie et de la vraie mort, et que c'est essentiellement un manque d'imagination qui les empêche d'accéder à cette connaissance" (44) [human beings . . . all have within themselves an absolute knowledge of real life and real death, and that it is essentially a lack of imagination that prevents them from coming to grips with this knowledge] (45). She is a doctor not only in order to save lives, as she tells one of her patients who wishes to die, but primarily because she wants to alleviate suffering.

Another character, Denise, is a taxi driver who "likes to get people moving" (Manion 1995, 37). She also likes art but "n'aime pas qu'on manipule le sens. Elle veut être séduite sur le coup, par la beauté simple et expressive des choses" (44) [does not want to feel that there is an implied meaning. She wants to be seduced instantly, by the simple and expressive beauty of things] (44). Denis, for his part, also wonders about meaning in his own way. He usually makes videos for animals, but at the end of this story he is trying one for humans, and several characters end up in his video (Rodriguez et al). With Denis's films, the reader must wonder if all the characters are not acting in a film, as in Peter Weir's *The Truman Show*. Symbolic images—the boat floating on the water (also found in *Pas pire*), the taxi roaming all over the streets of Montreal, the hotel room in Rome, and images of art dealing with diseases and illnesses—all express various theories on life and death and the fragility of life.

1953, CHRONIQUE D'UNE NAISSANCE ANNONCÉE (1995)

1953, Chronique d'une naissance annoncée is an even more complex story, in which Daigle alludes directly to *La Vraie vie* (101). In her review entitled "Acadian Spring," Sally Ross finds *1953* "very similar to her previous novels in that it is composed of multiple story lines that overlap and intertwine," and that in this text as in her previous ones, "France Daigle explores the act of writing and the complex relationship between fiction and reality" (8). Therefore, according to Ross, "the way historical events are recounted becomes a major focus" (8). In *1953*, the story of Bébé M's disease alternates with historical events, such as, "En 1953, le monde occidental fut témoin d'un autre grand moment littéraire outre la parution du *Degré zéro de l'écriture* de Roland Barthes" (18) [In 1953, the Western world witnessed another great literary moment, aside from the publication of Roland Barthes's *Writing Degree Zero*] (15). Ross explains that "There are innumerable literary and philosophical threads that bind together the real and the fictitious stories contained in *1953*" (8). The main threads are the year 1953 itself, the year of Daigle's birth, and all the events that occurred that year, but also the significance of the local paper *L'Évangéline*.[14] Ross states that *1953* is "a dense and complex work. On one level, it is the chronicle of the creation of a novel. On another level, it provides an amazing glimpse of Acadian society in the early 1950s, filtered, of course, through the eyes and choices of an Acadian woman in the 1990s" (9).

In her review entitled "L'Écriture du roman" ("The Writing of the Novel"), Francine Bordeleau further explains that *1953* has a dual structure: "On the one hand: the news that can be found in *L'Évangéline*. . . . On the other hand: the author's analyses supported by Barthes, Stalin and Communism present a choice selection" (23). On the one hand, there are simple characters such as the two nurses, Garde Vautour and Garde Comeau, who read the local paper to find out about world affairs, and, on the other hand, the author presents her comments and meditations on life and language, as Bordeleau suggests: "*In this coded universe* the 'definition,' that is to say the separation, between Good and Evil is now the main focus of language and is no longer aimed at creating a Marxist explanation of the facts . . . but to present reality as seen through the eyes of judgment" (23). Bordeleau also indicates the parallel between *1953* and *La Vraie vie* because "in fact, many chapters from *1953* recall this novel's main characters; therefore one can be read as a continuation of the other" (23). She adds that

Pas pire (1997)

Seduction and novelty are also present in Daigle's latest title to date, which can also be called a narrative on origins.[15] *Pas pire* (*Just Fine*) is a first-person narrative in which the narrator is named France Daigle (for the first time, page 115), suggesting an autobiographical text. However, several scenes, such as Daigle's own participation in Bernard Pivot's famous program, are fictitious. Therefore, the reader must question the role of the subject who says "I," as well as the use of reality and fiction. *Pas pire* is the story of France Daigle, the narrator of the text, who is afflicted with agoraphobia and who talks about it honestly. In this book, general comments (about deltas or astrology—the text is structured around the houses used in astrology—and about language issues) alternate with stories of the narrator's childhood in the town of Dieppe, in New Brunswick. However, the name Dieppe also recalls a town in Normandy, which was the stage of "une désastreuse opération expérimentale" (32) [that disastrous expedition] (23), causing the death of thousands if not millions of soldiers in 1942.

The narrator's memories go back to the beginnings of times: "Je me revois bébé . . . je viens de naître" (43) [I'm a baby again . . . I've just been born] (34). Yet, she also shares memories of her people, more specifically through smells, such as "l'odeur du bouillon de mon peuple" (50) [the smell of Acadian bouillon] (40), which is the "bouillon" of Acadian culture coming from the kitchen of her friend and neighbor Marie.[16] This "bouillon" parallels the "Bouillon of culture" served up weekly by Bernard Pivot for the French public interested in literature and art in general. At the end of *Pas pire*, there is an exceptional scene in which the author named France Daigle imagines that she was invited by Bernard Pivot to discuss her work, entitled *Pas pire*, for "Bouillon de Culture." Pivot is leafing through the very book that we are reading before interviewing his distinguished guest. This scene, placed at the end of the book, seems to summarize the whole story and guide our own reading. Pivot, literary critic *par excellence*, states: "Il y aurait encore beaucoup de choses qu'on pourrait dire de ce livre, beaucoup de métaphores et d'évocations qu'il serait intéressant d'explorer"

(154) [Much more could be said about this book; it would be interesting to explore many metaphors and allusions] (135).

Indeed, as Pivot states, we know that everything is not and cannot be said about this text. The story we are told combines fiction and reality, as suggested by Pivot who says that in this book, "on ne distingue pas très bien le réel de la fiction" (153) [one can't easily distinguish the real from the fictional] (134). As a response to Pivot, the author of *Pas pire* explains that one of the characters, the Minister of Culture, is fictitious, but she does not say anything about the reality or the fiction of the other characters. As a matter of fact, the questions supposedly asked by Pivot offer an interpretation of the symbolism and metaphors of this text but can also mislead the reader. This *mise en abyme* is humoristic on several levels and indicates Daigle's playfulness with language, but it also stresses the work involved in the structure of the text, its architecture, as her comments on her first text already suggested.

In her review of *Pas pire* entitled "Littérature acadienne: Espace et écriture" ("Acadian Literature: Space and Writing"), Blandine Campion states that "meaning . . . never presents unequivocal, monolithic truth" (D4). In another review of the same book, "Éloge du plaisir et de la lenteur, France Daigle et l'espace cérébral" ("Praise on Pleasure and Slowness: France Daigle and the Cerebral Space"), Campion suggests that the word, "ludique" (playful), is the term that best describes Daigle's relationship to the world in general and to writing in particular. Interviewed by Campion, France Daigle underlines her wish that her readers find "pleasure in playing" when reading her texts: "Mais c'est mon premier souhait: que le livre procure un plaisir de jeu, dans lequel on peut se laisser aller sans avoir forcément à questionner tous les éléments" (D1) [But this is my primary wish: that the book provides a pleasure in playing in which one can let go without necessarily having to question all its elements]. Campion goes on to say that the word, "jeu" (game/play), is present many times in *Pas pire* and that the author "'enjoys' deconstructing and reconstructing temporality as well as the different plots that she intermingles, creating echoes and parallel effects, multiplying discourses and cultural or historical references" (D2).

Therefore, what strikes France Daigle's reader is that her fiction is like a "casse-tête" (a puzzle). This image "crystallizes all the main elements present in France Daigle's writing, according to Campion. The puzzle evokes both the playful aspect of the text and the fragmented aspect of contemporary life present in France Daigle's books as well as fictions themselves, in which the use of the typographical white space plays an important part. Finally it reveals the element of reflection and of reconstruction of meaning so fundamental to the author's approach to writing" (D2). What France Daigle tries to accomplish when she writes is "apporter des petits plaisirs, tout en cherchant à voir le grand portrait à travers les fragments" [to bring small pleasures while at the same time trying to see the big picture beyond its fragments] as she states in the same interview with Campion (D2). However, she also confesses that "l'auteur de fiction n'est pas le maître absolu du sens de son œuvre" (*Pas pire* 45) [fiction writers are not the absolute masters of their works] (36). Many puns or comical situations—such as the parallel between a punk named Chuck Bernard and Bernard Pivot (same glasses, she says) or the meeting between Terry Thibodeau and the French writer on Terry's boat—suggest different readings according to the narrative threads the reader may choose to explore.

When reading France Daigle's texts, one is struck by their complex structure which forces the reader to participate actively in the reconstruction of the text. During the Congrès International d'Études Francophones in 1998 where she presented her work, France Daigle stressed her evolution as an artist and stated that the more she writes, the more she appropriates language. She indicated that she is leading toward something that belongs to her more and more.[17] She also mentioned her evolution as a writer to explain how fiction and reality work together and how "le langage et la forme du récit progressent" [language and the form of the story progress]. She described *Pas pire* as "un roman virtuel, pas encore écrit" [a virtual novel not yet written] and talked about a "livre-expérience" [an experimental book] which is "conçu à la lumière de [s]a propre expérience de vie et d'écriture" [conceived in the light of her own experience with life and with writing]. Such statements on language and style clearly indicate that her writing is self-reflexive. Yet, she also raises important questions on the role of "l'artiste multi-disciplinaire du vingtième siècle" [the twentieth century multidisciplinary artist] as depository of a mosaic of knowledge. For her, multidiscipline is "le résultat d'un rapprochement, d'un décloisonnement entre plusieurs médiums" [the result of a coming together, a decompartmentalization among several mediums], which is clearly the case in *Pas pire* with its references to cinema, painting, and theater.[18]

France Daigle's texts all display the same complexity in their construction, especially with the use of recurring images. Her characters and story lines inscribe her in the company of modern lesbian voices who challenge the position of the character, the author, and the text, particularly in the revision of gender construction and representation. Daigle's work must be read in the context of these multiple voices and in connection with more famous voices from other parts of francophone Canada, mainly Québec, such as Alonzo, Blais, and Brossard, or another voice emerging from New Brunswick, her compatriot Hélène Harbec, with whom she wrote *L'Été avant la mort*. France Daigle and the four authors I mentioned earlier may also be called "nouvelles Prométhées" [new Prometheas], to use Patricia Smart's term:[19] "New Prometheas, these women writers do not seem to want to steal fire, but rather to tame language and Totality by discovering their bodily qualities" (145).[20]

Notes

1. When no English translation has been published, I have included my own translation of the title of the work (Alonzo, Harbec, Daigle, et al . . .) with no date after the English title.

2. France Daigle has published nine "novels" to date, and I will deal mainly with the ones published in the 1990s. Daigle has also worked for the cinema: (1) narrator for the experimental film *Tending Towards the Horizontal* (film director Barbara Sternberg from Toronto. 33 min., 16 mm. color), 1988; (2) Scenario for "Portrait," 1987, not produced; (3) with Renée Blanchar, scriptwriter of *L'Arrangement*; work in progress for the Productions Phare-Est, Moncton, 1998; (4) with Jean-Marc Larivière, scriptwriter of *La Vraie vie;* work in progress for the Productions Phare-Est, Moncton, 1998. Daigle's professional awards include "Prix Eloize" for *Pas pire* (1998); "Prix France-Acadie" for *Pas pire* (1998); "Prix Pascal-Poirier d'excellence en littérature" given by the governor of New Brunswick (1991); Author-in-residence at the University of Moncton (1997); Grant from the Conseil des Arts of New Brunswick (1991 and 1993); Grant from the Conseil des Arts of Canada (1994 and 1996–97); member of juries for the Conseil des Arts of Canada (1995 and 1998). (Personal correspondence, April 1999).

3. Unless otherwise noted, all translations are my own. I would like to thank my colleague, Jeff Chamberlain, from George Mason University, for his thorough reading and for his help with the translations of this essay. However, any "contresens" is my own.

4. The 45 reviews I have read on Daigle's work were all published in Canada, except for Françoise Favretto's published in Belgium. My complete bibliography on Daigle is forthcoming.

5. Further references to this text will appear as *1953*.

6. *La Vraie vie, 1953, Chronique d'une naissance annoncée*, and *Pas pire* have all been published in English by The House of Anansi Press.

7. My essay is the first study focusing exclusively on Daigle published outside of Canada, except for a section in Runte's *Writing Acadia: The Emergence of Acadian Literature 1970–1990*. See Boudreau and Robichaud (1988), Cook (1994), Déléas-Matthews (1988), Gaudet (1988), Masson (1998), Ouellet (1993), and Plantier (1996 and 1998), all published within Canada.

8. The translation of Barthes's text comes from Susan Sontag's *A Barthes Reader*.

9. In this essay, Daigle deals with the evolution of her writing in *Sans jamais parler du vent*. She states that "je conçois ces trois livres comme une trilogie, tant au niveau de la forme qu'au niveau de certaines constantes thématiques" (43) [I envision these three books as a trilogy, on the level of form, as well as on the level of certain constant themes].

10. Plantier's book, *Le Corps du déduit*, has been an excellent point of departure for my own study. Plantier focuses on Daigle's works published in the 1980s but also includes a study of *La Beauté de l'affaire*. However, there are several problems in the references Plantier gives (or does not, as the case may be): for example, a text by France Daigle quoted on p. 107 and p. 118 in Plantier's analysis, "En me rapprochant sans cesse du texte" (*De l'avant-texte*) is not quoted in his selective bibliography established by Marguerite Maillet (159–61). The "Colloque de Moncton en août 1991" (110) has no reference in the bibliography either. The entry for Déléas-Matthews gives *Cultures du Canada français* as the journal where her essay was published (161), when it is in fact *Atlantis* (which is given in a note on page 118, but with the wrong volume number: 11 instead of 14). Boudreau and Robichaud's essay is said to have been published in *Dalhousie French Review* although it was published in *Dalhousie French Studies*.

11. Further references to this text will appear as *La Beauté*.

12. Manion's comments also allude to Daigle's *Film d'amour et de dépendance*.

13. Martin also states that "Ms. Daigle always lived in Moncton" (18), although Daigle herself stated in "Autoportrait" that she wrote *Sans jamais parler du vent* in Paris and that she also lived in Montréal for a while. A better knowledge of Daigle's biography or a closer reading of her own texts might have resulted in more accurate comments.

14. This local paper read by several characters deals with Acadian culture and is described by Daigle in *1953* as "un journal qui permettait aux Acadiens de ne pas être retranchés du réseau névralgique de la Terre" (21) [a newspaper that provided Acadians with a link to the nerve centres of the world] (18). *L'Évangéline* is also a long poem by Longfellow telling the dramatic story of the near genocide of the Acadian people in the 18th century.

15. See my review of Daigle's *Pas pire* in "Lectures acadiennes" (222–25).

16. "Bouillon de Culture" is a famous TV program in which Bernard Pivot invites artists to discuss their work. It is as popular as his previous TV program, *Apostrophes*. An invitation to this program may be as important to some artists as a nomination to l'Académie française [the French Academy], because it guarantees a broad audience. France Daigle's fictional visit to this program is ironic on many levels.

17. These comments were made by France Daigle at the CIEF on 28 May 1998, during a plenary session entitled: "L'Œuvre et l'artiste multi-disciplinaires" (Multidisciplinary Works and Artists).

18. Gabrielle Poulin calls this multidisciplinary technique "the contamination of genres" (18), and Boudreau and Robichaud call it "metaphorical contamination" (150, as quoted above).

19. Smart used this term to describe four women writing in 1985: Louise Bouchard, Carole Massé, Virginie Sumpf, and Esther Rochon. However, it can also apply to other women writers, as I suggest here.

20. I would like to thank a special friend, Sylvie Bompis, who was extremely generous with her time and went to the National Library of Ottawa and to Chap-

ters bookstore in Ottawa to retrieve the English versions of Daigle's texts. This work would not have been complete without her precious help.

Works Cited

Alonzo, Anne-Marie. *Galia qu'elle nommait amour*. Laval, Québec: Trois, 1992.

Barthes, Roland. *Le Plaisir du texte*. Paris: Seuil, 1973. Translated by Richard Miller under the title *The Pleasure of the Text*. (New York: Hill and Wang, A Division of Farrar, Straus & Giroux, 1975. Rpt. in Susan Sontag's *A Barthes Reader*. New York: Hill and Wang, 1982. 404–14).

———. *Le Degré zéro de l'écriture*. Paris: Seuil, 1972. Translated by Annette Lavers and Colin Smith under the title *Writing Degree Zero* (New York: Hill and Wang, 1977).

B. M. [Beaulieu, Michel]. "*Film d'amour et de dépendance* par France Daigle." *Livres d'ici* (November 1984): 21–22.

Blais, Marie-Claire. *Soifs*. Montréal: Boréal, 1995. Translated by Sheila Fischman under the title *These Festive Nights* (Toronto: Anansi, 1997).

Bordeleau, Francine. "L'Écriture du roman." [On *1953, Chronique d'une naissance annoncée*.] *Lettres québécoises* 79 (Automne 1995): 23–24.

Boudreau, Raoul, and Anne-Marie Robichaud. "Symétries et réflexivité dans la trilogie de France Daigle." *Dalhousie French Studies* 15 (Fall-Winter 1988): 143–53.

Brossard, Nicole. *Amantes*. Montréal: Quinze, 1980. Translated by Barbara Godard under the title *Lovhers* (Montreal: Guernica, 1986).

———. *Baroque d'aube*. Montréal: L'Hexagone, 1995. Translated by Patricia Claxton under the title *Baroque at Dawn* (Toronto: McClelland and Stewart, 1997).

———. *La Lettre aérienne*. Montréal: Éditions du Remue-ménage, 1988. Translated by Marlene Wildeman under the title *The Aerial Letter* (Toronto: Women's Press, 1988).

Campion, Blandine. "Éloge du plaisir et de la lenteur. France Daigle et l'espace cérébral." [On *Pas pire*.] *Le Devoir* (8 août 1998): D1–2.

———. "Littérature acadienne: Espace et écriture." [On *Pas pire*]. *Le Devoir* (2–3 mai 1998): D4.

Cook, Margaret. "France Daigle: Dualité et opposition." *Littéréalité* 5.2 (Winter 1994): 37–46.

Côté, Suzanne. "*L'Été avant la mort*." *Canadian Woman Studies/Les Cahiers de la femme* 7.3 (Fall 1986): 127.

Daigle, France. "Autoportrait." *Québec français* 60 (December 1985): 40.

———. *La Beauté de l'affaire: Fiction autobiographique à plusieurs voix sur son rapport tortueux au langage*. Outremont, Québec: NBJ & Moncton: Éditions d'Acadie, 1991.

———. "En me rapprochant sans cesse du texte [à propos de *Sans jamais parler du vent*, p. 35]." Rpt. in *De l'avant-texte ou du texte dans tous ses états*. 2 vols. Edited by André Gervais. Montréal: Nouvelle barre du jour, 1986. 31–45.

———. *Film d'amour et de dépendance: Chef-d'œuvre obscur*. Moncton: Éditions d'Acadie, 1984.

———. *Histoire de la maison qui brûle, vaguement suivi d'un dernier regard sur la maison qui brûle*. Moncton: Éditions d'Acadie, 1985.

———. *Moncton-Sable*, play. Mise en scène by Louise Lemieux. Moncton, 1997.

———. *1953, Chronique d'une naissance annoncée*. Moncton: Éditions d'Acadie, 1995. Translated by Robert Majzels under the title *1953, Chronicle of a Birth Foretold*. (Toronto: Anansi Press, 1997).

———. *Pas pire*. Moncton: Éditions d'Acadie, 1998. Translated by Robert Majzels under the title *Just Fine* (Toronto: Anansi Press, 1999).

———. *Sans jamais parler du vent: Roman de crainte et d'espoir que la mort arrive à temps*. Moncton: Éditions d'Acadie, 1983.

———. *Variations en B et K, Plans, devis et contrats pour l'infrastructure d'un pont*. Montréal: NBJ, 1985.

———. *La Vraie vie*. Montréal: L'Hexagone; Moncton: Éditions d'Acadie, 1993. Translated by Sally Ross under the title *Real Life* (Toronto: Anansi, 1995).

———, and Hélène Harbec. *L'Été avant la mort*. Montréal: Éditions du remue-ménage, 1986.

Déléas-Matthews, Josette. "France Daigle: Une Écriture de l'exil, une écriture en exil." *Atlantis* 14.1 (Fall 1988): 122–26.

Favretto, Françoise. "France Daigle: *Sans jamais parler du vent*: poème-roman." *25/Mensuel* (Revue belge) 82/83 (March/April 1984): 43.

Gaudet, Jeannette. "La Métaphore du cinéma dans *Film d'amour et de dépendance: Chef-d'œuvre obscur* de France Daigle." *Dalhousie French Studies* 15 (Fall-Winter 1988): 154–59.

Harbec, Hélène. *L'Orgueilleuse*. Montréal: Les Éditions du remue-ménage, 1998.

Jacquot, Martine. "De l'Acadianité à l'américanité: Une Poésie de l'errance." *Dalhousie French Studies* 15 (Fall-Winter 1988): 134–42.

Joubert, Lucie. "Découpages et dérapages." [On *La Vraie vie*.] *Spirale* 131 (March 1994): 4.

Lépine, Stéphane. "France Daigle, *Film d'amour et de dépendance: Chef-d'oeuvre obscur*." *Nos livres* 15.5958 (December 1984): 19–20.

Longfellow, Henry Wadsworth. *Évangéline: A Tale of Acadie* (1847). *Évangéline and Selected Tales and Poems*. Selected with Introduction by Horace Gregory. New York: New American Library, 1964.

Manion, Eileen. "Reality Bites." [On *La Vraie vie*.] *Books in Canada* 24.7 (October 1995): 37–39.

Martin, Frédérick. "L'Envers du décor et le décor du réel." [On *La Vraie vie*.] *Lettres québécoises* 72 (Winter 1993): 17–18.

Masson, Alain. "Écrire, habiter." *Tangence* 58 (October 1998): 35–46. [On Daigle: 39–42].

Mauguière, Bénédicte. "Memory, Identity and Otherness in Contemporary Women's Writing in Québec." In *Women by Women: The Treatment of Female Characters by Women Writers of Fiction in Québec since 1980*, edited by Roseanna Lewis Dufault, 54–67. Madison, Teaneck, N.J.: Fairleigh Dickinson University Press, 1997.

Ouellet, Lise. "De l'autobiographie à la fiction autobiographique dans la littérature féminine." *La Licorne* 27 (1993): 365–78 [On Daigle: 368–72].

———. "*Film d'amour et de dépendance* de France Daigle." *Le Papier* 3 (November 1984): 18.

Plantier, René. *Le Corps du déduit: Neuf études sur la poésie acadienne, 1980–1990* [On Huguette Légaré, Dyane Léger, and France Daigle]. Moncton: Éditions d'Acadie, 1996. [Daigle 101–51].

———. "Le Renvoi de la balle acadienne: *1953*, de France Daigle." *Tangence* 58 (October 1998): 56–65.

Poulin, Gabrielle. "Prophétie et fiction, *L'Été avant la mort* de France Daigle et Hélène Harbec." *Lettres québécoises* 43 (Fall 1986): 18–20.

Ricouart, Janine. "Lectures acadiennes." [On Gérald Leblanc's *Moncton Mantra*, Hélène Harbec's *L'Orgueilleuse*, and France Daigle's *Pas pire*]. *Trois* 15.1, 2–3 (1999): 216–26.

Robichaud, Anne-Marie. "*La Beauté de l'affaire* de France Daigle." *Eloizes* 17 (Fall 1991): 81-83.

Ross, Sally. "Acadian Publications. *Histoire de la maison qui brûle* and *L'Été avant la mort.*" *Atlantic Provinces Book Review* 13, no. 4 (November-December 1986): 14.

———. "Acadian Spring." [On *1953*] *Atlantic Books Today* 10 (Summer 1995): 8–9.

———. "Three Recent Acadian Literary Works." [On *Film d'amour et de dépendance.*] *Atlantic Provinces Book Review* 12, no. 1 (February/March 1985): 13.

Runte, Hans R. *Writing Acadia: The Emergence of Acadian Literature 1970–1990*. Amsterdam and Atlanta, GA: Rodopi, 1997.

Smart, Patricia. "Prométhées au féminin: L'Écriture d'une nouvelle génération de femmes." [On Louise Bouchard's *Les Images*, Carole Massé's *Nobody*, Virginie Sumpf's *L'Irrecevable*, and Esther Rochon's *Coquillage*.] *Voix et images* 12, no. 1 (Fall 1986): 145–50.

Weir, Peter, Dir. *The Truman Show*. Paramount Pictures, 1998.

Memory, Sexuality, and Patriarchy: Emancipatory Strategies in Contemporary Franco-Albertan Women's Writing

PAMELA V. SING

CLICHÉS REGARDING NON-QUÉBÉCOIS FRANCOPHONE WOMEN IN CANADA (stereo)typify them as Catholic, conservative, and traditionalist. Unquestioningly upholding the role attributed to them by patriarchal discourses, thereby actively maintaining the status quo, they can hardly be qualified as feminists.

In Western Canada, French-speaking communities are at their most fragmented and dispersed (Aunger 1996, 194), and therefore, the minority status of the "collectivity," if the notion is still indeed applicable, renders it a most fragile entity. There one would expect the cliché to be particularly applicable, if only because of the fear of threatening the chances for survival of an already endangered sociocultural construct. Predictions of its demise have been repeated for more than a century now (Morice 1908, ix; Joy 1972, 21; Bourgault 1977, 15), albeit without fruition: the will to survive has far from vanished. Franco-Albertans and -Colombians continue to lay claim to their right to "vivre en français" (live in French), working continuously toward the flourishing and renewal of their culture. Certainly literary critics have tended to view the literary production of Western Canadian francophone women in this light, from both formal and thematic perspectives. Claire Dyan-Davis, for example, has found the representation of women's roles in Western Canadian francophone women's novels to have little in common with modern reality, Franco-Manitoban, Fransaskoise and Franco-Albertan authors having perpetuated the conventional form and mentality of the nineteenth-century novel. Citing the main character in Marguerite-A. Primeau's *Sauvage-Sauvageon*, Maxine, "the most educated of the francophone West's heroines," Dyan-Davis criticizes the anachronistic manner in which contemporary novels portray women whose intellect and education are unable to empower them in any way:[1] "The position they occupy, although important, is determined by a value system that undermines the individual to the advantage of the community (193).[2] Louise Renée Kasper, in her "feminist reflections" on the first two novels of Simone Chaput, a contemporary Franco-Manitoban novelist, recognizes along with Dyan-Davis the tendency toward conventional readerly writing[3] and the textualization of the self-effaced woman. However, she nuances the latter's conclusions by foregrounding "the difficulty of becoming a woman in Chaput's texts, and concludes by stating her wishes for the creation of "subtle, aggressive, tender, impertinent texts (259).[4] Clearly, for both these critics, as represented in contemporary women's novels, the renewal of Western Canadian francophone culture is profoundly problematic.

Interestingly, in the Far West, where both sociocultural and literary realities are painfully fragile, the contemporary novel is, to date, uniquely feminine.[5] Elsewhere (Sing 2000), I have elaborated on this phenomenon. I have cited, among a number of hypothetical reasons, the lack of francophone literary institutions in Alberta,[6] and the conservative character of the community, both of which have somehow resulted in women solely playing the role of "la gardienne de la culture" (guardian of the culture). Regardless of its sociocultural, economic, or psychological reasons, of course, the question points to the analogy to be established between the emerging voices of unknown Franco-Albertan women novelists and their characters, and that of the invisible Franco-Albertan community, and begs the following question: how are the silent and invisible writers of such a community, itself silent and invisible vis-à-vis the rest of the world, to find the courage to question, contest, and expose dominant practices without bringing the walls of that community down around them? One has had a glimpse of the contemporary novel written in francophone Manitoba, which benefits not only from having two literary presses and a number of other cultural institutions, but also from having an existence officially recognized by Ottawa and Québec City. However, in francophone Alberta, where one would expect the question of cultural renewal to be at its most problematic, women's contemporary novels express a distinctly subversive world vision.

The novels that will be discussed here all refer to the patriarchal vision responsible for either the initial establishing or the survival of the French fact in Alberta. After a brief look at the sociohistorical conjuncture that fostered the French-speaking presence in this Western province, one will quickly see how, in the first contemporary Franco-Albertan novel written and published by a woman,

Marguerite-A. Primeau, mentioned earlier, an "underground" feminine voice inscribes a counterideology that belies the tensions overshadowed by the dominant "Canadian" ideology explicitly expressed in the novel. (Between the publication of Primeau's novel, in 1960, and 1989, sexuality is not treated extensively in any novel by a Franco-Albertan woman writer. Therefore, I feel that it is indispensible to acquaint the reader with Primeau's writing on the theme before discussing contemporary versions.) In the novel of the 1990s, this contentious voice leaves the underground to not only accuse the one voice, author of women's traditional silence, but also to openly denounce it.

The Call to the West

During the fur trade era of the first third of the nineteenth century, French-Canadian explorers, fur traders, and voyageurs arrived from Québec in what is now Alberta. Intermarriage between the third group and native women created a new race, the Métis, whose culture, while being predominantly Indian, did conserve fragments of Québécois francophone cultural practices and language. In the 1840s, the arrival in the West of French-speaking Roman Catholic missionaries strengthened the Métis communities' French character. From this period until the late 1870s, French, the first European language spoken on the Canadian prairies, was heard at least as often as English. Soon, however, increasing numbers of English-speaking Protestant Ontarians moved west. Hoping to counterbalance this tendency, the Church elected "prêtres-colonisateurs" (colonizing priests), who, from 1870 to 1930, sought hard to build up Alberta's French-Canadian population, campaigning extensively mostly in Québec and New England, but also in France, Belgium, and Switzerland, to encourage settlement in the West. Although projected objectives were not met, an ethnically heterogeneous group of French-speaking homesteaders nevertheless colonized scattered parts of Alberta. There, the Roman Catholic fathers attempted to construct a homogeneous population, ever mindful of the vision expressed by their superiors. Because the majority of pioneers were originally from Québec then, Franco-Albertan villages were modeled after those in the East.[7] Experience would reveal the impossibility of the nationalist project, but official versions of the enterprise emphasize the "pure laine," cohesive, collective characteristics of these settlements whose raison d'être consisted of remaining French-Canadian by keeping the

Catholic faith on the one hand, and conserving the French language and the sociocultural practices that went along with speaking that language, on the other.

Dans le muskeg

I need hardly recall the discourse that bound traditional French-Canadian women to silent obedience and complete submission to the masculine heads of households and of the Church. Subalterns destined to second their husbands, brothers, and sons, and devoted mothers, they were forbidden to express any autonomous will or desires. Naturally, they were deprived of any sexual identity.

It is, therefore, revealing to discover that in Marguerite-A. Primeau's first novel, the voice and body of a sensual, feminine character inscribes a subtly powerful outlaw sexual/textual presence. Unsurprisingly, this 1950s French-Canadian *roman des origines* (novel of beginnings) relegates such an illegitimate element to an underground space: the perturbing presence is incarnated by a secondary character. Now, until recently, critics have referred to *Dans le muskeg* (1960) as a novel that naively recounts "the first seeds of an innocent and happy bilingual identity" (Dubé 1994, 88), or as a well-written work marked by the absence of "the woman who is beautiful, attractive, sensual, stable, and neither embittered, silly, nor deceitful" (Tessier 1988, 195). However, the protagonist, a Montreal-born schoolteacher imbued with the imperialistic dream of establishing a Québécois village in northern Alberta, is "punished" because, for puristic, nationalistic, ideological reasons, he sacrifices his love for a sensual blond Métisse toward whom he feels a strong sexual attraction. From the first moment that Joseph Lormier becomes aware of Antoinette Bolduc, she has an unsettling effect on him that, further on in the text, contaminates the narrative level.

First introduced as one of several indigenous (i.e., Indian and Métisse) prostitutes who linger about the prairie train stations, Antoinette belongs to the paradigm of outlaw sexuality and voice, the only sources of "relief" from and on the endlessly flat, monotonous prairie.[8] Even more than the clinging red dress she wears, the "fluidité" (fluidity) and "légèreté" (lightness) of her spoken French, "le bercement des syllabes . . . la mollesse avec laquelle les sons se fondaient l'un dans l'autre" (17) [the lilting of her syllables, the softness with which the sounds blended together] fascinate and shock the future patriarch. Her physical proximity causes him to lose control of his actions: despite himself, he reaches out to the warmth and texture of her hair before guiltily retracting his hand.

Months later, the couple meet for the second time at a Christmas party. Lormier, for whom the unforgettable young woman has come to incarnate the prairies, is once again drawn by the lilting voluptuousness of the young woman's French. She, sensing not only the impact she has had on the schoolteacher, but also the kind of life she could lead as his wife, has abandoned her provocative demeanor, and taken up residence with relatives living in the same village as Lormier. The priest, aware that the ardent young woman has her eye on the schoolteacher, approves of the mixed couple, but shares his thoughts only with the reader. Over the winter, as Antoinette adopts the French-Canadian values taught to her by the Catholic nuns, Lormier "forgets" that she is Métisse, conscious only that "l'appel de l'amour brûle au fond de son regard" (80) [the call of love burns, hot, in the depths of her regard]. The spring sees their first kiss, and then, unexpectedly, he addresses the young woman using the intimate "tu" (you), calling her, in a trembling voice, "mon amour" (82) (my love). Just when their union seems inevitable, malicious gossip regarding Antoinette's past sends Lormier away to Québec where, in order to forget the Métisse, he marries a woman whom he will never love. He takes her back to Alberta, they have a daughter, and they lose their much coveted son at birth. The village of Avenir thrives under his direction until, with the Depression, an Irish merchant is the only one to succeed in saving the community. Furthermore, despite the unyielding disapproval of both fathers, Lormier's daughter and the merchant's son fall in love and wish to marry. The novel ends the day after the wedding ceremony that symbolizes the Canadian solution to the problem of minority francophone survival: bilingualism. Yet, if the reader follows the secondary narrative involving the blond Métisse, it is clear that the novel contests the official version of events.

As Lormier grows old, disillusioned, and embittered, reproachful of the wife who has not provided him with "his due," a son, and as this woman dies, virtually dispatched by her husband's indifference, Antoinette marries one of her own kind, but becomes increasingly French-Canadian. Transformed into the young, elegant, self-assured mother of a "gamin blond en costume marin" [a blond youngster in a sailors' suit], she is a woman "dont n'importe qui eût été fier" (102) [anyone would be proud of], observes Lormier. One day, as Lormier's wife lies dying, he, having fled her presence, chances upon Antoinette. Embracing her passionately, he declares his unhappiness and his undying love for her, but she pushes him away, reminding "M'sieu Lormier" of their respectful sociomarital identities before turning away, leaving him thereafter "seul avec ses regrets" (207) [alone with his regrets].

During the ceremony recognizing the new bilingual, Catholic couple, his daughter's voice declaring "Oui, je le veux" [I do] evokes in the tearful schoolteacher's mind the image of the Métisse: she with whom, had he adapted to the Far West rather than play the unyielding role of the nationalist patriarch, it would have been possible to define an Other Canadian-ness, a hybrid, "impure" one, created in the image of the prairie's sociogeographical beginnings and predisposed to strengthening the French fact in the Canadian West.

COURTEPOINTE

In 1991, the French translation of Franco-Albertan Marie Moser's first novel, *Courtepointe*, was published, (re)creating fragments of the story of three generations of Franco-Albertan women, the first of whom is married to another Lormier. Written and published in English in 1987, under the title *Counterpoint*, the novel confirms the threat of assimilation that insidiously pervades Primeau's first novel: the author and narrator are products of the years when it was illegal to teach French in Alberta's school system. More explicitly than Primeau, then, Moser's narrator remembers, imagines, and reinvents Alberta's francophone history, supplementing the latter, but also criticizing and undermining it.

This occurs most explicitly on the thematic level, but the author also incorporates into her English text French lexical elements that may be interpreted as constituting both a metonymical representation of women's roles in a francophone patriarchal society and a critique of this society. Consistently used, these French words, although small in number, form an official *his*torical subtext from which are absent realities, nuances, or differences corresponding to pertinent aspects of any number of *her*stories. The brief discussion that follows illustrates what I mean.

The titles *Monsieur* and *Madame* as well as their abbreviations appear in the English version of the novel, as does the derogatory and disapproved-of term *vieille fille* (old maid), but not so *Mademoiselle*, which lends respectability to independent, unattached women. The polite expression of a man meeting a married woman for the first time, "Enchanté, Madame" [I am delighted, Madam], appears in the text, but not so any terms of affection or endearment.⁹ Unsurprisingly, the nationalist slogan "L'union fait la force" [union gives strength] is cited in French, as are the title *Monsieur le curé* [Sir, when addressing the priest], and the words consecrating Him whom the clergy represents, *"Je crois en Dieu, le Père Tout-Puissant, Créateur du ciel et de la terre"* [I believe in God, the Father almighty, Creator of heaven and earth . . .].¹⁰ The expressions *fille du roi* (daughter of the king) and *sage-femme* (midwife), to which I will return in more detail further on, also appear in French, as do, finally, the epitaphs of the main character's grandmother and of a number of her contemporaries, all significant of one aspect or another of women's lives and hardships at the turn of the century. Whereas the first French expressions cited indirectly draw our attention to the conspicuous absence of words pertaining to the personal, particularly feminine, aspects of social life, the others, seemingly indicative of official and socially accepted titles, roles or values, are all subverted in the novel. The nationalist slogan will not prevent dissent in the couple or their eventual separation; the importance of the Church and its representatives and its rules will not prevent Céline from knowing a mystical presence that, in the end, proves to be more spiritually fulfilling and long-lasting than her relationship with her Catholic husband; and the respectability of the epitaphs will take second place to the social comment they carry. All this confirms a particularly important issue: by writing in English, using French for concepts, practices, and memories she knows intimately and that are therefore most authentically articulated in her mother tongue, Moser demonstrates the problem of reshaping language, itself related to that of imagining anew. This is undoubtedly the problem of every writer, yet the rebellion of a minority feminist writing has certain undeniable objectives that, in *Courtepointe*, are underlined by the novel's structure.

Courtepointe is organized into chapters alternating between first-person narration and omniscient narration, both the responsibility of the main character, who tells her own story as well as her mother's and that of her grandmother whom she has never met, but whom she recreates, using her imagination and bits of knowledge about the past. The novel therefore raises questions about the privileged status of official, public, but nevertheless subjective versions of history in relation to unofficial, personal, subjective versions, implying that the latter are perhaps all the more veracious because of their private nature.¹¹ When, upon her mother's death, Odette Dupré leaves her suburban Vancouver home, despite her husband's wishes, to travel back in time and eastward to her hometown, a Franco-Albertan village, she asserts the life force and creative energy of three generations of women. Her "memories" thus reveal details of women's experiences that patriarchal discourse dismisses as insignificant or inappropriate. This counter-discursive intention is indicated by the reproduction of the family's genealogical tree that precedes the first chapter, and which consecrates, at the top of the page, as the head of the family, Jeanne-Françoise de La Rochelle. Odette (re)invents her ancestor, "une orpheline de bonne famille" (32) [an orphan of good family] (13), as "une femme robuste avec des cheveux roux et un tempérament fougueux" (32) [a sturdy woman with flaming red hair and a temper that could be ignited by the smallest spark] (13), mother of "vingt marmots" (32) [a brood of twenty children] (13), and a "sage-femme" (32) [midwife] (13). Although this description seeks clearly to establish the morality of the ancestor, Jeanne-Françoise nevertheless escapes the category of a patriarchal woman from several points of view. A daughter of the king exiled to Québec, her exact identity is most likely uncertain.[12] However, she is a potentially carnal figure whose "flaming red hair" and temper connote an untamable character, while her aristocratic-sounding name attaches her, not to a man, but to a place. Her social status transforms her into royal chattel (sent to New France to marry a pioneer settler, her dowry was likely assumed by the royal treasury), but she is equally defined by the art of midwifery that places her under the sign of creation and in an autonomously feminine universe.

Ten generations later, Odette's grandmother, Céline, creator of the eponymous quilt, is the first woman of the family to settle in Alberta. She does so as the new wife of Calixte DesVallières, a man imbued with the nationalist mission consisting of extending Québec's geographical, cultural, and linguistic borders to Western Canada, and who reminds her that, without him, she would have become a *vieille fille* (old maid).

On their wedding night, Calixte reveals that, in his mind, the body of his new wife is like the land of the Far West: his for the taking. Céline, however, has been raised in a convent where she was taught that her body, "temple de l'âme" (38) [sacred vessel of the soul] (17), was to be kept pure, beyond the reach of "la souillure des hommes" (38) [pure and clean from the touch of men] (17). Claiming his rights as her husband, however, he ignores her shyness and bewildered, self-conscious pleas, which, written in free indirect speech, express both Céline's and Odette's sentiments: "Ne comprenait-il pas? Tout allait trop vite. De telles familiarités ... lui faisaient honte. Elle alla vers l'escalier pour éviter ses caresses, mais il était déjà près d'elle.—S'il te plaît, pas maintenant. Attends" (49) [She moved away, wanting to tell him that she had scarcely regained her breath from his first touch and would he please slow down because this was happening too quickly. His familiarity . . . made her ashamed. She walked to the stairway, trying to avoid his touch, but he was beside her. "Please, not now. Wait"] (23). She flees up the stairs, but he corners her in their bedroom, locks the door behind him, and amidst her repeated objections to his haste, orders her to undress, forces her hands away from her breasts in order to fix his gaze on her. He, on the other hand, takes the liberty of turning away from her before undressing, then, glassy-eyed, takes her unlovingly, unconcerned by the pain he is inflicting upon her. At the end of it all, ever respectful of pristine order, the man orders his wife to leave no feminine traces of the ordeal: "Ne laisse pas le sang tacher les draps, Céline" (50) [Don't let that virgin blood run on the sheets] (24).

The description of the new couple's wedding portrait, no doubt taken a short time before the wedding-night scene, but appearing in the text only toward the end of the novel, constitutes an eloquently silent critique of the patriarchal family structure that the husband intends to perpetuate: "une femme délicate . . . regardait timidement son mari, un bel homme à l'expression sévère" (278) [a delicate woman . . . looking shyly toward her husband, a handsome though stern-looking man] (160). Time however, will produce a woman who, having learned to distance herself from her husband's self-important seriousness, appears in a later family portrait, a "petit air amusé" on her lips, a "lueur d'ironie dans le regard" (278–79) [My grandmother's expression is one of amusement, I think, because of the way her lips are compressed in a smile. It is that glimmer of irony in her eyes, as though none of this is to be taken seriously . . .] (161).

The transformation takes place at St-Prosper-du-Lac in the future province of Alberta to which the couple travels the day after the wedding. The descriptions of the landscape, seen from Céline's point of view, are rich in sensual connotations. Justly, then, as her husband thinks only of colonizing the soil, of transforming it into a territory of French-speaking culture, Céline enters into communion with the prairie. Two narrative sequences are particularly significant in this respect.

Pregnant for the first time, Céline attends St-Prosper's St-Jean-Baptiste celebrations with Calixte who, along with a number of other town officials, must make a speech. Seated on the platform, the man sees his wife signaling to him that "quelque chose se passe" [something is happening], but he answers that now is not the time to disturb him. Consequently, as he is in the midst of propounding the official views about the importance of the past, French culture, and the Catholic faith, the woman enters another universe: "Autour d'elle, le terrain scintilla de couleurs, l'odeur de l'herbe devint insupportablement âcre et la voix de Calixte et le vent dans les feuilles se mêlèrent en un rugissement qui l'enveloppa, comme en pleine tempête" (95–96) [The field around her scintillated with colors, the scent of the grass became overwhelmingly pungent, and Calixte's voice and the wind in the leaves blended in a huge roar circling about her. She was at the center of some great force] (51). Ready to deliver, Céline's condition commands around her a circle of women whose activity interrupts Calixte's speech definitively. He is led away by a group of men solicitous of his nerves, as several pairs of women's strong able hands lay her down on the grass "sous les peupliers noirs" (97) [under the cottonwoods] (52). Soon, a gray-haired "sage-femme métisse" (97) [a gray-haired Métis woman] (52) appears and assists Céline who, clutching tufts of grass, implores the tree with which she identifies to give her strength. The intimate details of the delivery of a set of twins most certainly textualize a painful yet joyous feminine reality, the former aspect of which socially acceptable accounts inevitably neglect. The husband's reactions to the event are derisory in their stereotypically patriarchal flavor. Consider, first, his answer to the new mother, who apologizes for having interrupted his speech:

> —Non, non, c'était une merveilleuse façon de le finir, ponctué des cris d'une femme en train d'accoucher, un exemple frappant de notre développement futur dans l'Ouest. Une conclusion magnifique!
> —C'était moi, la conclusion? demanda-t-elle, étrangement déçue. (102)

> [—No, no, it was a marvellous way to end, punctuated by the cries of a woman about to give birth, a vivid illustration of our future growth here in the West. A marvellous finale.
> —I was a finale? She felt curiously disappointed.] (54–55)

Then, visibly delighted to now have "un héritier pour porter le nom des DesVallières, pour continuer [s]on œuvre," [an heir to the DesVallières name, to carry out (his) work], he names the boy Jean-Baptiste, "d'après le saint patron des Canadiens français" (102) [after the patron saint of French-Canadians] (55), leaving it to his wife to name the daughter who, he is certain, "sera belle" (102) [will be beautiful] (55). Céline complies, thinking of her own mother who died at a young age, and thereby instinctively and willfully contributing to the establishment of a women's tradition. Clearly in defiance of traditionally constructed gender-related clichés, Moser inscribes the boy under the sign of peaceful sleep, the girl, under that of wakeful curiosity. He will become a mild-mannered, sensitive artist, "heureux et patient" (140) [happy and patient] (77), a disappointment to his father, she, "qui aurait dû être un fils" (159) [who should have been a son] (89), an ambitious, determined doctor devoted to women's issues.

Céline discovers that this women's tradition, interpreted by Calixte, signifies that she has sole responsibility for the babies' care—when they awaken, crying during the night, "si elle ne se levait pas immédiatement, Calixte la poussait du coude pour la réveiller" (103) [If she didn't get up right away, Calixte would nudge her awake] (55). With the disappearance of her own individual identity, now melded to that of her infants, the novel introduces an ambivalent character. Taking some time for herself early one evening, the new mother walks toward the lake, a site associated with religious miracles and Métis legends and rituals. There, in the distance, a man in a boat waves to her. Céline immediately associates him with "les forces de la nature" and the "diable" (107) [these forces of nature and of the devil] (58). The mysterious figure will come into contact with the young woman on three other occasions, each time more intimately, and it is these contacts that will awaken Céline to her sexual self.[13]

When Jean-Baptiste is three, Céline, believing him to be drowning in the lake, attempts to rescue him. Unable to find him, she resolves to drown herself, or rather to abandon herself to the water, regretting only that she will do so "sans avoir jamais connu de joie" (149) [without having felt any joy] (82). However, she is drawn from the water by the man in the boat. A part of Céline watches as the dark-eyed stranger with a long black beard resuscitates her body. Forevermore marked by his touch and warmth, "elle se sentit tout autre, comme si une nouvelle femme l'habitait. Elle se souvenait de l'homme et de son étreinte et désirait encore sa chaleur" (151). [She felt different, as if a new person inhabited her body. She remembered the man and his embrace and she longed to feel his warmth again] (84).

A short time after this incident, the sight of her husband napping at his desk provokes in her "un sentiment qu'elle avait déjà ressenti, mais qu'elle avait réprimé: elle désirait Calixte. Elle voulait un autre enfant" (161) [She was moved by a feeling she had had before, but had suppressed: she desired Calixte. She wanted another child] (89). Although sexual desire is conflated with the Church-sanctioned wish for a child, Céline nevertheless reclaims her own body, and empowers herself as an erotic being: she arouses her husband, then drags him onto the floor. He protests "doucement" (161) [made quiet protesting sounds] (90), but continues to respond to her advances. Surprised by her own audacity, staring brazenly into her husband's shocked eyes, Céline discovers "le rythme de la volupté. Il la brûla de sa chair chaude et douce et elle éprouva plus de plaisir que jamais auparavant. Elle gémit et tomba sur lui, l'étreignant, vorace, certaine que son corps avait voyagé avec le sien" (161) [the rhythm of pleasure. He burned her with his hot, smooth flesh, and she felt more pleasure than she had ever felt before. She moaned and fell over him, clutching him ravenously, knowing his body had travelled with hers] (90). Yet, Calixte, furious, exclaims that it is a sin for a woman to behave like that, and barks: "Va te coucher immédiatement, femme! Et que ça ne se reproduise jamais! Mon Dieu!" (162) [Go to bed right now, woman. This had better not happen again. My God!] (90). Finding it impossible to forgive her, he thereafter avoids her, refusing to share her bed, even after spending the summer and autumn in the East, attempting to encourage settlement in the West. Céline, on the other hand, "se souvint de l'étreinte et de la chaleur du pêcheur et désira sa caresse une fois de plus" (164) [She remembered the fisherman's embrace and his warmth, and she longed for his touch again] (91), but tries to divert her thoughts. When finally Calixte returns to their bedroom, Céline suppresses her body's reaction: she will henceforth be the submissive wife he requires.

The necessity to repress her sexuality deprives the woman of vitality, but this does not become apparent until the next time "l'étranger" (the stranger) suddenly appears in her universe in the middle of Epiphany celebrations—his attire, dark eyes and black beard confirm that he is a Métis. They dance together, and the closeness of their bodies, his breath on her hair, leave Céline "alerte, pleine de vie. Son sang coul[e] délicatement dans ses veines, son cœur ba[t] rapidement dans sa poitrine. Elle se sen[t] flotter comme cette fois-là, sous l'eau" (175) [She felt alive. Her blood flowed lightly over her bones; her heart beat quickly in her chest. She felt herself floating, the way she had in the water] (98). He leaves as suddenly as he had appeared, but only after Céline acquiesces to one day board his boat. Her husband and aunt disapprove openly of Céline's behavior, but the latter "s'éloigna, . . . soulevée par une vague de bonheur. Elle s'était amusée, elle se sentait femme et elle ne voulait pas perdre cette sensation" (176) [walked away from her. She was lifted by a wave of happiness. She had enjoyed herself, she felt like a woman, and she didn't want to lose the feeling] (99). Odette's grandmother becomes a version of Aubert de Gaspé's Rose Latulipe (59–70), but she will not accompany the man identified as the devil until months later.

Calixte having given up on the prairies and returned to Ottawa, Céline descends one evening toward the lake where she first encountered the nameless fisherman. Soon, "des bras puissants la soulevèrent et elle sentit une douce chaleur l'envahir" (254) [strong arms lift[ed] her and [held] her and she remembered and she felt a gentle, encompassing warmth] (146). Accepting an invitation to accompany her savior "sur l'autre rive" (254) [across the lake] (146), she disappears until Odette's imagination and writing bring her back years later, a figure of freedom, the Muse of a new feminine reality.

MADELEINE AND THE ANGEL

Franco-Albertan Jacqueline Dumas's first novel, *Madeleine and the Angel*, published in 1989, is the most overtly critical, subversive, and disturbing of the three novels discussed here, and, to date, most likely in Western Canadian women's francophone literature. Multivoiced, although written in the first person, the novel inscribes great swaths of experience, some passages using colloquial English, others, unabashedly poetic prose, yet others, a hybrid style consisting of English words and French syntax, while, throughout, French words and expressions appear in italics, forming a linguistic paradigmatic critique of Franco-Albertan patriarchy.

Dumas's 1950s Franco-Albertan space is predominantly urban, marginal, patriarchal, brutal, cruel, and destructive. Located in a multicultural English-speaking territory, an isolated pocket of incestuous, secretive francophone culture is represented as existing only as the result of severe patriarchal control, and for women this means the colonization of their minds, feelings, and bodies. This is highlighted by the fact that the narrator's maternal grandmother, a loving, warm, nurturing woman of French origins who lives on a farm, is banished from her daughter's impoverished house.[14] The (son-in-)law deprives "his" women of arms that hug out of tenderness and words that question his authority. On the book cover and in a key passage of the novel, this horrific metaphor of the patriarchal woman appears:

Venus de Milo, your threatening, armless body: no arms to hug with; no arms to fend off the rapist . . . pornographic model gone numb . . . Woman, aphasic . . . Torched for flaming his desire . . . Your life-giving womb *crimen exceptum*, your life-giving womb a tomb. Prick up the throat, cattle prod up the ass, bayonet through the heart. Eliminate the details, but the flesh remembers. (113)

In this setting, then, as in Primeau's and Moser's novels, women's sexual desires and desirability are outlawed, but with a significant difference. Primeau's writing entrusts this private identity to a secondary, outlaw-cum-ideal female character whose role as mother and wife does not diminish at all her sexual power and whose Métis blood, like the seemingly evanescent narrative that textualizes her role, keeps her safely sheltered in a marginal zone located somewhere within the French-Canadian community. Moser's writing entrusts it to a discreetly rebellious grandmother who, once abandoned by her husband, crosses over to the sensuous, life-giving universe of a mysterious other. In both cases, female sexuality is preserved with the help of an outsider. Dumas, on the other hand, places emphasis on the seemingly impossible task of becoming an autonomous sexual woman. At the beginning of the novel, the narrator's mother lies dying in a hospital, her pain and "sinful wound" of a nature such that only a "Hecate, Queen of Witches" or "alabaster Virgin Marys" (2) could bring relief. The narrative immediately shifts to the respectful, loving relationships the narrator has with her daughter and her sister, Maria Goretti, then delves elliptically into the family past to reveal the obstacles that have had to be surmounted before the small female community of three could be created. The narrator's "healing" is therefore implied, but no outsider is there to help. A stubbornly cultivated, completely internalized streak of rebelliousness has been the only solution.

Madeleine and the Angel, then, is the story of several types of abuse, but also of one woman's, the narrator's, attempt to reclaim her eponymous mother from the clutches of her now-deceased father. The destructive influence and effects of the latter's perverted, psychotic, violent actions, all sanctioned, he used to claim, by "his" Angel or "the" Voices, are, however, infinitely far-reaching. The reader comes to realize the impossibility of the task as Pauline, having recently given birth to a child ("I sit here before the fire watching my tiny daughter . . . her perfect bum a peach offering to the moon. . . . You sweet darling, you smell of apples and bubble-gum" [2–3]), tells of dreams where she is attempting to save a female figure who resembles her mother, but whose face is indiscernible. The identity of this woman who has not loved, supported, protected, or guided her will always remain an unknown and unknowable black hole in Pauline's universe.

Her husband's victim and accomplice, Madeleine is the fully patriarchal woman: obedient, submissive, collusive, and although she figures in the novel's title, her own voice is almost never heard. Once, when "drunk," she beckons Pauline to her bedside, calling her "mon gros trésor mon p'tit chou-chou!" [my love my li'l darling] and "ma p'tite chérie" (104–5) [my li'l beloved] before telling her that, Michael the Archangel and Lucifer having "committed to a desperate struggle for [her] father's soul," it is the family's duty to "help him bear his cross" (107). Another time, during the first of a series of "exhilarating, spur-of-the-moment midnight [car] trips," Madeleine "chatter[s]," enthralling her daughters with stories of her youth, but the passage is told in free indirect speech and her "merr[y] recounting" is interrupted: " 'Hey old lady, you been drinking or something?' said my father. She put her hand over her mouth and laughed" (151). The father turns the radio on, "full blast," and the mother "sang along, not out loud, whisper-sang, whispering, not singing the words when she knew a song" (152). Out loud, Madeleine feels free to say only what satisfies, aids, and abets her husband. When, for example, "She used to catch us for him" (64). Pauline's sister recalls one of those times:

> He was chasing me once, remember mom, Madeleine? Remember? And you opened your arms just like that, to hug me. I went to you, you squeezed me so hard it took my breath away. I love you! I love you! you said. And then you called him. Michel! you called, Michel! I've got her! I've got her! (185)

On all other occasions, she obeys her husband's orders "without a word," and, at times, the daughters are forced to watch or listen as their father's accomplices:

> Neither Maria nor I tried to leave the room; we sensed that our presence was required, spectators, witnesses, that our role was not finished until the scene was shifted to the privacy of their bedroom . . . when he booted her backside for scrubbing the floor too quickly, or not quickly enough, or lifted her up by the hair for raising her head at the wrong time, and he solicited our response with a sly look in our direction, I did not consider even a secret complicity with her: I snickered. (78–79)

Clearly, the *divide et impera* strategy proves effective. Fear of the patriarch and distrust of one another incite inexplicable behavior, and prevent any form of feminine solidarity, as though collaboration with authority could spare one from becoming a victim. Neither daughters nor mother are spared, of course, and if the former eventually form a friendship, telling one another everything they can remember—from Pauline's thoughts of suicide to Maria's torrid roller-coaster love affair with a married woman—the latter becomes completely and irremediably alienated from herself and the world. At the end of the novel, she has killed her husband with an ax, but this does not free her. Immobilized, not by her act, but by "his" death, she withdraws into total silence. Her final act, an attestation of the denial that explains at least partially how she could have acted so complicitously with her husband, consists of sending Pauline's daughter a "silver-plated medal of the Assumption of the Virgin Mary" and a card that reads: "To our dear little granddaughter—may God protect you and show you His way through the intercession of His Immaculate Mother—from your Grandpa in Heaven who wants you to have this" (2–3).

This religious vocabulary is a particularly significant trait of Dumas's novel. A reminder that the Catholic church demanded of its feminine followers unquestioning obedience and respect toward male authority, regardless of the abusive character of that male authority, it also reveals the extent to which Madeleine has internalized her colonized status. The narrator's father exploits this conjuncture mainly in two ways. Posing as a priest, he metes out punishments such as the one described above, involving Madeleine having to recite the entire rosary. At other times, he is a priest and a sexed Christ-like figure, here on earth to do the Lord's bidding. He performs his first "miracle" late one morning when Pauline and Maria Goretti, respectively aged six and twelve, are "taking turns bouncing an India rubber ball hard off the side of the house." Their play awakens their father who, shouting his "wrath," stomps outside, sending both girls running off in different directions. Minutes later, he has spent his anger on the older sister. She was named after a twelve-year-old girl who was canonized because, just before dying, she forgave her murderer, a man who had responded to her refusal to give in to his desire by

> stab[bing] her with [his] long dagger, plunges it thirteen times into her breast and abdomen, tears open her intestines, pierces her lungs, grazes her heart. . . . He plunges the dagger into Marietta's back, one last time, and runs away. (18)

Pauline's sister lives up to the name of her patron saint in silence, and it is only when their father calls his wife to witness the consecration of his act that the narrator tells us this:

Maria Goretti is lying on her back on the beach, on the sandy scrub, her clothes soaked and muddy, one shoe missing, her hair wet and matted. She is not moving. . . . My father stands above her, tall, huge, a mountain. . . . He closes his eyes the color of the heavens and lifts his face to God: "*Seigneur, Mon Père* [Lord, My Father], hear my prayer, that these my wife and children may know it was You Who sent me." He kneels in the sand, bends over Maria Goretti, lays his head over her heart, "Take this the kiss of life," kissing her, putting his own wet lips on hers. . . . "*Lève-toi, ma fille à moi*, arise" [Get up, my own daughter]. Maria Goretti gets up on all fours, coughing and retching. (47–48)

This passage is representative of the entire novel in regard to the italicized textualization of the French language, used here in a perverse version of religious rites. French words are far more numerous and homogeneous in nature in *Madeleine and the Angel* than in Moser's novel. Aside from passages dealing with the maternal grandmother, French is associated with leering male characters, the father's peremptorily given orders, his rage, or, simply, his blasphemous way of being. His cursing betrays his profound frustration, but, more importantly for the women in his life, emphasizes their condemnation as abject nonentities under the complete domination of a demeaning, misogynous authority legitimized by the Church. Paradoxically, of course, one vein of French-Canadian profanity expresses irreverence toward sacred objects associated with Holy Communion. Michel combines religious curses with sexist insults or, when he wants a favor, with terms of endearment, which pervade and corrupt the home and the narrative text with a stifling, sulfurous atmosphere. One of the more degrading passages recounts the father informing Pauline about menstruation. Between "swigs" taken from a bottle of Teacher's, he finds the obscene, vulgar words to explain the difference between men's sexual organs and women's while cursing and silencing his daughter's queries. "How the hell does he know, *tabourette* (cripes), if I'll have any warning ahead of time? Shut up and listen. . . . At school *hostie* (fuck), well if it happens at school, tell the Sister Principal" (149–50).

Earlier, in relation to Moser's novel, the rapport between the use of French and strikingly memorable events was mentioned. In Dumas's novel, it is the father's devil voice, demonic acts, actions, and influence that take precedence over everything else: to the point that the Angel in him, the part of him with which Madeleine first fell in love, but which, throughout the novel, is present only as the alcoholic part of him that needs a drink, or as a repentant, shriveled creature the day after a drunken binge, is lost. When his wife "lifted the axe and split his head in two" (177), she apparently believed that she could recover the archangel. Before falling completely silent, for without Michel to second, she has no raison d'être, she wonders aloud, "The Devil's dead, you know. . . . But where's the Angel?" (169). The title of the novel, then, inscribes the useless quest for a feminine tradition and the impossibility of a "good," even decent life, under a patriarchy founded on one truth.

Saying it, and above all saying it in English, using French to simultaneously symbolize and punctuate the retelling of the terror and violent oppression at the base of this patriarchal regime, to stylize the father's altogether-too-unforgettable voice and discourse, is a preeminently emancipatory gesture. Pauline's explanation is explicitly clear:

> English was the language which allowed us to be inconspicuous, to appear normal. It was the link to the outside world, the language of sanity, of freedom, of escape from our daily rituals. French was not the language of culture, but that of oppression, of forced prayer, forced obedience, of unfulfilled dreams, the language of nightmares. (60)

I have discussed three women's novels, three impassioned critiques of the extraordinarily powerful authoritarian discourse characteristic of a minority culture located within a conservative region of Canada, three forms of communicative strategies created in order to reconstruct what has been suppressed in official discourse. Women's voices in the stories of Primeau, Moser, and Dumas wage battle, even war, with those their culture seems to have constructed to silence them. In 1960, it is a lilting, sensual voice that disrupts, troubles, and haunts the existing sociolect and its founding spokesman. During the last decade, the voices have become more assertive, motivated by a revisionary will that, without refusing the past entirely, emphasizes the need to preserve only that which will allow dialogue, exchanges, participation, mutual respect, and sharing. By daring to claim the right to create communities of multivoiced women, by daring to write a politicized space where taboo subjects—such as interracial couples, abortions, women's sexuality, both with men and other women—are raised, the women authors of contemporary Franco-Albertan novels certainly *do* "do gender."

Notes

1. Although lack of space prevents further elaboration of my reading of this novel, I would emphasize that in Primeau's novels "empowerment" is to be found

in the problematic, but nevertheless, willful glorification of the margins as a space where difference is recognized, valued, and respected.

2. Unless otherwise noted, all translations are my own.

3. It would be fair to note that Québécois women's writing of the 1990s, which Lori Saint-Martin has termed "métaféministe," tends also to be considerably more readerly than that of the "militantly feminist" 1970s or 1980s novels of authors such as Nicole Brossard or Louky Bersianik. On the other hand, francophone women's novels of Western Canada have never been rebelliously "unreaderly." In a minority milieu, where readers are far from numerous, can one afford to alienate potential consumers?

4. Chaput's third novel, *Le Coulonneux (The Pigeoner)*, published in 1998, while undoubtedly a "readerly" love story told with poetry and from multiple points of view, inscribes a troubled and troubling universe placed under the signs of freedom and wanderlust.

5. The category of children's literature is excluded here.

6. Alberta and British Columbia do not lack writers, but do most certainly lack the infrastructure necessary to support any efforts to create a specific francophone discursive space. Writers wishing to publish in French must turn to presses located in other regions of Canada's francophone minority, from Saskatchewan eastward to Ontario.

7. An eloquent example is the village of Rouleauville, established at the turn of the century in Calgary and considered to be a "little Québec" located on the banks of the Elbow River.

8. Marie Moser, *Counterpoint*, Toronto, Irwin Publishing, 1987 (124). All further references to the English version of the novel will be taken from this edition.

9. From this point of view, a discussion of the representation of the Albertan prairies in Nancy Huston's writing is pertinent and greatly enlightening, but in this paper I have chosen to deal only with Franco-Albertan writers of Québécois ancestry. I refer interested readers to Sing (1998).

10. Uttered by a sensual Métis fisherman, however, the original intent of the expression is subverted, so that the cliché becomes infused with a physicality far stronger than any socially accepted gentleman would dare to express in public.

11. To momentarily return to the subject of the English and French versions of the novel, it is clear from this perspective that, contrary to the novel's English title, the French translation of the title does not suggest the fragmentary character of *her*stories and of the work of memory as well as the contrapuntal effect they have compared to official *his*tory. Also, the frequent italicized recurrences in the English text of the expression *petit coup* or *petit-coup* accentuate more the modus operandi of women's stories.

12. Uncertain in the sense that the young girls and women exiled to Canada have been thought of as orphans, "gifts" from their families to the New World, or residents of La Salpêtrière and, therefore, possibly criminals, prostitutes, or simply judged to be wanton by French society. If certain researchers, concerned with the sullied reputation of "les filles du roi," claim the uprightness of *all* the young women sent to Canada, thus corroborating the identity Céline gives to her ancestor, "an orphan from a good family," recent studies confirm the variety of the group's sociocultural origins and mores. In the final analysis, the fact remains that, considered as a discursive historiographic construct, "les filles du roi" [daughters of the king] constitute a plurivocal, multiclass group, "le sujet d'angoisse et de rancœur chez les historiens canadiens" (Landry 1992, 25) [the source of distress and rancor for Canadian historians].

13. The text states explicitly that "depuis la naissance des jumeaux, la nuit, elle attendait avec impatience l'approche de Calixte" (143) [since the birth of the twins, she waited with anticipation for Calixte to move over her in the night] (78), not daring to show or express her pleasure (perhaps "anormal," [abnormal] after all, thinks she). However, the subject is treated narratively as a flashback in a chapter recounting events that occur three years after the twins' birth, and only after the textualization of her first distant encounter with the mysterious figure.

14. Heartbreakingly tender memories of "Mémère" [Granny] are simultaneously a means of psychological survival, a sort of haven to which the girls are able to escape in their imagination, reassurance of the fact that life at home is not the only possibility, and a longed-for "paradise lost" compared to which the horrors of the present seem magnified.

Works Cited

Aunger, Edmund A. "Dispersed Minorities and Segmental Autonomy: French-Language School Boards in Canada." *Nationalism and Ethnic Politics* 2, no. 2 (1996): 191–215.

Bourgault, Pierre. "Le Québec face au Canada français." In *Langue, littérature, culture au Canada français*, edited by Robert Vigneault, 13–19. Ottawa: Éditions de l'Université d'Ottawa, 1977.

Chaput, Simone. *Le Coulonneux*. Saint-Boniface: Les Editions du Blé, 1998.

———. *Un Piano dans le noir*. Saint-Boniface: Les Editions du Blé, 1991.

———. *La Vigne Amer*. Saint-Boniface: Les Editions du Blé, 1989.

Dubé, Paul. "Je est un autre: Et l'autre est moi". In *La Question identitaire au Canada francophone: Récits, parcours, enjeux, hors-lieux*, edited by Jocelyn Létourneau, 83–94. Ste-Foy: Les Presses de l'Université Laval, 1994.

Dumas, Jacqueline. *Madeleine and the Angel*. Saskatoon: Fifth House, 1989.

Dyan-Davis, Claire. "La femme, la tradition littéraire et le roman de l'Ouest." *Cahiers franco-canadiens de l'Ouest* 1, no. 2 (1989): 185–95.

Gaspé, Philippe Aubert, fils. *Le Chercheur de trésors, ou L'Influence d'un livre*. Montréal: Opuscule, 1968 (1837).

Joy, Richard. *Languages in Conflict*. Toronto: McClelland and Stewart, 1972.

Kasper, Louise Renée. "Réflexions féministes sur les romans de Simone Chaput." *Cahiers franco-canadiens de l'Ouest* 4, no. 2 (1992): 243–60.

Landry, Yves. *Les Filles du roi au XVIIe siècle, suivi d'un répertoire biographique des filles du roi*. Montréal: Leméac, 1992.

Morice, Adrien-Gabriel. *Dictionnaire historique des Canadiens et des Métis français de l'Ouest*. Montréal: Granger Frères, 1908.

Moser, Marie. *Counterpoint*. Toronto: Irwin Publishing, 1987. Translated by Gisèle Villeneuve as *Courtepointe*. Montréal: Québec/Amérique, 1991.

Primeau, Marguerite-A. *Dans le muskeg*. Montréal: Fides, 1960.

Sing, Pamela V. "La Voix métisse dans le 'roman de l'infidélité' chez Jacques Ferron, Nancy Huston et Marguerite-A. Primeau." *Francophonies d'Amérique* 8 (1998): 23–37.

———. "Le Far-Ouest francophone et sa littérature: Exiguïté et écriture." In *Pro-*

duire la culture, produire l'identité? edited by Andrée Fortin, 135–60. Ste-Foy: Les Presses de l'Université Laval, 2000.

Tessier, Jules. "La Dialectique du conservatisme et de l'innovation dans l'œuvre de Marguerite Primeau." In *Les Outils de la francophonie,* 186–204. Vancouver/Winnipeg: Centre d'études franco-canadiennes de l'Ouest, 1988.

Giving Voice to the Body: (Pro)creation in the Texts of Nancy Huston

PATRICE J. PROULX

> ... le problème des femmes écrivains a été moins d'apprendre à "écrire avec leur corps" que d'aimer, de valoriser et de respecter l'intégrité de leur corps écrivant.
> [... the issue for women writers is not so much learning to "write with their bodies" as it is loving, valorizing, and respecting the integrity of the body that writes].
> —Nancy Huston

> as a woman & a poet
> i've decided to wear my ovaries on my sleeve.
> —Ntozake Shange

BORN IN CALGARY, ALBERTA, NOVELIST AND CRITIC NANCY HUSTON ASSOciates her own "coming to writing" with her relocation to Paris in 1973. She claims that it was the French language that both authorized and inspired her to write—her self-imposed exile from her mother tongue allowed her to reinvent herself by means of the new idiom.[1] Huston immediately became involved in the French women's movement, publishing essays in such feminist journals as *Cahiers du GRIF* and *Sorcières*. All of Huston's works reflect her concern with the sociocultural construction of gender, in particular as it relates to issues of women and (pro)creation, prevailing theorizations of the mind/body dichotomy, and textual inscriptions of the female body. In an early text entitled *Mosaïque de la pornographie* (*A Mosaic of Pornography*) (1982), for example, Huston critiques the misogyny of the pornographic text through a study that juxtaposes male-authored narratives of the "fallen woman" with the memoirs of a prostitute, Marie-Thérèse, thereby effectively countering the male author-narrator's desire to situate the woman as object and as text. The thematics of contractual love is studied further in *A l'amour comme à la guerre* (*All's Fair in Love and War*) (1984), in which Huston analyzes the sociocultural and political implications of the historical figuration of woman's body as it relates metaphorically and metonymically to both war and prostitution.

In this essay, I propose to explore the conceptualization of the maternal and the nonmaternal body as it relates to artistic creation in selected fictional and nonfictional works by Huston. Through my analysis of her textual production, I plan to evoke the origins and the implications of restrictive metaphorizations of the female body (as mother, and as muse for the male creator, for example), while concomitantly analyzing patriarchal mythologies in which men seek to usurp women's generative function. Both personal experience and a critical engagement with feminist issues have led Huston to privilege an exploration of the maternal figure in many of her works. As a writer with two children, she has often felt compelled to address concerns relating to her own struggle to define herself as an artist and a mother. Alice Jardine contends that "The issue of how to think about the relationships among women/writing/maternity is among the most important in feminist thinking today, especially in France" (89). In furthering her argument, Jardine evinces the theoretical underpinnings of one of the myths underlying the unspoken belief that women must choose between creation and procreation: "Beauvoir provided what has remained, in spite of everything, *the* feminist myth: the baby *versus* the book. . . . Over the past few years this mutual exclusivity has been seriously questioned. . . ." (90). Huston herself will textually inscribe this image in a subversive manner, acknowledging its metaphorical resonance while at the same time undermining the implications of such cultural myths of mutual exclusivity. She suggests, rather, that the act of procreation provides artistic inspiration, affording her a fresh perspective on her work: "L'éditeur dit que mon roman est viable; il accepte de le mettre au monde, tout en me félicitant 'en premier lieu pour l'autre . . . oeuvre en gestation'—là aussi, les vieilles métaphores sortent toutes seules de la plume. Mais quel soulagement! c'est toi, ce sont les pas que tu m'as aidée à faire dans ces pages-ci . . . qui m'ont donné la force de retourner à ce manuscrit" (1990, 255) [The editor says my novel is viable; he agrees to bring it into the world, at the same time congratulating me "first of all for the other . . . work in gestation"—there, too, conventional metaphors flow from my pen. But what a relief! it's you, it's the steps you've helped me to take in these very pages . . . which have given me the strength to return to my manuscript].

In *Journal de la création (Journal of Creation)* (1990), one of her first works to explicitly trace out the baby versus the book myth, fragments of the journal recounting Huston's own pregnancy are interwoven with and serve as a springboard for her study of writing couples and their attempts to come to terms with the physical and metaphysical intersections between creation and procreation in their lives and in their work. She questions the seeming inability or unwillingness of certain well-known pairs (among them Virginia and Leonard Woolf, Sylvia Plath and Ted Hughes, Unica Zürn and Hans Bellmer, and Simone de Beauvoir and Jean-Paul Sartre) to effectively problematize the binary oppositions of mind/body, and creation/procreation.[2] The author, who often incorporates autobiographical elements in her theoretical studies, reflects upon the lived experience of the female artist and evokes the potential for an empowering maternal subjectivity. By means of this (auto)biographical strategy, Huston sets out to "prove" that woman is capable of creating *while* procreating: "Mon but en écrivant ce journal est de mettre en doute l'innocence—non pas de tel ou tel artiste, mais des métaphores dont se pare la création artistique, afin de continuer à paraître aussi asexuée et inattaquable qu'un ange . . . exterminateur" (62) [My goal in writing this journal is to question the innocence—not of a particular artist—but rather of the metaphors with which artistic creation endows itself in order to appear as asexual and irrefutable as an exterminating angel].

Much of the force and the originality of this work derives from the skillful interlacing of the nonfictional journal and the critical essay, a narrative strategy reflecting the author's desire to situate her own beliefs in relation to the objects of her study. As Janet Wolff posits, this approach has been gaining increased attention in recent years—feminist literary critics are "arguing the need to integrate the personal into academic work—what Miller refers to as 'getting personal' and Mary Ann Caws as 'personal criticism.' . . . But it is also about a more clearly political choice, about the decision to identify and select certain texts and situations as worth studying, and about the willingness to state the basis of one's commitment to them" (49).

An important theme in Huston's work has been a questioning of traditional mind/body dynamics, in which woman is primarily associated with the corporeal, man with the spiritual. The *Journal de la création* bears witness to Huston's search for an alternative paradigm which would acknowledge the fact that no barriers exist a priori between mind and body.[3] Contemporary philosopher Linda Alcoff, in an incisive study of mind/body dualism that critiques gender-based categorizations defining reason and knowledge as male, calls on women to "reconfigure the role of bodily experience in the development of knowledge" (17). If one starts from the premise that the mind is not and has never been separable from the body, "it also follows that our dominant conceptions and ideals of reason have been connected to bodies, have been expressions of bodily concerns or needs and reflections of embodied ways of being, and have had other interesting relations to the body that we have yet to discover..." (17).

For Huston, the urge to seek out the underlying reasons for the conflicted nature of her own relation to her physical and spiritual selves, as well as the ways of effecting a reconciliation between the two, serves as a motivating factor in her project. In the previous two years, she herself had experienced first a debilitating mental anguish and then a physical paralysis that required hospitalization. The author, therefore, does have a personal stake in attempting to reconceptualize well-established philosophical theorizations of the mind/body divide that could be associated with certain patriarchal mythologies of genesis.[4] Huston elucidates the polemics which essay to confer legitimacy on the expropriation of the female body in the birth process: "L'acte de l'esprit par excellence, le geste fondateur de toutes les philosophies, cosmologies et religions, consiste à *rejeter l'évidence des sens*. Nier que la vie, y compris la vie de l'esprit, s'origine dans le corps d'une femme.... Proclamer que l'intelligence engendre la matière et non le contraire" (1990, 24) [The act of the intellect par excellence, the founding act of all philosophies, cosmologies, and religions, involves *rejecting the evidence of the senses*. Deny that life, including the life of the intellect, originates in the body of a woman.... Proclaim that mind engenders matter and not the opposite].

In her biographical study, Huston looks at the physical and psychological obstacles confronting the female artist in general, as well as the fact that, in certain of the artist couples, the woman serves not only as muse but also as actual material for the work of the male partner.[5] Huston notes, in discussing Zelda and F. Scott Fitzgerald, that Scott based many of his female characters on his wife, ultimately concluding that he himself was responsible for her very existence: " 'Parfois je me demande si Zelda n'est pas un personnage que j'ai moi-même créé' " (55) [Sometimes I wonder if Zelda isn't a character that I myself created]. In this examination of artistic creativity as seen through chosen couples, Huston comments on several key narratives in which the male creator gives birth to a female creation,[6] thus obviating the need for woman in the generative process. She analyzes, among others, the Pygmalion myth; Edgar Allen Poe's updated version of this story, "Le Portrait ovale" ("The Oval Portrait"), in which a woman painted by the protagonist becomes more real than his own wife; and Villiers de L'Isle-Adam's *Eve future* (*The Future Eve*). In deconstructing the Pygmalion myth, for example, she convincingly traces out the misogynistic implications of separating the female body from the actual birth experience. Huston asserts that, through the use of tropological constructs which negate women's presence, the male creator endeavors to transcend the human condition, giving birth "par un acte de foi" (1990, 28) [by an act of faith].

Rosi Braidotti, in her discussion of the male appropriation of reproduction, points to the fact that, conventionally, heroes and divine beings do not trace their origins back to a woman: "one of the constant themes in the making of a god is his 'unnatural' birth: his ability, through subterfuges such as immaculate conceptions and other tricks, to short-circuit the orifice through which most human beings pop into the spatio-temporal realm of existence . . . it therefore inscribes an antimaternal dimension at the very heart of the matter" (68). The widespread acceptance of such attempts to marginalize the mother must be questioned. In her correspondence with American academic Sam Kinser, Huston admits to her own fantasy of circumventing the female body and being born from pure "spirit." She had imagined herself as Athena, born only of her father, springing fully formed from his head: "Sans mère; sans rien dans mon propre corps qui puisse faire penser à la mère; pur esprit, combattant avec la lance de ma langue et le bouclier de mes convictions de fer" (Huston and Kinser, 1984, 309) [Without a mother; without anything in my own body to make me think of the mother figure; pure intellect, battling with my tongue as spear and my will of iron as shield]. The forgotten figure in this story, as Huston acknowledges, is Athena's mother, Métis, swallowed by Zeus to prevent her from giving birth to a son who might overthrow the father. Huston believes in the necessity of disclosing the silencing of the mother on which this and countless other mythologies are based. She concludes that, if so many have considered the mother as having a harmful effect on their lives, "c'est peut-être parce que la maternité a été confinée dans ce lieu trop exigu qu'est la tête d'un homme" (310) [It is perhaps because the idea of maternity has been confined within that too-narrow space of a man's mind].

Huston is moved to question what she has termed elsewhere the "refus de l'enfantement" (1995, 156) [refusal to bear children] by numerous women writers and artists. Many of the female artists in Huston's study elected to remain childless as a means of demonstrating their commitment to the life of the intellect. When considering the situation of Virginia and Leonard Woolf, Huston proposes that "Il n'y a probablement jamais eu de tentative de couple aussi pure, aussi extrême que celle des Woolf . . . pour effectuer la reconversion à sens unique, du corps vers l'esprit" (1990, 87) [There has probably never been such a pure, extreme attempt to carry out the one-way reconversion, from body to mind . . . as that made by the Woolf's]. Nevertheless, almost all of the women, whether childless or not, struggled with such physical and psychological illnesses as anorexia (Woolf, Zürn), eczema (Plath), tuberculosis (Peignot), and mental distress that led to suicide (Plath and Zürn) or to institutionalization (Fitzgerald). Even in a couple (the Barrett-Brownings) in which both partners respected and praised the work of the other, Elizabeth Barrett-Browning exhibited uncertainty about her own artistic vision. Several lines from *Aurora Leigh* (1857) testify to her insecurity and bear out the pervasive influence of the Pygmalion myth in the artist's psyche: "Pygmalion souffrait-il de ces mêmes doutes? / . . . Mais non; Pygmalion aimait—et qui aime / Croit en l'impossible. Mais je suis triste: / Je ne puis aimer totalement une oeuvre à moi" (Huston 1995, 69–70) [Pygmalion, did he suffer from the same uncertainties? / . . . Of course not; Pygmalion loved, and he who loves / Believes in the impossible. Yet I am sad: / I cannot wholly love one of my own works]. Elizabeth Barrett-Browning has difficulty appropriating this (pro)creative metaphor for her own purposes.

Susan Friedman has written a groundbreaking article that illuminates both the controversial underpinnings and the liberatory possibilities of the childbirth metaphor used in conjunction with artistic creation. While the metaphor as used by women may seem to risk a "dangerous biologism," Friedman concludes that women's use of the metaphor, rather than suggesting an alignment with traditional stances on mind/body dynamics, "tend[s] to defy those divisions and reconstitute woman's fragmented self into a (pro)creative whole while uniting work and flesh, body and mind" (75). Friedman, like Huston, points to the role that male envy of woman's reproductive capacity may play in the construction of these metaphors of literary paternity, and underscores the reality of man's parturient status: "Confined to 'headbirths,' men cannot literally conceive and birth babies" (55).

Through her use of the journal form, a genre which by its very nature underscores the presence of the author in a spatiotemporal context, Huston brings her own experience of pregnancy to the forefront while carrying out her thought-provoking study of couples who have had to deal in some way with issues of maternity/paternity in their private lives and in relation to their public personas.

She writes that in one of her courses, entitled "Le Corps écrit" ("The Written Body"), she had the pleasure of announcing to the students that "tout en leur parlant du problème corps/esprit . . . j'allais subir devant leurs yeux une véritable métamorphose physique" (1990, 20–21) [while discussing the mind/body problem with them . . . I would be undergoing a veritable physical metamorphosis before their very eyes]. She then asks herself a question that touches upon the problematic nature of such bodily transformations in terms of perceptions of a mind/body hierarchy in which the mind predominates: "Peut-on faire confiance intellectuellement à quelqu'un qui enfle et gonfle de semaine en semaine?" (21) [Can one put his or her intellectual trust in someone who is swelling and filling out more and more each week?].[7]

It is by means of this (auto)biographical work that Huston cogently illustrates her own belief that both women and men must recognize the interconnection of mind and body in order to live (pro)creative lives. Despite the many and sometimes insurmountable difficulties encountered by the women artists in her study, Huston's vision of paradigmatic structures which interconnect such dichotomous pairings as mind/body is an optimistic one: "Toujours est-il que je me sens apaisée, guérie à force d'avoir pleinement éprouvé le caractère humain d'une grossesse humaine: elle m'a restitué mon corps, qui est un corps humain, c'est-à-dire pensant" (252) [Still, I feel soothed, healed by having experienced to the full the human nature of being pregnant: the pregnancy restored my body—a human, *thinking* body—to me].

Huston's *Journal de la création* establishes a theoretical framework for several of her fictional works to follow. Two texts in particular, *La Virevolte (Slow Emergencies)* (1994) and *Instruments des ténèbres (Instruments of Darkness)* (1996), exemplify her continued interest in complex gender issues surrounding both the fictional renderings and the nonfictional realities of women as mothers and artists. Many of the themes explored by Huston in her earlier critical studies—pregnancy, motherhood, mind/body dynamics and the idea of (pro)creation—resurface here and play out in fictional form. The female protagonists of the two novels are artists who struggle to come to terms with their own positioning in relation to the maternal sphere.

Lin Lhomond, in *La Virevolte*, is a dancer and choreographer with two daughters. The theme of dance as (pro)creation is reflected in the narrative style—the author attempts to convey the ephemeral quality and the nonlinear movement of this artistic form through certain passages which make use of the fragment and a typographical superimposition of phrases which seem to suggest that one phrase generates the next. To further the impression of nonlinearity, narrative segments are often self-contained, presented as vignettes. In "Festins fragiles" ("Fragile Feasts"), an essay in which she discusses her relationship to writing, Huston comments on the reasoning behind her choice of discursive style for *La Virevolte*. In keeping with the (pro)creation motif, she positions herself as a sculptor who shapes her text little by little: "Livre taillé, tailladé, dans la pierre, la chair. Scalpel, bistouri, ciseau. On commence avec un immense bloc de marbre et on finit avec un enchaînement hoquetant de cailloux, osselets dansants. Style par lequel je suis parvenue non par accumulation mais par coupes" (14) [A book carved, slashed in stone, in flesh. Scalpel, knife, chisel. You start with an immense block of marble and finish with a halting *enchaînement* of pebbles, dancing ossicles. I came to this style not by piling up but by cutting out].

La Virevolte opens with the birth of Lin's first child, an event rendered vividly as a "cataclysme de tout son être" (14) [hellish upheaval of self] (11). While it is a life-transforming experience, the protagonist does not feel that her new role as mother threatens in any way to place her identity as dancer under erasure: "Elle est toujours là. Elle n'est pas morte et elle n'est pas devenue quelqu'un d'autre. Non seulement elle est toujours elle-même, mais elle est mère" (15) [She is still there. She did not die or become someone else. Not only is she still herself, but she is also a mother] (12). In fact, Lin sees the healthy convergence of creation and procreation. She recalls her pregnancy in sensual terms that reflect both her body's connection to dance and the active nature of her role in the gestation process: "Avec Angela la grossesse avait été comme neuf mois d'orgasme: une stimulation perpétuelle de ce centre brûlant de la danse, le long cône vivant entre sexe et gorge. . . . Penser que, tout en vaquant à ses affaires quotidiennes, son corps tricotait patiemment les chairs, entassait les cellules, organisait l'existence de tout un autre individu" (56) [With Angela, pregnancy had been like nine months of orgasm—a perpetual stimulation of that burning center of the dance, the long vibrating cone from sex to throat. . . . To think that, as she went about her daily life, her body was patiently weaving tissues and stacking cells, organizing another human entity] (61). This image challenges theorizations of pregnant women which code them as passive receptacles for the male seed. A domestic iconography traditionally associated with women is reconceptualized and legitimized in a powerful way here, through the image of the knitting together of new life.

Lin takes a real physical and spiritual pleasure in her pregnancy and in her first years with Angela—a time during which her positions as mother and dancer seem to coincide. The narrative portrayal of the protagonist bathing her newborn, for example, humorously figures the interweaving of her life and her art: "Lin . . . lave les pattes de grenouille écartées en 5ème position grand plié" (15) [Lin . . . sponging the frog legs parted in fifth-position grand plié] (13). One of the dances she conceives at this time begins with the birth of a daughter, swaddled in white tulle, continues by tracing her growing independence from the mother, and leads to the latter's death, wrapped in the same material in which she had welcomed her daughter into the world. It emblematizes the relation she envisions with her child, while at the same time forcing the protagonist to face the unbearable realization that her children, like her artistic creations, exist in a limited spatiotemporal realm: "la danse déjà l'enfant mortelle de mon corps mortel mais maintenant ces deux filles aussi, ces fillettes remuantes et respirantes, qu'est-ce que j'ai fait" (64) [the dance already the mortal child of my mortal body but now these girls as well, now these clamoring clambering girls, what have I done] (71). As one possible response to this reality of the human condition, she choreographs a dance called the *Pietà*—it reinforces the elaboration of a matrofocal optic already present in her work, raising the issue of the mother's suffering through a stylization of the gestures associated with mourning: "Elle . . . laisse envahir son corps par l'indicible douleur des mères; s'acharne à styliser ces gestes immémoriaux que sont l'arrachement des cheveux, la lacération de la poitrine; traduit les flots de larmes en palpitations affolées des doigts, la mélopée funèbre en roulements géométriques sur le sol" (101) [She . . . allows her body to be invaded by the agony of maternal grief, stylizes the timeless gestures of tearing out hair and raking chest with nails, translates the flood gush of tears into skittering mad-bird hands, translates the raw throat of keening into geometrical rolls on the floor] (118).

Huston's privileging of dance in this text reflects a further thinking through of mind/body dynamics. Her protagonist, as a dancer, is strategically well placed to speak to the issues of women's literal and figurative embodiment of art. Critic Elizabeth Dempster postulates that the association of dance with a feminine, maternal space has been at the root of its characterization as a "derivative, diversionary and minor art" (38). She further suggests that dance has been identified with "a body which has been defined as a dependent, contingent object, lacking autonomy, lacking the capacity to speak of or otherwise represent itself and lacking transcendent symbology and function" (39). Thus, choosing dance as the preferred art form of the protagonist might seem to position woman solely in terms of her corporeality. Huston, however, seeks to undermine conventional associations that locate the dancing body as voiceless and intimates through her protagonist how the dancer is a generator of meaning. Wolff counters the idea that this art form is somehow intuitive, insisting that it necessarily implicates mind as well as body: "a knowledge of dance makes it clear that there is nothing unmediated going on here" (81).

Lin, in her creations, is especially concerned with transforming significant life experiences for women into dance. While some of her works incorporate goddess and mythological figures, she focuses in particular on women's domestic and child-rearing experiences.[8] For the protagonist, all events can potentially be reconfigured as dance. She recognizes the primordial importance of valorizing the maternal experience and its (pro)creative impulse. In one narrative sequence, for example, the protagonist can be seen rocking her child to sleep in the melancholy half-light of early morning. She ponders how to best capture the realities of such fleeting moments of life and to render them in her art: "Comment récupérer tout cela, comment s'en servir. . . . Toujours le travail de Lin a consisté à prendre les thèmes les plus ténébreux de la vie et à les transformer en lumière . . . les retraduisant ensuite en mouvement: rien ne doit exister qui ne puisse être transfiguré par le corps" (60) [How to recover this, how use it for the dance—always Lin's work, her love, her passion has been to take life's darkest themes and turn them into light . . . then bursting them back into movement—nothing must exist that cannot be folded into the body and there transfigured] (66–67). Once again, the focus remains on the intersection of mind and body. A quote from Dempster reinforces the conception of dance serving an integrative function in terms of traditional pairings in Western philosophy: "In moments of dancing the edges of things blur and terms such as mind/body, flesh/spirit, carnal/divine, male/female become labile and unmoored, breaking loose from the fixity of their pairings" (52).

While the form and content of Lin's dances make manifest her desire to place equal value on her roles as mother and dancer, the blurring of "edges" that necessarily occurs is not unproblematic. With the birth of Lin's second child, serious conflicts develop in her ability to reconcile the time and effort she must devote to her art with what she perceives as her limited capacity to embody the more nurturing role of mother. Although she may be part of a nontraditional couple, in the sense that her husband is very present for their children, the expectation remains that she will function as the primary caregiver. Huston's conceptualization of Lin includes allusions to the violence that threatens to erupt when her creative impulse is suppressed. At a time when she is feeling most conflicted, for example, she dreams that her second daughter contracts a serious disease. Frightened by the thoughts of illness or accidents befalling her children, she insists on forgoing a European tour: "Ce qui se passe en elle ces jours-ci n'est pas dicible" (88). [There is something too grim going on inside of her] (98). In response to this inner turmoil, Lin ultimately feels compelled to leave her family, thereby claiming her art as essential to her existence: "oui c'est pour cela que je suis au monde / et rien—non *rien*— / ne peut égaler cette jouissance de faire bouger les corps dans l'espace" (121) [Yes it is for this that I was born / and nothing—no, *nothing*— / can equal this joy of making bodies move through space] (132).

Although the protagonist becomes a well-known dancer and choreographer with her own company, and is seemingly fulfilled through her performances, the decision to break with her family haunts her life in different ways. She whirls around upon hearing children call out for their mothers, even years after her own are no longer young: "C'est Angela—la voix d'Angela—Lin virevolte. Son corps réagit avant son cerveau, elle n'y peut rien, ma fille, ma fille—elle virevolte" (133) [It is Angela—Angela's voice—Lin spins around. Her body responds to the voice before her brain, she cannot help it, my daughter, my daughter—she spins around] (147). This evocation of the novel's title situates her in her role as dancer, while concomitantly making manifest the enduring ties to her maternal role.

After many years of dancing, Lin is diagnosed with degenerative osteoarthritis in her hip. A botched surgery forces her to give up dancing and limit herself to choreography—she will no longer be able to embody her own creations. Nonetheless, the protagonist continues to incorporate life experiences in her art, using her own physical decline as inspiration for a dance to lyrically convey the realities of the aging body: "dansant l'infection et le déclin inévitables, sculptant l'artériosclérose et les varices, les secousses et les spasmes du mal neurologique—mais en beauté—oui, cela aussi—acceptez, acceptez cette musique-là aussi, cette trahison, la dissonance puissante de cette débâcle" (200) [dancing the inevitability of infection and decline, sculpting arteriosclerosis and varicose veins, the jerks and spasms of neurone damage—but beautifully—

yes, this, too—accept, accept this music, too, this betrayal, the powerful dissonance of this defeat] (227).

La Virevolte, then, depicts a woman who bears children whom she loves, yet feels she must abandon in order to express herself creatively at the highest level. Huston makes no moral judgment of her protagonist, choosing instead to limn the complex nature of the opposition that arises between her maternal and her personal desires[9]—while maternity is valorized, it is not made sacred. A reconciliation with her daughters takes place when they are older and begin spending vacations with their mother. Interestingly enough, one daughter will eventually use occurrences from her own life in her career as a comedian, verbally transforming episodes that her mother had realized as dance.

In *Instruments des ténèbres*, another fictional work from the 1990s with (auto)biographical elements, the theme of (pro)creation remains a leitmotiv. In this metafictional narrative, the protagonist reflects upon the gestational nature of writing while producing a text which leads to her own rebirth. Nadia is a childless, middle-aged American writer with an uncompromising view of the world, as revealed to the reader in her first journal entry: "qu'on se trouve au printemps ou en automne ou en hiver m'est parfaitement égal, le miracle de la vie ne me touche pas" (11) [I don't care whether it's spring or fall or winter; the miracle of life doesn't touch me] (11). She feels alienated from others as well as from herself, and unequivocally asserts the insignificance of her own existence through a symbolic renaming: "Mes parents m'avaient appelé Nadia, et quand il m'est devenu clair que I, le je, n'existait pas, je l'ai éliminé. . . . Nada. Le néant" (12–13) [My parents called me Nadia and when it became clear to me that 'I' did not exist, I cut it out. . . . Nada. Nothingness] (12). It is only through her writing that she will be able to recover the "I."

Nada's journal entries[10] segue into movements from "La Sonate de la résurrection" ("The Resurrection Sonata"), the story she composes not only as a way of thinking through the process of artistic creation, but also as a means of dealing with the death of her twin brother and the dysfunctional relationship of her parents to their children and to each other. As in a musical composition in which one section evolves from and plays off of another, the narrator draws inspiration from memories of her own life, as well as from authentic episodes in André Alabergère's *Au Temps des laboureurs en Berry* (*In the Days of the Berry Plowmen*) (1993), in order to recreate the story of Barbe Durand, a seventeenth-century French girl executed for hiding her pregnancy and allegedly causing the death of her newborn. Barbe, whose mother died in childbirth, lives her life in the margins, moving from family to family as a maidservant and becoming the "souffre-douleur de tous" (46) [everyone's scapegoat] (37). Although her pregnancy results from a rape, Barbe delights in her changing body and is hopeful at the thought of the new life growing inside. Nada's comments on the staging of these scenes serve to illuminate the exploratory aspect of her craft, while simultaneously recasting the Pygmalion myth in relation to a female artist: "Et l'histoire, pareille à une statue de bronze se dégageant peu à peu d'entre les ordures fourmillantes. D'avance, on sait très peu sur la forme que prendra la statue. (Jamais je n'aurais cru que la grossesse de Barbe se passerait ainsi.)" (261) [The book a bronze statue gradually emerging from writhing garbage. And, in advance, one has only the vaguest notion of the statue's ultimate shape. (I had not expected Barbe's pregnancy to go that way.)] (203).

Throughout "Le Carnet *Scordatura*" ("The Scordatura Notebook"), Nada engages in discussions of self-discovery and the creative process with her muse. Traditional paradigms of a female muse for a male creator are inverted with this imaginary male character who often takes issue with the protagonist's vision for the characters in her story, forcing her to reaffirm her beliefs on creativity. In her examination of self, she feels especially compelled to confront the enigmatic nature of her relationship with her mother, a talented violinist who was forced by her husband to renounce her musical career in order to care for her family, and who ultimately ends up in a convalescent home suffering from amnesia. It is tempting to see Nada's mother as an example of what the protagonist in *La Virevolte* might have become if she had had to abandon dance.

The tortured nature of her mother's relation to the childbirth experience—she had many children and numerous miscarriages that nearly killed her—scarred Nada for life. She had to help her mother eliminate the traces of each miscarriage before her father returned from work: "Etant l'aînée . . . c'est moi qui dus assister au carnage dans la chambre parentale, fausse couche après fausse couche car mon père ne cessait de la mettre catholiquement en cloque . . . de sorte que, plus d'une fois l'an, les draps s'emplissaient de sang et aussi de ces caillots noir veloutés et tremblotants qui avaient une vague ressemblance avec de la chair humaine" (37) [Being the eldest child . . . it was I who was privy to the regular bedroom carnage, miscarriage after miscarriage as my father continued to knock her catholically up and she . . . refrained from taking measures to prevent it and the sheets filled with blood and trembly velvety black clots of something like human flesh more than once a year] (30). It is not surprising, then, that Nada cannot envision a healthy relationship with her own body, especially in regard to its reproductive capacity. She assumes a sardonic stance when referring to the aftermath of abortion, which she compares to that of her mother's miscarriages: "(Ah! n'est-ce pas que mes scarabées sont plus propres, plus secs, plus discrets? Au moins leur meurtre ne laisse-t-il pas de taches)" (37) [(Ah! My beetles are so much cleaner, so much drier, and more discreet! At least their murder makes no mess)] (30). The protagonist undergoes several abortions and eventually becomes sterile. As Huston reveals in an interview in which she specifically refers to the mind/body problematics of this text, her protagonist "a digéré les théories d'un certain féminisme à la de Beauvoir qui séparent le corps et l'esprit, qui proclament que l'art est supérieur à la vie" (Roy 21) [digested the theories of a certain feminism advocated by Beauvoir which separates body and mind and which asserts that art is superior to life]. On a certain level, Nada's fictional characters will indeed replace the children whom she can no longer engender.

By means of her writing, Nada uncovers and works through painful, long-repressed memories, inscribing new possibilities for herself through her creation of Barbe. In order to reclaim her own twin brother, who died at birth, and to exorcise the guilt she feels in having survived him, the protagonist envisions a twin brother who will ultimately play a role in Barbe's salvation: "C'est justement le rôle que joue Barnabé pour Barbe, le rôle dont j'ai rêvé toute ma vie pour Nathan, ou Nothin' mon jumeau mort"(167) [This is the role Barnabé plays for Barbe, the role I have dreamed of all my life for Nathan, or Nothin', the dead twin brother] (130). This episode is emblematic of the way in which the narrator uses her composition of the sonata as a springboard for the reevaluation of her own life.

Later in the text, in a passage which recalls Huston's earlier discussion of the baby versus the book myth and which attests to Nada's fear of the tenuousness of her artistic authority, the narrator conjures up an image of text as developing fetus, dreaming that her mother wants to destroy her as yet unformed characters: "Pourquoi Elisa voulait-elle que j'assassine mes jumeaux? Ce livre encore embryonnaire, si absolument vulnérable, flottant entre l'existence et l'inexistence" (228) [Why would Elisa want to kill my twins? This novel still so inchoate, so utterly vulnerable, hovering between life and death] (176). The writing of Barbe's story allows the protagonist, finally, to mourn the loss of her own child: "Tu as énormément compté dans ma vie, mon ange. Et je m'excuse de t'avoir traité de scarabée, dans les premières pages de ce carnet" (345) [You matter a great deal to me, my darling. And I apologize for calling you a beetle in the first pages of this notebook] (266). Through the creative interplay between passages in the journal and in the sonata, Huston succeeds in illuminating that which lies in the shadows, underscoring the possibility of a "résurrection," or rebirth, for both her narrator and her readers.

All three of the texts examined in this essay engage the reader in a provocative questioning of the complex relationship between the artist and her work, between mind and body. It is Huston's contention that we cannot afford to accept gender-based distinctions of (pro)creation uncritically:

> Les institutions patriarcales ont privé non seulement les femmes de leur âme, mais les hommes de leur chair, et il faudrait bien du temps encore avant que les artistes ne deviennent des êtres pleins, non mutilés et non envieux. Avant que les femmes ne cessent de s'amputer de leur maternité pour prouver qu'elles ont de l'esprit; avant que les hommes ne cessent de déprécier la maternité tout en la mimant parce qu'ils en sont incapables. (1990, 230–31)

> [Patriarchal institutions have not only deprived women of their souls, but men of their flesh, and it will require a good deal of time before artists become whole beings, not maimed or envious. Before women stop cutting themselves off from maternity to prove they have a mind; before men stop disparaging maternity while at the same time mimicking it because they are incapable of giving birth].

Huston's texts successfully give voice to the maternal and the non-maternal body, while bodying forth the restorative potential of a (pro)creative theoretical stance.

Notes

All translations other than those for Huston's *La Virevolte* and *Instruments des ténèbres* are my own.

1. In fact, Huston explicitly connects her rejection of her native tongue to the fact that her English-speaking mother divorced her father and abandoned her when she was a young girl. A recent essay by Huston conjures up an image that vividly renders the pre-text which grounds her desire to embrace an alternate, more nurturing, language: "Donc, en matière de langue maternelle, quand j'avais six ans, elle a disparu. Ma mère. Avec sa langue dans sa bouche" (1995, 232) [So, as for my mother tongue, it disappeared when I was six. My mother, that is. With her tongue in her mouth].

2. Susan Friedman provides a useful definition of the terms at issue here: "Underlying these words is the familiar dualism of mind and body, a key component of Western patriarchal ideology. Creation is the act of the mind that brings something new into existence. Procreation is the act of the body that reproduces the species. . . . The pregnant body is necessarily female; the pregnant mind is the mental province of genius, most frequently understood to be inherently masculine" (52).

3. Adrienne Rich, in *Of Woman Born*, informs us that she has always recognized the inherent integration of mind and body: "As a woman thinking, I experience no such division in my own being between nature and culture, between my female body and my conscious thought" (95).

4. Theories of genesis through the ages that support a view of male as primary genitor include such early notions as the Aristotelian doctrine privileging the spiritual over the corporeal and positing that the male provides the soul, and Nichlaus Hartsoeker's notion of generation which was based on the "spermatic animalcule." This theory, according to philosopher Kelly Oliver, presupposes the fact that "the masculine element produces both the form and the material of the child in miniature and the tiny person merely grows in the maternal womb as the seed grows in the soil" (18–19).

5. She refers, for example, to several of Bellmer's portraits of Zürn in which he represents the vulva in place of her eyes. Huston, in a comment alluding to the significance of the gaze, indicates how this serves to negate Zürn's own artistic potential: "Une femme dont le sexe remplace le regard peut-elle être une artiste?" (215) [Is it possible for a woman whose gaze has been replaced by her genitals to be an artist?]. In addition, after describing episodes in the relationship between Georges Bataille and Colette Peignot in which the former seeks to realize his erotic vision through the body of Peignot, Huston writes: "Or, c'est en partie grâce à l'abjection réelle de Colette Peignot que Georges Bataille va réussir à élaborer son oeuvre" (183) [Thus, it is partly thanks to the real abjection of Colette Peignot that Georges Bataille will succeed in developing his work].

6. A citation from critics Sandra Gilbert and Susan Gubar, who examined the assumptions grounding metaphors of literary paternity, serves to illustrate the primacy of this issue: "Like the metaphor of literary paternity itself, this corollary notion that the chief creature man has generated is woman has a long and complex history. From Eve, Minerva, Sophia, and Galatea onward, after all, patriarchal mythology defines women as created by, from, and for men, the children of male brains, ribs, and ingenuity" (12).

7. Braidotti has this to say about the ways in which the pregnant woman challenges ideas of fixed bodily form: "The fact that the female body can change shape so drastically is troublesome in the eyes of the logocentric economy within which to see is the primary act of knowledge and the gaze the basis of all epistemic awareness" (64).

8. Marie Béïque, in a review of *La Virevolte* that includes a passage from a radio interview given by Huston, underscores the author's desire to imbue her text with the lived experience of women: "In this way, the author wishes to show the role that women can play outside of their traditional functions: 'I believe it is important to introduce female reality into the universal. It is something which concerns all of humanity'" (161).

9. Huston also admits that the autobiographical element of this text stems from her own mother's decision to leave the family to pursue a career when the author was a young child. She claims that the writing of the text was cathartic in

the sense that it enabled her to come to terms with the absent mother figure in her life, and to reach an understanding vis-à-vis her own loss and the loss suffered by her mother. See Beïque's review for more information on this aspect of the text.

10. These entries constitute what she refers to as "Le Carnet Scordatura" ("The Scordatura Notebook"), The reader learns that "scordatura" signifies a certain form of musical discord, and that the narrator feels herself to be an "instrument désaccordé" (34) [mistuned instrument] (27).

WORKS CITED

Alabergère, André. *Au Temps des laboureurs en Berry*. Bourges, France: Edition Cercle généalogique du Haut-Berry, 1993.

Alcoff, Linda Martin. "Feminist Theory and Social Science: New Knowledges, New Epistemologies." In *Bodyspace: Destabilizing Geographies of Gender and Sexuality*, edited by Nancy Duncan, 13–27. New York: Routledge, 1996.

Beïque, Marie. Review of *La Virevolte*, by Nancy Huston. *Recherches féministes* 9, no. 2 (1996): 161–62.

Braidotti, Rosi. "Mothers, Monsters, and Machines." In *Writing on the Body: Female Embodiment and Feminist Theory*, edited by Katie Conboy, Nadia Medina, and Sarah Stanbury, 58–79. New York: Columbia University Press, 1997.

Dempster, Elizabeth. "Women Writing the Body: Let's Watch a Little How She Dances." In *Grafts: Feminist Cultural Criticism*, edited by Susan Sheridan, 5–54. London and New York: Verso, 1988.

Friedman, Susan Stanford. "Creativity and the Childbirth Metaphor: Gender Difference in Literary Discourse." *Feminist Studies* 13, no. 1 (1987): 49–82.

Gilbert, Sandra M., and Susan Gubar. *The Madwoman in the Attic: The Woman Writer and the Nineteenth-Century Literary Imagination*. 1979. New Haven: Yale University Press, 1984.

Huston, Nancy. *Désirs et réalités*. Montréal: Leméac, 1995.

———. "Festins fragiles." *Liberté*, décembre 1994, 7–15.

———. *Instruments des ténèbres*. Arles: Actes Sud; Montréal: Leméac, 1996.

———. *Instruments of Darkness*. Toronto: Little, Brown and Co., 1997.

———. *Journal de la création*. Paris: Seuil, 1990.

———. *Mosaïque de la pornographie: Marie-Thérèse et les autres*. Paris: Denoël/Gonthier, 1982.

———. *Slow Emergencies*. Toronto: Little, Brown and Co., 1996.

———. *La Virevolte*. Arles: Actes Sud; Montréal: Leméac, 1994.

Huston, Nancy, and Sam Kinser. *A l'amour comme à la guerre, correspondance*. Paris: Seuil, 1984.

Jardine, Alice. "Death Sentences: Writing Couples and Ideology." In *The Female Body in Western Culture: Contemporary Perspectives*, edited by Susan Rubin Suleiman, 84–96. Cambridge: Harvard University Press, 1985.

Oliver, Kelly. *Family Values: Subjects Between Nature and Conflict*. New York: Routledge, 1997.

Rich, Adrienne. *Of Woman Born: Motherhood as Experience and Institution.* Tenth Anniversary Edition. New York: W. W. Norton, 1986.

Roy, Monique. "Celle par qui le scandale arrive." Review of *Instruments des ténèbres*, by Nancy Huston. *Châtelaine* (septembre 1996): 20–21.

Wolff, Janet. *Resident Alien: Feminist Cultural Criticism.* New Haven: Yale University Press, 1995.

Feminist Discourse and Children's Literature in Québec: Some Theoretical and Historical Foundations

LUCIE GUILLEMETTE

THIS ESSAY IS PART OF ONGOING RESEARCH IN THE FIELD OF FEMINIST and literary studies. My purpose is to describe and analyze the place of feminist thought in a few Québécois novels for young people that have been written by women during the last ten years. These include works by Louise Leblanc, Ginette Anfousse, and Marie-Danielle Croteau, all of which have been published, respectively, in three collections available from Les Éditions de la courte échelle: Premier Roman, Roman Jeunesse, and Roman+. My main objective is to select paradigms of feminist language from children's fiction and to focus particular attention on those feminine voices responsible for dissolving the oppositional categories at the source of the oppression of women in male discourse. One must remember that these dichotomies are the direct inheritance of a philosophical tradition formed by patriarchal thought. Accordingly, they are not sexually neutral, but are expressed through a system of binary oppositions in which a woman's role is always inferior to that of a man: nature/culture, body/mind, object/subject, darkness/light, etc. With respect to methodology, feminist reading consists of abolishing these heterosexual couplings of classical philosophy, which has down through the ages presented the subject of knowledge as exclusively male and consequently superior to all things female. Relativist feminism attempts to dissolve the philosophical framework whereby the reason-endowed male mind dominates nature, the body, and the female.

In *Gynesis* (1985), Alice Jardine speaks of a feminine space that is capable of destabilizing the antinomian patterns of male thought. Within the context of postmodernism, it is essential to articulate this "other-than-themselves" (25)—that is, to outline a discursive strategy appropriate for producing the "woman-in-effect" (31).

The author develops the concept of "gynesis," described as a process by which language is attributed to newly defined spaces within narratives undergoing a crisis of legitimation. This crisis is the loss of male authority, the very authority that has traditionally excluded the feminine from its narratives. "The crises experienced by the major Western narratives have not, therefore, been gender-neutral. They are crises in the narratives invented by men" (Jardine 1985, 24).

Before the feminine can be understood in new ways, however, it must be given a new definition. The term "feminine" is used here in a constructivist sense. The feminine attests to the experience of women in the world. Identity and gender are thus posited as artifacts. Indeed, quite a few feminists maintain that gender is a social construct, and certain feminist theoreticians rightly describe it as cultural sex. Author Toril Moi states:

> Among many feminists it has been long established usage to make "feminine" (and "masculine") represent *social constructs* (patterns of sexuality and behaviour imposed by cultural and social norms), and to reserve "female" and "male" for the purely biological aspects of sexual difference. Thus "feminine" represents nurture, and "female" nature in this usage. "Femininity" is a cultural construct. . . . patriarcal oppression consists of imposing certain social standards of femity on all biological women, in order precisely to make us believe that the chosen standards for "femininity" are *natural* (122–23).

I propose to demonstrate that bipolar structures such as nature and culture, same and other, masculine and feminine are not depicted in a relationship of opposition and inequality in the contemporary works of children's literature treated in this paper. At the core of these fictional works one finds feminist ideas actualized through random and heterogeneous forms that question accepted notions of center, truth, and meaning. My objective is to highlight the constructed dimension of the feminine gender that underlies certain texts written for children during the last decade. Accordingly, I will focus on the discourse of female characters who succeed in developing what Jardine calls "space coded as *feminine*, as *woman*" (Jardine 1985, 25)—that is, a feminine speech that revises and abolishes the binary structures reproduced in the master narratives or, as Lyotard puts it, the great philosophical, historical, and scientific discourses.

Let us examine how the use of a feminine subject in contemporary children's literature relativizes the systems of opposition upon which the master narratives are founded. The questioning is threefold: (1) how do women writing for a young audience succeed in relativizing patriarchal systems of opposition so as to make feminine identity possible; (2) in what way do these authors convey the experience of small girls and adolescents, then introduce new feminine values at the twilight of the twentieth century; (3) into what type of feminist discourse do these writings fall with regard to depicting the inequalities that exist between the sexes?

The object of my investigations here is the feminine voice. I will focus on texts whose *énoncé* (utterance) moves away from a homogenizing patriarchal logic and whose feminine, enunciative *I* leads to the development of a narrative framework that breaks with the traditional structures legitimated by masculine thought. I will use a few illustrations from novels published during the last decade to show how a young female character denounces inequality between the sexes and articulates a form of speech that allows her to relativize the apriorities of a male culture and consequently develop her own identity and systems of reference. This feminist discourse is at odds with the binary schemata that have resulted from a particular metaphysical tradition I wish to examine here. The language of the feminine that one observes in certain Québécois novels for young people is indicative of a self-representative practice. This is one of the mainsprings of the fragmentation of the feminine gender created by a patriarchal society.

As is the case for women's literature produced in a culture dominated by men, children's literature produced in a culture dominated by adults reflects the relationship between a woman writer and the apriorities of patriarchal thought. In a collection of writings entitled *Écriture féminine et littérature de jeunesse* (*Feminine Writing and Children's Literature*), Margaret Higonnet maintains:

> The status of both women and children is problematic. Although they presuppose a biological given, they nevertheless function within a cultural field. Both are still formed within the epistemological framework of a system of oppositions. As Simone de Beauvoir has shown, the second sex will be represented as the antithesis of the first and, by the same token, the Child as the antithesis of the adult. (1995, 17)[1]

In other words, literary practices regarding childhood and adolescence often give rise to a cultural discourse on sex, which, at this time, points to "the loss of paternal fiction" (Jardine 1985, 67). From the standpoint of feminist writers whose heroines are young girls, the need to free oneself from preconceived notions of gender takes the form of a quest for identity, determined through a process of criticism of male dictates. Cultural discourses on sex are veritable markers of experience that make it possible to place children's literature within a particular context. In paternal fiction, the author portrays girls as naturally quiet, submissive, and obedient, thus reinforcing the kind of stereotyped behaviors that are in keeping with the principles of a legitimated social ethic. Conversely, when a principle of equality is advocated, the writer will attempt to enhance the value of feminine words and action in order to highlight the constructed dimension of cultural and sociosexual roles. As one is aware, these roles are identified with gender in the language of feminist theories. The result with regard to the characterization of women is this: in the first case, the heroine reproduces paternalistic norms and conforms to prescribed models that serve to keep her in a state of passivity and submission. One has only to look at the "good little girls" educated to become good wives and mothers, who figure in the stories of the comtesse de Ségur. In the second case, the protagonist defines her own systems of representation and has the ability to interpret—even to deconstruct—the beliefs and values inculcated by the adults in her world. During the last years of the twentieth century, writers like Louise Leblanc, Ginette Anfousse, and Marie-Danielle Croteau presented girls who attempted to arrive at a highly individual definition of feminine gender based on personal life experience.

What distinguishes children's literature published in Québec during the last twenty years or so is an enunciative practice that employs the narratorial *I*. We are beginning to understand how cultural discourses about sex govern an author's choice of form, Margaret Higonnet affirms (1993, 116). It becomes necessary, then, to describe and analyze the feminine voice of the child and the adolescent who reveals through word and action the social and cultural roles she is expected to assume by adults in a patriarchal society. By using the narratorial *I*, the female character seeks to develop her own systems of reference.

Following in the footsteps of several generations of militant feminists, author Louise Leblanc abolishes the subordination characteristic of girls' relationship with boys. The writer preaches female emancipation by giving the floor to a little girl who successfully challenges the arbitrary division of the sexes. Leblanc has written a series of novels about Sophie, all available in the collection First Novel from Les Éditions de la courte échelle. Published between 1990 and 1998, the series includes nine novels intended for children age seven to nine. The first book of the Sophie series, *Ça suf-*

fit, Sophie! (That's Enough Maddie), portrays a little girl with a strong sense of reality. Although only nine years old, Sophie has already learned to distrust conventional wisdom and to question certain myths set forth in books and movies. As a result, the knowledge she acquires will differ significantly from the images evoked by female characters usually portrayed as flawless and shielded from the ups and downs of normal life: "Dans les livres et dans les films, les héroïnes, elles ont toujours l'air en forme. Alors que moi, je suis très, très fatiguée." (43) [In books and movies, the heroines always seem to be in great shape. But as for me, I get very, very tired].[2] Sophie imagines this speech while dreaming of having left home. Even in her dreamworld, however, the little girl represents herself as a creature with solidly material concerns, one very different from movie heroines unruffled by mundane considerations such as hunger or thirst. A thought that occurs to her while daydreaming is that grand gestures like leaving home are not necessary for becoming a heroine. The story presents the world of dreams, traditionally associated with the irrational, as a legitimate place from which one can articulate a logical, reasonable feminine discourse.

Published in 1991, Louise Leblanc's *Sophie lance et compte (Maddie in Goal)* remains a timely illustration of the abolition of sexual differences.[3] Nine-year-old Sophie dreams of becoming a hockey goaltender. So it's no surprise when the little girl exclaims during Christmas celebrations, "pour une fois, je n'avais pas reçu de poupée en cadeau" (8) [for once, I didn't get a doll for a present]. This is a feminine *I* liberated from all narratorial authority, one that assumes responsibility for a cultural discourse where there seems to be no opposition between the sexes. Having decided to participate in an all-boy hockey match, Sophie first outlines a plan. Next, she employs various strategies to convince her brother Laurent to lend her his hockey equipment. Finally, she goes before her teammates, fully prepared to confront the adversary. "Un chocolat blanc dans une boîte de chocolats bruns, voilà comment je me sens" (45) [A white chocolate in a box of dark chocolates, that's how I feel], she muses. Although the successful realization of her dream brings many difficulties, Sophie triumphs because she succeeds in mocking the prejudices of the majority.

The domination/submission relationship modeled on the biological superiority of the male over the female is relativized in *Sophie vit un cauchemar (Maddie in Trouble)*. The children in Sophie's school wish to choose a new leader. A believer in the principle of "might makes right," Lapierre is firmly convinced the job belongs to him. Sophie's friend Clémentine, however, sets about to replace the criterion of brute force by a more rational consideration. "Il n'y a pas que la force" (15) [Brute force isn't the only thing that matters], she maintains. Clémentine's remark causes Sophie to ponder the attributes other than force that make a good leader. On her grandmother's advice, she proposes that a leader be chosen democratically—that is, through the electoral process. The tyrannical Lapierre tries again to intimidate the group by claiming that he will get the others to vote for him by force: "Si vous ne votez pas pour moi, vous êtes tous des tartes. Je suis le plus fort" (27) [If you don't vote for me, you're toast. I'm stronger than everyone else]. However, Clémentine has not yet had her say. Toughened by karate lessons, the little girl tosses her adversary easily to the ground, and the children escape a male dictatorship based on "might makes right." Elections are called. Yet, the two candidates, Sophie and Lapierre, must prove their courage by stealing something from a store. Seriously upset by the circumstances of the theft, Sophie withdraws and names Clémentine in her place. The latter is elected by popular acclaim. In Sophie's words, "[elle] a toutes les qualités voulues. Elle est la meilleure en classe, la plus réfléchie et . . . la plus forte" (58) [she has everything we need. She's the best one in the class, she's the smartest and . . . she's the strongest].

Notable in this story is the way in which the female characters take a stand not only for equality between the sexes, but also for objectivity and equity in the organization of a social microcosm. Louise Leblanc makes it quite clear that, in the popularity contest shown here, female reason wins the day. The feminist message is thus convincingly expressed through an activity linked to reason. This use of female reason is depicted throughout the series as the crucial condition for solving the problem of sexual inequality. The traditional schema in which man is a thinking subject superior to woman is destabilized here through feminist discursive strategies.

The story of *Sophie devient sage* (*Good Little Maddie*) (1997) again addresses the issue of sexism. Tanguay and Sophie both aspire to play the role of Masto, an elephant, in the school play. Tanguay maintains that this role should be played by a boy: "Masto est un éléphant, pas une éléphante" (23) [Masto is a male elephant, not a female], he tells Sophie, who promptly retorts, "Il n'y a pas de raison! Tu n'es qu'un sexiss . . . (*sic*)" (24–25) [That's not so! You're just being sexiss . . . (*sic*)]. Sophie's words show that sexism is simply not a reasonable attitude. This is why she presents her rival with arguments intended, as she says, to make him see reason: "J'ai plus de ressemblances avec Masto que toi!" (24) [I have more in common with Masto than you do]. To accomplish two goals—to get the role and to bring her mother home—Sophie decides to play at being a "good little girl." In the end, the girl and the boy agree to share the role so ardently desired. Sophie's little brother Julien brings this about when he suggests to the teacher: "Mais l'éléphant doit être vraiment gros. Il faudrait deux élèves pour jouer le rôle" (59) [But the elephant must be really big. We need two kids to play the role]. Sophie and her adversary must team up and work together. Once again, the discourse of sexual equality wins over traditional ideas of inequality.

The feminine experience is also the main theme in Ginette Anfousse's Rosalie series, published in the collection Roman Jeunesse. Intended for children ages nine to twelve, the adventures of young Rosalie Dansereau are recounted in six stories printed between 1987 and 1998. With the publication of her novel *Les Catastrophes de Rosalie (Rosalie's Catastrophes)* in 1987, author Ginette Anfousse began a dialogue with the comtesse de Ségur and *Les Malheurs de Sophie (Sophie's Misfortunes)* (1859). Two little girls living a century apart, one in the nineteenth-century French countryside, the other in a large North American city, are confronted with the demands of the adult world. Anfousse's text, however, depicts a child who has been emancipated from traditional social roles. On several occasions, nine-year-old Rosalie questions the values being conveyed to her by the seven women who have assumed responsibility for her upbringing after the death of her parents. She considers her own personal experience of the world to be of primary importance and never hesitates to challenge conventional wisdom. Upset over a friend who has lost his dog, she says to her aunt Florence:

> Je ne veux plus que tu me dises que la mort, c'est la vie. Ni que la peine donne de la maturité et de la spiritualité! Parce que moi, Rosalie, je ne sais pas ce que ça veut dire! Je ne veux pas que tu me répètes que mon père et ma mère sont heureux dans leur ciel. Et que le chien de Marco est allé les retrouver! Je veux . . . je veux juste que Marco n'ait plus de peine. Parce que même si son chien n'était qu'un chien, même s'il était vieux, même s'il était laid comme une vadrouille et qu'il aboyait tout le temps, c'était *son* chien! Et . . . c'est la peine de Marco, sa peine à lui, qui me fait pleurer. (61)

> [Don't tell me any more that death is just a part of life. Or that suffering brings maturity and spirituality! Because I, Rosalie, don't know what that means! I don't want you to tell me that my father and my mother are happy in heaven. And that Marco's dog has gone to meet them! I just don't want Marco to suffer. Because even if his dog was only a dog,

even if he was old, even if he was as ugly as a dust mop and barked all the time, he was still his dog. And . . . it's seeing Marco so sad . . . that makes me cry].

Narrated in the first person, Rosalie's account breaks with the sociohistorical model of silence and submission taught to young Sophie in the novel by the comtesse de Ségur. This process of self-representation frees Rosalie's words from all narrative patronage. Thus, like many fictional heroines, Rosalie becomes the author of a text referred to in fiction as a *mise en abyme*. This consists of a brief reflection by the little girl after receiving instructions at school: "Pour mon pire malleur, les sept sœur de mon père on décidé de m'adopté. C'est pour ça aujourd'hui que je suis toute seul. . . . Comme vous voyez, se n'ai pas drole la vie d'une orfeline qui n'a pas eu la chance de vivre dans un orfelinat"[4] (22) [Oh, woe is me, my father's seven sisters have decided to adopt me. That's why I'm all alone today. . . . As you can see, it's no picnic being an orphan when you're not lucky enough to live in an orphanage]. Entitled "The Orphan," the text expresses clearly the enunciative traces of a child who writes a beginner's French. It constitutes the self-representation of a first-person narrator, one who deconstructs the isolation and anonymity generally associated with the term *orphanage*. The subject of the enunciation is autonomous and therefore manages to challenge parental and narrative authorities for the purpose of self-representation.

The relationship between girls and boys is the main theme of *Le Héros de Rosalie (Rosalie's Hero)*, a story in which Rosalie falls in love for the first time. The object of her devotion is Pierre-Yves Hamel, a boy who attends the same school as Rosalie and whom she gets to know through the romance of their respective cats. Pierre-Yves will, in fact, remain the love interest throughout all the novels in the series. From the very first, Rosalie makes sure that her future Romeo will regard her with respect. Pierre-Yves is convinced that the book he is reading "c'est exactement le genre de livres qui n'intéresse pas les filles" (34) [is exactly the kind of book that doesn't interest girls]. Outrage over such a sexist comment causes Rosalie to lie: she tells her friend that she has about twenty books in the same collection, when she actually has only four. "Mais mon mensonge avait fait son petit effet. Pierre-Yves avait subitement perdu son air de conquérant" (34) [But my lie certainly was effective. Pierre-Yves dropped that superior look of his right away]. Although juggling truth and lies, her words render inoperative the traditional dynamic of dominating male/submissive female.

The following scene has Rosalie and Pierre-Yves leafing together through the books in question and exchanging opinions on an equal basis. The young girl insists, too, that Pierre-Yves is first and foremost a friend and confidant.

Flattered for a time by the attentions of a young American during a trip to Florida, Rosalie realizes afterward that this is no substitute for the special bond she has formed with Pierre-Yves during their moments together: "Mais je savais bien, moi, que c'était avec mon grand héros vicking que j'avais tellement de choses en commun" (*Les Vacances de Rosalie* 72) (*Rosalie's Vacation*) [But I knew I had more things in common with my great Viking hero]. When Pierre-Yves catches her by surprise on the arm of her American admirer, the little girl must learn to deal with the shaky new world of love relationships: "Je voulais demander à Marco Tifo si un gars pouvait réellement se laisser mourir d'amour" (69) [I wanted to ask Marco Tifo if a guy could really die of love]. Although her knowledge of men is necessarily limited at this point, Rosalie instinctively knows how to play her cards right to regain her boyfriend's attention. Seeing Pierre-Yves chatting with a young American girl, the twelve-year-old girl throws herself in front of the fishing boat he is on, thus forcing him to come to her aid: "Pierre-Yves me reparlait enfin. Mieux, j'avais risqué le tout pour le tout et mon grand héros avait pu, encore une fois, jouer les héros" (80) [Finally, Pierre-Yves talked to me again. I threw caution to the winds, and my big hero had another chance to act like a hero]. The story's action points to a shrewd and clear-sighted protagonist who discovers, little by little, the intricacies of male psychology.

It is the weaknesses of the stronger sex, in particular, that capture Rosalie's attention during her American odyssey. "C'est si fragile, un héros!" [A hero's a fragile thing] she muses when new problems develop in her relationship with Pierre-Yves (*Le Grand rêve de Rosalie* 66) (*Rosalie's Big Dream*). Notable here is how the female character departs from the commonly held view of a "hero": "Mais tu n'as pas à te rendre malade comme une sapristi de mocheté de fille, parce qu'au fond, il n'y a rien de changé entre nous" (66) [You don't have to make yourself sick over it like some silly girl, because everything's basically the same between us], she tells her friend. Indeed, our heroine has decided to become a tap-dancing star and is afraid her project will permanently alienate Pierre-Yves. Yet, Rosalie is astonished to learn that both he and her best friend, Julie, are ready to help make her dream come true. The male hero depicted in the Rosalie series is obviously not a rigid, inaccessible being who holds himself aloof from the concerns of his peers.

In *Rosalie à la belle étoile* (*Rosalie Goes to a Concert*) (1998), however, the heroine has eyes only for the lead singer of a heavy metal-type rock group. "Je viens de rencontrer le gars le plus hallucinant de la planète" (30) [I've just met the most absolutely gorgeous guy on the planet], Rosalie confides to Julie. Although still close to Pierre-Yves, the protagonist is temporarily swayed by Roy Richard's good looks. In fact, she believes that her boyfriend has lost interest in her and shudders at the idea of his falling in love with another girl: "Je te jure que je vais en mourir" (34) [It would kill me, I swear], she tells Julie. Actually, what Rosalie is looking for is diversion, because she feels that a breakup with Pierre-Yves is inevitable: even their cats have lost interest in each other. Julie, who has always been more interested in computers than boys, is unimpressed by her friend's melodramatic words. Julie the computer buff becomes the voice of reason to the extent that Rosalie, vexed by her friend's indifference, openly insults her. In a sarcastic aside, Rosalie snarls that "si elle continuait à faire la sainte nitouche, elle finirait comme une sapristi de mocheté de vieille fille, toute seule, à taper, le reste de ses jours, sur son ordinateur" (33–34) [if Saint Julie keeps on acting like this, she'll end her days like some horrible old maid, all alone, typing away on her computer]. However, insults do not seem to bother the smartest girl in school, who is gifted, above all, with a generous heart. So Rosalie easily convinces her to lie to their parents and to accompany her to a concert given by Roy Richard's band. When the plan is discovered, however, Rosalie insists on taking the blame.

Because of her escapade, she is punished by her family and deprived of the companionship of both boyfriend and cat. Later on, she forgets the whole Roy Richard episode in her joy at being united with the companions she thought that she had lost. Notable in this scenario is how Rosalie deconstructs certain belief systems linked with the social roles attributed to boys and girls. Here, it is the female who seeks to seduce someone new while at the same time expecting fidelity from her boyfriend. The most striking aspect of the novel, however, is the theme of feminine solidarity expressed in the relationship of Rosalie and Julie, close friends with radically different personalities.

Practices of feminine self-representation are emphasized still more in Ginette Anfousse's 1991 novel *Un Terrible secret* (*An Awful Secret*). The text is part of the collection Roman+ intended for adolescents. The protagonist is Marilou Brochu, a sixteen-year-old girl with a passion for words and writing who spends much of her time leafing through dictionaries. Because of her strong language skills, Marilou is the editor of the school newspaper. Yet, journalism and writing are not the only fields in which she shines. Marilou is also known as the "super-planteuse-de-machos-toute-catégorie" (the supergirl-match-for-any macho) (16), a reputation that is echoed in her discourse: "Je ne leur [les garçons] demande pas d'inventer le moteur à deux temps, seulement d'imaginer autre chose que de foncer bêtement sur nous avec une moto" (31–32) [I'm not asking them to invent the two-stroke motor, just to think that maybe there's something else to do besides charging at us with their motorcycles].

Far from being the dupe of noisy boys craving attention at all costs, the feminine *I* deploys a discursive space that corresponds to this "other-than-themselves," to use Jardine's expression. Note that the protagonist's discourse attempts to abolish the domination/submission structure that appears to define relations between the sexes in her school. One boy goes so far as to suggest that Marilou write a column about her "féminisme enragé" (ferocious feminism) (55). It is hardly surprising that the girl places so high a value on her friendship with Colombe: alliances between girls produce a solidarity which, she believes, is precarious in a man's world: "plus je pensais aux amitiés entre filles . . . plus je les trouvais fragiles" (41) [The more I think about girls' friendships . . . the more fragile they seem]. Indeed, Marilou is viewed as a girl with "du tempérament" (with a temper) (124), because she is not afraid to "foncer sur une dizaine de machos" (53) [take on a dozen machos] if necessary.

Reflecting upon the behavior of her schoolmates, Marilou casts a critical eye on the practice of seduction in a patriarchal context: "Je vous jure que je connais des filles qui passent, disons, au moins trois quarts d'heure, chaque matin, à se crêper la frange pour eux. À s'agrandir les yeux aussi. À s'épaissir les lèvres. À s'étrangler la taille. À s'écrapoutir les fesses, les cuisses et j'en passe . . ." (31) [I swear I know girls who spend at least forty-five minutes every morning teasing their bangs for them. And making their eyes bigger. And their mouths fuller. And pinching in their waists and squeezing into skin-tight jeans . . . and who knows what else]. Throughout a self-reflexive account addressed to a narratee, the young girl contests Simone de Beauvoir's myth of the eternal feminine and Betty Friedan's memorable "feminine mystique." It is obvious that Marilou sees nothing very liberating in the behavior of her schoolmates. In colorful terms, she describes the boys as "des tas de zouaves qui aiment les tartes" [a bunch of jerks who like tarts] and the girls as "des tas de dindes qui aiment les épais" (89) [a bunch of turkeys who like dummies], and she decides to make this the subject of a newspaper column. One senses that the knowledge derived from dictionaries has served to make her aware of the constructed dimension of social roles. Thus, Marilou poses as an autonomous subject of enunciation, who views her classmates in the third person, as a *them* that is part of her field of observation.

Marie-Danielle Croteau gives us another example of a feminine identity that derives from traditional systems of representation in a trilogy published between 1993 and 1997 by Les Éditions de la courte échelle. A teenage girl is the main character of her three novels, entitled respectively *Un Vent de liberté* (*A Wind of Freedom*) (1993), *Un Monde à la dérive* (*A World Adrift*) (1994), and *Un Pas dans l'éternité* (*Anna in Search of Herself*) (1997). Anna Dubois, an orphan who has been living with her grandfather Théo on an island in Québec ever since the death of her parents, dreams of going around the world: "Certains se gavent de hamburgers, moi, j'avale des kilomètres. Sur papier, bien entendu. Je collectionne les récits et les guides de voyages, les atlas, les cartes géographiques et les timbres. Malheureusement, tout cela ne fait que me creuser l'appétit" (1993, 16) [Some people stuff themselves with hamburgers, but I swallow kilometers. On paper, of course. I collect travel writings, guides, atlases, maps and stamps. Unfortunately, all this only gives me a bigger appetite].

Eager to make her own discoveries, Anna leaves on an expedition aboard a sailboat that her tutor has made for her birthday: "Je ne savais pas encore qu'il n'est pas nécessaire de s'éloigner beaucoup pour être dépaysée" (1994, 24) [I didn't know yet that it's not necessary to go far to have a change of scenery]. As is the case for many contemporary heroines, however, she finds that indetermination and contradiction make the road to identity a difficult one: "J'avais besoin que l'on me ramène au centre de moi-même" (1994, 82) [I needed to find my center].

Born in California to parents who died shortly after her birth, Anna has spent her existence on an island with a man who is similarly distanced from his origins. Théo has spent his youth traveling across America rather than earning a traditional living as a fisherman. Of her benefactor Anna relates that, "[Théo] s'est installé à San Francisco et il a eu ma mère avec une Québécoise, qu'il avait rencontrée là-bas. Elle est repartie un jour en lui laissant le bébé sur les bras. Il n'est revenu ici qu'à la mort de mes parents" (1993, 17) [Théo settled in San Francisco and had my mother with a Québécoise he met there. She took off one day and left him with the baby. He only came back here when my parents died].

Like her hazy American origins, Anna's feminine identity is not an innate characteristic. It emerges, rather, from the artificial constructs used within the discourse of the narrative instance: education and social position. Anna says she has "disguised herself as a girl" to go to the billiard room—that is, she has worn heels that are too high, a skirt that is too short, and a blouse that is too skimpy. Although her clothes inevitably attract the attention of many of the boys there, they fail to impress the one boy who will eventually become her friend. In other words, there are flaws in the categorical logic of gender or cultural sex, because it does not express Anna's real needs and wants. Anna must therefore search for the roots of her identity within her personal experience.

Upon the death of her grandfather, the young girl finds herself alone in the world. There is now a "switch" or change of voice in the narrative structure of the novel: Anna starts to alternate between the *she* and the *I*. The first-person narrative of the story's beginning is interrupted because of the difficulty she has in recounting events that have led her to regret her very existence. "Ça y est, je glisse vers moi. Il ne faut pas. Je dois rester en dehors de ce récit, sinon j'en mourrai. Sinon Anna en mourra" (1997, 18) [There I go, I'm sliding towards myself. I shoudn't do this. I have to stay outside this story. Otherwise, I'll die from it. Otherwise Anna will die from it]. In fact, she feels guilty for the death of her grandfather, who has perished in a fire. For Anna Dubois, recourse to the third person represents a heterogeneous form of thinking that is expressed by a narrative plurality. This polyphony tends to dissolve the referential structure posed by a conventional narrator. From this narrative choice there results a relativization of the dichotomous schema of same and other, which does not appear in a strict relation of opposition. Fragmented, the narrative voices shatter all identifying structures of same and other.

The path to self-identity carved out by such female protagonists as Sophie, Rosalie, Anna, and Marilou reveals the attitudes adopted by girls to criticize paternalistic norms and to free themselves from various sources of oppression. Now, the knowledge necessary to fuel a discourse founded on the equality and emancipation of women in children's fiction comes from feminist demands that were first heard in America, then Europe, during the second half of the nineteenth century. The theoretical foundations of the feminist thinking of writers of children's fiction in Québec can in effect be systematized by using the constructivist principles found in the writings of John Stuart Mill, the influential nineteenth-century feminist thinker and author of a work entitled *The Subjection of Women*, published in 1869. He was strongly in favor of the equality of the sexes, and his philosophy served as a catalyst for theories on gender that were formulated a century later. Like Elaine Showalter, Toril Moi, and Judith P. Butler after him, Mill stipulated that feminine character is not a natural given so much as the result of conditioning. In *The Subjection of Women*, he maintained that "all women are brought up from the very earliest years in the belief that their ideal of character is the very opposite to that of men" (16), and that women are taught early on to renounce responsibility for their own lives and submit to the will of others. He further maintained that women must acquire the right to form their own opinions and act upon them without any physical or moral interference from their peers. In keeping with Mill's thesis, the relation of subordination that exists between human beings among couples of all sorts—man and woman, parent and child, master and slave—works to the detriment of human progress. Mill believed that "authority on the one side and subordination on the other prevent perfect confidence" (25).

In a 1973 study that takes "the side of little girls," Elena G. Belotti refers to Mill's ideas to demonstrate that girls' characters are the logical product of a historical, cultural, and social context, rather than the expression of a natural, innate identity: "Mill analyzes educational influences and indicates, furthermore, the simplest and surest way of arriving at a knowledge of woman that is not, as is often the case, a mere reflection of man's view of her" (7). One observes how Belotti makes use of certain philosophical theses based on a constructivist principle to describe the young female character.

The use of a discourse based on the feminine *I* in contemporary children's novels demonstrates that happiness and individual freedom go hand in hand with the emancipation of girls from imposed cultural roles. Many protagonists reject the summary and reductive models of the feminine questioned by Mill. These works of fiction portray woman as a creature of body and soul whose search for self-knowledge makes her capable of transforming the symbolic order of patriarchy. Indeed, the writers I am concerned with here reject a feminine condition that places girls in a position of inferiority with respect to knowledge and culture. Made uneasy by the ingrained assumptions and oppositions of a patriarchal society, these fictional heroines denounce, in their turn, prejudice, public opinion, and force of habit—that is, the "tyranny of custom" condemned so strongly by John Stuart Mill. Contemporary writers, it would seem, have learned to combine Mill's philosophy with certain modern feminist ideas to create female protagonists who defy patriarchal standards by inventing a highly individual identity.

Notes

1. My translation.
2. All translations of primary texts are my own.
3. In 1992 *Sophie lance et compte* won the Livromagie award.
4. Rosalie's text without the spelling errors: "Pour mon pire malheur, les sept soeurs de mon père ont décidé de m'adopter. C'est pour ça aujourd'hui que je suis toute seule. . . . Comme vous voyez, ce n'est pas drôle la vie d'une orpheline qui n'a pas eu la chance de vivre dans un orphelinat."

Works Cited

Anfousse, Ginette. *Les Catastrophes de Rosalie*. Montréal: La courte échelle, 1987. Translated by Linda Gaboriau as *Rosalie's Catastrophes*. Charlottetown: Ragweed Press, 1994.

———. *Le Grand rêve de Rosalie*. Montréal: La courte échelle, 1992. Translated by Linda Gaboriau as *Rosalie's Big Dream*. Charlottetown: Ragweed Press, 1995.

———. *Le Héros de Rosalie*. Montréal: La courte échelle, 1988.

———. *Rosalie à la belle étoile*. Montréal: La courte échelle, 1998.

———. *Un Terrible secret*. Montréal: La courte échelle, 1991.

———. *Les Vacances de Rosalie*. Montréal: La courte échelle, 1990.

Belotti, Elena Gianini. *Du côté des petites filles: L'Influence des conditionnements sociaux sur la formation du rôle féminin dans la petite enfance*. Paris: Éditions des femmes, 1973.

Butler, Judith P. *Gender Trouble: Feminism and the Subversion of Identity*. New York: Routledge, 1990.

Croteau, Marie-Danielle. *Un Pas dans l'éternité*. Montréal: La courte échelle, 1997.

———. *Un Monde à la dérive*. Montréal: La courte échelle, 1994.

———. *Un Vent de liberté*. Montréal: La courte échelle, 1993.

Higonnet, Margaret R. "Diffusion et débats du féminisme." In *Ecriture féminine et littérature de jeunesse*, edited by Jean Perrot and Veronique Hadengue, 17–24. Paris: La Nacelle, 1995.

———. "La Politique dans la cour de récréation: La Critique féministe et la littérature enfantine." In *Culture, texte et jeune lecteur. Actes du Xe Congrès de l'International Research Society for Children's Literature*, 109–33. Nancy: Presses universitaires de Nancy, 1993.

Jardine, Alice. *Gynesis: Configurations of Woman and Modernity*. Ithaca and London: Cornell University Press, 1985.

Leblanc, Louise. *Sophie prend les grands moyens*. Montréal: La courte échelle, 1998.

———. *Sophie devient sage*. Montréal: La courte échelle, 1997.

———. *Sophie vit un cauchemar*. Montréal: La courte échelle, 1996. Translated by Sarah Cummins as *Maddie in Trouble*. Halifax: Formac Publishing Co. Ltd., 1998.

———. *Sophie lance et compte!* Montréal: La courte échelle, 1991. Translated by Sarah Cummins as *Maddie in Goal*. Halifax: Formac Publishing Co. Ltd., 1992.

———. *Ça suffit, Sophie!* Montréal: La courte échelle, 1990. Translated by Sarah Cummins as *That's Enough Maddie*. Halifax: Formac Publishing Co. Ltd., 1991.

Lyotard, Jean-François. *La Condition postmoderne: Rapport sur le savoir*. Paris: Minuit, 1979.

Mill, John Stuart. *The Subjection of Women*. Indianapolis: Hackett, 1988 [1869].

Moi, Toril. "Feminist, Female, Feminine." In *The Feminist Reader. Essays in Gender and the Politics of Literary Criticism*, edited by Catherine Belsey and Janet Moore, 117–132. New York: Basil Blackwell, 1989.

Ségur, Sophie, Comtesse de. *Les Malheurs de Sophie*. Paris, Gallimard, 1997 [1864].

Showalter, Elaine, ed. *Speaking of Gender*. New York: Routledge, 1989.

Huguette Bertrand: "Internaute" Pioneer Poet: An Introduction to *Entre l'ombre et la lumière*

MYLÈNE CATEL

BECOMING "CONNECTED" TO THE INTERNET PROMISES VAST OPPORTUnities for authors, particularly women, who still have relatively limited access to traditional modes of publishing. Many talented academic women writers bemoan the fact that poetry does not sell anymore, that they are not read, that they cannot find an editor. Yet, they seem reluctant to adopt a revolutionary multimedia mode of diffusing their work. Huguette Bertrand, however, as an "Internaute," to use an expression from cyberjargon for a surfer and a searcher, has been innovative in establishing a home page for posting her own work and introducing other francophone women writers. Bertrand defies critics who predict that a profusion of bad prose and poetry will inevitably render the Internet a vehicle of bad taste. She argues that publishing on-line allows women writers, especially those marginalized by the established male-dominated and/or profit-dominated world of publishing, a unique chance to express themselves and to receive immmediate feedback. Through her membership in L'Union Nationale des Écrivains Québécois (UNEQ), Bertrand's inspiring presence has been felt via her creative multimedia web pages since 1995.

In contrast to publishing poetry on paper in a traditional manner, which may require an immense effort and compromise only to reach a limited, elite milieu, publishing on the Internet can be extremely liberating. A few words from an unknown Internet reader, such as, "Thanks for your words for my sad nights," can alleviate feelings of alienation and inadequacy engendered by fruitless efforts to fund printing and circulating a slim volume of poems. Although she does register her work with the Bibliothèque Nationale du Canada, Bertrand is not concerned about her "droits d'auteur" (author's rights of copyright and royalties). She considers her work as a gift. To those obsessed with being "recognized" as a poet, Bertrand replies, "Everything is ephemeral, it is relative." Not content to disseminate only her own work, she has been instrumental in establishing hyperlinks to connect her readers to multimedia sites created by other francophone women writers.

It seems apparent that the Internet will remain and grow. Therefore, women (especially as professors and students), have the responsibility to support unique endeavors, such as those of Huguette Bertrand, and to empower themselves. Women need to make their presence felt by supporting the creation and globalization of an on-line women's community. Then and only then will women be able to fulfill their timeless destinies as *mothers of tales*.

Entre l'ombre et la lumière

Entre l'ombre et la lumière (Between Shadow and Light) is an unfinished piece by Huguette Bertrand, produced and presented on the Internet with all rights reserved. For the sake of convenience, a printed version is provided below, but it would be better for the reader to consult this mixed-media work on-line because it implies visual, aural, and reflective stimulation. The underlying theme is the "shadow-light" metaphor conveyed through a network of twenty "espaces" (spaces).

In this work, it is a question of space and time and exchanging energies (from the earth to women's spaces, back to Mother Nature and maternal archetype) while meditating on a woman's passion, also a passion for writing. Mirrored in the various mental (emotional, intellectual, sensual) spaces the reader enters and leaves, a fluid movement (ebb and flow) is created between the space (a photo landscape reworked by Huguette Bertrand herself), the music, and the text that bring one's attention back to the space and music while "multiplying" the interpretive gaze of the otherness of it all. An intricate relationship is woven between Huguette Bertrand's own "shadows" and the referentiality of language. Closely linked to the unconscious, and hence the shadows of women's space, are a Jungian archetype, and a means of self-discovery.

Thus a woman poet's shadow could be called a dark mirror in the sense that it re-presents an image, but unlike mirrors it does not suggest a wholeness. On the contrary, shadows double, triple, and multiply the body, disfiguring it, and yet one could not be without them. Redirecting the shadow themes, metaphorically, I read Bertrand's work as it traces the alienation of a shadow in particular (or several shadows) cut from its body: a woman's lonely attempt to work in a more-than-challenging male-dominated space (the Internet). The new turn introduced by Huguette Bertrand in the borrowed and appropriated shadow tales sheds light on a different understanding of the modern cybertext.

Appropriating space in the very space opened by the alienation of shadow(s) founded on the opacity of narration, Huguette Bertrand's work establishes direct, simultaneous relationships between words and things. The shadow remains above all the thing of the thing, the word of the word, the narration of the narration, the shadow of light, the light of the shadow. The title indicates after all an in-between space—shadow/light—although it mostly reflects a darkened light, sometimes melancholic, sometimes compassionate, sometimes violent, sometimes explosive, not unlike the trauma of birth.

Overshadowed then by a dis/located symbolism ("mixed" media), the text fails to adhere to any specific form and never gives the reader a sense of closure but rather forces him or her (more likely her) to pass it on. It is an open space after all! Oscillating between the acute and convex reverberations of (un)conscience, remembrances in *Entre l'ombre et la lumière* can never be separated from its manifestation in cyberspace. Displaced and dislocated shadow-lights form an eccentric women's cyberspace, ceaselessly inaccessible, ever-changing, removing readers and critics from the possibilities and condition of one "fixed" condition of existence. This is one of the lessons to be learned from Huguette Bertrand's very own space of creation.

Works Cited

Bertrand, Huguette. *Entre l'ombre et la lumière*.
http://francomedia.qc.ca/~s.o.s.fr//Poesie/Musique/espace0.html

Entre l'ombre

      et la lumière

      poésie en image

      de Huguette Bertrand

GÉMISSEMENTS

Silencieusement
  la Terre gémit en son
  dedans
  nous respire à chaque
  seconde
  sème des pensées
  amoureuses
  sur nos vivants déchaînés
  espère
  suffoque
  éclate
  en mille désirs
  sur nos corps
  achevés

Derrière l'ombre

    la lumière

Longue traversée
dans ce désert fou
accablé de mirages
vaste contrée
amoureuse
de nuits étoilées
venues tisser nos pas
sur le temps
incommensurable
abandonné
dans l'explosion
d'un silence
absolu

À L'OMBRE
DES DÉSIRS

À travers nos chevauchées
nuitamment étoilées
la puissance de nos désirs
nous emporte
vers des voies orageuses
à la conquête de nos sens
toujours fruités

les mots soupirent
devant les gestes
accordés aux envolées
intimes
subjuguées par l'éclair
passé maître
dans l'art du frisson

Sous un bruissement
   d'ailes
   la mer s'illumine
   en reflets onduleux
   verse dans nos
   mémoires
   des regards salins
   dispersés en mille
   vagues
   dans un rêve d'oiseau
   envolé vers de plus
   grands espaces
   toujours plus haut

MÉMOIRE D'OMBRE

Fantaisiste
la Terre déambule
devant le chaud regard
d'un soleil provoquant
se couvre d'un édredon
d'amours mortes
épaves éparpillées
sur les rives charnelles
d'un océan de rêves

MIRAGE

Mordre dans la lumière crue
embellit la mémoire
des pas fleuris
offerts en bouquets
cultivés dans les sables
d'un rêve assassiné

trop cru
trop rauque
pas assez bouquet
pas assez offrant
trop fleuri
trop assassiné
par des futurs imaginés

        LA MÉMOIRE
        DES PAS
        IMAGINE
        DES LUMIÈRES
        FLEURIES

À même le jus humain
le temps se cherche des
avenirs
se répand
sur la broussaille des
jours
torpille nos heures
ensommeillées au fond
de l'oeil
lorsqu'enfin éclatent
les douces brises
efflorescentes
que bercent les vagues
de nos mémoires
intimes

                      Arrêtez le temps
                        Arrêtez l'espace
                          Arrêtez la lumière
                            Arrêtez les avenirs

                    ARRÊTEZ TOUT !

                    SILENCE . . .

                    une brise efflorescente passe

Dans l'ombre de l'infini

> Dans l'infini
> les mots s'élancent
> s'entrechoquent
> étranges anarchistes
> projetés
> sur les écrans
> de nos imaginaires
> font bouillonner nos sens
> livrés aux fantasmes
> désirs censurés
> par la foulée des jours
> de courses folles

ÉCLATS   ET LUMIÈRE

La nuit s'endort
dans ses rêves
amochés
par les errances du jour
au coeur des villes navrées
parmi les salutations d'usage
les départs
les retards
l'appétit
à plein ventre
en plein coeur
à vendre
un jour ou l'autre
au centre
d'une lumière
éclatée

incandescence

    Coup de grisou
    dans l'espace ensanglanté
    la lune expire

    tacheté rouge
    le temps lui lance
    des soupirs flamboyants

    la nuit éclate
    de rire
    devant cette lune
    éclaboussée
                            le ciel
                            grimaçant
                            s'emporte
                            contre
                            une marée
                            de nuages
                            rouges

ORAGE À L'OMBRE

Ô rage d'ombres
rugissantes sous la ouate
d'un matin gris
abandonne à la pluie
une spirale emportée
sur le galbe
des nuages
jusqu'aux courbes des arbres
violés
par le vent ennuyé
et frileux

À travers les nuances de l'ombre
un foyer de lumière éclate
effusion dans l'âme
du présent
rongé par les heures
fléau des jours
sur des terres convulsives
toujours nous ramène
vers les nuits percutantes
des passions mauves

                                                L U M I N A N C E

un jet de lumière traverse un regard
  boréal
    transperce les échos
    échoués sur les battures
    d'une mémoire farcie
    de gestes givrés
    mémoire étreinte sur la banquise
    allumée bleue
    dans l'ombre amoureuse
    d'un graffiti
    sur le tableau inspiré nu
    glaciaire

                    R
                    E
                    G
                    A
                    R
                    D

                            B
                            O
                            R
                            É
                            A
                            L

Errance obscure
 d'une lune automnale
 affectée par l'ombrage
 des sommeils arrimés
 à la beauté des nuits
 accrochées aux branches
 des amours lapidées
 par les vents épris
 de ténèbres
 abyssales

CHAIRS

D'OMBRE

Sous les paupières
les chairs d'ombre défilent
en demi-teintes
veilleuses amoureuses
dans le couloir
d'un regard
enjoué

Sur les eaux tumultueuses des naissances
   glissent quelques mots
   envoûtés par les berges
   aspirées
   vers des lumières aperçues
   dans ce lointain
   lumières entre toutes lumières
   situées
   à la frontière des sens

                    présage des tendresses amovibles
                    itinérance de peaux vives
                    à même la terre la crasse
                    les chimères
                    et l'amour au quotidien des horloges
                    horrifié

LUMIÈRES CHIMÉRIQUES

LUEURS DE RÊVES

> Par une fenêtre
> les ombres
> de la nuit
> projettent
> sur nos sommeils
> des lueurs
> de rêve
> que l'aube
> s'approprie
> pour supporter
> le jour
> effrayé

À L'OMBRE
DES PIERRES

À même le sang du vivant
l'amour bouillonne
crache des oiseaux
sur les jours
s'agite dans la pénombre
évidée de tous les bruits
rencontrés au hasard
se prononce animé
à travers des silences
bave du désir
de reconnaître
au coeur de la pierre
des visages
rassemblés

EN PLEINE LUMIÈRE

Arbre desséché
un enfant aspire
au plein des choses
émerveillé
par le verbe ciselé
en sa forme originelle
ténor du désir
de l'amour
et tous ses plaisirs
que la chair propose
dans un verre de rhum
à la santé du poète

                       allongée
                  une croix rebelle
              reprend ses mystères
                     inassouvis

(en hommage au poète Alphonse Piché 1917–1998)

Dans la nuée
    d'un ciel
    raisonnable
    un parfum se répand
    sur le sommet jouissif
    d'une chair vive
    ses pentes douloureuses
    que le temps cet amant
    grise
    de fruits aimantés
    aux jours insolents
    amant givré
    dans la gourmandise
    pleure des perles
    sur les cris

CRIS À L'OMBRE

Quand les ombres se rêvent

    Elle est là au loin dans sa
    vie
    grignote des utopies
    boit à la source de toutes
    les libertés
    marchande de fleurs
    et de beautés
    reprend la course
    refait le pas
    toujours renouvelé

                            Elle est là au loin dans
                            sa vie
                            court sur les eaux vers
                            le soleil
                            de ses rêves
                            désordonnés
                            refaçonnés par le bleu
                            nuit
                            de ses sourires
                            ensommeillés

http://www.espacepoetique.com/Poesie/Musique/espace0.html

Entre l'ombre et la lumière
                poésie en image
            de Huguette Bertrand

Marguerite . . . or She Who Sees Behind the Mirror: A Translation of Hélène Rioux's *Marguerite . . . ou celle qui voit derrière le miroir*

JULIE RIEMAN

Translator's Introduction

In "Marguerite . . . or She Who Sees Behind the Mirror," Hélène Rioux describes the end of an old woman's life and addresses the universal themes of life's small pleasures, human isolation, and the perils of aging. This story is a sort of scrapbook of the meager highlights and everyday events that make up the life of a spinster, and yet, Miss Marguerite's end could be that of any elderly woman—any woman's dialogue with death.

Translating a text from one language into another always presents problems—some that are common to nearly all translations and others that arise from the particular culture or language in question. "Marguerite . . ." had some of both.

There was the question of cultural references, which could either be transposed into a target language equivalent or made understandable while keeping as much of the original flavor as possible. The "convent school" where Miss Marguerite was educated could have become a "parochial school," and the "ministry" in which she worked a "government department," but I chose to retain the Québécois cultural references so that the reader, too, can travel.

In this story, there was also a challenge in dealing with punctuation. Both the French language and Rioux's particular style make a slightly different use of certain punctuation marks than is common in English. In addition, there was the usual conflict between the tendency toward conciseness in English and that toward a certain "flow" in French. I tried to preserve Rioux's punctuation wherever possible, because it is vital to the characteristic rhythm that distinguishes her style. However, there were sentences in which the story would simply not have flowed in English had I retained the original punctuation. Therefore, some semicolons became periods, and a stray dash and set of periods made their way into the English version—a clear and conscious case of the maxim *traduttore, traditore* [translator, traitor].

When translating a text from one language into another, something is always lost, yet something is always gained. I felt that, in this case, some of Rioux's characteristic rhythm (derived from her style of punctuation) was lost in my English version of the story. What was gained, I believe, was another writer, another culture's picture of the universal dilemmas of old age . . . as well as an introduction to this incisive and gifted author.

Montréal, le 14 juillet 1999
Chère madame Rieman,

Tout d'abord, j'aimerais vous dire que je suis très touchée par votre traduction. Etant moi-même traductrice, je sais qu'il n'est pas simple de rendre un climat, de faire passer une émotion d'une langue à une autre . . . Ici, c'était un climat de détresse, la vulnérabilité d'un personnage, la cruauté que la vie démontre dans des détails. Je trouve votre Miss Marguerite très émouvante.

Je vous envoie le recueil dont cette nouvelle est tirée—vous ne l'avez peut-être pas. Dans votre introduction, vous écrivez que la nouvelle décrit les derniers jours d'une personne âgée. C'est cela, bien sûr. Mais c'est aussi la conclusion d'une suite de rendez-vous avec la mort, rendez-vous donnés aux différents âges de la vie. Dans mon recueil, tous les personnages sont féminins, je l'ai voulu ainsi. La mort s'incarne deux fois seulement, dans la première nouvelle, avec le personnage le plus jeune, et dans la dernière, sous les traits de cette femme en blanc, immobile dans le miroir. Cette apparition, pour moi, n'est pas seulement un fantasme de personne âgée. Je voulais dire que la mort est peut-être toujours là, et que seules les personnes très jeunes, ou très vieilles, sont capables de la voir. . . .

Veuillez agréer, chère madame Rieman, l'expression de mes sentiments les meilleurs.
Hélène Rioux

[Montreal, July 14, 1999
Dear Ms. Reiman,

First of all, I would like to say that I was very touched by your translation. Being a translator myself, I know that it isn't easy to create an atmosphere, to transpose an emotion from one language to another. . . . Here, it was an atmosphere of distress, the vulnerability of a character, the cruelty that plays out in the details of life. I found your Miss Marguerite very moving.

    I am sending you a copy of the collection from which this story is taken, in case you don't have it. In the introduction to your translation, you write that this short story describes the last days of an elderly person. That is, of course, true. But it is also the conclusion of a series of meetings with Death, meetings that take place at different stages of life. In my book, all of the characters are female—that was deliberate. Death actually appears only twice: in the first story, with the youngest character, and in the last story, in the form of a motionless woman in white in a mirror. For me, this apparition is not just the delusion of an elderly person. What I wanted to say was that Death is, perhaps, always there, and that only the very young or the very old are capable of seeing it. . . .

With my very best wishes,
Hélène Rioux]

—What are you doing in my mirror?
—I am a reflection of you.
—I don't recognize my face.
—I am looking at you.
—Don't look at me.
—I am waiting for you.
—Is it time already?
—Perhaps.

Marguerite . . .

or She Who Sees Behind the Mirror

> The walls
> the walls
> have ears
> and the mirrors
> the eyes of a lover.
> —Jean Cocteau

She is still there. She has been there constantly, for a week now, always motionless. In the bathroom, at the back of the mirror. She is white, and very still.

Always in the same position. Just three-quarters of her, but head erect, eyes staring strangely. Her light garment seems to float about her. She remains there, observing, without uttering a word. There is nothing one can say about her, neither that she is gentle nor that she is menacing. She is like no one. Her silence is white, like her stillness.

She arrived just like that, without warning, as they say. One evening, when turning on the light, Miss Marguerite noticed her silhouette over the basin, caught her eye. Since then, she has been there continually, night and day.

Miss Marguerite just turned 88. She's completely white-haired and very timid. So stooped that she looks like a hunchback. So wrinkled, so sprinkled with brown spots—those marks that are tactlessly called age spots—so covered with them that she's like a shriveled apple, left for days in the kitchen, on a corner of the counter, abandoned or forgotten. For this is how life treats us, no different than fruit, plants, animals. That characteristic odor, both sweet and rancid, which emanates from her person, they call it the smell of old people, and that odor comes from her. Hair, she has almost none; only a tiny bun at the nape of her frail neck. Putting her hair up like that exhausts her, as it has become increasingly difficult for her to lift her arms. The trouble is that she can't imagine doing her hair any other way. Her deformed feet can hardly stand shoes; indoors she wears woolen slippers as she goes about her tasks. She has no walker, but instead leans on the furniture, moving forward with small steps, resting often. Her dresses are trimmed with lace collars; on what remains of her bosom, a cameo at the end of a silver chain. When she speaks, her voice is very soft, with a hint of confidentiality, her turns of phrase exquisitely polite.

Her life has unfolded quietly. She was a civil servant, always within the same ministry. She rarely went out. There was the occasional concert with a friend from the convent school, her only friend in fact, who was taken prematurely by cancer. For years, they had season tickets for a series of musical evenings with the local symphony. Miss Marguerite especially loved the great symphonies. These outings, which were usually preceded by dinner in a quiet restaurant where they shared harmless confidences, stirred up feelings in her which occupied her thoughts for months. The head waiter, for example, a very handsome man, had been charming, as usual. He had even added a drop of well-aged brandy to their coffee, assuring them it was excellent for the heart. This kind of attention disconcerted yet pleased her. Or perhaps the evening had been exceptionally mild; it had been pleasant to walk to the concert hall, and what a privilege to see this virtuoso with one's own eyes performing the "Pathétique." Yes, there was enough fuel to feed innocuous daydreams for months.

With the exception of these excursions, there was very little else really. Nice big books (she had a predilection for sagas with scores of characters), music, keeping house, her stamp collection. She had also corresponded regularly with philatelists from all over the world. Her album is now in a drawer of the bureau, with a small set of tweezers and sacks of transparent envelopes containing stamps that she hadn't had time to put in their proper places.

She hadn't been pretty: she was of medium height, her legs a bit heavy, complexion muddy, eyes a lifeless, pale blue. She was without deformity or grace, one of those people with whom life, from the outset, had not been generous. Yet never a bitter word, never a regret. She was, as they say, good-natured.

She lived with her mother, first in the big family house where she and her brothers had spent their childhood. Then, when they had been forced to sell it due to family debts and the fact that maintenance had become a burden, they moved into this apartment in a very quiet residential neighborhood, where she still lives—a four-room apartment without a balcony, yet sunny, on the third floor. On the walls, now yellowed with age, hang oval frames, family portraits; there are crocheted antimacassars on the armchairs. The little pink marble clock stopped long ago. The clockmaker said they no longer make these delicate mechanisms; it would cost too much to repair them. So a cheap alarm clock was bought to keep the time; it sits near the marble clock on the buffet and tick-tocks infernally. Apart from that, nothing has really changed.

When her mother was alive, in the evening after supper, they liked to drink a small glass of raspberry liqueur while playing dominoes or Scrabble. Sometimes one of her brothers stopped in and stayed an hour or two. One of them worked at the post office, another was an accountant and the third a Latin teacher. Strangely, in this family they all remained single. A sterile branch. If the Latin teacher had unmentionable tendencies, this was never discussed, and the two naive women seemed to suspect nothing. Only the accountant came to visit, with his longtime girlfriend, a woman by the name of Laure, who had dyed hair and a raspy voice. Miss Marguerite and her mother, accepting her as a slightly odd relative, had never made any disagreeable comments. Every winter, Miss Marguerite's brother spent a month with Laure in Florida, and from one year to the next, this woman's skin grew to look more and more like old leather. The postal worker's breath usually smelled of cheap gin, and he had a fixed sort of stare. That was how daily life passed: with small, always predictable pleasures.

Miss Marguerite retired at sixty-five. On her last day, they invited her to lunch at a restaurant, and her co-workers gave her farewell cards and a much-too-flashy rhinestone brooch that she never dared to wear.

Life went on, even more quietly. That was when Miss Marguerite learned to cook. She excelled at desserts. She cut out recipes from newspapers, magazines. Between games with her mother, she liked to savor a slice of banana cake, a macaroon. Their sight deteriorated, gradually their fingers became deformed; while they watched television, they squeezed small rubber balls for their arthritis or rolled Chinese exercise balls in the palms of their hands. They followed the adventures of soap opera characters with interest, never missing an episode. These they discussed, trying to find solutions to the myriad of problems whose existence they might never have imagined had it not been for television. Afterwards, Miss Marguerite played patience[1] while her mother dozed in her armchair. She still plays patience, but less and less often; her patience is exhausted.

Her brothers died, one after the other. Her mother shriveled up, in sorrow's embrace, then died very quietly. Miss Marguerite found herself all alone.

At Social Services, Miss Marguerite is classified as being independent, yet she can barely get down two flights of stairs, clinging to the banister. The street began to frighten her. The social worker advised her to call the grocery store and have her food delivered. But this is the only outing she still has—this trip to the supermarket, where she can touch the food, compare prices, take her coin purse out of her handbag and exchange a few words with the cashier. She doesn't want to give this up.

Before the woman in white arrived, other people came into the house, but only at night. They moved objects around, rummaged in her papers. The others were shadows that moved stealthily about the small apartment. Miss Marguerite could bolt the door, close all the windows, but still they managed to slip in. Perhaps they came through the walls.

And then, there is the hole. A large hole in the wall, behind the toaster. That was where they lay low and waited for nightfall. When evening arrived, they came out silently, one by one. In the dark, she sometimes, with terror, felt soft breath on her neck. From then on, she always left a light burning.

At first, she was afraid there might be mice. She confided this to the social worker. To reassure her, the social worker brought her some traps, but no rodents were ever caught. The social worker looked in the kitchen cupboards and told her that she saw nothing unusual, that the noises were the kind one hears in any house, that the hole was caused by wear. You know, she said, these quickly built apartments are not of the same quality as the solid old houses of yesteryear. Be that as it may, Miss Marguerite would have liked to have a cat. But without a balcony, the poor animal would have been very unhappy; and how would Miss Marguerite have managed to empty the litter box? She gave up the idea. When Miss Marguerite dozed off, there would be rustling and scratching, and she would awaken with a start. They were there, bent over peeking into her drawers. An undeniable presence.

The cupboard doors opened by themselves. Things disappeared. A sugar bowl, a tortoiseshell comb. And sometimes, more important things, like her bank book.

One day, the television stopped working. Since then, Miss Marguerite has lived shut up in silence. The days are long, from one dawn to the next. During the day, she sits by the window, watching life go by in the street. But she is afraid to open the window.

For all intents and purposes Miss Marguerite no longer sleeps. She sometimes dozes for a few minutes in her armchair—nods off, as she puts it with a smile—seated before the blank screen. At these times, she's a carbon copy of her mother at the end of her life. Miss Marguerite is afraid of falling asleep and waking up to find that the furniture has been moved and that new ghosts have invaded the house.

Then her glasses disappeared into thin air. She gropes her way along, bumps into the furniture. Large bruises cover her thin legs.

How could she go out of the house? She's almost blind. How could she venture out alone into that jungle? People say that hoodlums with hair dyed red or purple steal old ladies' handbags, then push them, knock them down, and sometimes even kick them before running off with their loot. Some of these old people find themselves with broken arms or hips, pitiful forms moaning on the sidewalk. Others sometimes have spells and have to ask strangers for help. That's the kind of incident they write about in the papers. She would like the social worker to assign a volunteer to accompany her. She had a volunteer for a few months, and she always looked forward to this visit with pleasure. When they returned to the apartment, she would offer the woman some tea and cookies. But the volunteer moved to a different neighborhood, and Social Services explained to Miss Marguerite how snowed under they were with work. They did send her an aide who comes every Thursday, vacuums, cleans the bathroom—a young woman full of get-up-and-go, who cleans the mirror with window cleaner. Yesterday was Thursday, and Miss Marguerite anxiously awaited her arrival so that she could show her the woman in white. But no one rang the bell. Wasn't it Thursday? Sometimes, Miss Marguerite gets the days mixed up.

A nurse also comes to take her blood pressure, but she never has much time to chat. When Miss Marguerite talks to her about her nocturnal visitors, the nurse nods her head in an understanding way, and Miss Marguerite has the impression that she's talking to the wall.

And how can she telephone, now that the phone no longer emits its familiar ring, so reassuring when it's there that no one even notices it? The line has been cut off. Yes, they also cut off her phone. Inexorable silence.

She should just decide to go and knock on someone's door. But Miss Marguerite is timid, and proud. She has never asked anyone for help.

There are still some canned goods in the cupboard. Enough food to last until the Social Services nurse comes. But the can opener, where has it gone? The cookies, she wouldn't consider eating them; there are little worms in the package. They even sabotage her food. Tears roll hotly from her tired eyes, down her wrinkled cheeks.

One evening, about a week ago, as she approached the basin in the bathroom, she saw the white form standing in the depths of the mirror. Since then, the others have not ventured out of their hiding place. There is only the woman in white and the silence in the house, the broken television, the cut telephone line and the lost glasses.

The woman in white does not speak—these apparitions are usually mute. She makes no hostile gestures. She doesn't come out of the mirror. Her constancy and her immobility make her almost reassuring.

When the Social Services nurse came for her weekly visit, no one answered the door. Nor did they the following day. When she called, no one answered the phone. The police were asked to come and force the door.

Upon entering, they were hit by an acrid smell that permeated the overheated apartment.

They found Miss Marguerite in the bathroom, crumpled in a strange position on the floor. She had broken her hip in a fall and could not get up. She was undoubtedly too weak—it was obvious that she had not eaten for several days—she must have had a sudden dizzy spell. The nurse, a specialist in gerontology, said that this sometimes happens to the very elderly.

They discovered a number of odd things: the sugar bowl in the drawer of the bedside table, a tortoiseshell comb and savings passbook in the refrigerator, which was full of moldy leftovers in plastic containers. The nurse remarked that very old people sometimes exhibit this type of strange behavior. They sometimes lose their memory, or even their minds. They also noticed that the television was on, but that the knobs for the sound and picture were on the lowest settings, so that it was impossible to see or hear what was happening on the screen. They wondered why the telephone was unplugged, what the can opener was doing in the first aid kit and why Miss Marguerite had put her glasses under the bed.

They noted that the mirror in the bathroom had been broken, and the nurse ventured that Miss Marguerite had felt dizzy, grabbed onto the sink, and that in the process, her head had hit the mirror, making her lose her balance. It was difficult to know how long her agony had lasted.

Notes

1. Called solitaire in the United States.

Work Cited

Rioux, Hélène. "Marguerite . . . ou celle qui voit derrière le miroir." In *Pense à mon rendez-vous*. Montréal: Editions Québec/Amérique, 1994.

Contributors

SANDRA BEYER is associate professor of French at the University of Texas at El Paso, where she served as director of the Women's Studies program from 1990 to 1996 and is now serving as chair of the Department of Languages and Linguistics. She is coeditor of a forthcoming book, *A World of Difference? An International Study of Women in Higher Education*, and has published articles and presented papers on Marcel Proust, Simone de Beauvoir, Marguerite Yourcenar, and Anne Hébert.

MYLÈNE CATEL is assistant professor of French at the State University of New York in Potsdam. She received a grant to participate in an institute on the Internet in Foreign Language Instruction at Michigan State University. She has participated in conferences related to feminism and social change. She is a poet who publishes regularly on the Internet.

PEGGY DEVAUX is a doctoral candidate at the University of Alberta in Edmonton, Canada. Her research interests include English- and French-Canadian literatures, lesbian feminist writers, and ethnic/immigrant writing. Her Ph.D. dissertation will focus on Arab-Canadian authors.

ROSEANNA DUFAULT is professor of French and chair of Modern Languages at Ohio Northern University, where she teaches courses in Québec and francophone studies. She is the author of *Metaphors of Identity: The Treatment of Childhood in Selected Québécois Novels* and *Women By Women: The Treatment of Female Characters by Women Writers of Fiction in Québec since 1980*, both published by Fairleigh Dickinson University Press. She also has published articles on Anne Hébert, Marie-Claire Blais, Gabrielle Roy, Louise Maheux-Forcier, and Ying Chen in various journals and anthologies. She is vice president of the American Council for Québec Studies.

KARIN EGLOFF is associate professor of French at Western Kentucky University. Her research interests include twentieth-century

French literature, French-Canadian literature, and film studies. She has published a book on André Langevin and is currently finishing a manuscript about adolescence in recent French-language cinema. She is the author of several articles on Québec and contemporary French women writers.

PAULA RUTH GILBERT is professor of French, Canadian, and Women's Studies at George Mason University, where she also served as dean of the College of Arts and Sciences from 1987 to 1991. She currently teaches courses on North American francophone women writers, Gabrielle Roy, nineteenth-century French and symbolist poetry, violence and gender, introduction to Women's Studies, reading the arts, cultural studies, comparative Québec and Canadian fiction, and socially constructed worlds. She is the author of *The Aesthetics of Stéphane Mallarmé in Relation to His Public* and *The Literary Vision of Gabrielle Roy: An Analysis of Her Works*, and she is the editor of *Traditionalism, Nationalism, and Feminism: Women Writers of Québec*. She has published numerous articles and reviews on both Québec studies and nineteenth-century French poetry. She has recently completed a critical reader on Violence and Gender and is currently writing a book entitled *Violence and the Female Imagination: Québec Women Writers Confront Gendered Cultures*, for which she has received a National Endowment for the Humanities Fellowship.

KAREN L. GOULD is dean of Arts and Letters and professor of French and Francophone Studies and Women's Studies at Old Dominion University in Norfolk, Virginia. She is the author or coeditor of five books, including *Postcolonial Subjects: Francophone Women Writers* (1996) and *Writing in the Feminine: Feminism and Experimental Writing in Québec* (1990), and more than forty articles and essays on Québec women writers and on Claude Simon. She has served as editor of the interdisciplinary journal *Québec Studies* (1988–93), as president of the Association for Canadian Studies in the United States (1993–95), and as president of the International Council for Canadian Studies (1999–2001).

MARY JEAN GREEN is the Edward Tuck Professor of French and former associate dean of the faculty for the humanities at Dartmouth College. She is the author of *Fiction in the Historical Present: French Writers and the Thirties* (1986), *Louis Guilloux: An Artisan of Language* (1980), and *Marie-Claire Blais* (1995); coeditor of *Postcolonial Subjects: Francophone Women Writers* (1996); and author of the recently published *Women and Narrative Identity: Rewriting the Québec National Text.*

LUCIE GUILLEMETTE is professor of French at the Université du Québec at Trois-Rivières. Her fields of study include feminist theory and narratology, women's writings, the contemporary novel, and children's literature. She has published numerous articles in journals, including the *Revue canadienne des études américaines/ Canadian Review of American Studies, Voix et Images, Francophonies d'Amérique, Simone de Beauvoir Studies, Lurelu,* and *Dalhousie French Studies,* and she has participated in collectives devoted to the contemporary novel and women's writings. She is currently researching types of knowledge in novels written by women in Québec.

SUSAN IRELAND is associate professor of French at Grinnell College. She is the author of articles on the contemporary French novel, Québec women writers, and postcolonial Algerian literature. She is also a coeditor of *A Feminist Encyclopedia of French Literature* (1999).

LUCIE LEQUIN is associate professor of Québec Literature and chair of Études françaises at Concordia University in Montreal. She coauthored with her colleague Maïr Verthuy a book entitled *Multi-culture, multi-écriture: La Voix migrante au féminin en France et au Canada* (Paris: L'Harmattan, 1996). They have also written an anthology of women immigrant writings, *Féminin pluriel* (Québec: Nota Bene, 1999). In addition, she has published several chapters in books and journal articles. Currently, she is preparing a book, *L'Ecriture des femmes migrantes au Québec,* and is working on the relationship between ethics and literature.

KAREN MCPHERSON is assistant professor of French and Francophone Studies at the University of Oregon. She is the author of *Incriminations: Guilty Women/Telling Stories* and has published articles on Anne Hébert, Simone de Beauvoir, and Marie-Claire Blais. She is currently working on a book called *Archaeologies of an Uncertain Future: Recent Generations of Canadian Women Writers.*

JANE MOSS is the Robert E. Diamond Professor of French and Women's Studies at Colby College in Waterville, Maine. Her numerous articles on French and Québec theater have appeared in a wide variety of scholarly journals, including the *American Review of Canadian Studies, Québec Studies, Theatre Research International, Mosaic, Canadian Literature, Signs, Atlantis, Modern Language Studies, The French Review, L'Annuaire théâtral, Theatre Research in Canada, Sites,* and *Dalhousie French Studies.* She has also contributed essays to books on Québec and francophone women writers. She was president of the American Council for Québec Studies from 1992 to 1995 and is managing editor of *Québec Studies.*

MAUREEN F. O'MEARA is associate professor of French at the University of Dayton in Ohio. Her research interests include French seventeenth- and eighteenth-century narratives, stories of encounter between the French and the Native Americans, and narratives by francophone women writers of the Americas. Her articles have appeared in journals, including *Studies on Voltaire, MLN, Esprit créateur,* and the *Rocky Mountain Review of Language and Literature.*

ALICE A. PARKER is professor of French and Women's Studies at the University of Alabama. Her publications cover a range of French and francophone women writers from the eighteenth century to the present. *Liminal Visions of Nicole Brossard* (Peter Lang, 1998), analyzes Brossard's poetry, fiction, and theory from the vantage points of current critical and feminist theory. Her present project is a broad study of myth and memory in women's writing.

PATRICE J. PROULX is associate professor of French and a member of the Women's Studies faculty at the University of Nebraska at Omaha. Her research interests include the notion of identity and exile in the works of contemporary French and francophone women writers. She is a coeditor of *The Feminist Encyclopedia of French Literature* (Greenwood Press, 1999). Her articles have appeared in such journals as *The French Review, Europe Plurilingue,* and *Women in French,* and she has essays in the edited collections *Elles écrivent des Antilles: Haïti, Guadeloupe et Martinique* and *Multi-culture, multi-écriture: La Voix migrante au féminin en France et au Canada.*

ANNABELLE M. REA is professor of French at Occidental College in California. She has received support from the governments of Québec and Canada for her articles, conference papers, and reviews on Québec literature, primarily on Anne Hébert. She has also written on George Sand and currently serves as president of the Sand Association in the United States and as a member of the editorial board of George Sand Studies. In addition, she made many contributions to the study of women writers as chair of Women in French from 1990 until 1995.

JANINE RICOUART is associate professor of French at George Mason University where she teaches nineteenth- and twentieth-century francophone literature, film, and women's studies. She published a book entitled *Ecriture féminine et violence: Une étude de Marguerite Duras* and edited two books, both published in 1999: *Marguerite Duras Lives On*, and *Relectures de Madeleine Monette*. She also published several essays on francophone women writers, including Marie-Claire Blais, Jovette Marchessault, Madeleine Monette, and Marguerite Duras. She translated Jane Gallop's "Keys to Dora," a chapter from Gallop's *The Daughter's Seduction*, published in *Trois*, Summer 1998. An excerpt from her translation of Mireille Best's short story "Le Livre de Stéphanie" is published in *The Vintage Book of International Lesbian Fiction* (Vintage, 1999). She has also written book reviews for *The French Review*, *Lambda Book Reports*, and *Trois*. She is currently working on a book length manuscript dealing with class issues and francophone literature.

JULIE RIEMAN has worked for ten years as a professional translator, mainly in Brussels, Belgium. She received her master's degree in Translation and Interpretation (French/English) from the Monterey Institute of International Studies in 1985. Her most meaningful achievement has been the translation from German and French into English of 100 pages of poetry written by prisoners of the Dachau concentration camp. She currently makes her home in Boise, Idaho.

LORI SAINT-MARTIN is professor of literature at the Université du Québec in Montréal. Her publications include fiction, literary translations, and academic studies, including, most recently, *Mon père, la nuit* (short stories, Québec: L'Instant même, 1999); *Le Nom de la mère: Mères, filles et écriture dans la fiction québécoise au féminin* (Québec: Nota Bene, 1999); two edited volumes on Gabrielle Roy; and *Contre-voix: Essais de critique au féminin* (Nuits Blanches, 1977).

MILÉNA SANTORO is assistant professor of French at Georgetown University, Washington, D.C., where she enjoys teaching courses on the literature and culture of Québec. She has written articles on Québécoise and French women writers, including Nicole Brossard, Madeleine Gagnon, Esther Rochon, Hélène Cixous, and Jeanne Hyvrard. Currently, she is working on a book, *Mothers of Invention: Feminist Authors and Experimental Fiction in France and Québec.*

PAMELA V. SING is assistant professor at the Faculté Saint-Jean of the University of Alberta and head of the French sector. She teaches French, Québécois, and Franco-Canadian literatures. She has published a book, *Villages imaginaires: Edouard Montpetit, Jacques Ferron, et Jacques Poulin* (Montréal: Fides, 1995), and numerous articles in anthologies and journals, the most recent ones dealing with women's writing in Québécois and Franco-Canadian literatures.

EILEEN SIVERT is associate professor of French at the University of Minnesota. She has published numerous essays on nineteenth-century French literature as well as work on Marie-Claire Blais and Jovette Marchessault. She is currently writing a book on women novelists of Québec.

Index

Abandonment: in *La Cage*, 29–30; fear of in postfeminist theater, 119; in *La Memoria*, 144, 147, 149, 151, 156–57; in Proulx, 164; in *La Danse juive*, 182; in *La Dot*, 208; in Moser, 277, 280; in Huston, 298–300

Abortion: in *Laurence*, 109, 179; in Franco-Albertan literature, 284; in Huston, 301

Abuse: and francophone women writers, 20, 186; and misogyny, 36; of power, 49–50, 140; in feminist theater, 121–22; in Proulx, 161, 162, 165; of power in *L'Écho*, 187–88, 189; sexual, in *L'Écho*, 193, 195–200; in Dumas, 280–82

Adolescence: and literature, 19; in *Le Vent majeur*, 67–68; in Théoret, 97; in *Un Homme est une valse*, 131–32; and incest in *L'Écho*, 192, 199–200; and children's literature, 308–9, 315

Agent/agency: of women in Brossard, 36, 38–39; of names in *Baroque d'aube*, 43–44; of death in *Le Vent majeur*, 59–60; men as, of violence, 61–62; in *L'Été*, 90; Montreal as, of change, 103–4; female, in *La Memoria*, 142, 144, 150; separation from and the cultural law, 171; of the daughter in *Laurence*, 179–80; women's, and the "other family romance," 183; and dismemberment in *L'Écho*, 199; the mother as, of cultural subversion, 203–15; women as, of culture in *Le Bonheur*, 215

Agnant, Célie, 18. Works: *La Dot de Sara*, 203–10, 213, 214

Alienation: in *Entre les fleuves*, 18–19; and postfeminist theater, 110–11; in *Un Homme est une valse*, 134; between mother and son in Proulx, 165; and exile, 204; and exile in *Les Lettres*, 221–22; and immigrant writers, 235; and masculine language in Daigle, 251; from the self in Dumas, 282; in Huston, 299

Alonzo, Anne-Marie. Works: *Galia qu'elle nommait amour*, 248, 262

Ambivalence: in father-daughter bonds, 18, 170, 171–72; of the narrator in *Le Vent majeur*, 61, 72–73; and gender in Harvey, 133; and the mother in *La Memoria*, 155–56; toward the mother in Proulx, 165; and exile, 204, 225; and identity in Moser, 277

Androgyny: of the couple in *La Cage*, 32; of mourning in *Le Vent majeur*, 70–71; in *Un Homme est une valse*, 131–32; in Daigle, 253

Anfousse, Ginette: works for children/adolescents, 19, 306, 309, 312–17

Anger: in *Baroque d'aube*, 43; in *L'Été*, 91; in postfeminist theater, 122; in *La Memoria*, 156–57; in Proulx, 166; in "La Gifle," 173; in *La Danse juive*, 181–82; in *L'Écho*, 188, 191–92, 195; in Moser, 278; in Dumas, 282, 283

Anonymity: in *Baroque d'aube*, 38; in *L'Été*, 93; in *Un Homme est une valse*, 136; in Proulx, 163; in children's literature, 313

Anxiety: in *Baroque d'aube*, 41–42, 44–45; and women writers, 74; in *Laurence*, 104; sexual, and feminist theater, 111; and sex drive in *Un Homme est une valse*, 132, 141; in Daigle, 256

Appelle-moi (Bourget), 111, 112–15

À propos de l'amour (Teasdale), 172–73

Asexuality: in *L'Écho*, 194–95, 199; and creativity in Huston, 290

INDEX

Art: and the legend of La Corriveau, 23; seduction of, in *Baroque d'aube*, 42; role of in life, 42–44; in *Vertige*, 48–49; and death, 54–55, 68; in *Le Vent majeur*, 60–61, 67–68; communal, theater as, 111; in postfeminist theater, 118–19; in *Un Homme est une valse*, 135, 137; and objectification of the body in Proulx, 161–63, 166–67; world of in Proulx, 165; in *La Dot*, 209–10; and Daigle, 252–53, 257, 259–61; and life in Huston, 296; women's embodiment of in Huston, 296–97; and mind/body dualism in Huston, 297–99, 301

Aurélie, ma soeur (Laberge), 122

Authority: of the mother, 23–24; mother's obedience to, 25; male, absence of in *Baroque d'aube*, 44–45; narrative, in *Les Cathédrales sauvages*, 65; and *Laurence*, 96, 178; of the Church in *Laurence*, 98; and the power relationship in "La Gifle," 173; paternal, in *L'Écho*, 187, 200–201; patriarchal, in Dumas, 279–80; collaboration with in Dumas, 281–83; artistic, in Huston, 301–2; male, loss of and "gynesis," 307; and children's literature, 307, 310, 313; and John Stuart Mill, 318–20

Autobiography/autobiographical writing: and death, 54; and Gagnon, 62, 65, 66, 69, 73–74; and Théoret, 96, 97; and *La Memoria*, 142; and incest/abuse, 186, 197; and *L'Ingratitude*, 210; and *Entre les fleuves*, 237; and Daigle, 253, 255, 259; and Huston, 290, 294, 299

Autonomy: and the need to work in *L'Été*, 92; and love in postfeminist theater, 126; and closeness in *Laurence*, 179; and tradition, 203; and women's submission, 270; feminine, in Moser, 274; of the sexual woman in Dumas, 280; and the body in Huston, 296–97; in children's literature, 313, 317

Avec l'hiver qui s'en vient (Laberge), 121–22

"Baby versus book": in Huston, 19, 289–90, 301–2

Balance/equilibrium: in *Baroque d'aube*, 43; in the language of Brossard, 50; of erotic power, 110–11; and independence, 139; in *Laurence*, 179; of the family in *L'Écho*, 187; of cultures in *Les Lettres*, 233; of cultures in *Entre les fleuves*, 235, 241, 244–46; and culture in Western Canada, 269

Baptism: in *L'Été*, 90, 91–92

Baroque d'aube (Brossard): 16, 36–45, 47, 50, 248

Barthes, Roland: and Oedipal rivalry, 171; and Daigle, 249–50, 258

Baudelaire: and the "tombeau" form, 73–74; and hair in *L'Écho*, 189; and paradise in *L'Écho*, 189–90; and world-weariness in *L'Écho*, 190–91

Beauty: recognition of in *La Cage*, 30–31; in *Vertige*, 45–46; of the fire in *Le Vent majeur*, 61; and death in *Le Vent majeur*, 68; of Gagnon's work, 74; in *L'Été*, 82, 89; of the birdcage in *L'Été*, 82–83, 90; and universal love in *L'Été*, 92; and passion in postfeminist theater, 126; of woman in Proulx, 162; of the mother in "Friperie," 176, 177; in *L'Écho*, 190; of life in *Les Lettres*, 227; in Daigle, 253–54, 257; women's, in Primeau, 270; of the daughter in Moser, 276–77; of physical decline in Huston, 298–99

Beauvoir, Simone de: and Huston, 290, 301; and children's literature, 308, 316–17

Bernadette et Juliette (Bourget), 111–12

Bersianik, Louky, 169, 203

Bertrand, Huguette: and Internet publishing, 322–23. Works: *Entre l'ombre et la lumière*, 19, 323–45

Birth/rebirth: of the individual, in *La Cage*, 30–31; of a character and myth in Brossard, 37; of a child, as myth, 38; and mourning in Gagnon, 55–56; in *Les Cathédrales sauvages*, 57, 66; (figurative) in *Le Vent majeur*, 61, 67–71; (figurative) and death in *Le Deuil du soleil*, 74; and women's life writing, 74; (figurative) on Grosse Île, 90; in the convent in *Laurence*,

102; into tradition-bound culture, 105; and feminist theater, 109; (figurative) of the present in *Les Lettres*, 228; and exile in *Les Lettres*, 230–31; (figurative) and curiosity in *Les Lettres*, 232; in *Entre les fleuves*, 238, 239, 241–43, 246; and Daigle, 258–60; in Primeau, 271; in Moser, 276; in Dumas, 280–81; in Huston, 291, 292, 295–302; trauma of, in *Entre l'ombre et la lumière*, 324

Blais, Marie-Claire, 262. Works: *Soifs*, 248

Blood: in *Baroque d'aube*, 40; as common origin in *L'Été*, 90; in postfeminist theater, 121; in *La Memoria*, 151; in *La Danse juive*, 182; and incest in *L'Écho*, 190–94, 196; (figurative) and recovery in *L'Écho*, 200; (figurative) and exile, 204; in *La Dot*, 206; virgin, in Moser, 275; and miscarriage in Huston, 301

Bloody Mary (Théoret), 95–96

Body, the: as subject of francophone writing, 16; liberation of in *La Cage*, 30; beauty of in *La Cage*, 30–31; gender's inscription on, 36; wisdom of and lovemaking in *Baroque d'aube*, 41; in *Baroque d'aube*, 44–45; in *Vertige*, 45–47, 48–49; female, in Brossard, 50; and sense of loss in Gagnon, 55–56; and history, 81; and storytelling in *L'Été*, 83, 84, 86–87; repossession of in *L'Été*, 85; and folk medicine in *L'Été*, 87; and desire in *L'Été*, 90; and postfeminist theater, 108–9, 110, 113, 118, 120–21, 123, 125; in *Un Homme est une valse*, 132, 136, 138, 139; women's, and memory in Brossard, 143–44; in *La Memoria*, 147, 150, 154; objectification of in Proulx, 161, 162, 163; male, in Proulx, 163; female, in Proulx, 166–67; and separation of mind in Proulx, 168; of the father in "La Gifle," 173–75; and somatophobia, 180; of the father in *La Danse juive*, 180–82; and paternal law in *L'Écho*, 187–88; and medical imagery in *L'Écho*, 188–89, 199; female, rejection of *L'Écho*, 189; and self-destruction in *L'Écho*, 190–93; men's, in *L'Écho*, 191–92, 196, 199; and amputation in *L'Écho*, 194; asexuality of in *L'Écho*, 194–95; and surrender in *L'Écho*, 196; social, and dismemberment, 199; and recovery in *L'Écho*, 199–200; in *Les Lettres*, 218; and space in *Entre les fleuves*, 236; and exile in *Entre les fleuves*, 237, 241; and the water motif in *Entre les fleuves*, 240; and rebirth in *Entre les fleuves*, 243; presence of in Daigle, 252; and silencing of the lesbian voice, 255, 262; sensual, in Primeau, 270; of the wife in Moser, 274–75; and drowning in Moser, 277; and empowerment in Moser, 278; submission of in Moser, 278; and patriarchal control in Dumas, 279–80; in Huston, 288–93, 295–302; male domination of, 306; in *Entre l'ombre et la lumière*, 323–24; in children's literature, 320

Bonheur a la queue glissante, Le (Farhoud), 203–4, 213–14

Boundaries: and women's creative potential, 37; and pleasure in *Baroque d'aube*, 38; blurring of in Brossard, 40, 203; violation of in Brossard, 41; of the known world in *Baroque d'aube*, 42–43; and sexual difference in Brossard, 50; and female desire in Laurence, 104; masculine and feminine, in *Un Homme est une valse*, 133; and the prison of the past in *La Memoria*, 152; violation of in *L'Écho*, 196

Bourget, Élizabeth, 17, 114–15, 119–20, 126–27. Works: *Appelle-moi*, 111, 112, 114; *Bernadette et Juliette*, 111–12

British rule: in Québec, 79–80, 85–86

Brossard, Nicole, 16, 262; view of gender, 36, 39–40; role of writing and language in the works of, 39, 40; and narrativity, 39; as explorer, 46; as feminist, 47; and the eroticism of writing, 49; and women's memory writing, 143–44; and desire, 249–50; and autobiography, 255. Works: *Baroque d'aube*, 36–45, 47, 50, 248;

Vertige de l'avant scène, 36, 43, 45–50; *Journal intime*, 36, 37–38; *Le Désert mauve*, 40

Cadieux, Elizabeth. Works: *La Nuit*, 111
Cage, La (Hébert), 16, 23, 27–32
Canada: and francophone women's writing, 11–12, 15–20; immigration to, 18; francophone presences in, 18; interest in translation in, 19; traditional family structure in, 23–24; history of in *L'Été*, 78–79; and exile in *Les Lettres*, 230; and immigrant writing, 235; in *Entre les fleuves*, 240, 243; and Daigle, 248, 262; and stereotypes of non-Québécois women, 267
Castration: in postfeminist theater, 122; and the mythical mother in Proulx, 165; symbolism of, 171
Ça suffit, Sophie! (Leblanc), 309–10
Catastrophes de Rosalie, Les (Anfousse), 312
Cathédrales sauvages, Les (Gagnon), 17, 55, 56–73; significance of part and chapter titles, 56–57; and *L'Écho*, 199
Catholic(ism): and women writers, 12; and family structure, 23–24; theology, and the role of the mother, 25; and education in *Laurence*, 101; and feminist theater, 108–9, 121–22; and Western Canadian women, 267; and Western Canada, 269–70; in Primeau, 272; in Moser, 273, 276; in Dumas, 282; in Huston, 300–301
Cemetery: in *Le vent majeur*, 60–61, 68, 69; in *Les Cathédrales sauvages*, 63–64
Censorship: and feminist theater, 108–9; and Bourget, 111
C'était avant la guerre à l'Anse-à-Gilles (Laberge), 121–22
Change: family as an agent of in *La Cage*, 32; in Brossard, 44; resistance to in *Laurence*, 100; Montreal as an agent of in *Laurence*, 103–4; and feminist theater, 108, 109; and women's memory writing in Brossard, 144; in the body in *La Danse juive*, 180–81; and exile, 204; in *La Dot*, 208–9; and exile in *Les Lettres*, 225, 229–30; in *Entre les fleuves*, 240, 241; in children's literature, 317, 318
Chant pour un Québec lointain (Gagnon), 55
Childhood: and the mother-monster in "Le Torrent," 26–27, 32; and memory in Brossard, 38; and transmission in *Les Cathédrales sauvages*, 62–63; and storytelling in *Le Vent majeur*, 69; in *L'Été*, 85, 91; in postfeminist theater, 119; lost, and incest in *L'Écho*, 191–92, 196, 199–200; and storytelling in *La Dot*, 206–7; in Daigle, 259
Cholera: in *L'Été*, 78–79, 82, 84. See also Epidemic; Typhus
Church, the: in "Le Torrent," 24–25; in *Laurence*, 98, 101; in Daigle, 252, 254–55; and Western Canada, 269, 270, 273, 278, 282, 283
Closure: and writing in *Les Cathédrales sauvages*, 66–67; in *Le Vent majeur*, 72; in *Un Homme est une valse*, 140; in *La Memoria* 147, 153
Communication: and lesbian love in *Vertige*, 47–48; and self-creation/knowledge in *Le Deuil du soleil*, 73–74; in Théoret, 96–97; in feminist theater, 112, 114; nonverbal, in Proulx, 166; of pain in *L'Écho*, 187, 191, 193, 196; and the legacy of words in *La Dot*, 208–9; strategies of, 284
Community/collaboration: and the individual in Brossard, 37; and mythmaking, 37–38; and women's creativity, 41; and the voyage in *Baroque d'aube*, 41–42; and storytelling in *L'Été*, 83–85, 89; loss of in *L'Été*, 89–90, 93; in *Un Homme est une valse*, 131; of women born of incest, 199–200; in *La Dot*, 208, 209; and exile in *Les Lettres*, 218–23, 230–33; and Western Canadian women, 267–68; in Primeau, 271, 280; of women and Internet publishing, 323
Conan, Laure, 11
Confession: of rage in *La Cage*, 29; in

L'Été, 89–90; in *Un Homme est une valse*, 136; of fear of loss in *La Memoria*, 148–49; in *L'Écho*, 197; in Daigle, 253

Connection/communion: between death and creation in *Le Vent majeur*, 60–61; with the universe in *L'Été*, 89–90; male-female in *Un Homme est une valse*, 139–40; and healing in *La Memoria*, 148, 149; between the past and future, 151; between mother and daughter, 156; between father and daughter, 177; with the mother in *Entre les fleuves*, 241–45; in Daigle, 251, 253, 261–61; of mind and body in Huston, 294; of the body to dance in Huston, 295

Consciousness, female: in *La Cage*, 27–28; and myth in Brossard, 36; absence of, 79; and writing in *Un Homme est une valse*, 133; male, in Proulx, 167–68; in *L'Ingratitude*, 210

Construction/reconstruction: of gender in Proulx, 160–61; of the present in *Les Lettres*, 228; of the self in *Les Lettres*, 230, 232, 233; of text and Daigle, 248, 253–56, 261–62; image of in Daigle, 252–53, 255; of multiple narratives in Daigle, 254; of temporality in Daigle, 260; of meaning in Daigle, 261; of gender in Daigle, 261–62; of a heterogeneous population in Western Canada, 369–70; of gender-related clichés in Moser, 277; sociocultural, of gender in Huston, 288–89; of metaphors of literary paternity, 293; in children's literature, 309, 315–18

Control: by the priests in "Le Torrent," 23–24; by the mother in "Le Torrent," 26; of the keys in *La Cage*, 28; and life, 42–43; *Vertige*, 49–50; lack of and storytelling, 84; by the father in *Laurence*, 98; of one's own life in *Laurence*, 104–5; loss of and passion in postfeminist theater, 126; of the gaze in *Un Homme est une valse*, 130–31; of discourse in *Un Homme est une valse*, 134, 137; of circumstance in *Un Homme est une valse*, 135–37; of women in Proulx, 167–68, 270–71; patriarchal, and Franco-Albertan culture, 279–80

Convent/convent hospital: in *Laurence*, 97–100, 179; and the teaching of submission, 101–3; in post feminist theater, 122–24; and the female body in Moser, 274–75; in *Marguerite*, 346

Corriveau, La: as represented in *La Cage*, 16, 23–24, 27–28, 31

Corriveau, Marie-Josephte, 23–32; legend of in Québec, 23

Couples: as subject of in the work of francophone women dramatists, 17; priests and mothers as in "Le Torrent," 25; androgynous in *La Cage*, 32

Courtepointe/Counterpoint (Moser), 272–79

Creativity/creation: as subject of francophone writing, 16; and memory in Brossard, 37, 38; and death in Brossard, 40, 60–61; in *Baroque d'aube*, 43, 44–45; in *Vertige*, 46–47, 49–50; in Brossard, 50; and death, 55; and the legacy of writing in *Le Vent majeur*, 72–73; and catastrophe/trauma/death in *Le Vent majeur*, 60, 61, 67–68, 72; and gender in Gagnon, 61–62; and death in Gagnon, 73; and mourning in *Le Deuil du soleil*, 73–74; and the limits of history in *L'Été*, 80; and storytelling/dance in *L'Été*, 85–86; of herbal remedies in *L'Été*, 87–92; and the need to work in *L'Été*, 92; in *Un Homme est une valse*, 132; of future memories in *La Memoria*, 150; in Proulx, 161, 162; and culture in *Les Lettres*, 227; in *Entre les fleuves*, 238; in Daigle, 252–55, 258; in Moser, 274; in Huston, 288–302; of an on-line women's community, 323, 324

Croteau, Marie-Danielle: works of for children/adolescents, 19, 306, 309, 317–20

Culture: French and Catholic, 12; American mediatic, 12; in *Vertige*, 46–47; and Québec in *L'Été*, 93; and the Church, 101; and urbanity,

103–4; resistance to in *Laurence*, 105; defiance of in postfeminist theater, 123; submission to in postfeminist theater, 124; women's and women writers, 169; and parricide, 171; and "the name of the father," 172; daughter's position in, 173; of the father in "La Gifle," 175; and men in *Le Bonheur*, 214; and legacy in *Le Bonheur*, 215; and meaning in *Les Lettres*, 218; and writing in *Les Lettres*, 221; and transformation in *Les Lettres*, 223–24; admiration of in *Les Lettres*, 224–25; and exile in *Les Lettres*, 226–29, 231–33; and perspective in *Entre les fleuves*, 235–36; collision of in *Entre les fleuves*, 237; and space in *Entre les fleuves*, 238, 245, 246; Acadian and Daigle, 259–60; and Western Canadian women, 267–68; of Québec in Moser, 274; man as embodiment of, 306; and *Marguerite*, 346; and children's literature, 308

Daigle, France, 19, 248–55. Works: *La Beauté de l'affaire*, 252–55; *La Vraie vie*, 255–59; *1953, Chronique d'une naissance annoncée*, 258–62
D'Amour, Francine: *Les Dimanches sont mortels*, 170
Dance: and the legend of La Corriveau, 23; as recovery in *L'Été*, 85–86, 88; intimate, in *L'Été*, 90; in feminist theater, 117; in *Un Homme est une valse*, 134, 140, 141; in *La Memoria*, 150; in Proulx, 167–68; and sexuality in Moser, 278–79; and (pro)creation in Huston, 294–99
Danse juive, La (Tremblay), 18, 170, 180–82
Dans le muskeg (Primeau), 270–72
Death: as subject of francophone writing, 16; in Gagnon, 17, 53–75; in *Marguerite*, 20; of Anne Hébert, 23; of La Corriveau, 23; in "Le Torrent," 24–25, 26; of the husband in *La Cage*, 31; of the protagonist in *La Cage*, 31; and myth in Brossard, 36; in *Baroque d'aube*, 40; in *Le Désert mauve*, 40; in Brossard, 40, 43, 49–50; in Gagnon, 53–55; discourse about, 54; and writing in Gagnon, 54–59, 69–70, 72–73; and mourning/remembrance, 54–55; witnessing of in *Les Cathédrales sauvages*, 57–59, 61–62; and creation in *Le Vent majeur*, 59–61; as symbolized by the setting sun in *Le Vent majeur*, 61; and fire in *Le vent majeur*, 61; and creativity in Gagnon, 61–62; and transmission in *Les Cathédrales sauvages*, 62–64; and the legacy of writing in *Le Vent majeur*, 67–69; and art in *Le Vent majeur*, 68; as inspiration in *Le Vent majeur*, 68, 71–72; and writing the other in *Le Vent majeur*, 69–70; of the other in *Le Deuil du soleil*, 70; as theme in Gagnon, 73; and writing in *Le Deuil du soleil*, 73–74; confronting and Gagnon, 74; and women's life-writing, 74; on Grosse Île, 78–79, 80, 81; and life, 81, 92–93; odor of, in *L'Été*, 82; and grace in *L'Été*, 83–85; and the immigrants' struggle in *L'Été*, 85; environment of in *L'Été*, 91–92; in postfeminist theater, 122–23; in *Un Homme est une valse*, 139–40; and writing in *La Memoria*, 143; and the prison of memory, 146; and time in *La Memoria*, 151; and the mother in *La Memoria*, 156–157; and the mother in Proulx, 164; and sex in Proulx, 166; and the father's strategy in "La Gifle," 174–75; in *L'Écho*, 189, 192–93, 196, 198; and the "mort vivant" in *L'Écho*, 199; (figurative) and exile, 204; in *L'Ingratitude*, 210, 212–13; in *Le Bonheur*, 213, 215; and exile in *Les Lettres*, 217, 231, 233; in *Entre les fleuves*, 239–40; and Barthes, 249–50; and Daigle, 257, 259; in Moser, 273–74; in Dumas, 280, 282; in Huston 295, 296, 299–302; in *Marguerite*, 346, 348; in children's literature, 312, 314, 317, 318
Depression: and writing in *Un Homme est une valse*, 133; and loss in *La Memoria*, 143; and incest in *L'Écho*, 188, 189, 197; in *Entre les fleuves*, 246

"Déracinement" (uprooting): and the poet in *La Memoria*, 143; and exile, 205; in *Les Lettres*, 218–19
Derrida, Jacques: *Aporias*, 53–54
Desert mauve, Le (Brossard), 40
Desire, carnal: discourse of in *Un Homme est une valse*, 17; in Brossard, 38–39, 41, 42–43, 45–46; and writing, 38; and pleasure, 38–39; and women's creativity, 41; meaning of, 42–43; writing of in *Vertige*, 47, 48; and fire in *Les Cathédrales sauvages*, 57, 58; in *Le Vent majeur*, 72; men's, destructiveness of in *Le Vent majeur*, 72–73; as "un manque" in *Le Deuil du soleil*, 73–74; in *L'Été*, 84, 89, 90; female, in *Laurence*, 104; and postfeminist theater, 108–14, 116–18, 120, 122, 123, 126–27; in *Un Homme est une valse*, 133–36, 138–41; and memory writing in Brossard, 143–44; men's, and women's role, 171; and father-daughter relationships, 172; of the daughter in "Friperie," 176; of the daughter in *Laurence*, 179; of the father in *La Danse juive*, 180; and father-daughter relationships, 182–83; in *L'Écho*, 189–90; of matricide in *L'Ingratitude*, 211; and Barthes, 249–50; in Moser, 278; in Dumas, 280, 282
Destruction: transmission of in "Le Torrent," 27; and myth in Brossard, 36; and witnessing in *Les Cathedrales sauvages*, 57–59; and desire in *Les Cathédrales sauvages*, 58; and storytelling in *Les Cathédrales sauvages*, 59, 63; of men in *Le Vent majeur*, 72–73; in *La Memoria*, 150; in Baudelaire, 189; of the clocks in *L'Écho*, 195; in *Le Petit Prince*, 198; in Huston, 301–2
Deuil du soleil, Le (Gagnon), 55, 56, 62, 69–79
Devil, the: in *Laurence*, 99; in Moser, 277, 279; in Dumas, 281, 283–84
Dialogue: in postfeminist theater, 110, 112, 124; in *Un Homme est une valse*, 130; in *Les Lettres*, 217–18; in *Entre les fleuves*, 244; and gender, 249; in Primeau, Moser, and Dumas, 284; with death, in *Marguerite*, 346; in children's literature, 312
Discovery: in *Baroque d'aube*, 45; in *Vertige*, 49; of the self in *Le Vent majeur*, 70–71; and the body in *L'Été*, 86–87, 90; of the world in *L'Été*, 92–93; and sex in *Un Homme est une valse*, 140; and Freud's Wunderblock, 145; in *Le Bonheur*, 214; and sexual pleasure in Moser, 278; of the self in Huston, 300; in children's literature, 317
Discourse: authoritarian, in the works of Franco-Albertan women novelists, 19; of the mother in *La Cage*, 27–28; masculinist, in Brossard, 37; as a means of feminine resistance, 36, 40; in Brossard, 44; and phallocentricism, 47; Western, and Gagnon, 53–54; and transmission in *Les Cathédrales sauvages*, 63; authoritarian, and *Laurence*, 96–97; of the convent, 101; in *Un Homme est une valse*, 130–33, 135, 137–40; feminine, in *Un Homme est une valse*, 135–37; of the city in *Un Homme est une valse*, 136–37; the feminine in, 160–61; of the father in "La Gifle," 173; cultural, in *Les Lettres*, 217–18; multiple, in Daigle, 260; patriarchal, and Western Canadian women, 267, 270; patriarchal, in Moser, 274; and Western Canadian literature, 284; patriarchal, in Dumas, 284; feminist, and children's literature, 306–20; male, and oppression of women, 306; in children's literature, 308–11, 316, 318–20
Discourse, of female desire/sexuality: in *Un Homme est une valse*, 17, 133; and postfeminist theater, 109–12, 114, 116–18, 120, 126–27
Dis/order: in "Le Torrent," 26; in *Laurence*, 101; in "La Gifle," 174; and father-daughter relationships, 182–83
Domination: of women in Proulx, 163, 167–68; male, in *L'Écho*, 188; of women in Dumas, 283; male, and reason, 306; male, and the Internet, 322–23, 324; male, and children's literature, 310–11, 313–16

Dot de Sara, La (Agnant), 203, 205–10, 213, 214
Double Mélodie (Laberge), 110, 122, 124–26
Dowry, cultural: as legacy in *La Dot*, 209; as legacy in *L'Ingratitude*, 212; and marriage in *L'Ingratitude*, 212–13
Dream: the protagonist's, in *La Cage*, 29; and myth, 37–38; in *Baroque d'aube*, 40–41, 44–45; and the other in *Le Deuil du soleil*, 70; in *Le Vent majeur*, 71–72; in *Les Cathédrales sauvages*, 73; in *L'Été*, 89; in *Laurence*, 103–4; in Proulx, 163; the daughter's in "Friperie," 177; in *L'Ingratitude*, 210; in *Entre les fleuves*, 240; in Dumas, 280–81; in Huston, 301–2
Dream/aspiration: the husband's, in *La Cage*, 29; in *Baroque d'aube*, 38; in *Vertige*, 47; in *Les Cathédrales sauvages*, 65–67; in *L'Été*, 81, 85, 87–90, 93; in postfeminist theater, 112, 118–19; in *Un Homme est une valse*, 130–31, 137, 140; and incest in *L'Écho*, 192; in *L'Ingratitude*, 211–13; in Primeau, 270; in Huston, 298, 301; in children's literature, 310, 314–15, 317
Drowning: in *Entre les fleuves*, 239–40, 243–44; in Moser, 277
Deuil du soleil, Le (Gagnon), 55, 56, 69, 74–75
Duo pour voix obstinées (Pelletier), 115–16, 118–19
Dumas, Jacqueline, 19. Works: *Madeleine and the Angel*, 279–84
Dupré, Louise. Works: *La Memoria*, 17, 142–58
Duty: of women in rural families, 24; and the convent in *Laurence*, 101; in postfeminist theater, 122; freedom from in *L'Ingratitude*, 211; in Daigle, 252–53; in Dumas, 281

Écho du Silence, L' (Gourdeau), 18, 186–201
Education, of women: in *Les Cathedrales sauvages*, 62; lack of, in *L'Été*, 80; in *Laurence*, 98, 101, 102; in Théoret, 103, 105; in feminist theater, 112; of the daughter in "Friperie," 176; and maternal transmission, 203, 207; in *Le Bonheur*, 214; of women, and empowerment, 267–68; in children's literature, 318
Ego, the: and myth in Brossard, 36; of men in feminist theater, 114–15; of the sister in *Laurence*, 179
Empowerment: of evil through words, 39–40; objects of, in *L'Été*, 82; and postfeminist theater, 108; through slapping in "La Gifle," 175; and education, 267–68; and sexual desire in Moser, 278; and maternal subjectivity in Huston, 290; of women, and Internet publishing, 323
Encore une partie pour Berry (Harvey), 131
Enfants du Sabbat, Les (Hébert), 27
Entre l'ombre et la lumière (Bertrand), 19, 322–45
Entre les fleuves (Ltaif), 18–19, 235–46
Entre raison et déraison (Théoret), 96
Environment: effect on women in *Baroque d'aube*, 41–42, 43; and death in *L'Été*, 91–92; and the convent in *Laurence*, 101; urban, in *Laurence*, 101; and recovery in *L'Écho*, 200; and estrangement, 204; in *Le Bonheur*, 215; in Daigle, 250–51, 255
Epidemic: in *L'Été*, 78–79; and history in *L'Été*, 80, 81, 82, 87. See also Cholera; Typhus
Equality: and relationships in the works of francophone women dramatists, 17; and postfeminist theater, 109–110, 114, 119–20, 124; in *Un Homme est une valse*, 130; and love in Proulx, 167; of voices in *Les Lettres*, 217–18, 233; and mind/body dualism in Huston, 297–98; sexual, in children's literature, 311–12, 314, 318–19
Eroticism: of writing, 49; in postfeminist theater, 108–9, 111, 114, 118–22, 124–27; in *Un Homme est une valse*, 140–41; in Moser, 278
Été avant la mort, L' (Harbec), 249

Été de l'Île de Grâce, L' (Ouellette-Michalska), 17, 78–93

Evil: and Hébert, 32; genealogy of in Brossard, 39–40; in *Laurence*, 99–100; in Proulx, 164–65; in *L'Écho*, 190–93, 196; in Daigle, 258–59

Exile: questions of in Canada, 18; and transmission of women's cultural heritage, 18; in *Les Lettres*, 18; in *Entre les fleuves*, 18–19; of Nancy Huston, 19; as theme in francophone literature, 20; from the maternal tongue, 38; of the immigrants in *L'Été*, 80, 85–86; in the works of immigrant writers, 105; and the poet in *La Memoria*, 143; and possibility in Proulx, 160; and the legacy of words, 203–5; in *La Dot*, 206; in *L'Ingratitude*, 211; in *Les Lettres*, 217, 220–24, 231, 232; and immigrant writers, 235, 237; in *Entre les fleuves*, 239–40, 244, 246; in Moser, 274; and Huston, 288

Existence: and women's creativity, 41; everyday, liberation from in *Baroque d'aube*, 41; in *Vertige*, 46–47; transformation of in *L'Été*, 89; affirmation of in postfeminist theater, 121; and the cycle of, 153–54; and gender in *Le Bonheur*, 213–14; in *Les Lettres*, 231; in *Entre les fleuves*, 238; in Daigle, 256; in Huston, 291–92, 298, 299; and *Entre l'ombre et la lumière*, 324

Expedition: and myth and memory in Brossard, 37; funding of in *Baroque d'aube*, 42; in Daigle, 259; in children's literature, 317. *See also* Voyage; Journey

Fairy tale: of La Corriveau, 27–28; and the protagonist's adoptive family in *La Cage*, 32; and maternal images in Proulx, 165

Family: and the "detached daughters," 15; as subject of francophone writing, 16, 27; liberation from traditional structure, 16; traditional, as a prison in *La Cage*, 23, 27–32; in "Le Torrent," 23–27; in *Les Fous de Bassan*, 27; in *Le Temps sauvage*, 27; in *Les Enfants du Sabbat*, 27; adoptive, in *La Cage*, 30; and the protagonist's independence from in *La Cage*, 31; and the symbolism of the grenade in *La Cage*, 31; in the work of Hébert, 31–32; and traditional aspect of in "Le Torrent," 32; and the immigrants' struggle in *L'Été*, 85; traditional/patriarchal/rural in Théoret, 96–98, 101; urban, in *Laurence*, 98; criticism from in *Laurence*, 105; and individuality, 105; and postfeminist theater, 109–10, 116, 119, 122; structure of and the name of the father, 172; dynamics of in "Friperie," 177; and the daughter's rebellion in *Laurence*, 178–80; visions of and the detached daughters, 183; middle class, and incest, 186, 187; patriarchal, in *L'Écho*, 187–88; and violence in *L'Écho*, 192; and the legacy of abuse in *L'Écho*, 197, 200; in *La Dot*, 205–6, 208–10; in *Le Bonheur*, 213, 215; and exile in *Les Lettres*, 220, 221, 225–26; in Moser, 274, 275; in Dumas, 280, 281; in Huston, 297–300; in children's literature, 315

Fantasy: of La Corriveau, 27–28; gratification of, 53–54; in *L'Été*, 89–90; in *Un Homme est une valse*, 134, 138; men's, and women's role, 171; of paternal approval in *Laurence*, 179; in *L'Écho*, 196–97, 199

Farhoud, Abla, 18. Works: *Le Bonheur a la queue glissante*, 203–4, 213–14

Fate: in *Laurence*, 98, 178–79; of women in Proulx, 166; in *L'Écho*, 196

Father-daughter relationships: in francophone writing, 18, 20, 169, 170–71

Fear: and the death of La Corriveau, 23; and Hyacinth, in *La Cage*, 30–31; in *Baroque d'aube*, 40, 41–42, 44–45; in *Les Cathédrales sauvages*, 57–58; in *Le Vent majeur*, 61; in *L'Été*, 89–91; paternal, in *Laurence*, 99–100; of ridicule in *Laurence*, 103; of the city in *Laurence*, 104; and eroticism in theater, 111; of commitment in postfeminist theater, 112; of losing one's lover in postfeminist theater, 118–19; of the future in *Un Homme est une valse*, 135–36; and the sexes in *Un Homme est une valse*, 140; in *La Memoria*, 148–49; of pity in Proulx, 164; of the mother in Proulx, 165; and father-daughter relationships, 172, 173; of the body's fleshiness, 180–81; and surgery in *L'Écho*, 188–89; and incest in *L'Écho*, 188–89, 193, 196; of the city in *La Dot*, 208; of foreigners in *Les Lettres*, 219–21, 225; of the rapidity of life in *Les Lettres*, 224; of the patriarch in Dumas, 281–82; and the usage of French in Dumas, 284; in Huston, 301–2

Feminine, the: break with the masculine in Brossard, 50; in *L'Été*, 86–87; in *Laurence*, 96; representation/definition of in *Un Homme est une valse*, 134–35; in Proulx, 160–61; and writing in Théoret, 178; and words in Moser, 273; and children's literature, 307–8, 316–17

"Feminine mystique, the," 316–17

Feminism: voices of, 11; in the texts of francophone women writers, 12; and religious icons, 47; and location, 49–50; and desire, 50; in Théoret, 95–96; and theater, 108–12, 119; in Proulx, 167–68; and father-daughter relationships, 170–71; and "the name of the father," 172; and the father-daughter relationship in "Friperie," 177–78; and Théoret, 178; and the father's body, 180; and incest/abuse, 186; and non-Québecois francophone women, 267; and rebellion in writing, 273; and Huston, 288–89, 301; and children's literature, 306–20

Feminist criticism: history/tradition of, 11, 12; and view of gender, 36; and Théoret, 105; and rejection of patriarchal power, 169–70; and parricide, 171; and identity, 248; and Huston, 290

Feminist movement: in Québec, 11; and *Le Vent majeur*, 70–71

Feminist Québec theater: and postmortems, 108–27

Femininity: of the narrator in *Le Vent majeur*, 70–71; of transmission in *Le Vent majeur*, 71–72; and postfeminist theater, 110; and writing in *Un Homme est une valse*, 133; of the daughter in "Friperie," 177; and the symbolism of hair in *L'Écho*, 189–90; rejection of in *L'Écho*, 194–95; of the Western Canadian novel, 268–69; in Primeau, 270; and autonomy in Moser, 274; and virginity in Moser, 275; and children's literature, 307

Feminization: of myth and memory in Brossard, 16, 37; of space in *Entre les fleuves*, 235–36, 244

Fertility, female: as symbolized by the grenade in *La Cage*, 31; women as "blobs of," in *Baroque d'aube*, 42

Fiction: by francophone women writers, 15, 16; representation of culture in, 37–38; construction of in *Baroque d'aube*, 41, 45, 50; and reality in *Baroque d'aube*, 41; and life, 42–43; and lesbian love in *Vertige*, 48; and significance of for women in *Vertige*, 49; and women's alternative history, 79; role of and history, 81; and the imagination in *L'Été*, 85; and Théoret, 97; and *Un Homme est une valse*, 131, 138; and memory in *La Memoria*, 142; and transformation in *La Memoria*, 154; father-daughter relationships in, 170–71; and the detached daughter, 182–83; rejection of in *L'Écho*, 195; and *Entre les fleuves*, 237; and Daigle, 255, 256, 258–61; in Huston, 294; and children's literature, 308–9

Film: and postfeminist theater, 111; and *La Memoria*, 152, 156; in Proulx, 162, 165; in *Les Lettres*, 230; and gender, 249; and Barthes, 250; and Daigle, 256, 257, 261; in children's literature, 310

First-person narration: in "Le Torrent," 25; in *Vertige*, 45–46; in *Le Vent majeur*, 59–60; in *Les Cathedrales sauvages*, 62–63, 66–67; and *Le Vent majeur*, 72; in *L'Été*, 80; in *La Memoria*, 142; in francophone literature, 186; in Daigle, 259; in

Moser, 273–74; in children's literature, 313, 318
Fous de Bassan, Les (Hébert), 27, 169
Fréchette, Carole, 17, 109, 111, 120, 126–27 Works: *La Peau d'Élisa*, 120
Freedom: in *Un Homme est une valse*, 132, 134, 135, 137–38; in *Laurence*, 178–79; and father-daughter relationships, 182–83; and the mind in *L'Écho*, 195; and dismemberment in *L'Écho*, 198–99; in *La Dot*, 203, 207, 213; in *L'Ingratitude*, 210–12; in *Le Bonheur*, 215; in *Entre les fleuves*, 239; in Daigle, 250–51; in Moser, 279; in Dumas, 282; and English in Dumas, 284; and the childbirth metaphor, 293; in children's literature, 309, 312, 316, 319–20
"Friperie" (Turcotte), 18, 170, 175–77
Freud: view of women, 36; and murder in *Le Vent majeur*, 59–60; and the *tablette magique*, 145; and writing about the Oedipal complex, 171, 172; and "Friperie," 177; and *L'Écho*, 191–92, 195
Fulfillment: quest for in francophone drama, 17; and art in *Le Vent majeur*, 60–61; in *L'Été*, 87–88; in post feminist theater, 112, 119–20; in *L'Ingratitude*, 211–12; in Moser, 273; and dance in Huston, 298
Future, the: of francophone women writers, 15, 16, 20; and children's literature, 19; in *Vertige*, 45–46, 48; and sexual difference in Brossard, 50; and women narrators, 72; and creativity in Gagnon, 74; and death in *L'Été*, 82; and storytelling in *L'Été*, 84, 89; and urban optimism in *Laurence*, 104–5; and postfeminist theater, 109; fear of in *Un Homme est une valse*, 135–36; and the past in *La Memoria*, 144, 146, 149–51, 153–54, 156; women's, and the "other family romance," 183; and love in *L'Écho*, 188–89; and the journey into in *L'Écho*, 189–90; and hope for in *L'Écho*, 200–201; and the legacy of words in *La Dot*, 207–9; in *L'Ingratitude*, 210–11; and exile in *Les Lettres*, 222, 224–25, 227–28, 231–32; in Moser, 276

Gallop, Jane, 11; and men's disembodiment, 173–74
Games: in *Un Homme est une valse*, 130, 131, 133–40; of chess in "La Gifle," 172–75; of power in "Friperie," 177; children's, in *La Dot*, 207
Gagnon, Madeleine, 16, 169; and loss, 53–74; and death writing, 54–55; own experience of loss, 56–57; and transmission of textual legacies, 73. Works: *Chant pour un Québec lointain*, 55; *Les Cathédrales sauvages*, 55, 56–73; *Le Vent majeur*, 55, 67–73; *Le Deuil du soleil*, 55, 56, 69, 74–75; "Mon corps dans l'écriture," 55; *Le Vent majeur*, 59–60; *Lueur*, 62–63, 72
Gaze: control of in *Un Homme est une valse*, 130–31; female, in *Un Homme est une valse*, 132, 137; male, in *Un Homme est une valse*, 132, 137; of the mother in "Friperie," 176; of the father and daughter in "Friperie," 177; in *Les Lettres*, 220; of otherness in *Entre l'ombre et la lumière*, 323
Gender: as subject of francophone writing, 16; in *Les Lettres*, 18; cultural construction of in Huston, 19, 288–89; reversal of in *La Cage*, 30, 31; its inscription on women, 36; and the relationship between the individual and community in Brossard, 37; and literature/words in Brossard, 39–40; and survival in *Baroque d'aube*, 40; and first-person narration in *Vertige*, 45–46; and religious icons, 47; and the significance of in Gagnon, 61–62, 69–72; and transmission in *Le Vent majeur*, 71–72; in *Laurence*, 96–97, 105; in postfeminist theater, 114, 121–22, 126–27; in *Un Homme est une valse*, 132–33; and *Une Homme est une valse*, 133; role of in Proulx, 160, 161; nature of in Proulx, 161; meaning of in Proulx, 167–68; and power relationship in "La Gifle," 173; and conventions of greatness, 174–75; and writing in Théoret, 178; expectations in *Laurence*, 179; and exile in *Les Lettres*, 218–20, 223–24; and space in *Entre*

les fleuves, 243, 246; and Franco-Canadian lesbian writers, 248–62; construction of in Daigle, 261–62; and clichés in Moser, 277; in Franco-Albertan literature, 284; and mind/body dualism in Huston, 290–91, 294; and procreation in Huston, 302; and children's literature, 307–9, 318, 319

Gender identity, 19; in *Laurence*, 17; in *Homme invisible à la fenêtre*, 17; and the childbirth metaphor in *Le Vent majeur*, 70–71; in Théoret, 95–96; binary, and gay theater, 109; in postfeminist theater, 110

Gender roles: in *Un Homme est une valse*, 17; in *Laurence*, 96, 99, 105; and postfeminist theater, 108, 114; in Proulx, 160; and the patriarchal mother, 169–70

Genesis: of storytelling in *Les Cathédrales sauvages*, 58–59; in Huston, 291

Genealogy: in *Baroque d'aube*, 39–40; female, and cultural law, 171, 172; in *La Danse juive*, 182; story of in *La Dot*, 207; in Moser, 274

Generations: of Franco-Canadian writers, 16; of rural families, 24; and the passing on of the male name, 30–31; and time, 38; dreams of, 38; of postfeminist theater, 111, 119; of women in *La Memoria*, 157–58; of female relationships, 172; and the war of the sexes, 174–75; and incest in *L'Écho*, 186–87, 195, 197, 200–201; of women in *La Dot*, 205, 206; of women in *L'Ingratitude*, 210; and exile in *Les Lettres*, 225; of francophone women in Moser, 272, 274

Geography: influence of on the individual, 18; and transmission of women's cultural heritage, 18; in *Les Lettres*, 220, 228, 229; in *Entre les fleuves*, 235–36, 238, 245; of Québec in Moser, 274

"Gifle, La" (Teasdale), 18, 170, 172–75

God/Christ: in "Le Torrent," 25–26; in *La Cage*, 27–28; in *Baroque d'aube*, 42; and mourning in *Les Cathédrales sauvages*, 58–59; in postfeminist theater, 122–23; in *La Memoria*, 155; and the father in *L'Écho*, 192–93, 198; freedom from in *L'Ingratitude*, 211; in Daigle, 254–55; in Moser, 273; in Dumas, 282–83

Gourdeau, Gabrielle. Works: *L'Écho du silence*, 18, 186–201

Grave(s): significance of in *Le Vent majeur*, 60–61, 72–73; and writing in *Les Cathédrales sauvages*, 67; in *L'Été*, 78–79; in *La Memoria*, 147; in Proulx, 164, 166; and silence in *L'Écho*, 195–96

Grand rêve de Rosalie, Le (Anfousse), 314–15

Grosse Île: in *L'Été de l'Île de Grâce*, 17, 78–93; and history of, 80, 81, 83–84; force of and dance, 85–86

Harbec, Hélène, 262. Works: *L'Orgueilleuse*, 248; *L'Été avant la mort*, 249

Harvey, Pauline. Works: *Un Homme est une valse*, 17, 130–41; *Encore une partie pour Berry*, 131

Healing: in *L'Écho du silence*, 18; writing as, 56, 72–73; in *L'Été*, 91; and women's memory writing in Brossard, 144; and trauma/loss in *La Memoria*, 148, 149, 152–53; and shame in *La Danse juive*, 181; in *L'Écho*, 188–89, 194, 199–201; in Dumas, 280; in Huston, 294

Hébert, Anne, 16, 23–32; *La Cage*, 16, 23, 27–32; death of, 23; treatment of the family, 24–32. Works: "Le Torrent," 23–28, 31–32; *Le Temps sauvage*, 26, 27; *Les Fous de Bassan*, 27, 169; *Les Enfants du Sabbat*, 27

Heritage: cultural, of francophone women, 18, 20; the husband's, transmission of in rural families, 24; the husband's, transmission of in *La Cage*, 28–29; in Brossard, 44; and writing in Gagnon, 62–63; and women narrators, 72; and women's life writing, 74; and storytelling in *L'Été*, 86; and women's lineage, 203–4, 206–7, 210; in *Entre les fleuves*, 244

Héros de Rosalie, Le (Anfousse), 313–14
History: constraints of in Brossard, 37, 38; and myth, 37–38; feminine resistance to, 39; of Argentina, in *Baroque d'aube*, 42; and the exclusion of women in *Baroque d'aube*, 43–44; of women and *Vertige*, 47; and writing in *Le Vent majeur*, 69; of Québec and Canada, 78–80, 93, 95–96; alternative, in Ouellette-Michalska, 79; of Grosse Île, 80, 81, 83–84; and the body, 81; and storytelling, 84, 87; denouncement of, 86; of Québec in *Laurence*, 96, 97–98; silencing of women in, 143–44; and trauma, 150–51; and gendered reality in Proulx, 168; and the father's conflation with patriarchy, 172; on the side of the father in "La Gifle," 174; in *L'Écho*, 195; women's, and tradition, 203; and cultural legacy in *L'Ingratitude*, 212; and identity in *Le Bonheur*, 215; and exile in *Les Lettres*, 219, 222; in *Entre les fleuves*, 236–40, 243, 246; in Daigle, 251, 253, 258, 260; of Alberta in Moser, 272; of women's roles in Moser, 272; and subjectivity in Moser, 273–74; and children's literature, 306–20
Heterosexuality: of the narrator in *Le Vent majeur*, 70–71; and postfeminist theater, 108–9
Home/household, the: as a prison in *La Cage*, 28; in Laurence, 97, 99; rupture with in the works of immigrant writers, 105; and postfeminist theater, 110, 112, 119; and incest in *L'Écho*, 186, 195–96, 198; in *La Dot*, 208–10; in *Le Bonheur*, 214; and exile in *Les Lettres*, 218–20, 222–23, 232–33; and women's submission, 270; in Moser, 273–74; and sexism in Dumas, 283; in children's literature, 310
Homeland: and storytelling in *L'Été*, 85, 86; in *La Memoria*, 147; and exile, 204; and the legacy of words in *La Dot*, 205, 208; and rebellion in *L'Ingratitude*, 212; in *Les Lettres*, 218–19

Homme est une valse, Un (Harvey), 17, 130–41
Homme gris, L' (Laberge), 121–22
Homme invisible à la fenêtre (Proulx), 17, 160–61
Homme qui peignait Staline, L' (Théoret), 96–97
Homoeroticism: and the myth of Hyacinthus, 30; and gay theater, 109
Homosexuality: in *Le Vent majeur*, 70–71; and gay theater, 109
Horizon, the: significance of in Brossard, 44, 45; in *Vertige*, 45–46, 47, 49; in *Le Vent majeur*, 60–61
Huston, Nancy, 19; and (pro)creation, 288–302. Works: *Mosaïque de la pornographie*, 288–89; *À l'amour comme à la guerre*, 288–89; *Journal de la création*, 289–91, 294; *La Virevolte*, 294–99; *Instruments des ténèbres*, 294, 299–302
Hysteria: and postfeminist theater, 110–11; in "La Gifle," 175; in *L'Écho*, 188

Ideology: in francophone literature, 24; Hébert's rejection of, 24; mother's adhesion to in "Le Torrent," 25–27; patriarchal Catholic, in postfeminist theater, 121–22; and writing in Harvey, 131, 133; cultural, and "the name of the father," 172; in Primeau, 269, 270
Identity: of Québec, 11; as subject of francophone writing, 16; cultural and ethnic, in Canada, 18; cultural, in *Les Lettres*, 18; and gender, 19; cultural, as theme in francophone literature, 20; of the self in "Le Torrent," 26–27; and memory in Brossard, 36–37; in *Vertige*, 46–47, 49–50; of the "authors" in *Les Cathédrales sauvages*, 64; collective, and convent education, 102; and independence in *Laurence*, 104; personal, and rupture, 105; and postfeminist theater, 111, 119–20; in *Un Homme est une valse*, 130, 131, 137; sexual, in *Un Homme est une valse*, 132, 133; in *La Memoria*, 147–48; and gender in Proulx, 160,

163; female, and women writers, 169; and exile, 204; and the legacy of words in *La Dot*, 205, 208–9; in *Le Bonheur*, 215; in *Les Lettres*, 219–21, 223, 226–30, 232; and immigrant writing, 235–36, 238; in *Entre les fleuves*, 239, 241–44, 246; and Franco-Canadian lesbian writers, 248; sexual, 248–49; and Daigle, 250; sexual, and women's submission, 270; in Primeau, 270–72, 280; in Moser, 274, 277; in Dumas, 281; in Huston, 295; in children's literature, 307–9, 317–20

Illusion: and witnessing in *Les Cathédrales sauvages*, 57–58; of happiness in postfeminist theater, 115; of love in postfeminist theater, 126; in *Un Homme est une valse*, 138; and marriage in *L'Ingratitude*, 212–13

Ils étaient venus pour . . . (Laberge), 121–22

Images/imagery: in *Baroque d'aube*, 43–44, 45, 50; in *Vertige*, 49; in *Les Cathédrales sauvages*, 57; and women in *Le Vent majeur*, 70–71; in *Le Vent majeur*, 72; of the butterfly in *L'Été*, 82; and grace in *L'Été*, 93; and destiny, 103–4; in postfeminist theater, 121; and reality in *Un Homme est une valse*, 134–35, 137; in *La Memoria*, 145–46; funereal, in Proulx, 164; maternal, in Proulx, 165; and incest in *L'Écho*, 186; of the paternal rod in *L'Écho*, 187–88; medical, in *L'Écho*, 188–89, 193; of hair in *L'Écho*, 189; of the journey in *L'Écho*, 189–90; of the body in *L'Écho*, 191; of physical handicaps in *L'Écho*, 198; Creole, in *La Dot*, 206; of life in *La Dot*, 207; in *Entre les fleuves*, 236, 238–41, 243, 244; in Daigle, 251–55, 257, 261–62; in Primeau, 272; in Huston, 289, 295, 301–2; in *Entre l'ombre et la lumière*, 323–34; in children's literature, 310

Imaginary, imagining: and women's creativity, 37; in *Baroque d'aube*, 41–42; and *Vertige*, 47, 48–50; in *L'Été*, 80, 81, 82; and the audience in L'Écho, 193; and self-mutilation in *L'Écho*, 194; and parental overbearance in *L'Ingratitude*, 211; and exile in *Les Lettres*, 220–22, 226–28; and exile in *Entre les fleuves*, 237; in Moser, 272, 273; and Huston, 292, 300

Imagination, the: in *Baroque d'aube*, 38, 40; and reality in Brossard, 40; men's, in *Baroque d'aube*, 42; and trauma in *Le Vent majeur*, 67–68; and the childbirth metaphor in *Le Vent majeur*, 70–71; and the protagonist in *L'Été*, 81–82; and transformation in *L'Été*, 85; and Montreal in Théoret, 96; in *Un Homme est une valse*, 130; in *La Memoria*, 145, 152–54, 157; in *La Dot*, 209–10; in *L'Ingratitude*, 213; poetic, of Québec, 221–22; in *Entre les fleuves*, 238, 239; in Daigle, 253, 257; in Moser, 273–74, 279

Immigrants: in *L'Été*, 78–79, 85–86, 88–90, 93; in Québec society, 79–80; in *Laurence*, 98; in postfeminist theater, 120; in Québec in *Les Lettres*, 219, 220–30, 233; in *Entre les fleuves*, 235–36, 242

Immigrant writers, 16, 20, 105, 204–5, 217, 235

Immigration: to Canada, 18; in the works of immigrant writers, 105; and exile, 204; experience of in *Les Lettres*, 217, 221, 223–24, 230–32

Immortality: and storytelling in *Les Cathédrales sauvages*, 63; and the protagonist in *L'Été*, 81–82

Incest, father-daughter: in *L'Écho*, 18, 186–201; in *La Danse juive*, 182; and francophone culture, 279–80

Independence: of Québec, 11; in *La Cage*, 29–30; female, in Théoret, 95–96; in *Laurence*, 97, 98, 104, 180; and postfeminist theater, 109–12, 115; in *Un Homme est une valse*, 138–39; and tradition, 203, 211; in *L'Ingratitude* and *La Dot*, 213; in Moser, 272–73; in Huston, 296

Individual(s): his/her sense of self, 18; and community in Brossard, 37, 38; in *Vertige*, 49–50; death of in Gagnon, 54–55; and the history of the

body, 81; and grace in *L'Été*, 83; in *L'Ingratitude*, 211; and Western Canadian women, 267–68; and identity in Moser, 277; in children's literature, 319–20
Inequality: and gender in *Laurence*, 96, 105; and the power relationship in "La Gifle," 173; and children's literature, 308, 312
Ingratitude L' (Ying Chen), 203–4, 210–13
Inheritance: and writing in Gagnon, 62–63, 72; of the father's power, 171–72; of strength in *La Dot*, 207–8; of cultural legacy in *L'Ingratitude*, 213; of tradition, 306
Innocence: loss of in *Les Cathédrales sauvages*, 58, 61; flowers as a symbol of in *L'Écho*, 196; in Primeau, 270; in Huston, 290
Inscription: on the body in *L'Écho*, 187–88, 190, 191, 194, 196, 199
Inspiration: and the function of writing in the prose of Gagnon, 17; writing as a means of, 20; religion and for Brossard, 47; in *Le Vent majeur*, 60–61; in *Les Cathédrales sauvages*, 64–65; death as in *Le Vent majeur*, 68; death as, in Gagnon, 70, 73; of the mother-daughter relationship, 170; in "La Gifle," 174; women as in *La Dot*, 205–6; of the French language and Huston, 288; and procreation in Huston, 289, and physical decline in Huston, 298–99; and memory in Huston, 299–300
Instruments des ténèbres (Huston), 294, 299–302
Internet publishing, 19, 322–24
Interpretation: male, and the history of francophone literature, 20; of ideology in "Le Torrent," 25–26; of myth, 39; in Brossard, 50; and *Un Homme est une valse*, 134; of the symptoms of incest, 191–92; of "M" in *Entre les fleuves*, 243; of *L'Été avant la mort*, 249; in Daigle, 260; in children's literature, 309
Intimate/intimacy: in *Les Enfants du Sabbat*, 27; in Brossard, 44; in L'Été, 90; and feminist theater, 108–9, 120; in postfeminist theater, 110, 120, 126–27; in *Un Homme est une valse*, 133–35; and exile in *Les Lettres*, 223; of *Entre les fleuves*, 236
Irony: in *Le Vent majeur*, 73; in feminist theater, 115–16; in *L'Écho*, 197; in Moser, 275
Isolation: of rural families, 24; of mother and son in "Le Torrent," 24–25; of Grosse Île, 86–87, 93; in *Laurence*, 101; in postfemininst theater, 110; and the legacy of words in *La Dot*, 208; in *Les Lettres*, 226; of Franco-Albertan culture, 279–80; in *Marguerite*, 346; in children's literature, 313

Jansenism: and transmission of ideology in "Le Torrent," 26–27; and feminist theater, 108–9
Jardine, Alice. Works: *Gynesis*, 306–7
Jocelyn Trudelle trouvée morte dans ses larmes (Laberge), 121–22
"Jouissance" (pleasure): in *Vertige*, 49; maternal, and feminist theater, 108–9
Journal intime (Brossard), 36, 37–38
Journal: as form in Huston, 19, 293–94; in *Le Vent majeur*, 69
Journal de la création (Huston), 289–91
Journal pour mémoire (Théoret), 96
Journey: in *Baroque d'aube*, 42–43, 248; of birth in *Les Cathédrales sauvages*, 66; between the other and the self in *Le Deuil du soleil*, 70; and *Laurence*, 97–98, 100, 103–4; in *Un Homme est une valse*, 141; in *La Memoria*, 150, 151; into the future in *L'Écho*, 189–90; and exile, 205; in *Le Bonheur*, 214, 215; and exile in *Les Lettres*, 225; in Daigle, 250–51. See also Voyage
Juxtaposition: in *Baroque d'aube*, 40, 41–42, 45; in *Vertige*, 46–49; in *Laurence*, 100; in *L'Écho*, 188, 192–93, 195–96; solitary, in *Le Bonheur*, 213–14; in *Mosaïque*, 288–89

Kristeva, Julia: and Brossard, 50; and feminine discourse in Proulx,

160–61; and matricide in *L'Ingratitude*, 211; and the name "Kora," 246

Laberge, Marie, 17, 109, 120, 121–22, 126–27. Works: *C'était avant la guerre à l'Anse-à-Gilles*, 121–22; *Avec l'hiver qui s'en vient*, 121–22; *Ils étaient venus pour . . .* , 121–22; *Jocelyn Trudelle trouvée morte dans ses larmes*, 121–22; *Deux tangos pour toute une vie*, 121–22; *L'Homme gris*, 121–22; *Aurélie, ma soeur*, 122; *Pierre, ou la consolation*, 122–24; *La Double mélodie*, 122, 124–26

Language: in Brossard, 16, 39; experimentation with by women writers in Québec, 17; in erotic discourse in francophone drama, 17; as a means of feminine resistance, 36; symbolism of in Brossard, 37; as embodiment of culture in Brossard, 37; and myth, 39; in *Baroque d'aube*, 41–42, 44–45; in *Vertige*, 46–47, 48, 49; reordering of in Brossard, 50; and loss in Gagnon, 55–56; in *Les Cathédrales sauvages*, 66; and women in *Le Vent majeur*, 70–71; in *L'Été*, 82–85, 90; discovery of in *L'Été*, 92–93; in *Laurence*, 96–97, 101, 103; in postfeminist theater, 110–12, 116–18, 119–20, 122, 126–27; in *Un Homme est une valse*, 130, 132–33, 136–37; and the poet in *La Memoria*, 143; and loss, 153; and vision, 154; and Théoret, 178; of the daughter in *Laurence*, 178; women's, and the "other family romance," 183; in *L'Écho*, 193, 195–96, 199–200; in *La Dot*, 206; in *Le Bonheur*, 213; and exile in *Les Lettres*, 221, 222; in *Entre les fleuves*, 237, 240–42, 245; and Daigle, 249–53, 255, 258–62; in Western Canada, 269–70; reshaping of, in Moser, 273; and Québec in Moser, 274; and hybridity in Dumas, 279, 284; religious, in Dumas, 282–83; French, and Huston, 288; feminist, and children's literature, 306; and "gynesis," 307; in *Entre l'ombre et la lumière*, 323–24; and *Marguerite*, 346–48; feminist, and children's literature, 306–9, 316

Laurence (Théoret), 17, 18, 95–106, 170, 178–80

Law: in *La Cage*, 28, 29; protagonist's defiance of in *La Cage*, 31; in *Laurence*, 102–3, 178; in feminist theater, 122; cultural, and women's subordination, 171; of the father, 172; paternal, in "La Gifle," 174; in *La Danse juive*, 182; and the body in *L'Écho*, 187–88; and violence in *L'Écho*, 192; of silence in *L'Écho*, 197; paternal, and dismemberment in *L'Écho*, 198–99; and exile in *Les Lettres*, 229

Leblanc, Louise: works of for children/adolescents, 19, 306, 309–12

Legend(s): of La Corriveau, 15–16; in *Baroque d'aube*, 44–45; in postfeminist theater, 122–23; and women's memory writing, 144; of Ariadne's thread, 151–52; and women in *La Dot*, 205–7; and *Entre les fleuves*, 245–46; of the Métis in Moser, 277

Lesbianism/lesbian writers: in *Vertige*, 47–48; and feminist theater, 108–9, 120; in *L'Écho*, 188; and Franco-Canadian women writers, 248–62; voices of in Daigle, 248, 249, 255, 261–62

Lettres chinoises, Les (Ying Chen), 217–33

Liberation: from traditional family structures, 16; of body and mind in *La Cage*, 30; keys as a means of in *La Cage*, 31; of woman's intelligence in *La Cage*, 31; of women through writing, 50; sexual, in postfeminist theater, 112, 115, 122; of the discourse of desire/sexuality, 120, 126–27; and dismemberment in *L'Écho*, 198–99

Life: affirmation of and writing in the prose of Gagnon, 17; passion for in francophone drama, 17; and transmission of women's cultural heritage, 18; and myth in Brossard, 36, 42–43; banality of, in *Baroque d'aube*, 42; control of, 42–43; and words, 43; as a gamble, in Brossard, 44; phenomenology of in *Vertige*,

46–47; and writing, 54, 58–59, 67; quality of and technology/science, 54; and the death drive, 55–56; and beauty in death, 68; and the necessity of writing in *Le Vent majeur*, 69; and the necessity of linking death, mourning, and writing in Gagnon, 68; and rupture with the past in *Le Vent majeur*, 72–73; and death as inspiration, 73; last phase of, Gagnon's, 74; and death/the absurd in *L'Été*, 78, 81, 92–93; struggle for in *L'Été*, 79–80; and the imagination/imaginary, 81–82; eternal, in *L'Été*, 82; joy of in *L'Été*, 82; and transcendence, 84; and storytelling in *L'Été*, 84, 86; and the immigrants' struggle in *L'Été*, 85; significance of in *L'Été*, 87–89; miracle of, and the symbolism of the child in *L'Été*, 91–92; transformation of in *L'Été*, 92; as subject of Théoret's writing, 97, 99; and convent education, 102–3; and women's education in Théoret, 103; of female sexual discourse, 109–110; everyday, and postfeminist theater, 110; and women's desire in postfeminist theater, 117; role of passion in in postfeminist theater, 123; and sex drive in Harvey, 132; and game/art, 135; death in and memory, 146; the fight for in *La Memoria*, 148; and loss in *La Memoria*, 151–52; of passion, 156; as a maze in Proulx, 160; and the mother in Proulx, 164; and writing in Proulx, 168; refusal of in *Laurence*, 179–80; and death in *L'Écho*, 189, 192–93, 198; zest for and maternal transmission, 203; daily, of women in workers in Haiti and Québec, 205; and the legacy of words in *La Dot*, 205–9; in *L'Ingratitude*, 211–13; everyday, and exile in *Les Lettres*, 220, 222–24, 228, 231–32; daily, in *Entre les fleuves*, 245; in Daigle, 252–53, 256–61; in Primeau, 271; social, and words in Moser, 273; under patriarchy in Dumas, 284; in Huston, 291, 292–93, 295–302; in *Marguerite*, 346, 348

Liminal space: and Brossard, 37–38, 47; and Gagnon, 62, 73; in postfeminist theater, 110

"Livre rêvé, le": Gagnon's pursuit of, 54–55; and *Les Cathédrales sauvages*, 65–67; and separation of mind and body, 168; and the male experience, 169; and mother-daughter relationships, 170; and Oedipal rivalry, 171; and "the name of the father," 172; migrant, and exile, 205

Loss: and writing in *La Memoria*, 17; in francophone literature, 20; in Gagnon, 53–74; and mortality, 54; and language in Gagnon, 55–56; Gagnon's, 56–57; of innocence in *Les Cathédrales sauvages*, 58; and writing in *Les Cathédrales sauvages*, 58–59, 61–70; and creativity in *Le Vent majeur*, 60–61, 69, 70; of power in history, 81; and storytelling in *L'Été*, 84; of community in *L'Été*, 89–90, 93; of hope in *L'Été*, 92; and the poet in *La Memoria*, 143; and women's memory writing, 144–48; fear of, 148–49; of clairvoyance, 149–50; acceptance of, 151; and writing, 153, 154; of the mother, 155; of the mother in "Friperie," 177; and exile in *Les Lettres*, 226–28, 233; in *Entre les fleuves*, 239–40, 246; in Huston, 301–2; of male authority and "gynesis," 307; in children's literature, 315

Love: in *Baroque d'aube*, 44–45; lesbian, in *Vertige*, 47–48; women's, and the law, 50; and fire in *Les Cathédrales sauvages*, 57; of words, in *Les Cathédrales sauvages*, 62, 63; in *Le Vent majeur*, 68, 71–72; in *L'Été*, 88–90; universal, 92; in postfeminist theater, 110–12, 114–26; physical, in *Un Homme est une valse*, 136, 137, 138–40; in *La Memoria*, 156–57; in Proulx, 162, 165, 167; in *Laurence*, 178; romantic, myth of, 179–80; romantic, in *L'Écho*, 188–89; in *La Dot*, 209; maternal, in *L'Ingratitude*, 210–11; in *Les Lettres*, 217, 219–20, 227, 229–33; in *Entre les fleuves*, 242, 243; in Primeau, 270–72; in Dumas, 280–81, 283–84; and artistic vision in Huston, 293; of dance in Huston, 297; of

children in Huston, 299; in children's literature, 313–15
Lovemaking: in *Baroque d'aube*, 41; in *Vertige*, 49; Gagnon's experience of, 73; in postfeminist theater, 112–13, 116–19, 122–24; in *Un Homme est une valse*, 133–34; memory as defense against in *La Memoria*, 142–44; cycle of, in *La Memoria*, 146; in Proulx, 162; of childhood in *L'Écho*, 191–92; and gender in *Le Bonheur*, 213–14; and exile in *Les Lettres*, 220, 221, 224
Lover: ideal, as imagined by female writers, 30; language and, in *Vertige*, 49; in *Le Vent majeur*, 71, 72; and postfeminist theater, 110, 111, 114, 115, 117–18, 120, 122–23, 126; in *Un Homme est une valse*, 137–39; in *La Memoria*, 144, 149, 150; in Proulx, 162, 163, 166; in *La Danse juive*, 180; lesbian, in *L'Écho*, 188, 189–90; and rape in *L'Écho*, 195–196; men as in *La Dot*, 205–6; and dowry in *L'Ingratitude*, 212–13; and exile in *Les Lettres*, 233
Ltaif, Nadine, 105. Works: *Entre les fleuves*, 18–19, 235–46
Lucidity: and the name "Ludivine" in *La Cage*, 30; and love in postfeminist theater, 122, 124, 126; in *Un Homme est une valse*, 131; in *Les Lettres*, 224–25, 230–31; of the daughter in *La Danse juive*, 181
Lueur (Gagnon), 62–63, 72

Madeleine and the Angel (Dumas), 279–84
Maillet, Antonine, 19, 248–49, 255
Malheurs de Sophie, Les (Anfousse), 312–13
Marchessault, Jovette, 109, 169; and sexuality in theater, 108. Works: *Des Cailloux blancs pour les forêts obscures*, 170
Marginalization: of the mother in *La Cage*, 27–28; of societal outcasts and the chosen family in *La Cage*, 29–30; and Franco-Albertan space, 279–80; in Huston, 292, 299–300; of women writers, and Internet publishing, 322–23
Marguerite . . . ou celle qui voit derrière le miroir (Rioux), 19–20, 346–48
Marriage: as necessity in *La Cage*, 28–29; in traditional plot, 31; in *L'Été*, 87–88; in *Laurence*, 98, 99, 101, 102, 104, 178–80; in postfeminist theater, 118–20; in Proulx, 162; in *La Dot*, 209–10; in *L'Ingratitude*, 212–13; and the Métis, 269; in Primeau, 271–72; in Moser, 272, 274
Maison Trestler, La (Ouellette-Michalska), 80, 86, 96
Maternity: as subject of francophone writing, 16; as cause for the death wish in *La Cage*, 29; of the male persona in *La Cage*, 31; in Brossard, 38; and feminist theater, 109; in *La Memoria*, 155; in Proulx, 165; lack of in "Friperie," 176; in Huston, 289, 290, 292–94, 297–99, 302; in *Entre l'ombre et la lumière*, 323–24
Matricide: in "Le Torrent," 24, 32; in *L'Ingratitude*, 211
Memoria, La (Dupré), 17, 142–58
Memory/memories: as subject of francophone writing, 16, 20, 142; in Brossard, 16, 143–44; and mourning in *La Memoria*, 17; and the transmission of women's cultural heritage, 18; in *Baroque d'aube*, 36–45, 47, 50; in *Vertige*, 36, 43–50; and pleasure, 38; and women's silence, 43–44; and the symbolism of names, 43–44; and patriarchy, 44; and writing, 54, 56; translation of into words, 56; in *Les Cathédrales sauvages*, 63; and writing in *Le Vent majeur*, 70; and women narrators, 72; and the story of Grosse Île, 79; women's collective, 79; of the immigrants' struggle, 79–80; of the sick in *L'Été*, 83–84; and storytelling in *L'Été*, 84; in postfeminist theater, 114, 121–25; in *Un Homme est une valse*, 133–34; and fiction in *La Memoria*, 142; and writing in *La Memoria*, 143–44; and Freud's Wunderblock, 145; and the question of mourning, 146–47; and remaking of the self, 147–49; sharing

of, 149–150; and trauma, 150–51; role of and mourning, 150–51; and labyrinth of life, 151; and the mother in Proulx, 164–65; mother as in "Friperie," 177; in "La Chevelure," 189; and incest in *L'Écho*, 193–94, 199; transmission of in *L'Écho*, 195; and exile, 204; of fathers in *La Dot*, 205–6; and the legacy of words in *La Dot*, 206–8; collective, and cultural legacy in *L'Ingratitude*, 212; in *Les Lettres*, 220, 226–28; in *Entre les fleuves*, 240; in Daigle, 259–60; in Moser, 273–74; in Huston, 299–301

Metaphor: in *Vertige*, 48; in *Les Cathédrales sauvages*, 58, 66; of birth in *Le Vent majeur*, 70–71; of sexuality in feminist theater, 111, 120–21; in *Un Homme est une valse*, 138, 139; and Freud's Wunderblock, 145; of the parapalegic, 164; of the mother, 169–70; of "the name of the father," 172; of the daughter's position in "La Gifle," 173, 174, 175; of warfare in *L'Écho*, 193–95; and alcohol in *L'Écho*, 198; of insects and animals in *Entre les fleuves*, 238–39, 241, 243; and imagery in Daigle, 251–52, 259–60; of the patriarchal woman in Dumas, 279–80; and the female body in Huston, 288–89; and creativity in Huston, 290; and (pro)creation in Huston, 293; of shadow and light in *Entre l'ombre et la lumière*, 323–24

Migration: in *Les Lettres chinoises*, 18; in Théoret, 96; in Harvey, 130

Mind, the: liberation of in *La Cage*, 30; and myth, 39; and good art and literature, 42–43; and articulation in Théoret, 97; and game playing in *Un Homme est un valse*, 140–41; and Freud's Wunderblock, 145; in *La Memoria*, 147, 151–52; in Proulx, 167; and separation from body, 168; and trauma in *L'Écho*, 193; freedom of in *L'Écho*, 194–95; and recovery in *L'Écho*, 199–200; and memory in *Les Lettres*, 228; in Primeau, 272; in Moser, 274–75; patriarchal control of in Franco-Albertan culture, 279–80; in Huston, 291, 293, 301, 302

Mirror image: in Brossard, 43; in "Friperie," 176; in *L'Écho*, 197, 199–201; in *Entre l'ombre et la lumière*, 323–24

"Mise en abyme": and *Les Cathédrales sauvages*, 65; in postfeminist theater, 124; in children's literature, 313

Misogyny: and the history of francophone literature, 20; in the work of Brossard, 36, 42; absence of in *Baroque d'aube*, 44–45; in feminist theater, 122; in Dumas, 283; of pornography in *Mosaïque*, 288–89; and birth in Huston, 292

Modernity: and feminine resistance to literature and history, 39; in *Baroque d'aube*, 40, 43–44, 248; and death, 53–54; in Théoret, 95–96; in *Laurence*, 98, 101, 102; and exile in *Les Lettres*, 218–19, 225–230, 232, 233; and Daigle, 250–51, 253–54, 256, 261–62; and Western Canadian women, 267–68; in children's literature, 320

"Mon corps dans l'écriture" (Gagnon), 55

Monde à la dérive, Un (Crouteau), 317–20

Monologues: in postfeminist theater, 108–9, 110, 112, 120; in *L'Écho*, 190–93, 195

Montreal: as the center of the international francophone community, 12; in Théoret, 17, 95–96; in Brossard, 38–39, 47, 49; in *Laurence*, 98, 99–100, 101, 103–5, 178; in feminist theater, 112; in *Un Homme est une valse*, 130, 136–37, 140; in Proulx, 162; in *La Danse juive*, 180; in *La Dot*, 206, 208; in *Les Lettres*, 217, 219, 221, 224, 227, 228, 231–33; and Ltaif, 235; in *Entre les fleuves*, 241–43; in Daigle, 256, 257; in Primeau, 270

Morality: rural, in *Laurence*, 99–100; and urban corruption in *Laurence*, 101; in Moser, 274

Mortality: in the work of Brossard, 36, 40; and mythmaking, 37–38, 40; and loss in Gagnon, 54, 55–56; and writing in *Les Cathédrales sauvages*, 58–59, 67; and creative potential in Gagnon, 74; in Huston, 296

Mosaïque de la pornographie (Huston), 288–29

Moser, Marie, 19. Works: *Courtepointe/Counterpoint*, 272–79

Mother, the: and transmission of women's cultural heritage, 18; and defiance of patriarchal legacy, 18; in "Le Torrent," 24–25; in Catholic theology, 25; in *Le Temps sauvage*, 27; in *Les Enfants du Sabbat*, 27; in *La Cage*, 27–28; the name "Ludivine" as suggestive of, 30; powerlessness of, 32; as object of blame in literature, 32; and mourning in *La Memoria*, 145, 147, 154–158; and death in Proulx, 164; and son in Proulx, 164–65, 167–68; pre-Oedipal, 169–70; patriarchal, 169–70; and female genealogy, 171–72; power of in "Friperie," 177; and daughters in Laurence, 178–79; as perpetuators of tradition, 203; in *Entre les fleuves*, 241–43; marginalization of in Huston, 292; of tales, and Internet publishing, 323

Mother-daughter relationship/union/bond: in francophone literature, 18, 20; in Proulx, 165; and women writers, 169–71; and cultural legacy in *L'Ingratitude*, 213; in *Entre les fleuves*, 241–43

Motherhood, glorification of: in "Le Torrent," 23–25; and feminist theater, 108–9; in Proulx, 165; in Huston, 294

Mother/maternal tongue, the: as medium in *Vertige*, 46, 49; and the Nom/non du Père in Brossard, 50; and Huston, 288

Mourning: and the function of writing in the prose of Gagnon, 17, 53–74; and memory in *La Memoria*, 17; in francophone literature, 20; and writing, 54–57, 63–64; and birth in Gagnon, 55–56; and humanity in *Les Cathédrales sauvages*, 58–59; and writing in *Le Vent majeur*, 61, 67–69; and death of the other in Gagnon, 70; and the feminist movement in *Le Vent majeur*, 70–71; and androgyny in *Le Vent majeur*, 70–72; Gagnon's experience of, 73; and writing/creativity in *Le Deuil du soleil*, 73–74; as women's territory, 74; in postfeminist theater, 122–23; and women's memory writing in *La Memoria*, 144–45, 153–54; the question of in *La Memoria*, 145–47; and the role of memory, 150–51; and exile in *Les Lettres*, 228; in Huston, 296, 301–2

Muse: in Huston, 289, 291–92, 300

Mutilation: in Proulx, 162, 163; in *L'Écho*, 188, 193, 194, 198–99

Murder/killing: in "Le Torrent," 26–27; in *Le Vent majeur*, 59–61, 68–69; and writing in Gagnon, 67–68, 72–73; (figurative) in postfeminist theater, 115–16, 118; in Proulx, 162; of the mother in "Friperie," 177; in *La Danse juive*, 182; and daughters in writing, 182–83; in *L'Écho*, 189, 192–93, 196; and suicide in *L'Ingratitude*, 211; and cultural legacy in *L'Ingratitude*, 213; in *Entre les fleuves*, 237, 239, 241; in Dumas, 282; in Huston, 300–302; in children's literature, 315

Myth: in Brossard, 16; "baby versus book," in Huston, 19; in *Baroque d'aube*, 36–45, 47, 50; in *Vertige*, 36, 43, 45–50; and dreams, 37–38; and history, 37–38; and literature, 37–38, 42–43; and language, 39; and mortality, 40; and life, 42–43; and writing, 44; and women's creativity, 46; in *Un Homme est une valse*, 134; of the mother in Proulx, 165; cultural, and "the name of the father," 172; of romantic love, 179; of Pygmalion in Huston, 291–93, 300; in children's literature, 310

Mythology: cultural, and the female experience, 20; and Hyacinthus in *La Cage*, 30; and gender reversal in *La Cage*, 30–31; symbols of in *Baroque d'aube*, 40; and names in *Entre les fleuves*, 236, 241, 245; patriarchal, in Huston, 289, 291, 292, 297

"Name of the father, the": and Western culture, 172, 178–80; in *Laurence*, 179–80

Narcissus/narcissism: and the myth of Hyacinthus, 30; in *Le Vent majeur*, 71–72; in feminist theater, 119; of the daughter in "Friperie," 177; in *L'Ingratitude*, 212

Nationalism, 12, 121–22; in Western Canada, 269–70; in Primeau, 272; in Moser, 273, 274

Nepveu, Pierre: and urbanity in Montreal, 95; 103–4; and *Les Lettres*, 221–22, 226–28

Noël, Francine. Works: *Maryse*, 170

Nous parlerons comme on écrit (Théoret), 95–96, 97

Obedience: in "Le Torrent," 26; to one's husband in *La Cage*, 31; in *Laurence*, 101; and model of power in *L'Écho*, 187, 200–201; in *L'Ingratitude*, 210; and francophone women, 270; in Dumas, 281, 282; in children's literature, 309

Object(s): female protagonist of *La Cage* as, 28–29; transformation of in *L'Été*, 82; and grace in *L'Été*, 92; sexual, in postfeminist theater, 108–9, 114, 122; woman as, in *Un Homme est une valse*, 138–39; man as, in *Un Homme est une valse*, 140; woman as, in Proulx, 162, 168; the father as in *La Danse juive*, 181; of obssession in *Les Lettres*, 227; and space in *Entre les fleuves*, 236; sacred, and irreverence toward in Dumas, 283; woman as in *Mosaïque*, 288–89; of Huston's study, 290; the body as in Huston, 296–97; woman as, and seen as inferior, 306

Oedipus complex/rivalry: and murder in *Le Vent majeur*, 59–60; in literature, 169, 171; and the mother-daughter union, 170; women's role in, 171; and the daughter, 171–72; and novelistic form and content, 172

Ombre de toi, L' (Provost), 110, 118–20

Oppression, patriarchal: and francophone women writers, 20, 49; and postfeminist theater, 109–110;

mother as the victim of in *L'Ingratitude*, 211–12; and the usage of French in Dumas, 284; of women in male discourse, 306; and children's literature, 307, 318–19

Orgasm: in *Un Homme est une valse*, 137–39; and pregnancy in Huston, 295

Orphanage/Orphans: in *La Cage*, 29–30; in *L'Été*, 79–80, 92, 93; in *L'Écho*, 197; and exile in *Les Lettres*, 226; in children's literature, 313, 317

Other, the: and *Les Cathédrales sauvages*, 65–66; in *Le Vent majeur*, 68–69, 70, 71; in *Le Deuil du soleil*, 70; and desire in *Le Deuil du soleil*, 73–74; in *Un Homme est une valse*, 136; parapalegic as in Proulx, 168; in Moser, 280; in *Gynesis*, 306–7; in children's literature, 318

"Otherness": awareness of in Canada, 18; in *Le Vent majeur*, 71–72; and writing in Proulx, 168; and exile in *Les Lettres*, 218, 220; and hybridity in Primeau, 272; in Moser, 274; in *Entre l'ombre et la lumière*, 323

Other family romance, the: and women writers, 169, 170, 172, 183

Ouellette-Michalska, Madeleine, 16, 17, 132. Works: *L'Été de l'Île de Grâce*, 78–93; *La Maison Trestler*, 80, 86, 96; and Harvey, 132

Pain. See Suffering

Paradoxes: in *Vertige*, 48; in Harvey, 130–31; and exile, 205; in *Entre les fleuves*, 236–37; in Daigle, 256; in Dumas, 283

Pas dans l'éternité, Un (Crouteau), 317–20

Passion: in francophone drama, 17; and writing, in *Un Homme est une valse*, 17; in *Vertige*, 48; in folk medicine, 87; in postfeminist theater, 111, 116–26; in *Un Homme est une valse*, 130, 132, 138–39; in Proulx, 161, 162; aesthetic and carnal, in Proulx, 163; in *Entre les fleuves*, 242; in Daigle, 253; in Primeau, 271–72; for dance in Huston, 297; in *Entre*

INDEX 383

l'ombre et la lumière, 323–24; in children's literature, 316
Passivity, female: and postfeminist theater, 110; in *La Memoria*, 156; of the mother in Proulx, 165–66; and cultural legacy in *La Dot*, 209; and cultural legacy in *L'Ingratitude*, 212; and pregnancy in Huston, 295; in children's literature, 309
Past, the: and Franco-Canadian women writers, 16, 20; and rituals in *Baroque d'aube*, 41; and personal equilibrium, 43; and sexual difference in Brossard, 50; and death in *Le Vent majeur*, 68–69, 72–73; and life writing in Gagnon, 74; and death in *L'Été*, 82; and storytelling in *L'Été*, 84; in feminist theater, 118–19; in *Un Homme est une valse*, 136; in *La Memoria*, 143; and the future in *La Memoria*, 144–50, 153–54, 156; and narrative in *La Memoria*, 151; and the present in *La Memoria*, 157; in Proulx, 164; and incest in *L'Écho*, 188–90, 198, 200–201; and the legacy of words in *La Dot*, 207, 209; in *Les Lettres*, 218; cultural, in *Les Lettres*, 219, 221–23, 225–28, 230, 232; and *Entre les fleuves*, 237, 239; and Daigle, 250, 254; in Moser, 273–74, 276, 284; in Dumas, 280, 284; in Primeau, 284
Patriarchy/patriarchal legacy: defiance of, 16, 18; in *Laurence*, 99–100; defiance/survival of in francophone literature, 18, 20; figurative war against in *La Cage*, 31; in Brossard, 44; and Théoret, 96–97; and feminist theater, 108–9; and postfeminist theater, 109–110, 119, 121–22; and the mythical mother in Proulx, 165; and writing, 169; and the symbolic power[lessness] of mothers, 169–70; and the father, 172; and the daughter's double bind, 175; in *La Danse juive*, 182; and father-daughter relationships, 182–83; and symbolism of the phallus in *L'Écho*, 188; and complicity with the psychiatric profession in *L'Écho*, 191–92; father as the symbol of in *L'Écho*, 200–201; and rebellion

in *Entre les fleuves*, 245–46; and Western Canadian women, 267–69; in Primeau, 270–72; in Moser, 272, 274–76; Franco-Albertan, and language in Dumas, 279–80, 284; as embodied in the woman in Dumas, 281; in Huston, 289, 291, 302; and tradition, 306; and children's literature, 308, 315–16, 319–20
Peau d'Elisa, La (Fréchette), 110, 120–21
Pelletier, Maryse, 17, 109, 119–20, 126–27. Works: *Duo pour voix obstinées*, 115, 118–19; *Un Samouraï amoureux*, 116–18
Perspective: in *Un Homme est une valse*, 130–33, 138; and memory in *La Memoria*, 150–51; and gender in Proulx, 161; female, and women writers, 169; in *L'Écho*, 188. 195–98; in *La Dot*, 209; in *Les Lettres*, 217–20, 223–24; in *Entre les fleuves*, 235–39, 244; in Daigle, 252; in Moser, 275; in Huston, 289
Perversity: in *Laurence*, 99; in Proulx, 164; in Dumas, 280–81, 283
Phallocentricism: effect on women, 36; and the text of *Vertige*, 47; and representation, 50
Pierre, ou la Consolation (Laberge), 110, 22–24
Play: in the husband's absence in *La Cage*, 29–30, 32; and the name "Hyacinth" in *La Cage*, 30; in *Un Homme est une valse*, 130–32, 134, 138–40; and father-daughter relationships in "La Gifle," 172–75; with language in Daigle, 260; in Dumas, 282
Playwrights, women: and postfeminist theater, 108–11, 117–18, 124, 126–27
Pleasure: in *Baroque d'aube*, 38–39, 40, 41, 44–45; and death, 40; and women's creativity, 41; and lesbian love in *Vertige*, 47–48; the birdcage as a source of in *L'Été*, 82–83; and storytelling in *L'Été*, 86–87; and transformation in *L'Été*, 87–93; in *Laurence*, 99, 102; in feminist theater, 109–110, 114, 117, 120–22;

in *Un Homme est une valse*, 135–36, 137–38, 140–41; in Proulx, 166; in childhood and *L'Écho*, 192; and maternal transmission, 203; and the spoken word in *La Dot*, 205–10; and freedom in *L'Ingratitude*, 211; in *Le Bonheur*, 215; and exile in *Les Lettres*, 221; and Barthes, 249–50; of the text and Daigle, 250, 253–54, 260, 261; in Moser, 276–79; and pregnancy in Huston, 296; and dance in Huston, 298; in *Marguerite*, 346; in children's literature, 315
"Poésie en prose" (prose poetry): and *La Memoria*, 142–43
Political sovereignty: in Québec, 18
Pornography: in *Baroque d'aube*, 41–42; and feminist theater, 111; in Dumas, 280
Possession: and the legacy of writing, 67; in sex, 118; in *Un Homme est une valse*, 139–40; of body parts in Proulx, 163; and misogyny in *Mosaïque*, 288–89
Postmodernity, 12, 46; and Franco-Canadian lesbian writers, 248–62; and Daigle, 250, 253–54; and *Gynesis*, 306–7
Poverty: in *Laurence*, 98, 100–101, 178; in *La Danse juive*, 181; in *La Dot*, 208
Power: of the priests in "Le Torrent," 24; of the mother in "Le Torrent," 26; as represented by the keys in *La Cage*, 28, 31; over the wife and family in *La Cage*, 28; and myth, 37–38; of the writer, in *Baroque d'aube*, 41–42; in Brossard, 42–43; as agent of change in Brossard, 44; inequality of, 49; abuse of, 49–50; in *L'Été*, 80; stories of in history, 81; of forgetfulness in *L'Été*, 82; of the protagonist in *L'Été*, 84, 85; in postfeminist theater, 110–11, 119; of desire in feminist theater, 117; struggle for in *Un Homme est une valse*, 133, 137, 139–41; of the past in *La Memoria*, 147; of the man in Proulx, 163; and the mother in Proulx, 165; of pre-Oedipal mothers, 169–70; symbolic, of patriarchal mothers, 169–70; patriarchal, of the father, 169–70; the father's, and the daughter, 171–72; challenging of, 172; and the father-daughter relationship, 173–74, 182–83; male, through disembodiment, 173–74; as a game in "La Gifle," 174–75; game of in "Friperie," 177; of the mother in "Friperie," 177–78; model of in *L'Écho*, 187; abuse of, in *L'Écho*, 187–88; of words in *La Dot*, 210; in *Entre les fleuves*, 241; sexual, in Primeau, 280
Pregnancy: and feminist theater, 109; and incest in *L'Écho*, 192–93; in Moser, 275–76; in Huston, 289–90, 293–94, 296, 299–300
Present, the: and pleasure in *Baroque d'aube*, 38, 40–41, 50; and rituals in *Baroque d'aube*, 41; and symbolism in *Baroque d'aube*, 42; and personal equilibrium, 43; in *Vertige*, 45–47; and technology, 54; and history, 80; of the odor of death in *L'Été*, 82; of British soldiers in *L'Été*, 85–86; of folk medicine in *L'Été*, 87; of transformation in *L'Été*, 87–88; in postfeminist theater, 118–19, 120–21; eternal, in *Un Homme est une valse*, 143; in *La Memoria*, 144, 146, 149, 150, 153, 157; and the past in *L'Écho*, 188–89; and transmission in *La Dot*, 206–8; and exile in *Les Lettres*, 225–28; and *Entre les fleuves*, 237; and obedience in Dumas, 281
Priests: in "Le Torrent," 23–25, 26–27; in Western Canada, 269; in Primeau, 271; in Moser, 272–73; in Dumas, 282
Primeau, Marguerite-A., 19, 267–70. Works: *Dans le muskeg*, 270–72
Private, the: and myth, 37–38; and incest, 186; and exile in *Les Lettres*, 223; and subjectivity in Moser, 273–74; in Primeau, 280; and maternity in Huston, 293–94
Procreation: in Huston, 19; and sexuality, 24; and women's life writing, 74; and creativity in Huston, 288–302
"Prière" (prayer): writing as in *Le Deuil du soleil*, 73–74; and feminist theater, 108–9, 122

Prostitution: in *L'Écho,* 190, 191; in Primeau, 270–71; in Huston, 288–89

Proulx, Monique, 160–168. Works: *Homme invisible à la fenêtre,* 17; *Le Sexe des étoiles,* 160–61, 170

Provost, Sylvie, 17, 119–20, 126–27. Works: *L'Ombre de toi,* 118–19

Psyche: inscription of gender on, 36; and myth, 37–38, 44; of women and religious icons, 47; of the artist in Huston, 293

Psychoanalysis: in Gagnon, 55–56, 59–60, 72–73; and "Friperie," 176; and *Laurence,* 179; in *L'Écho,* 191–92, 195; rejection of in *L'Écho,* 200–201

Public, the: and myth, 37–38; in *Laurence,* 98; in *La Danse juive,* 181–82; and incest/abuse, 186; in *Le Bonheur,* 214–15; and exile in *Les Lettres,* 223; in Daigle, 259–60; and maternity in Huston, 293–94

Québec: and francophone women writers, 11–12, 15–20; independence of, 11; 1970s feminist movement in, 11; francophone nationalist movements in, 12; political sovereignty in, 18 ; and the legend of La Corriveau, 23; family structure in, 23–24, 27; and "Le Torrent," 24–25; and the role of the mother, 25; sin and, 26; and the feminist movement in *Le Vent majeur,* 70–71; history of, 78–80, 93, 95–96, 98; and Irish immigrants, 79–80; and language in *L'Été,* 90; in Théoret, 95–96; in *Laurence,* 97–99, 101–5; and feminist theater, 108–10, 122; and hybrid genre, 143; feminist writing in, 170; fate of women in, 178–79; and memory in *L'Écho,* 194; and the legacy of words in *La Dot,* 205, 206, 208, 209; in *Le Bonheur,* 213, 214; and exile in *Les Lettres,* 218–24, 226, 228, 230; and Ltaif, 235; in *Entre les fleuves,* 241–43, 246; and Daigle, 262; and Western Canadian women, 268; and Western Canada, 269; in Primeau, 271; in Moser, 274; children's literature in, 306–20; in children's literature, 317, 319

Québécois: definition of, 11–12; and absence of a father, 24–25; and the deconstruction of women, 163; and identity in *La Dot,* 209–10; in *Le Bonheur,* 214; in *Les Lettres,* 219, 221, 222, 225; and Western Canada, 269, 270; children's literature and feminist thought, 306; and *Marguerite,* 346

Rage: of the mother in "Le Torrent," 25, 26–27, 32; in Proulx, 164–65; in francophone writing, 170; in *L'Écho,* 192–93

Rape: spousal, in *La Cage,* 29; in *Le Vent majeur,* 59–62, 68–69; in *Les Cathédrales sauvages,* 64; in *Laurence,* 104–5; in feminist theater, 121–22; in *L'Écho,* 195–96; in Dumas, 280; in Huston, 300

Realism : in postfeminist theater, 110, 115, 118–19

Reality: in *Baroque d'aube,* 37–38, 41, 44–45; and culture, 37–38; constraints of, 38; liberation from, 41; in *Vertige,* 45–50; phallagocentric and *Vertige,* 47; and lesbian love in *Vertige,* 48; in *Laurence,* 100–101; and women's education in *Laurence,* 101–3; in postfeminist theater, 115; in *Un Homme est une valse,* 130, 134–35, 138; and the self in *La Memoria,* 148; and male narrativity in Proulx, 168; gendered, in Proulx, 168; in *Les Lettres,* 218, 227–28; linguistic and cultural, 235–36; in *Entre les fleuves,* 237, 238, 242–43; and Daigle, 255, 258–61; and Western Canadian women, 267–68; in Moser, 272, 276, 279; in Huston, 294, 296, 297–99

Reason/reasoning ("raisonnement"): in Brossard, 40–41; and love in postfeminist theater, 124; in *Un Homme est une valse,* 138; in *La Memoria,* 147, 157; historical, and patriarchy, 172; of the father in "La Gifle," 174–75; in *L'Écho,* 195; in *Entre les fleuves,* 238, 239, 244; and mind/

body dualism in Huston, 290–91; and male domination, 306; in children's literature, 310; and children's literature, 311–12, 315

Recovery: and writing in *La Memoria*, 17; writing as a means of, 20; and grace in *L'Été*, 85; and loss in *La Memoria*, 142, 157; and incest in *L'Écho*, 189–90, 199–200. *See also* Healing

Relationships: as subject of francophone writing, 16; and traditional gender roles in *Un Homme est une valse*, 17; women's, with themselves, 36; between the individual and community in Brossard, 37; between body, language, and text in Brossard, 46; lesbian, in *Vertige*, 47–48; between the narrator and words in Gagnon, 62; of the "authors" in *Les Cathédrales sauvages*, 64; in *Le Vent majeur*, 68–69; in *L'Été*, 88, 90; amorous, in postfeminist theater, 109–11, 112, 114, 115, 119, 125–27; in *Un Homme est une valse*, 130, 134–37, 139; in *La Memoria*, 144, 149, 150, 156; in Proulx, 160, 165–67; with one's body in *La Danse juive*, 180; incestuous, in *L'Écho*, 186, 189–91, 200–201; between generations of women in *La Dot*, 205; long-term, in *La Dot*, 205; father-daughter, in *La Dot*, 205–6; between women in *La Dot*, 206; with the mother in *L'Ingratitude*, 210; discovery of in *Le Bonheur*, 214; modern, in *Les Lettres*, 229–30; lesbian, 248; with modernity in Daigle, 250–51; between sensations in Daigle, 253; to language in Daigle, 255; between fiction and reality in Daigle, 258; to writing and Daigle, 260; with the husband in Moser, 273; in Dumas, 280; among women/writing/maternity in Huston, 289; and parents in Huston, 299–300; with the body in Huston, 301; between the artist and her work in Huston, 302; between words and things in *Entre l'ombre et la lumière*, 324; in children's literature, 313–15

Remembering: and writing, 54; in postfeminist theater, 118–20; in *La Memoria*, 146, 148, 149, 156; in Proulx, 164–65; in *La Dot*, 209; and exile in *Les Lettres*, 227; in Moser, 272, 278, 279; in Dumas, 280–82

Repression: in *L'Écho*, 18, 193; of the convent in *Laurence*, 103; and feminist theater, 108–9; and postfeminist theater, 109–110, 122; of aggression in "La Gifle," 175; in *L'Écho*, 194, 195; of sexuality in Dumas, 278–79; of memories in Huston, 301

Resentment: in father-daughter relations, 18, 170; in postfeminist theater, 118–19; in *Le Bonheur*, 214

Resistance: female, of gender's implications, 36; female, to narrative/history, 39, 40, 43–44; cultural, in Théoret, 97; to tradition in *Laurence*, 104–5; in Proulx, 166; female, lack of in "La Gifle," 173; of daughters in writing, 182–83; in *L'Écho*, 193; to change in *Les Lettres*, 229–30

Revenge: in *L'Écho*, 18; in "Le Torrent," 26

Revolt: in *Laurence*, 97–98, 105; and postfeminist theater, 110–11

Rhythm: of dance in *L'Été*, 85, 88; of the text in *Un Homme est une valse*, 131, 134, 138–39; of writing in *L'Écho*, 188–89; in *La Dot*, 206; of pleasure in Moser, 278; in *Marguerite*, 346–47

Rioux, Hélène, 19–20. Works: *Marguerite . . . ou celle qui voit derrière le miroir*, 19, 20, 346–48

Rituals: words as in mythmaking, 39; and time in *Baroque d'aube*, 41; and death in Gagnon, 53–54; purification, in *L'Été*, 91; and tarot cards in *La Memoria*, 149–50; of ice cream, in "Friperie," 176; in *L'Écho*, 198–99; funereal, in *La Dot*, 210; and sex in *Les Lettres*, 224–25; of the Métis in Moser, 277; religious, in Dumas, 283; and English in Dumas, 284

Roles: of women in *Laurence*, 17; stifling, in traditional narrative, 39; in *L'Été*, 79–80; reversal of, 110–11,

132, 138, 199; of leadership and feminist theater, 109; familial, and postfeminist theater, 109–10, 122; in Proulx, 160; of women in the patriarchal order, 169; of the father in francophone writing, 170; of the lover in *L'Écho*, 189–90; of the father in *L'Écho*, 192–93; of the doll in *L'Écho*, 196; of the audience in *L'Écho*, 196; of the surgeon in *L'Écho*, 199; false, of mothers, 203; of women in *La Dot*, 206; of God and Church in Daigle, 254–55; of the book in Daigle, 255; of Western Canadian women, 267–68; of the nationalist patriarch in Primeau, 272; women's, in Moser, 272; and words in Moser, 273; of the female character in Primeau, 280; of the daughters in Dumas, 281; as mother and dancer in Huston, 295, 297–98; of women as inferior to men's, 306; sociosexual, in children's literature, 309, 315–17, 319–20

"Roman archéologique" (archaeological novel): and Gagnon, 62–63; of rural life in *Laurence*, 105

"Rupture": in the works of immigrant writers, 105; in *Un Homme est une valse*, 134; in *Les Lettres*, 233

Romanticism: lack of in sex, 112–13, 114, 115; in Pelletier, 116–17; in *La Memoria*, 155–56; of the heroine's head in Proulx, 165–66

Rosalie à la belle étoile (Anfousse), 315

Rootlessness: in Harvey, 131; in *Les Lettres*, 218, 220, 221, 225–26, 230–32; in *Entre les fleuves*, 244

Rural society/life: in *Laurence*, 17, 97–98, 99, 100, 104–5

Sacrifice: by women, in *L'Été*, 17; by women in rural familes, 24; of the mother in *Laurence*, 98; and the convent in *Laurence*, 101; of the daughter in *Laurence*, 179; in *L'Écho*, 193–94, 198–99

Samouraï amoureux, Un (Pelletier), 110, 116–18

Sauvage-Sauvageon (Primeau), 267–68

Science: in Brossard, 41–42, 44, 46; in *L'Été*, 87; in *L'Écho*, 195; in *Baroque d'aube*, 248; and children's literature, 307, 313

Sea, the: in *Baroque d'aube*, 40–42, 44–45; in *Le Vent majeur*, 60–61; in *L'Été*, 91; in *Entre les fleuves*, 239–43; in Daigle, 250–51

Seduction: as symbolized by Buenos Aires in *Baroque d'aube*, 42; of the translator in *Baroque d'aube*, 50; of the narrator's vision in *Le Vent majeur*, 61; in postfeminist theater, 112, 115–17, 120, 124–25; of the mother in "Friperie," 177; of daughters in Laurence, 178–79; and daughters in writing, 182–83; of beauty/art in Daigle, 257–59; in children's literature, 315–17

Self, the: transformation of in *Les Lettres*, 18; and writing, 63–64; and the other in *Le Deuil du soleil*, 70; and femininity in *Le Vent majeur*, 71; and sex in *Un Homme est une valse*, 140; and memoir, 142; remaking of in *La Memoria*, 147–49; in Proulx, 162, 167–68; in francophone writing, 170; sense of, and the cultural law, 171; sense of, and the mother in "Friperie," 176; in *L'Écho*, 193–94; and exile in *Les Lettres*, 220, 221, 225, 232, 233; quest for/recognition of and Ltaif, 235–37; in *Entre les fleuves*, 238, 240, 242, 243, 246; sexual, in Moser, 277; fragmented, and mind/body dualism, 293; in Huston, 295, 300; -abandonment, in postfeminist theater, 117–18; -abuse, in *L'Écho*, 191; -assertiveness, in *Laurence*, 100; -censorship, in "Le Torrent," 27–28; -conception/actualization, and women's memory writing in *La Memoria*, 144; -consciousness, in *Laurence*, 103; -consciousness, in Moser, 274–75; -derision: in *L'Écho*, 193; -destruction: in "La Gifle," 175; -destruction, in *L'Écho*, 190, 191; -determination, in *Laurence*, 97; -esteem: in *L'Écho*, 188, 190; -identity, in "Le Torrent," 26–27; -loathing: in *La Danse juive*,

181; -loathing, in *L'Écho*, 191; -love, and the myth of Hyacinthus, 30; -mutilation, 162; -portrait, in *Vertige*, 48–49; -portrait, in Proulx, 163; -possession, in Harvey, 133; -preservation, in Brossard, 44; -promotion, in Harvey, 131; -recognition/acknowledgment, 71–74, 89–90, 125–27, 179–80, 225; -reliance, in *Laurence*, 97–98; -worth, and the "other family romance," 183

Senses, the: in *Baroque d'aube*, 38, 41–42; in *Vertige*, 46–47; and mourning in *Le Deuil du soleil*, 70; and storytelling in *L'Été*, 84; amputation of in *L'Écho*, 198; and the legacy of words in *La Dot*, 207–8; in *Entre les fleuves*, 239; and Daigle, 253; rejection of in Huston, 291

Sensuality: in the absence of the husband in *La Cage*, 29–30; and the elicitation of in *La Cage*, 31; in *Vertige*, 46–47; in postfeminist theater, 109–110, 114, 123, 125; of the mother in "Friperie," 176; in Baudelaire, 189; in *L'Écho*, 189–90; in *Le Bonheur*, 215; in Primeau, 270; in Moser, 275, 280; and pregnancy in Huston, 295; in *Entre l'ombre et la lumière*, 323–24

Sex: and postfeminist theater, 108–12, 114, 116, 119; and writing, 132–33; and the self, 140; in Proulx, 161–62; in *La Danse juive*, 180; in *L'Écho*, 196; and exile in *La Dot*, 208; and exile in *Les Lettres*, 224–25; in Primeau, Moser, and Dumas, 280; in children's literature, 318

Sexe des étoiles, Le (Proulx), 160, 170

Sexes, the: and the necessity of literature, 39; power struggle between, 119; in *Un Homme est une valse*, 130–31, 133–34, 140; and children's literature, 308–10, 316, 319

Sexism: absence of in *Baroque d'aube*, 44–45; in postfeminist theater, 114–15; and patriarchal control in Dumas, 283; in children's literature, 311–12, 313

Sexual difference: in Brossard, 36–37; and the necessity of literature, 39; and the past, 50 and writing in Gagnon, 69–70; in *Le Vent majeur*, 71–72; in *Un Homme est une valse*, 132–33, 140–41; and children's literature, 307, 310

Sexuality: as subject of francophone writing, 16; as means of procreation, 24; and the relationship between the individual and community in Brossard, 37; and feminist theater, 108–10, 111–14, 119–22, 124, 126–27; in *Un Homme est une valse*, 131–32, 137–38; and writing in *Un Homme est une valse*, 133; and truth in *Un Homme est une valse*, 136, 139; and art in Proulx, 167; of women in Proulx, 168; and the daughter's vulnerability in "La Gifle," 173–74; paternal, in *L'Écho*, 187–88, 194–95; in Primeau, 269–71, 280; and the self in Moser, 277, 280; and desire in Moser, 278; repression of in Moser, 278–79; in Western Canadian literature, 284

Shame: in *L'Écho*, 18; and feminist theater, 108–9; of the daughter in "Friperie," 176; in *La Danse juive*, 181, 182; and incest in *L'Écho*, 190–91, 199–200; and virginal sex in Moser, 274–75

Silence: of women in rural families, 24; of the father in *Le Temps sauvage*, 27; and the necessity of mythmaking, 39; of women, as prey, 42; and the sanctity of art, 43; of women in history, 43–44; in *Vertige*, 45–50; collective, and Gagnon, 53–54; in *Les Cathédrales sauvages*, 57–58; and trauma in *Le Vent majeur*, 60; in *Laurence*, 103; in Proulx, 166, 167; of father-daughter bonds in feminist writing, 171; women's, and parricide, 171; in "La Gifle," 175; and incest in *L'Écho*, 186–87, 193, 197–201; and exile, 204; in *L'Ingratitude*, 210; in *Le Bonheur*, 213–14; of the lesbian voice, 249, 255; and desire, 249–50; of Western Canadian women, 268; women's traditional, 269; in Dumas, 282–84; of the dancing body in Huston, 297

Silencing: in *L'Écho*, 18; in "Le Torrent," 27–28, 32; of the mother in *La Cage*, 27–28; and desire in *L'Été*, 90; of women in *Laurence*, 100–101; of women and feminist theater, 108–9, 122, 124; of women in history, 143–44; in *L'Écho*, 195–96; in Dumas, 283; of the mother in Huston, 292

Sin: sexuality as, 24; mother as bookkeeper of, 25–26; of unwed mothers in *Laurence*, 102; in postfeminist theater, 122; male, in Proulx, 161–62; original, and women in Proulx, 168; in Dumas, 280

Smart, Patricia: and *Laurence*, 100–101; and mother-daughter relationships, 170

Society: family structure in, 23, 27; restrictions of and the ideal lover in *La Cage*, 30; as proper object of blame in literature, 32; and death, 53–54; and death discourse, 54; pressures of in feminist theater, 115; limitations of in Proulx, 160; and gender expectations in *Laurence*, 179; and prostitution in *L'Écho*, 191; values of in *Le Bonheur*, 215; and exile in *Les Lettres*, 222, 223, 228–29, 233; Acadian, and Daigle, 258; patriarchal, in children's literature, 315

Solidarity: in francophone literature, 19, 20; in *La Cage*, 31, 32; in Brossard, 37; in *L'Été*, 92; in *Laurence*, 178–79; rebellion against in *L'Ingratitude*, 211–12; in *Entre les fleuves*, 246; patriarchal, in Moser, 272; feminine, in Dumas, 281–82; feminine, in children's literature, 315, 316

Solitude: in *Marguerite*, 20; delight of in *La Cage*, 29–30; in *Vertige*, 45–46; in *Les Cathédrales sauvages*, 64; in Théoret, 96; in *Laurence*, 104; in postfeminist theater, 115; in *Un Homme est une valse*, 134–35, 139; in *Les Lettres*, 226; in *Entre les fleuves*, 239–40

Sophie devient sage (Leblanc), 311–12
Sophie lance et compte (Leblanc), 310
Sophie vit un cauchemar (Leblanc), 310–11

Space: as subject of francophone writing, 16; creation of through writing, 18–19; in Brossard, 37, 38–39, 40–42, 44–47, 50; ontological, and connection, 41; and women's creativity, 44–45; and the title of *Vertige*, 46; in the cultural imaginary, 47; of a book, 65–66; in Gagnon, 74; safe, in *L'Été*, 83–84; for the protagonist in *L'Été*, 87–88, 93; and Montreal in Théoret, 95–96, 99, 103–4; of the convent in *Laurence*, 100–103; of female intimacy, 108–9; traditional social, 110; and writing in *Un Homme est une valse*, 131–33; and absence in *Un Homme est une valse*, 136–37; poetic, in *La Memoria*, 143; empty, in *La Memoria*, 148–49, 153; of Western culture, and "the name of the father," 172; of culture, daughter as a prisoner in, 173; the daughter's, in *Laurence*, 179; safe, and the diary in *L'Écho*, 193; safe, and healing in *L'Écho*, 199–200; geographical, in *Les Lettres*, 217–18, 220, 221, 223, 225, 229–31; public and private in *Les Lettres*, 223; between people in *Les Lettres*, 229, 230; and identity in *Les Lettres*, 231–32; textual, in *Les Lettres*, 233; feminine, in *Entre les fleuves*, 235–46; multicultural, and immigrant writing, 235–36; movement within in *Entre les fleuves*, 236, 238–43, 246; and schizophrenia in *Entre les flueves*, 238; literary, in *Entre les fleuves*, 238; closed and open, in *Entre les fleuves*, 240; gendered, in *Entre les fleuves*, 246; underground, in Primeau, 270; Franco-Albertan, in Dumas, 279–80; politicized, in Primeau, Moser, and Dumas, 284; of a man's mind and maternity in Huston, 292; feminine, maternal, and dance in Huston, 296–98; feminine, in *Gynesis*, 306–7; and language, 307; in *Entre l'ombre et la lumière*, 323–24; and children's literature, 307, 316

Status quo: maintainence of in *La Cage*, 29; and sense of exile, 204; and legacy in *Le Bonheur*, 215; and non-Québécois francophone women, 267

Stereotypes: of women in traditional narratives, 39; of men in *Les Lettres*, 230–31; of non-Québécois francophone women, 267; patriarchal, in Moser, 276; and children's literature, 309

Sterility: in feminist theater, 121–22; in Huston, 301

Stories/storytelling: and myth, 39; in *Les Cathédrales sauvages*, 57–59, 63, 64, 67; and catastrophe/death in *Le Vent majeur*, 60, 68, 69, 72–73; of Grosse Île, 78, 79–80; and the protagonist in *L'Été*, 80, 81, 83–86, 88; of power in history, 81; and dance in *L'Été*, 85–86; as sense of accomplishment in *L'Été*, 87–88; end of in *L'Été*, 93; of parricide, 171; in *Laurence*, 178; and the body in *La Danse juive*, 181–82; of incest in *L'Écho*, 193; writing of in Daigle, 251, 255; in Dumas, 281; in Huston, 299–302; in children's literature, 318

Submission: and the patriarchal legacy, 18; in "Le Torrent," 25; to spousal rape in *La Cage*, 29; in *Laurence*, 100–101; of love in feminist theater, 116, 120; in *Un Homme est une valse*, 135; of loss and survival in *La Memoria*, 142, 153; of the woman in Proulx, 163; and love in Proulx, 166; and father-daughter relationships, 172; of incest in *L'Écho*, 200–201; of love among women in *La Dot*, 206–8; in *Les Lettres*, 217–18

Subjection of Women, The (Mill), 318–20

Suffering: of francophone women writers, 20; of the community in *L'Été*, 84–85; and storytelling in *L'Été*, 86–87; of the protagonist in *L'Été*, 89–90; in the convent in *Laurence*, 101–2; and lovemaking in postfeminist theater, 117; and love in postfeminist theater, 122; in Proulx, 164; and incest in *L'Écho*, 187, 190, 191, 194, 197, 198; and exile, 204; in *L'Ingratitude*, 211–12; and exile in *Les Lettres*, 222–24, 226–27; in Daigle, 257; of the artist in Huston, 293; of the mother in Huston, 296;
and amnesia in Huston, 300; in children's literature, 312–13

Suicide: in feminist theater, 121–22; in *La Memoria*, 150–51; in *L'Écho*, 188, 192–93, 197; as revenge in *L'Ingratitude*, 210, 211; in Dumas, 282; and Huston, 293

Superiority: in *L'Été*, 90; in feminist theater, 114; male, in "La Gifle," 173, 174–75; of art over life in Huston, 301; of men as expressed through binary oppositions, 306; male, and children's literature, 310–11, 313, 319–20

Surrealism: and *Baroque d'aube*, 42–43

Survival: of Franco-Canadian women writers, 16, 20; in *L'Écho*, 18; of Catholic francophone culture, 23–24; in the husband's absence in *La Cage*, 29–30; in *Baroque d'aube*, 40; in *Les Cathédrales sauvages*, 58–59, 65; in *L'Été*, 90; in *Un Homme est une valse*, 134, 137; and memory in Dupré, 143–48, 157; and writing in *La Memoria*, 152–53; and incest, 18, 188–89, 190, 193–95, 198–201; in *La Dot*, 206; and exile in *Les Lettres*, 226, 227; and Western Canadian women, 267–69; minority francophone, in Primeau, 271; in Huston, 301

Symbolism: of Jesus in "Le Torrent," 25; of keys in "Le Torrent," 26, 27–28; of the keys in *Le Temps sauvage*, 26; of Perceval in "Le Torrent," 26; of books in "Le Torrent," 26–27; of keys in *La Cage*, 27–28; of the snake in *La Cage*, 28–29; of the baby's death's head in *La Cage*, 29; of the grenade in *La Cage*, 31; of the owl in *La Cage*, 31; of language in Brossard, 37; and mythmaking, 39; in *Baroque d'aube*, 41–42; of Buenos Aires in *Baroque d'aube*, 42; of the sea in *Baroque d'aube*, 45; and the semiotic in Brossard, 50; writing as in Brossard, 50; of fire in *Les Cathédrales sauvages*, 58, 72–73; and narrative in *Les Cathédrales sauvages*, 59; of the setting sun in *Le Vent ma-*

jeur, 61; and transmission in *Les Cathédrales sauvages*, 63; of the bonfire and cigarette in *Le Vent majeur*, 72–73; of Gagnon's recent texts, 74; in *L'Été*, 91–92; of the patriarchal mother's power[lessness], 169–70; and the father's patriarchal power, 169–70, 171–72; of castration, 171; of the father in "Friperie," 176; and daughters in *Laurence*, 178–79; of the father's daughter, 183; of the phallus in *L'Écho*, 188; of nursing as profession in *L'Écho*, 188–89; of the lover in *L'Écho*, 188–89; of hair in *L'Écho*, 189; of the male psychoanalyst in *L'Écho*, 191–92, 195; of the flowers in *L'Écho*, 196; of dismemberment in *L'Écho*, 198–99; of the name "Eva" in *L'Écho*, 200; of the father in *L'Écho*, 200; of the importance of memory, 204; of the cold in *La Dot*, 208; of motion in water in *Entre les fleuves*, 241–42; of rewriting in *Entre les fleuves*, 242; of the birth of self in *Entre les fleuves*, 243; and feminism in *Entre les fleuves*, 245–46; of the name "Kora" in *Entre les fleuves*, 246; of titles in Daigle, 255–56; of images in Daigle, 257, 260; of usage of French in Dumas, 284; and the body in Huston, 296–97; of renaming in Huston, 299; in *Entre l'ombre et la lumière*, 324

Syntax: in Brossard, 41–42, 46, 49

Taboo, cultural: and the patriarchal legacy, 169–70; and imagination/dreaming in *L'Ingratitude*, 213; in Franco-Albertan literature, 284

Teasdale, Christiane. Works: "La Gifle," 18, 170, 172–75

Temps sauvage, Le (Hébert), 26, 27

Tentation de dire, La (Ouellette-Michalska), 84

Terrible secret, Un (Anfousse), 315–16

Théâtre des Cuisines, 109, 120

Théâtre expérimental des femmes: and sexuality in theater, 108, 109, 111

Théoret, France, 11, 16. Works: *Laurence*, 17, 18, 95–106, 170, 178–80; *Nous parlerons comme on écrit*, 95–96, 97; *Bloody Mary*, 95–96; *Entre raison et déraison*, 96; *L'Homme qui peignait Staline*, 96–97; *Journal pour mémoire*, 96; *Une Voix pour Odile*, 97

Third-person narration: in *Le Vent majeur*, 68; in *L'Été*, 80; in children's literature, 318

Time/temporality: in Brossard, 16, 37, 38, 39, 40–42, 44–46, 48–49; and myth in Brossard, 38–39, 40–41; in *Baroque d'aube*, 41–42, 44–45; in *Vertige*, 46, 48–49; and writing, 56; in *Les Cathédrales sauvages*, 57, 63, 65; in *Le Deuil du soleil*, 73; and death in *L'Été*, 82; and storytelling in *L'Été*, 84; passing of in *L'Été*, 93; in postfeminist theater, 111, 118–19, 123, 124, 126–27; in *Un Homme est une valse*, 138; in *La Memoria*, 148–51, 153; and writing in Proulx, 168; and transmission in *L'Écho*, 197–98; and reincarnation in *La Dot*, 207; and marriage in *L'Ingratitude*, 231; conception of in *Les Lettres*, 223, 225–26, 228–29; and space in *Entre les fleuves*, 236; construction of in Daigle, 260; in Moser, 273–75; and space in *Entre l'ombre et la lumière*, 323–24

"Torrent, Le" (Hébert), 23–28, 31–32

Tradition: of feminist criticism, 11–12; French intellectual, 12; French-Canadian, 12; of women writers in Québec, 17; of gender roles in *Un Homme est une valse*, 17; of marriage in narrative, 31; and regard for myth, 38–39; and vertigo in *Vertige*, 48; of narration and *Vertige*, 49; decline of in Gagnon, 53–54; transmission of, in *Les Cathédrales sauvages*, 63; of "tombeau" form in *Le Deuil du soleil*, 73–74; and point of view, 80; resistance to in *Laurence*, 96, 104–5; of rural Québec in *Laurence*, 98–99; and education in *Laurence*, 101; and objectification in Harvey, 132; and the marginality of the daughter's story, 172; of language, plot, and narrative structure, 178; and model of power in *L'Écho*, 187; and powerlessness in *L'Écho*, 199; mothers as perpetuators of, 203; and exile, 204; as legacy in *La Dot*, 209; in *L'Ingratitude*, 211, 212–13; and men in *Le Bonheur*, 214; and exile in *Les Lettres*, 218–21, 225–26, 229, 230; in *Entre les fleuves*, 243, 245–46; and the novel in Daigle, 251–52; and Western Canadian women, 267; women's, of silence, 269, 270; women's, and naming in Moser, 277; feminine, in Dumas, 284; and mind/body dualism in Huston, 290–91, 293, 297; and pregnancy in Huston, 295; and the muse in Huston, 300; and patriarchy, 306; and exclusion of the feminine, 307; and publishing, 322; and children's literature, 319–20

Transformation: in *Vertige*, 46–47; in *Le Vent majeur*, 60; in *Les Cathédrales sauvages*, 65–66; and power in *L'Été*, 80–81; of the history of Grosse Île, 81; of objects in *L'Été*, 82; and grace in *L'Été*, 83; of stories into writing in *L'Été*, 84; of the community in *L'Été*, 84–86; and the imagination in *L'Été*, 85; and desire in feminist theater, 117; in *La Memoria*, 153, 154, 156; and incest in *L'Écho*, 191, 200–201; in *La Dot*, 209; in *Le Bonheur*, 214; and exile in *Les Lettres*, 217, 219, 221, 223–24, 228–30, 232, 233; in *Entre les fleuves*, 240; of reality in Daigle, 255; in Primeau, 271–72; in Moser, 274, 275; in Huston, 294, 295, 297

Translation: interest in, in Canada, 19; mythmaking as, 39; role of in *Baroque d'aube*, 43; of memory into words, 56; of trauma into words, 60, 68–69; writing as in *Le Deuil du soleil*, 73; in *L'Été*, 87–93; of the self in *Entre les fleuves*, 238; and dance in Huston, 296, 299; of *Marguerite*, 346–48

Transmission: of values/heritage/ideology in "Le Torrent," 23–27; of the husband's heritage in *La Cage*, 28–29; in Gagnon, 62- 75; and sexual difference in Gagnon, 69–72; in *Les Cathédrales sauvages*, 72; men's role in, 72–73; as theme in *Le Vent majeur*, 73; and self-creation/knowledge in *Le Deuil du soleil*, 73–74; through storytelling in *L'Été*, 84; of memories in *L'Écho*, 195; of abusive tendencies in *L'Écho*, 197; maternal, of patriarchal values, 203

Trauma: in *La Memoria*, 17, 147–48; in *Le Vent majeur*, 58–60, 67–68; and creativity in *Le Vent majeur*, 60–61; and creativity in Gagnon, 61–62; and writing in Gagnon, 62–63; of abandonment in *La Memoria*, 147; in *Le Désert mauve*, 147; and mourning in *La Memoria*, 150, 152–53; and the father's law, 172; in *L'Écho*, 186, 188, 189, 193, 194, 196, 199; of cultural values, 203–5; of tradition in *La Dot*, 206; of birth, in *Entre l'ombre et la lumière*, 324; and *Marguerite*, 346

Travel: in Brossard, 38, 44; in *Entre les fleuves*, 238–40; and *Marguerite*, 346; in children's literature, 317–18

Tremblay, Lise. Works: *La Danse juive*, 18, 170, 180–82

Truth: in *La Cage*, 29; and *Baroque d'aube*, 37–38, 44–45; in *Vertige*, 47, 49–50; and death in Gagnon, 54–55; and mourning in *Le Deuil du soleil*, 70; and sexuality in Harvey, 136; in *La Memoria*, 157; in *L'Écho*, 195; and love in *Les Lettres*, 229–30; and Barthes, 249–50; and Daigle, 260; and patriarchy in Dumas, 284; and children's literature, 307, 313

Turcotte Elise. Works: "Friperie," 18, 170, 175–77

Typhus: in *L'Été*, 82, 84, 85, 87, 89–91. See also Epidemic; Cholera

Urbanity: and survival in *Baroque d'aube*, 40; in Théoret, 17, 95–96, 100, 101, 103–5; and exile in *Les Lettres*, 226, 233; in Dumas, 279–80

Vacances de Rosalie, Les (Anfousse), 314

Values: transmission of in "Le Torrent," 23–25; and phallocentrism, 36; of the West, 44; women as producers of, 50; in *L'Été*, 91; rural, in *Laurence*, 99, 100, 101; in feminist theater, 119; system of and women's role, 171; patriarchal, and transmission of, 203; cultural, and exile, 204, 205; and identity in *Le Bonheur*, 215; and Barthes, 249–50; and Western Canadian women, 267–68; in Primeau, 271; and words in Moser, 273; in children's literature, 308–9, 312

Vent de liberté, Un (Crouteau), 317–20

Vent majeur, Le (Gagnon), 55, 59–60, 67–68

Vertige de l'avant scène (Brossard): and the importance of myth and memory, 16, 36, 45–50

Vertigo: in *Baroque d'aube*, 44–45; in *Vertige*, 45–46, 47, 48

Victim: La Corriveau as, 23; and Hébert's blaming of, 32; women as, in Gagnon, 61–62; women as, in feminist theater, 121–22; of desire in *Un Homme est une valse*, 140; woman as, in Proulx, 162; parapalegic as in Proulx, 164; of incest in *L'Écho*, 188, 191, 193, 194, 197–201; mother as, of society in *L'Ingratitude*, 211–12; woman as in Dumas, 281–82

Violence: familial, in "Le Torrent" and *Les Fous de Bassan*, 27; gender as, 36; and misogyny, 36; and memory, 38; in *Baroque d'aube*, 40; and storytelling in *Les Cathédrales sauvages*, 59; against women in Gagnon, 61–62; and creativity in Gagnon, 61–62, 67–68; and closure in *Le Vent majeur*, 72; urban, in *Laurence*, 98; in "La Gifle," 173, 175; of the father in *Laurence*, 178; in *L'Écho*, 198; in Dumas, 280–81; and the usage of French in Dumas, 284; and the creative impulse in Huston, 298; in *Entre l'ombre et la lumière*, 324

Virevolte, La (Huston), 294–99

Virgin Mother: and the absent-father motif, 25; and the change of name in *La Cage*, 30; sexual, in *Le Vent majeur*, 59–61; and death of innocence, 61; of men, in *Le Vent majeur*, 72–73; and paternal law in *L'Écho*, 192; and rebellion in *L'Ingratitude*, 212; in Dumas, 280, 282

Virginity: loss of in *L'Écho*, 196; loss of in Moser, 274–75

Virtual reality: in Brossard, 37, 40, 46

Vision(s): of the androgynous couple in *La Cage*, 32; in *Vertige*, 45–46, 48–49, 50; in *Les Cathédrales sauvages*, 59; in *Le Vent majeur*, 60–61, 67–68; in *LEte*, 82, 91, 93; in *La Memoria*, 150, 154; the father's, in "La Gifle," 174–75; of the detached daughters, 183; utopian, in *L'Écho*, 199–200; patriarchal, and Western Canadian women, 268–69; in Western Canada, 269–70; artistic, and Huston, 293, 294

Voice(s): of feminism, 11; of francophone women writers, 15, 19; male and female, in *Les Lettres*, 18; of the mother in *La Cage*, 27–28, 30; in Brossard, 37, 39, 43, 44–45, 248; and role of mythmaking, 39; of patriarchy, absence of in *Baroque d'aube*, 44–45; in *Aporias*, 53–54; and death/loss in Gagnon, 54–56, 63–64; and witnessing in *Les Cathedrales sauvages*, 57–59; and transmission in Gagnon, 62–63; of the dead, in *Les Cathédrales sauvages*, 65; multitude of in *Les Cathédrales sauvages*, 66; of the narrator in *Le Vent majeur*, 68; of the protagonist in *L'Été*, 84; of the immigrants in *L'Été*, 86; of unitary discourse, 96; narrative, in *Laurence*, 97–98, 101; of female sexuality in postfeminist theater, 122; male and female in Harvey, 134–35; in *La Memoria*, 146, 153, 157–58; of the mother in Proulx, 163–64; and sex in Proulx, 166; man's, and female authorship in Proulx, 168; in *Les Fous de Bassan*, 169; of patriarchal culture, 172, 173; of the father in "La Gifle," 174; and incest/abuse in *L'Écho*, 186, 190, 198; of authority, and maternal transmission, 203; in *Le Bonheur*, 214–15; in migrant literature, 217; in *Les Lettres*, 217–18, 233; of immigrant writers, 235; in *Entre les fleuves*, 235–38, 241, 246; and Franco-Canadian lesbian writers, 248–62; in *Soifs*, 248; in *L'Or-*

gueilleuse, 248; and gender, 249; in Daigle, 249, 250, 253, 255, 261–62; of Western Canadian women, 268; feminine, in Primeau, 268–72; in Dumas, 279–81, 283–84; women's, in Primeau, Moser, and Dumas, 284; in Huston, 298; feminine, in children's literature, 306, 308–9, 315, 318

Voix pour Odile, Une (Théoret), 97

Voyage: in *Baroque d'aube*, 41–42, 44; and *Vertige*, 47; of the sick in *L'Été*, 82–83; into the future in *L'Écho*, 189–90; and exile in *Les Lettres*, 222; in *Entre les fleuves*, 240. See also Expedition; Journey

Voyeurism: and feminist theater, 111, 126–27; in *Un Homme est une valse*, 137

Waltz: in *Un Homme est une valse*, 134, 136–38, 140–41; in *La Memoria*, 149–50

War: against the patriarchal order in *La Cage*, 31; and storytelling, 84; in *Un Homme est une valse*, 140; as metaphor in *L'Écho*, 193–95; with culture in Primeau, Moser, and Dumas, 284

War of the sexes: in *Un Homme est une Valse*, 139; in Proulx, 167; in "La Gifle," 174–75; and rebellion in *L'Ingratitude*, 212

Water: in *Baroque d'aube*, 43–44, 45; in *Les Cathédrales sauvages*, 59; in *L'Été*, 91; in feminist theater, 117; in *L'Écho*, 190–91; in *La Dot*, 206; in *Le Bonheur*, 214; as motif in *Entre les fleuves*, 237–43, 246; symbolism of in Daigle, 257; in Moser, 277–79

Wedding: in *La Cage*, 28; in *L'Été*, 88, 92; in Primeau, 271; night of in Moser, 274–75

Witch: as represented in *La Cage*, 16, 23; and sexuality in feminist theater, 108

Womb, the: as symbolized by the grenade in *La Cage*, 31; in *Vertige*, 46–47; and loss in Gagnon, 55–56, 63; and writing in *Les Cathédrales sauvages*, 66; in *Entre les fleuves*, 241–43, 246; in Dumas, 280

Woman/women: in Canada, 15; experiences/perceptions of as subject of francophone writing, 16; in *La Cage*, 16; in *L'Été*, 17; changing roles of in Laurence, 17; and their use of language in francophone drama, 17; in rural families, 24; identity as in *La Cage*, 31; powerlessness of, 32; as "discontents," 36; and effects of misogyny, 36; creativity of, 37, 41, 44–45, 46; and the imprisonment of narrativity, 39, 42; and language in *Vertige*, 46–47; and space in *Vertige*, 47; history of and *Vertige*, 47; and fiction and narration, 49; liberation of in Brossard, 50; and libidinal law, 50; violence against in Gagnon, 61–62; as sole narrators in *Les Cathédrales sauvages*, 67; and imagery/language in *Le Vent majeur*, 70–71; and the legacy of writing, as the heart of lifewriting, 74; and exclusion from Canadian history, 79; collective memory/consciousness of, 79; life of in *L'Été*, 81; and urbanity in Théoret, 95–96; urban, and condemnation of in Laurence, 99–100; education of in Théoret, 103; urban threat to in Laurence, 104; and urban optimism in Laurence, 104–5; and autobiographical writing, 142; and memory writing, 143–44; bonds between, and parricide, 171; fate of in Québec, 178–79; and closeness and autonomy, 179; and somatophobia, 180; and the "other family romance," 183; and incest, 186; and the transmission of abuse in *L'Écho*, 197–98; community of and incest, 199–201; and cultural legacy in *L'Ingratitude*, 212–13; as agents of culture in *Le Bonheur*, 215; roles of in francophone patriarchal society, 272; oppression of in male discourse, 306; and Internet publishing, 322–24

Women writers, francophone: in Québec, 11–12, 15–20, 27; in Canada, 15–20; in North America, 16; as a study of the women of today, 16; generations of, 16; and the importance of myth and memory, 16; tradition of, 17; and father-daughter bonds, 18; contemporary, in Canada, 18; and the necessity of recording the contributions of, 20; and the vision of the ideal lover, 30; accomplished, as symbolized by Buenos Aires in *Baroque d'aube*, 42; and disloyalty to civilization, 49–50; and confrontation of death, 74; and meaning, 95–96; and development of a female perspective, 169; and the diminishing role of the father, 170; and father-daughter relationships, 170; and the father, 171–72; and male superiority in "La Gifle," 173; and the "other family romance," 183; and Ltaif, 235; as the "new Prometheas," 262; Western Canadian, and sexuality, 269; and the refusal to bear children in Huston, 292–93; and Internet publishing, 322–24

Words: as rituals in mythmaking, 39; as smallest unit of the problematic of gender, 39–40; and life, 43; and women's silence in history, 43–44; juxtaposition of in *Vertige*, 46–47; discovery of in *Vertige*, 49; translation of memory into, 56; and witnessing in *Les Cathédrales sauvages*, 58; and trauma in *Le Vent majeur*, 60; play on in *Le Vent majeur*, 61; relationship with in Gagnon, 62; transmission/legacy of in Gagnon, 63–65, 68–70; and death in *Le Vent majeur*, 68–69; and love in *Le Vent majeur*, 71; transmission of in *Les Cathédrales sauvages*, 72; and memory in fiction, 79; of exile and death, 80; and storytelling in *L'Été*, 83, 84; and desire in *L'Été*, 89; and feminist theater, 108–9, 112, 124–26; in *Un Homme est une valse*, 130, 132, 134; of woman's desire, 136; and the *tablette magique*, 145; and [the cycle of] loss in *La Memoria*, 146, 149, 153, 156; and internalization in "La Gifle," 174; of the father in *Laurence*, 178–80; play on in *L'Écho*, 186, 192–93, 198–99; and sensorial memory in *La Dot*, 207–8; as a means of expression in *La Dot*, 210; and cultural legacy in *L'Ingratitude*, 213; and silence in *Le Bonheur*, 214; in *Les Lettres*, 225, 229–31; in *Entre les fleuves*, 237, 238; in Daigle, 255; feminine, absence of in Moser, 273; and patriarchal authority in Dumas, 279–81; French, in Dumas, 283; in *Entre l'ombre et la lumière*, 324; in children's literature, 313, 316

Worldview: phallocentric, 36; and Church teaching, 101–2; of the father in *Laurence*, 178

World Wars, the: and Gagnon, 53–54; and the Montreal experience, 95; in *Laurence*, 98; in *L'Écho*, 193, 195–97; Québec, and equilibrium, 235–36; and space in *Entre les fleuves*, 236

Writing: by francophone women, 11–12, 15; as subject of francophone writing, 16; the future of for Franco-Canadian writers, 16; in the prose of Gagnon, 17; and sexual passion, in *Un Homme est une valse*, 17; in *La Memoria*, 17; Ltaif's use of, 18–19; as a means of inspiration and recovery, 20; memory in Brossard, 37–38; as subject of in Brossard, 39; and myth in Brossard, 44; phenomenology of in *Vertige*, 46; of women's lives, 46–47; of desire in *Vertige*, 47; and sense of presence in *Vertige*, 48; eroticism of for Brossard, 49; the female body in Brossard, 50; as a symbol of renewal, 50; and phallocentricism, 50; and mourning in Gagnon, 53–74; of life, 54; and remembering/memory, 54, 56–57; and death/loss, 54–55, 56–57, 62; as healing in *Les Cathédrales sauvages*, 56–57, 58–59, 63–64; as an escape in *Les Cathédrales sauvages*, 59; and transmission/legacy of in Gagnon, 62–74; "coming to" in *Le Vent majeur*, 68–69, 72–73; and the other in *Le Vent majeur*, 69–70; and mourning in *Le Deuil du soleil*, 73–74; and storytelling in *L'Été*, 84, 86–87; in *Laurence*, 103; and the theater, 111; of love stories, 116; about romantic love, 116–17; in *Un Homme est une valse*, 131–34, 138–41; women's autobiographical, 142; and memory in *La Memoria*, 143–44; and memory in Brossard, 143–44; and Freud's Wunderblock, 145; and loss in *La Memoria*, 152–52; and "mourning work," 153; and the cycle of life, 153–54; in Proulx, 166; and otherness in Proulx, 168; in the feminine, 178; and the "other family romance," 183; in *L'Écho*, 188, 191; immigrant, and *Les Lettres*, 217–18, 221, 228, 229, 231–33; and Ltaif, 235–37; in *Entre les fleuves*, 239, 242, 245, 246; women's migrant, 244; and gender, 249; and Barthes, 249–50; and Daigle, 250–55, 257–61; readerly, and Western Canadian women, 268; feminist, and rebellion, 273; in Moser, 279; and Huston, 290, 294–95, 299, 301–2; in *Entre l'ombre et la lumière*, 323–24; in children's literature, 308, 316

Ying Chen, 18; and father-daughter relationships, 170. Works: *L'Ingratitude*, 203–4, 210–13; *Les Lettres chinoises*, 217–33

Youth: in *Baroque d'aube*, 40, 42; in Harvey, 131; and storytelling in *La Dot*, 206–7; and curiosity in *Les Lettres*, 232; in Dumas, 281